Wings across the World

Wings across the World

An Illustrated History of British Airways

Harald Penrose

Cassell

London

By the same author

I Flew with the Birds
No Echo in the Sky
Airymouse
Cloud Cuckooland
British Aviation: the Pioneer Years
British Aviation: the Great War and Armistice
British Aviation: the Adventuring Years
British Aviation: Widening Horizons
British Aviation: the Ominous Skies

CASSELL LTD.
35 Red Lion Square, London WC1R 4SG
and at Sydney, Auckland, Toronto, Johannesburg,
an affiliate of
Macmillan Publishing Co., Inc.,
New York.

First published 1980

ISBN 0 304 30697 5

Aircraft drawings by David Gibbings

Maps by the Kirkham Studios

Typeset by Inforum Ltd, Portsmouth
Printed and bound in Great Britain by
Fakenham Press Limited, Fakenham, Norfolk

Contents

In the Beginning 1918-19

Across the shell-torn wastes of Flanders the great guns sullenly thundered — but though action was massively concentrated on war, the future peace-time policies of Great Britain were having consideration. Among those planners was a remarkable yet now forgotten man, George Holt Thomas, greatest of pioneer aviation industrialists, who had built up the biggest aircraft production enterprise in the world, the war-time Aircraft Manufacturing Co Ltd, known as Airco. Tall, trimly bearded, hooknosed, he was a dominating and impressive figure, whose wealth stemmed from the *Daily Graphic* and topical London magazines inherited from his father. Through common motoring interests with the famous Farman brothers of France he began in 1909 to participate in aviation and established his initial Aircraft Supply Co in 1912 to build under licence their simple, easy-to-fly, pusher biplanes — which his powerful political affiliations ensured were purchased by the army. When war came he engaged the most brilliant aircraft designer of the day, Geoffrey de Havilland, and his creations went into massive production, particu-

larly the DH 4 and the DH 9A.

Even the disasters of the Somme in 1916 did not cause Holt Thomas to abandon thought of the post-war world, and that October he registered 'Aircraft Transport & Travel Ltd' (AT & T) with capital of £50,000. In January 1917 his friend Lord Montagu of Beaulieu, on return from a mission to Delhi, expressed conviction that an air route to India must be a peace-time priority, and this spurred Holt Thomas, aided by influential friends including the newspaper magnate Lord Northcliffe, to induce Lloyd George as Coalition Premier to institute a Civil Aerial Transport Committee.

Chaired by Northcliffe, this was formed that summer to 'consider the method of regulating civil aviation activities' and the extent to which 'trained personnel and aircraft which the conclusion of peace may leave surplus to the requirements of the naval and military air services of the United Kingdom and Overseas Dominions' could be used.

In February 1918 the Committee's Report was issued comprising an introduction and reports from each of the five special commit-

Civil aviation in full swing at Cricklewood with Handley Page Transport's civil version of the famous 0/400 war-time bomber. Services were operated to Paris and Brussels, and there was joy-riding as well.

tees, with the bulk as detailed appendices. State support for aerial transport services was recommended and the importance of establishing Empire air routes was urged. Based on the premise that each State owns its own air, the Committee stressed the importance of approaching Allied and friendly governments to institute an International Aeronautical Convention, and assigned the duty of regulating internal air transport to the Air Ministry, who would issue certificates of airworthiness for aircraft, and competency licences to pilots, navigators and ground engineers. Even C.G. Grey, caustic editor of *The Aeroplane*, mildly approved, pointing out that: 'What is wanted is an Aerial Lloyd's. It is distinctly in the best interests of the aircraft industry that every aeroplane intended for public service or for hire by private persons should be compulsorily inspected not only when new, but at regular and frequent intervals.'

Encouraged that cessation of air raids on London was a sign of forthcoming German defeat, a large audience on 30 May filled the Central Hall, Westminster, to hear Holt Thomas lecture to the Royal Aeronautical Society (RAeS) on 'Commercial Aviation' and the possibilities of a profitable air service between London and Paris. Because de Havilland had designed fifteen types of Airco aeroplane it was not difficult to formulate civil variants on which Holt Thomas based his thesis, and his assumption of 40 passengers per day in each direction seemed reasonably cautious, so his

estimated single fare of £5 was regarded as oracular.

However, 33-year-old Frederick Handley Page, famed for Britain's biggest bombers, urbanely criticized Thomas's choice of single-engined 450 hp biplanes assumed capable of carrying twelve passengers. 'When one considers that a load of over six tons has been carried on *some* machines', he said, meaning his new four-engined prototype, 'it is evident they could be used for commercial purposes affording comfort for passengers as an aspect that should not be neglected.' Here was the warning of formidable competition from this massive, strong-willed, already balding young man.

The DH 16 was a successful expedient to accommodate four passengers by widening the fuselage of a DH 9A and fitting a coupé lid.

Six months later the German nation was collapsing in revolution. On 4 October an armistice was formally requested — addressed not to the Allied Commander-in-Chief but to President Wilson of the USA who had pronounced Fourteen Points as fundamentals for Peace negotiations. Twenty days later Wilson invited the Allies to proceed on that basis. Lloyd George and Clemenceau agreed. The Kaiser abdicated and escaped to Holland. At 5 a.m. on 11 November, in a railway carriage in the Forest of Compiègne, the Armistice was signed. In England and France great crowds blocked the streets dancing and cheering in all-embracing chaotic frenzy. The ensuing Parliamentary election reinstated the Coalition.

All war contracts were cancelled. The RAF had sufficient aircraft for a decade or more. Undismayed, Holt Thomas began setting the stage for the airline traffic which he was certain would eventually replace all forms of surface transport. Brig-Gen Francis Festing, Deputy Master-General of Personnel, was appointed managing director of AT & T and in November Holt Thomas announced that a regular scheduled air service between London and Paris would open as soon as existing restrictions were lifted.

Interest in flying was widespread, for it had been assiduously cultivated week after week in the war with thrilling reports of aerial battles, and 'air aces' became popular heroes. But this extensive publicity had a double-edged effect:

Geoffrey de Havilland when chief designer of Holt Thomas's war-time Aircraft Manufacturing Co Ltd.

though it made a vast cross-section of people air-minded, it also induced belief that flying was a dangerous pursuit, for more young pilots had been killed in accidents than ever brought down in battle. The gamble for Holt Thomas was whether the masses would accept flying as a system of every day transport. Meanwhile the Allies and Germany were still nominally at war, so only military flights were permissible.

The RAF therefore commenced a route survey to Delhi on 13 December, flying a four-engined Handley Page V/1500 which just managed to achieve its destination five weeks later with only two engines still functioning. The Air Ministry also established the 86th (Communications) Wing RAF at Hendon, commanded by Lieut-Col Primrose, to operate DH 4s hastily converted by Holt Thomas's Airco business to carry two passengers protected by a hinged coupé cover, so that officials on urgent business could be flown to France or Germany. Six draughty Handley Page twin-engined 0/400s were allocated to take mails and personnel to the Occupation Armies in Flanders and Germany.

The Peace Conference in Paris demanded greater comfort for the carriage of Prime Minister and Cabinet, so two further 0/400s were painted silver and modified with special cabins having respectively six and eight chairs and were duly named *Silver Star* and *Great Britain*. At best they were very primitive airliners: noisy, vibrating, with only the drumming fabric cover shielding the occupants from the battering slipstream. The DH 4As were no less cold, but the cramped cabin with passenger seats facing each other at least had plywood sides, and windows could be slid open if a passenger was air-sick.

It was with this type of single-engined machine instead of twelve-seaters that Holt Thomas now intended to open his airline. Interviewed by the *Observer*, he said: 'I am just as enthusiastic over commercial transport as I was ten years ago over aircraft for military use; but the first point I have to recognize in linking the world by aerial routes is that unfortunately British celestial rights apparently end in mid-Channel. It is therefore unlikely that the French Government will allow an all-British enterprise to run Mail to Paris, or the Italians to Rome, nor the Norwegians from Aberdeen to Stavanger. An aerial service between London and Paris must include rights of Franco-British capital, Franco-British aircraft construction, Franco-

Captain 'Jerry' Shaw (*centre*) and the DH 9 with which he flew Major Pilkington to Paris on the first occasion on which British civil aircraft were permitted to fly abroad.

British pilots, and be an international combine in every detail.

'Facing these facts, I have started a company of national importance at Christiania to link my company Aircraft Transport & Travel Ltd under the same direction as my aircraft company and other aviation enterprises. Similarly I have formed an allied company in France and another in Italy. I expect through Tata Ltd of India to link longer journeys from London, through France and Italy, to India. Arrangements are also complete for a link to South Africa, from Cape to Cairo.'

Not to be outdone, Handley Page implied to reporters that it would be his massive four-engined V/1500 which would be used for his own proposed London–Paris service. 'The journey will take 2½ to 3 hours at the same fare as the first-class ticket for train and steam boat. Fifty passengers will be carried and experiments are being conducted to silence the engine noise.' Meanwhile he was quietly buying back from the Ministry of Munitions sixteen 0/400s of which all except four were still being constructed at his factory and therefore could readily be modified for civil use.

1919

Dawning 1919 found Britain involved in complex reorganization. Demobilization centres were dealing with 50,000 exits a day, yet it was essential to maintain a large Army of Occupation and extend communications by land, sea, and air. Concurrently sources of employment were swiftly diminishing because war-time fac-

tories were closing or being reorganized into smaller units. Adroitly Handley Page converted his into a public company, extending its nominal £150,000 with an issue of 500,000 £1 preference shares — and Holt Thomas persuaded Maj-Gen Sir Sefton Brancker to resign his post as Comptroller General of Equipment and join him in developing commercial aviation.

In the Commons Lord Weir, Secretary of State for Air and mastermind behind the immense war-time aircraft production, announced on 2 January that draft legislation controlling civil aviation was being formulated. Five days later, at a meeting convened by the London Chamber of Commerce, Maj-Gen Sir Frederick Sykes, latterly Chief of Air Staff, comprehensively pictured *Commercial Aviation in the Light of War Experience*. 'Aviation is but a dozen years old', he said, 'and is today a child of war and a military development pure and simple.' Ranging over every aspect affecting civilian use of aircraft, he stressed that public confidence in the safety and security of flying must be engendered so that aviation could take its proper place in relation to older transport. Britain's immediate targets must be the routes to India, Cape to Cairo, European services, and short-haul runs at home. Turning to organizational requirements, he dealt with personnel, aerodrome management, air charts based on aerial survey, weather, navigational problems, and necessity of directional wireless because 'night flying would increase the difficulties of the indispensable aerial navigator'.

On 11 January he was appointed Controller-General of Civil Aviation following Lord Weir's resignation on re-joining his Glasgow engineering business. Next day Winston Churchill became Secretary of State for War and Air. Things began to move despite the complexity of national reorganization, now handled by the Ministry of Reconstruction under direction of the formidable Sir Eric Geddes with mandate to plan a more generous social order with better conditions of employment, education, and housing.

Establishment of a Department of Civil Aviation (DCA) within the Air Ministry followed on 12 February. Concurrently Churchill presented a Bill granting 'powers in addition and not derogation of powers conferred by the Air Navigation Acts 1911 and 1913', providing among other things 'the conditions under which goods and mails be conveyed in aircraft in to and from the British Isles'. Entitled The Air Navigation Act 1919, the Bill received Royal Assent on 27 February. It was generally accepted that civil flying would become legal at the beginning of the governmental financial year on 1 April, the Act remaining in force until 1 January 1920.

While Lloyd George and Arthur Balfour were battling for Britain at the Peace Conference in March, Handley Page with his unfailing publicity aplomb was exhibiting at Selfridge's great London store the impressively big fuselage of one of the 0/400 bombers converted to cabin saloon furnished with impracticable, lushly upholstered lounge chairs for sixteen passengers. Encouraged by an invitation to tender for ten-seat, twin-engined aeroplanes for China, he also commenced modifying his available 0/400s into a more reasonable airliner, renamed the 0/700, and was secretly devising a more powerful version with equal-span wings instead of long overhangs.

Holt Thomas was more cautious. He would still use the DH 4As, but knowing that a two-seater could not be a paying proposition, he was making a similar conversion of the bigger, more powerful DH 9A, which became the DH 16 by separating the standard fuselage sides with longer struts for width to accommodate two pairs of passengers facing each other in an enclosure extension of the pilot's cockpit, and to maintain correct trim, the pilot was moved forward to under the centre section, with wings re-rigged to eliminate stagger.

Not to be outdone by his contemporaries of pre-war days, Robert Blackburn on 23 April registered the North Sea Aerial Navigation Co Ltd for which he was building a cabin version of his twin-engined Kangaroo bomber, which had superficial resemblance to the 0/400 but was considerably smaller and had much less carrying capacity. As endorsement of intention he issued publicity maps showing his proposed air connections between Hull, Copenhagen, Stockholm, Helsingfors, and even Petrograd, normal diplomatic relations having been reconstituted with the Union of Soviet Socialist Republics in February.

Hopefully, that even earlier pioneer Alliott V. Roe formed an Air Transport branch equipped with his company's Avro 504K open-cockpit biplanes modified to carry two passengers, intending to give the civil population everywhere their aerial baptism. Several young ex-RAF pilots followed his lead, and with their war-time gratuities purchased 504Ks from the Disposals Board for a quarter the original cost and hoped to reap a golden harvest. Some later became distinguished airline pilots.

By entering a four-engined V/1500 bomber, loaned by the Air Ministry, for the recently announced *Daily Mail* £10,000 prize for the first aeroplane to fly the Atlantic, Handley Page hoped to gain still more publicity for his proposed airline. He therefore engaged 25-year-old Major Herbert Brackley, DSO, DSC, former C.O. of an 0/400 bomber squadron, as pilot. On 1 April 1919 it was ready for test at Cricklewood, the 700-yard Handley Page aerodrome, and on that day, though Brackley made his flight, the ban on civil flying was extended for two months.

Immediately Handley Page and Holt Thomas protested with united voice at delay in permitting commercial flights within the United Kingdom whatever the problems were of sorting out the complexities of international sovereignty and rights of aerial passage under consideration by the International Commission on Air Navigation. The Air Ministry took heed, and agreed that local passenger flights at specified aerodromes by approved operators could take place during the Easter holiday weekend.

That 'Victory Easter', as the Press euphemistically termed it, was chilly with hail and rain but did not prevent several thousand indulging in the thrill of aerial joy-rides at two guineas a

head. Nor did Handley Page remain aloof from this money-making indulgence, for at Cricklewood he plied an 0/400, piloted by Major Leslie Foot, which carried a total of 600 people, six at a time crowded in the rear cockpit and two in the gunner's nose cockpit. Few realized that the small print on their tickets excluded all claims for injury or death. Such 'blood-chits' became commonplace even with the earliest airlines.

Whether the zest with which people took to the thrills of joy-riding was a true augury for civil transport was questionable. *The Aeroplane's* editor optimistically forecast that 'of the total population, two million will want the experience of having been up in an aeroplane, and a large proportion will go on joy-riding as often as they can afford; so ultimately one might reckon there would be some five million joy-rides to be given before pleasure-flying markets began to decline'.

That international aviation might soon be

operative was indicated by publication of an official map giving approved air routes within Great Britain, and, more importantly, to the Continent. Of the 337 aerodromes existing at the Armistice, five were now designated 'approved' entry and departure ports with Customs facilities — Hounslow on the west of London as the main base, Lympne in Kent as Channel entry, Hadleigh in Suffolk for the Netherlands, and New Holland in Lincolnshire for Scandinavia. Then on 30 April the *London Gazette* at last printed the new Air Navigation Directions (AND) giving schedules of aircraft registration and airworthiness certification; overhaul and examination; licensing of pilots, navigators, and engineers; log books; Rules of the Air; signals; prohibited areas; arrival and departure procedures; and control of import, export, and unloading of goods. There was a rush for the pilot and engineer examinations that same day. Ex-naval Flt Lieut Howard Saint gained the first pilot's licence, and the first two

The HP V/1500 before its Atlantic bid. Full of optimism, Frederick Handley Page told reporters in 1919 that he proposed using his four-engined V/1500 for the London–Paris service, but it was far too uneconomical to use and he abandoned the idea.

Winston Churchill seated in a Short 27 machine. He had been an early aviation enthusiast, for he took lessons in piloting at the Naval Flying School, Eastchurch, in 1913.

With the R. 34 safely moored after the world's first trans-Atlantic airship flight, her commander, Major G.H. Scott, is welcomed by the senior officer of the Hazelhurst base, USA.

but bad weather forced return and the flight was not completed until the 5th, during which Major Orde-Lees left by parachute when above Aberdeen 'to drop in on a friend'.

Appalling weather, with hail and rain, typified that first week of flying, during which on 3 May a DH 4A of the Communications Flight, with Sir Frederick Sykes as passenger, crashed at Kenley after stalling at 50 feet, killing the pilot, Capt E.M. Knott. Outwardly undismayed, the Controller-General three days later was lecturing on Civil Aviation to the Liverpool Chamber of Commerce.

The even more adventurous prospect of flying the Atlantic soon turned newspapers from the stir created by the introduction of civil aviation in the UK. Forestalling a non-stop British attempt, the Americans began a stage-by-stage flight to England on 8 May using three large Curtiss flying-boats. On 16 May, having completed an initial 1,000-mile leg to Newfoundland, they took off for the Azores, their route patrolled by 27 destroyers strategically located, and a depôt ship half-way, but on 18 May Sopwith test pilot Harry Hawker, accompanied by navigator Lieut Cdr MacKenzie-Grieve, left Newfoundland in their single-engined Sopwith to fly the Atlantic direct. Nothing was heard for eight days, and then a small Dutch steamer semaphored Lloyd's station on the Butt of Lewis that the Sopwith crew was aboard after being forced down in mid-Atlantic. The nation was as jubilant as though conquest of that great ocean had been achieved.

A navigational expert explained the hazard: 'Using astronomical observation, MacKenzie-Grieve was 115 miles off course in a run of 800 miles. With such large errors possible, dependence on dead reckoning is out of the question. Experimental "directional wireless" has given promising results and must become the method of future air navigation, but it is not yet sufficiently developed to be reliable.' However, despite the great risks and navigational problems one of the Curtiss flying-boats reached Plymouth Sound in the afternoon summer haze of 31 May, alighting within sight of the steps from which the *Mayflower* set sail 300 years earlier. There was no official welcome, nor even a car to take the crew to their hotel.

A fortnight later Capt John Alcock, a pre-war aviator, with Lieut Arthur Whitten Brown navigating without aid of wireless, flew their twin-engined Vickers Vimy ex-war bomber

ground engineers' licences were issued to H.M. Woodhams and Bill Kelly, both of A T & T — just in time, for the Air Navigation Act became operative next day, and the *Daily Mail* had already hired the company's open-cockpit DH 9, crewed by Saint and Kelly, to initiate civil flying by carrying newspapers from Hendon to Bournemouth. Precisely at midnight on 30 April the engine was started, and a few minutes later the machine took off; but clouds were low, the night was dark, the engine gave trouble, and Saint crashed on Portsdown Hill above the lights of Portsmouth, receiving severe injuries, though Kelly escaped with a shaking.

Certainly Handley Page was not to be outdone, so he had secured a contract to deliver newspapers to Manchester and Scotland. One of his four certificated 0/400s, piloted by Lieut-Col Sholto Douglas and carrying eleven passengers, therefore departed more cautiously that evening, reaching its initial destination after three hours against strong head winds. Next morning Douglas headed for Edinburgh,

non-stop across the Atlantic from St John's, Newfoundland in 16 hrs 12 mins to their touch-down and pile-up in a bog near the village of Clifden, County Galway, Ireland. Declaimed Winston Churchill on presenting the prize: 'It is only ten years since Blériot flew the English Channel — but it is not so safe and easy as it sounds to fly the English Channel. Yet think of the broad Atlantic, that terrible waste of desolate water, passing in tumult and repeated in almost ceaseless storms and shrouded with an unbroken canopy of mist. Across this waste, through this obscurity, went two human beings, hurtling through the air, piercing cloud and darkness, finding their unerring path, despite every difficulty, to their exact objective across those hundreds of miles where they arrived almost on schedule time . . . When we study the prodigious efforts made by so many to traverse the Atlantic by air, to bridge the gulf of waters, to annihilate space and time which divides these great communities, can we not feel that they also symbolize the attempt to unite, not merely in the sense of eliminating distance, but to unite into one harmonious association all those great communities of the English-speaking democracies, which, combined together, working in true comprehension and perfect freedom, constitute an absolute guarantee for their own safety, and the surest promise of a future advantage and security of the world?' Then as his peroration he announced: 'I am happy to tell you that I have received His Majesty's gracious assent to an immediate award of the Knight Commandership of the Order of the British Empire to both Captain Alcock and Lieutenant Brown.'

The Australian government had given spectacular token a month earlier towards the fulfilment of that unity of democracies by offering a similar prize of £10,000 for the first Australian to fly from Britain to that Commonwealth within an elapsed time of 720 hours.

With glowing optimism Handley Page gave a splendid lunch party at Prince's Restaurant, London, to announce the formation on 14 June of his subsidiary, Handley Page Transport Ltd. Passenger and freight agents had been appointed for services all over the world, and he had secured a cheerfully resolute team of penurious pilots, of whom Sholto Douglas was made chief at £500 a year. All had flown 0/400s in the war: Wilcockson big and calm; press-on

At the Savoy Hotel, 20 June 1919, Alcock receives the *Daily Mail* £10,000 prize from Winston Churchill, then Secretary of State for War. This was his reward for the first non-stop Atlantic flight, accomplished by Alcock and Brown in a Vickers Vimy.

McIntosh; Foot the charmer; lively young Wally Hope; monocled Vaughan Fowler; steady Dismore, who initially did engine overhauls in company with NCO pilots Perry and irrepressible Rogers, both of whom at first had the lower status of flying freight services. Then one day at Cricklewood a bowler-hatted figure appeared and stiffly said to Douglas: 'Good morning. My name is Woods Humphery. I'm the chief engineer.' In deference to Douglas's military seniority he did not mention his own rank of Major, nor that he was a professional marine engineer.

As an operational trial a Cricklewood–Bournemouth weekend summer service had been initiated on 5 June, but was doomed to closure within ten weeks by competition from the London & South Western Railway. Meanwhile all was made ready for a London–Paris service, which with growth of traffic was planned to extend to Lyons, Marseilles, Turin, Florence, Rome, thence Brindisi to connect with P & O ships to Egypt and India, or to board the flying-boats proposed by Sir Frederick Sykes for the Mediterranean — and lest they were built by some other company Handley Page ensured that a twin-float seaplane version of the 0/400 was designed in readiness.

Eleventh-hour signature by Germany of the Peace Treaty terms on 28 June gave encouragement that all this could soon become effective. A nation-wide day of Peace celebrations was organized for 19 July. The air of triumph was reinforced by the pioneering four-day sky-voyage across the Atlantic of the British airship R.34 which arrived at Mineola, USA on 6 July. No aeroplane carrying a commercial payload could have achieved such distance, so the government saw this as vindication of airships for trans-Atlantic travel; but in fact R.34, carrying negligible load, had saved only six hours on SS *Aquitania*'s record.

On the eve of her return six days later, the Department of Civil Aviation unexpectedly announced that in view of the Peace celebrations, specially licensed commercial aircraft would be permitted to fly beyond the British shores from the Customs aerodrome of Hounslow during a six-day period commencing the 15th. Major Pilkington of the famous glass business happened to see a brief paragraph in the *Evening News* of 14 July announcing this concession, and rang Capt Donald Greig, the tennis-star flight manager of A T & T, saying he had an important meeting in Paris at 10.30 next morning and wished to charter a machine to take him there. Delightedly Greig established a stupendous fare of £42, and nominated as pilot one of the older demobilized officers, 27-year-old, ginger-moustached Capt 'Jerry' Shaw, whose considerable experience of the Paris run with the Communications Squadron led him to join A T & T. A 7 a.m. start was essential to reach Paris in time.

In later years Shaw recalled: 'Woodhams prepared my favourite DH 9 which had the early registration K 109. I had no passport, so skipped the obligation. Likewise it was mandatory to land at Hounslow for Customs clearance, but passing over Cricklewood I spotted a Handley Page 0/400 being prepared for take-off, and believing rivalry was afoot, I headed directly for the Channel. It was pouring, and clouds became lower and lower until at Beauvais we were at only 200 ft and the great hill ridge was hidden. I tacked to and fro seeking a gap, presently discovered a slight rift, scraped over the hill at tree level, and with fifteen minutes in hand landed at Le Bourget where nobody showed the slightest interest although this was the official Port of Entry. French Air Force officers smuggled us on to a tram which sped through the Military barrier without the normal inspection of papers, thence by taxi to the city. So elated was Pilkington that we made a new bargain to fly him back next day. May be it wasn't so much the money or being first to fly commercially there that pleased me — but a night in Paris!'

Mid-July at last opened the way for the establishment of international airlines, whether aeroplane or airship. The Air Ministry announced: 'Pending final signature of the International Convention a provisional agreement to allow flying between France and Great Britain from Monday, August 25 has been agreed between the respective governments'.

Publication of the Convention on 21 July showed it was based on the British Air Navigation Directions, but specifically dealt with questions of admission to foreign territory and legal-

Below: The Instone DH 4A was originally *City of Cardiff* but was renamed *City of York* for their cross-Channel service in 1921. *Bottom:* An RAF DH 4A of 86 (Communications) Wing at Hendon.

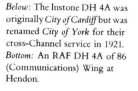

Feet

Metres

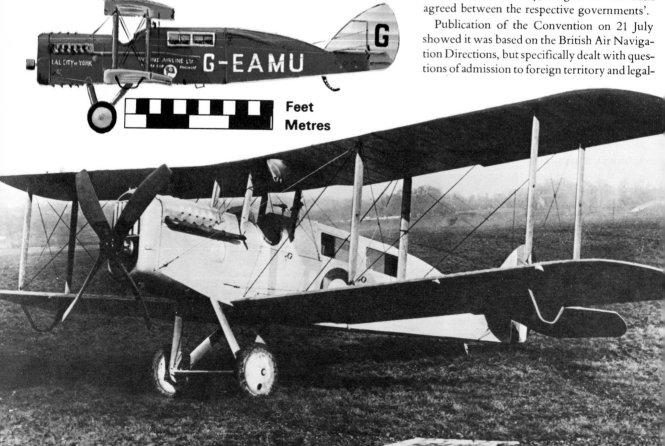

ity of crossing into another State; rules of departure, landing, and right of way; prohibited transport such as munitions; freedom of movement of State aircraft (military, customs, police); establishment of an International Convention for Air Navigation (ICAN); and finally provisions on co-operation, international radio, and a Court of Appeal for disagreements.

Two days before the permitted opening of A T & T services Lieut C.R. McMullin beat the gun by flying a DH 9 to Le Bourget with 'spares for the Paris service'.

Marking the historic occasion of the official commencement of cross-Channel scheduled operations, *The Aeroplane* reported: 'On August 25 the service was started. A DH 4A machine left Hounslow at 9.10 a.m. with a pilot, a Press representative, a number of newspapers, a consignment of leather, several brace of grouse, and a number of jars of Devonshire cream. The machine arrived at Le Bourget at 11.40 a.m. Left Le Bourget at 12.40 p.m. and reached Hounslow at 2.45 p.m. Bookings cover the entire first week of the service. The machines will leave for Paris every day that it is humanly possible to go. Whether there are passengers or not, they will go to scheduled times. The Postmaster has not yet given permission for letters to be carried. In America they found it eventually cheaper, and obviously quicker to send letters over long distances by air. The Post Office should realize the advantages of the speed of air transport. The aerial service would be put on a secure basis if they carried the mails.'

Pilot on that flight with G-EAJC was burly Lieut 'Bill' Lawford, who had learnt to fly in 1913, and at 35 was the oldest of the team. His journalist passenger was George Stevenson-Reese. However, *The Aeroplane* was misleading. The wily Frederick Handley Page was first with an 0/7 carrying seven journalists from Cricklewood, piloted by Major Leslie Foot, arriving at Le Bourget 90 minutes before Lawford's machine, and was followed that afternoon by another 0/400 piloted by Sholto Douglas, who flew home next day with his wife and Gertrude Bacon, known earlier as an 'intrepid balloonist'.

However none of these was scheduled. The inaugural flight of the official timetable that opening day was by Major Cyril Pattison, flying the A T & T Ltd DH 16, K 130, carrying four fare-paying passengers, one being Bruce Ingram, editor of the *Illustrated London News*.

Maj-Gen Sir Frederick Sykes, Brig-Gen Francis Festing and Holt Thomas were present to see the start, attended by a host of photographers. Take-off was at 12.40 p.m., after a delay of ten minutes, and the machine landed at Le Bourget 2 hours 25 minutes later.

'What would have been thought some 50 years ago', wrote the delighted Ingram, 'if any one had seriously made the announcement that our business men would in a few years be able to have lunch in London and tea in Paris, and return to London in time for dinner? And yet all this has now become possible. One cannot hope to describe adequately the interest, the sense of security, and the comfort which such a journey gives — to say nothing of the time saved, the avoidance of inconvenience caused by change from train to boat, then from boat to train again, with the usual scramble for places, and the irritating delays at the Customs in the journey between London and Paris.'

Inevitably there were difficulties. In the course of the first operational month only three days were officially fit for flying, thirteen considered unfavourable, and eight unsuitable, yet only two of the 56 scheduled flights were cancelled — one because squalls reached 100 mph, the other through mechanical defect.

Handley Page lost out to his rival by a week in starting his scheduled services. On 2 September he began his bid against Holt Thomas with a flight to Paris by Douglas in G-EAAF, the 0/7 civil version of the 0/400. A relatively unimpeded passenger space in the deep fuselage had been obtained by replacing the transversely crossed tie-rod bracing with a Vee of steel tubes at each station, enabling a row of cane seats to be fitted each side of a central gangway. His publicity leaflet stated: 'The accommodation is arranged as follows: after-cabin to seat six, forward-cabin to seat two passengers, and for those who prefer to travel in the open, two seats are arranged in front of the pilot. An observation platform with a sliding roof is fitted in the after-cabin.'

In smallest print at the bottom of the sheet was a somewhat disguised disclaimer of all legal liability: 'The Company do not hold themselves out to be and will not act as Common or General Carriers of Passengers or Goods'.

The A T & T fares to Paris were advertised in *The Aeroplane* as £21 single and £42 return. 'This fare includes free conveyance by motorcar to Hounslow Aerodrome from any point within a mile of Piccadilly Circus, and also from Le Bourget into Paris. A passenger called

Major-General Sir Sefton Brancker (*right*), the Director of Civil Aviation, and Alan S. Butler, Chairman of the De Havilland Aircraft Company.

for at an hotel in London at 11 a.m. arrives at the door of his hotel in Paris by 4 p.m. the same afternoon.'

With an air of jovial friendliness and no compunction, Handley Page undercut these fares to £15 15s single and £31 10s return. The battle was on. Compared with A T & T machines his airliners gave an impression of luxury with curtains and brackets of flowers between each pair of seats. Though 'the aeroplanes are fitted with every convenience for the comfort of passengers', toilets were unthought-of, nor were safety belts, but at least the windows could be opened. There was no radio and therefore no navigational safety.

By publicizing far and wide that his airline used only twin-engined aircraft, Handley Page was gulling the public into belief that they were safer than his rivals'. In fact they could not sustain level flight if one engine failed, so an extended powered glide preceded an inevitable forced landing. Their best attribute was the slow landing speed which in the months and years to come would prove a vital feature in the many emergency landings — but the light wing loading also meant that the machine rose and fell abruptly in the slightest turbulence. The real criterion of success was not the aeroplane but the skill, enthusiasm, devotion, and determination of the pilots — and theirs was the spirit which had taken the RAF to victory, though they must steady down and remember they were civilians licensed to fly by the Department of Civil Aviation.

To help them the DCA had issued a map and data with bearings for the *Aerial Route London (Hounslow)—France (St Inglevert)*, describing

the sequence in what now seems absurd detail; yet to pilots of those days it was precisely the way they navigated.

'From Hounslow Aerodrome (Civil) the route runs direct to Waddon aerodrome (Military) the course being 122° True. The Reservoirs 3½ miles S of Hounslow, and Hampton Court Palace 5 miles S.S.E. of Hounslow form prominent landmarks. Croydon military aerodrome is situated against the S.W. border of Waddon. When above Waddon, a good landmark being the open tanks containing blue liquid situated in Sutton Town, the course changes to 142° and continues so for 13 miles to Marlpit Hill, distinguished by the neighbouring Railway Station marked "Edenbridge" in white characters on the ground. A course of 97° is to be followed from this point to Ashford. The route is clearly marked by the main line of the South-Eastern & Chatham Railway . . . '

Despite that unmistakable iron guide, stretching on and on, straight as a die, every detail and landmark on its way to Ashford was described. At that town course changed to 146° for Lympne near Folkestone, thence 114° across the Strait of Dover to St Inglevert 29 miles distant, and with another change of course and great attention to landmarks, finally to Le Bourget.

Flying carefree and smoothly at a modest 80 mph and maybe 1,500 ft high on a sunny day, pilots subconsciously experienced great pleasure peering down at the unfolding English countryside and the fair land of France — but it was very different on days of fog, or obscuring rain and ceiling of low cloud. They were hemmed in.

On those occasions they might either select a southern route through the Redhill Gap in the 800-ft North Downs, or initially steer north past Alexandra Palace and then east around London's outskirts, turning south to the Thames, follow it to Gravesend, then through the Wye Valley to Ashford and the coast. A phone call to Lympne before starting secured a report of local weather, and one to the Paris office might reveal the temporary conditions at Le Bourget — if the French telephone system was working, for it was in parlous condition as aftermath of war. Blind-flying instruments had not been developed, and altimeters were unreliable: but the biggest problem was the compass, for it oscillated wildly after turns or on a blind and accidentally sinuous course. In the absence of proper instruments, balance could only be maintained by using whatever horizon there was as datum, driving pilots to fly low in conditions of bad visibility, and then safety depended on intimate knowledge of the country over which they flew. The Handley Pages, even though fitted with huge wheels for aileron operation, were very tiring to fly because of the sheer physical force necessary to keep on level keel. An old-timer commented: 'Pilot fatigue induced by such heavy controls had not been envisaged by designers or operators. The open cockpits were not heated and we were weighed down by heavy flying clothing restricting our movements. In mist and rain we frequently had to raise our goggles to see at all by peering round the windscreen in the face of an icy wind.' Ever present was the looming possibility of engine failure, so constant watch for suitable landing fields was the invariable practice.

Signature of the International Air Convention had been agreed by all contracting States except the neutral countries, Norway, Sweden, Denmark, Switzerland, and Holland, each refusing because Clause 5 bound signatories to forbid flight over their territory by non-contracting States — which meant an embargo on aircraft of the late enemy countries. In a move to secure cohesion Holt Thomas brought airline representatives of all countries together at The Hague — including Deutsche Luft Reederei, the cause of it all — and after three days' discussion, chaired by Sir Sefton Brancker, it was unanimously agreed to establish an International Air Traffic Association (IATA) as a controlling authority.

In September *The Aeroplane* recorded: 'During the past week, two fresh companies announced that they were starting London–Paris services. Both are French, the Compagnie Messageries Aériennes and Farman Frères'. The competing service began on Tuesday 15 September with the arrival of a single-engined ex-war Breguet which it was decided to operate on days alternating with Handley Page Transport — who triumphantly announced that in the past week they had carried 40 passengers. As counter-blast Holt Thomas paid public tribute to General Festing as organizer, Capt Donald Greig as manager, and the pilots Arthur Bayliss, Allan Riley, E.H. 'Bill' Lawford, and Charles R. McMullin — all of whom, whatever their RAF rank, basked in the soubriquet 'Captain'.

In the Hounslow office of A T & T, Greig had given the job of clerk to his young prospective brother-in-law, Capt Henry Spry Leverton, ex-prisoner of war, and his task was to ensure that all log books and inspection records were properly maintained. He was also in charge of the essential leather helmets and flying coats loaned to passengers to reduce the rigours of flying in the noisy and cold DH 9s and DH 16s; all too often they retained these items as souvenirs of their flying adventure. Sydney St Barbe was therefore put in charge of A T & T affairs at Le Bourget, where he cautiously took charge of the valuable clothing when passengers disembarked. From this developed a system of personal liaison, meeting passengers, explaining details of their journey, checking luggage and passports, taking them to the aircraft, and conversely receiving those from Paris and even placating them with a drink.

As Geoffrey Dorman, long the airline correspondent of *The Aeroplane*, recorded: 'One passenger thus tended was Albert Plesman, a big, bluff, handsome Dutchman who was due to fly by A T & T from London to Paris, but the regular machine became unserviceable, so Spry Leverton did what was then considered highly irregular. He approached the rival airline, Handley Page Transport Ltd, and asked if they had room for an A T & T passenger, with the result that Plesman travelled in one of the 0/400s.' That was to have repercussions, for on 7 October KLM Royal Dutch Airlines was officially established with Plesman as manager, and because of the Netherlands' non-alignment over the Air Convention it was decided to use

Starting an aircraft engine, 1919-style: this was achieved by turning a quick-release fitting on the propeller hub through shafting from a Ford T truck, as devised by Captain 'Benny' Hucks, RAF, a famous pre-war pilot.

pilots and aircraft hired from A T & T for the cross-Channel service. Further, a manager would be required for KLM's business in England: who better than Spry Leverton?

Handley Page made his next move by opening a Cricklewood–Hounslow–Brussels service on 23 September — even offering lunches at 3s packed in small baskets. But behind the scenes he was having problems. His trans Atlantic venture with the four-engined V/1500 had been cancelled and a programme of demonstrations substituted, but a forced landing through engine failure put the machine out of action for repairs. At this point the new Type W.8 airliner derived from the 0/400 was ready for flight. Because Capt Geoffrey Hill, the firm's test pilot, was ill, and Brackley still in the USA, Sholto Douglas was instructed to make the test flight but became so nettled at Handley Page's typical refusal to pay extra for these duties that he stormed out of the factory and re-joined the RAF, leaving the W.8 to await Hill's return.

Though share values of every company were dropping, a few business houses were contemplating use of communications aircraft. Shortly after the Paris Air Convention of the League of Nations was signed on 13 October, S. Instone & Co Ltd, steamship owners, led the way with purchase of a 375 hp Eagle-powered DH 4A and engaged Lieut Franklyn Barnard to fly it. The shipping founders were the brothers Einstein, who had changed their name by deed poll; now it was Sir Samuel Instone who controlled the business, and his younger brother Capt Alfred Instone was initiator of the aircraft interest to expedite transit of shipping documents between London and Continental ports and so save demurrage charges.

The Postmaster General was also convinced of aerial possibilities and announced that an Air Mail Service would be available on and after 10 November (though in fact bad weather prevented it that day). Various London Post Offices and certain provincial P.O.s would accept express letters for air carriage to France, Italy, Spain, and Switzerland at a surcharge fee of 2s 6d, and the mail would be loaded into a special DH 4A of A T & T distinguished by a pennant inscribed 'Royal Mail'.

That the letters might never reach their intended destination became evident within a few days. Jerry Shaw, flying a DH 4A from Paris with a single passenger aboard on a day of poor visibility, lost all sense of direction over

the Channel. Petrol was running low, and still no sight of England. Distrusting his compass, he climbed into the dark cloud hoping to take a sun-bearing on emerging, but inevitably stalled and spun blind through the enveloping opaqueness, centred the controls, and was lucky to recover from the whirl and achieve level flight low above the waves. Hope had almost gone when he discerned a distant plume of smoke, discovered it was a small coaster, and used it as focal point to circle in search of land. Light was fading. There was nothing. His only chance was to ditch alongside the ship. He came gliding down. The water drew closer. He switched off the engine. The ship's side became a swaying black cliff. Waves reared menacingly. Back with the stick: tail steeply down. Crump! Wild lurch — and lo! the 4A was resting on the water, tipped nose-down, wings awash.

Suddenly he remembered his passenger and turned in his seat. The coupé lid was wide open. He saw a bowler hat, a face beneath it, a figure clad only in undervest and pants. 'I realized we were for it', the man drawled with American inflection, 'so I crammed down my hat as a crash helmet and undressed in case we had a chance to swim!'

All ended well. They and the mail bag were hoisted aboard the *Harlech*, which proceeded to Weymouth, where next morning Jerry, in high

Right: De Havilland DH 16 (Aircraft Transport & Travel, 1919).
Bottom: Vickers Vimy Commercial (of the famed 'Go-Easy' Instone Air Line, 1919).

18

spirits, mystified the anxious Hounslow office by sending a telegram: 'Landed at Weymouth, proceeding to Waterloo'.

Towards the end of November the Report of the newly formed Advisory Committee for Civil Aviation was issued as a White Paper on *Imperial Air Routes*, and disclosed that a Cairo–Karachi route had been opened for military purposes, and would be available for civil traffic at an early date; similarly the route from Cairo to the Cape had been surveyed and a chain of landing places established. Of possible methods of financing such commercial air services, the Committee firmly decided that private enterprise with State aid should be adopted.

Implementing the prospect of long-distance airlines across the world was the steady stage-by-stage progress of the twin-engined Vickers Vimy ex-bomber entered for the £10,000 Australia flight contest. Piloted by Capt Ross Smith (who had surveyed the route while in the

RAF) and his brother Lieut Keith Smith, they had left Hounslow at 9.10 a.m. on 12 November, and after many adventures at last crossed the Timor Sea and landed at Port Darwin on 10 December, having flown 11,500 miles in 124 flying hours, thus forging the first great Empire link. This splendid victory for the Vickers organization was skilfully emphasized on 15 December when the new Science Museum building at South Kensington was presented with the actual Vimy which Sir John Alcock and Lieut Arthur Whitten Brown had flown the Atlantic six months earlier. Tragically, three days later Alcock was killed in the course of ferrying a Vickers four-seat commercial amphibian flying-boat to Paris for the first post-war Exposition Aéronautique.

Dominating the aircraft on display was Handley Page's W.8 biplane airliner, resplendent in ivory livery and glittering twin black nacelles housing the 450 hp Napier Lions. Robert Bager, successor to Sholto Douglas as

The first flight from London on Britain's first regular daily international service was by an Aircraft Transport & Travel DH 16 carrying four passengers.

chief pilot, had flown it to Le Bourget on only its second flight, and with wings folded it had been towed on its own wheels to the exhibition hall. At once it became news, for this was the world's first real contribution towards swift and safe but reasonably economic air transport carrying twelve to fourteen passengers with more comfort than ever before; and this time there were even toilet facilities!

Feet
Metres

Trial and Tribulation 1920-23

Hounslow, the main airport of England, was a primitive grass airfield 800 yards square on what remained of Hounslow Heath, on the west side of London. The nearby Thames was its signpost, particularly at dusk, for there was no radio to guide the way. Homeward-bound across the Dover cliffs, pilots flew north seeking a glint of the river at Tilbury, followed it through the heart of London checking distance by the passing bridges, picked up the L & SW Railway to Richmond and headed for the faint rotating light of the airport's gas-burning beacon which automatically operated half an hour after sunset for three hours. To show the landing area, petrol flares were hastily set in an 'L' across the grass, the shorter arm marking the end of the run, and at the last moment a magnesium flare beneath the wing could be fired electrically to reveal the ground more clearly. For machines that touched down at 50 mph or less it was relatively safe, for even in windless conditions they pulled up within 300 yards despite lack of wheel brakes.

Night or day, the airport offered negligible facilities. Petrol and oil was available, but no repair services, nor even a buffet in the shed used for a waiting room. At the Bath Road end were huts and six Bessoneaux canvas hangars in the east corner and on the west was a substantial double-fronted hangar with CUSTOMS painted on the left eave and DOUANE on the other. A 15-ft weather map of the cross-Channel shores painted on the door displayed weather reports written in chalk. Despite hazards of phone wires and cables, railway signals, trees, and a disused 'wireless' mast, Hounslow was regarded as easy and large, though subject to fog.

Pilots viewed Cricklewood with greater caution. A fully loaded 0/400 had to lumber up a ridge in the middle of the airfield and aim for a gap between the factory hangars, lifting with barely 100 yards in hand, then scrape low across Cricklewood Broadway, slowly gaining height. Nevertheless, on 10 January 1920 Cricklewood was approved as a Port of Entry, and Customs facilities made available on 18 February. Although his airline service had been running several months, Handley Page made this the occasion of formal inauguration with full

Press chorus, and Capt McIntosh took off in style with the recently converted G-EAMA direct for Paris. His erstwhile C.O., Major Brackley, after a discouraging six months with the V/1500 in the USA, had sailed back to England shortly before Christmas and was allocated the pioneering task, with Capt Fred Tymms as navigator, of piloting an 0/400, chartered by the *Daily Telegraph*, across 'darkest Africa' to the Cape, but they crashed in the Sudan, and it was Col van Rynveld with Capt Quintin Brand flying a Vickers Vimy who first achieved the Cape by air, though it took six weeks.

Pertinently, C.G. Grey observed: 'RAF officers and men in Asia and Africa are the real pioneers of our Imperial air routes. We know that Ross Smith under direction of General Borton surveyed the Australian route — but who were the unnamed pioneers who trekked across the Arabian Desert in Ford cars? Who were they who sweltered down the Red Sea coastline surveying the route to Aden, and who pushed into the African bush to build aerodromes along the upper reaches of the Nile and into the region of the Great Lakes? Few have done more distinguished service for Imperial aviation than these anonymous pioneers of the air routes.'

Sir Frederick Sykes exhorted: 'We have charted the earth, we must chart the air — but direct assistance is necessary. Subsidized competitors are in the field. The Imperial Dominion Governments must adopt a considered policy towards aviation. The first route to be helped must be Egypt to India.' But the early optimism of Handley Page and Holt Thomas was beginning to sag. There was not the great rush of passengers they expected on the Paris route. However, the former's intention of bringing air transport to South Africa, India, and Burma led him to register Handley Page (South Africa) Ltd and Handley Page Indo-Burmese Transport Ltd, and he was encouraged by a contract for carriage of air mail between Brazil and the Argentine. He also had his W.8 airliner ready for the Civil Aircraft Competition sponsored by the Air Ministry and was certain it would be a winner. Moreover the rival Aircraft Manufacturing Co's impressive DH 18 entrant was suddenly withdrawn. The company was in trouble.

First sign was Holt Thomas's resignation. He announced to the Press: 'By the amalgamation recently announced, the Birmingham Small Arms Co Ltd (BSA) acquired control of my company. Their interest lies in our large factories adaptable for motor bodies and engineering; naturally their first step is to cut expense not likely to be remunerative in the near future. Could I honestly advise my co-directors, in view of the government's apathetic attitude, to continue an expensive technical department devoted to aircraft design?' Sombrely, C.G. Grey said: 'It has been left to newcomers in the industry to shut down one of the oldest firms'.

Off to Norway! A typical impression of a Handley Page civil 0/400 climbing away — but this one was scrapped in 1920 after a pile-up.

For the time being it remained an entity and advertised the new single-engined airliner, which had just made its maiden flight, as 'the Airco 18 saloon airliner carrying pilot and eight passengers, capable of a speed of 121 mph at 5,000 feet with full load and a climb of 10,000 feet in $20\frac{1}{2}$ minutes'. In fact it was a drastic revision of de Havilland's DH 14 successor to his DH 9A, with 5 ft greater span and 50 hp more, and the pilot aft of the eight-seat cabin. Chief drawback was a much higher landing speed than previously experienced because the wing loading had been increased from the $9\frac{1}{2}$ lb/sq ft of the DH 9A to 12 lb/sq ft — whereas the Handley Page 0/400, loaded at only 8 lb/sq ft, touched down at very slow speed.

Soon BSA confirmed that the aviation side of Airco was to be closed. Thereupon Holt Thomas came to the rescue of his protégé, advising de Havilland to approach the new directors — who eventually offered him design rights, jigs, and work in hand for a nominal sum. Holt Thomas urged D.H. to form a new company and promised limited capital on condition that Arthur Turner, the Airco financial expert, was made chairman. This was eagerly accepted, for RAF repair contracts had been transferred and assurance given that A T & T would not cancel their order for six DH 16s.

Meanwhile Winston Churchill on 12 March had told Parliament that 'civil aviation must fly by itself'. A step in that direction was a much-publicized demonstration to Air Ministry technicians, politicians, and Press of the Marconi Company's development of direction finding (D/F), using a Handley Page 0/400 piloted by Major Foot. 'Wireless' stations at Pevensey, Lowestoft, and Chelmsford took radio bearings on the machine from which its position was calculated at Marconi's and transmitted to Foot while guests 'listened in' and were told what was going on.

The problems of circumnavigating London, either northward or southward, in poor visibility had already led to reconsideration of Hounslow's suitability as the main Customs Airport. A location south of the metropolis was considered essential, and eventually Croydon was chosen, comprising the adjacent airfields of Beddington and Waddon used as one. The flying area would be Waddon, on the east side of Plough Lane which separated them, but a level crossing would be made for aircraft to taxi to the ex-RAF hangars and huts of Beddington while traffic was stopped by a man with a red flag. The new aerodrome was far from ideal. In the northeast corner of Waddon was the wartime National Aircraft Factory — recently purchased by the Aircraft Disposal Co Ltd (ADC) — and behind it the Wallington water tower, both presenting a dangerous obstruction. Not only was the landing area rough and narrow but it had a ridge which could make aircraft invisible from the tarmac apron, and when the wind blew from the southeast the Purley valley caused down-draughts. However the die was cast, so the war-time huts adjacent to Plough Lane were converted to offices and a Customs

Engine check of a HP civil 0/400, while the maintenance party waits and the aerodrome policeman stands by to prevent stowaways or other intruders.

building, though a control tower still had to be made.

Quick to realize a potential source of new revenue, Trust Houses Ltd applied for a licence to convert and extend the original canteen into an hotel — whereupon the chairman of the Bench jocularly inquired whether that meant passengers might arrive in such condition that alcohol was required for their revival!

On 25 March 1920 this, the embryonic London Terminal Aerodrome, managed by Major S.T.L. Greer, ex-RFC, was formally opened by Lord Londonderry. *Flight* reported: 'It would appear that exclusive Wallington is anything but pleased with its new neighbour. A suggestion that the air terminus be named after that district has created strong opposition in the local council. Therefore Croydon is to become still more famous by adopting the newly born infant.'

One by one, the DH 4s, 9s, and 16s of Aircraft Transport & Travel came flying in and were duly housed in the two big RAF hangars. The Instone DH 4A *City of Cardiff* was also an early arrival, though their newly acquired resplendent blue and silver Vimy Commercial was not hangered there until 30 April, by which time A T & T had received its first DH 18 and the pilots were learning to handle it. Because of cheaper maintenance facilities at Cricklewood, Handley Page continued activities there, but as his pilots still had to fly across or around London to pick up passengers he privately mourned that this cost extra petrol, yet he held out for

another year, and at least was gratified in May that the PMG awarded the contract to him when the rival A T & T tried to negotiate increased rates for the carriage of mail but failed. To ensure safer delivery he fitted his aircraft with 'wireless'.

That month international aviation took a step forward with signature of the ICAN Regulations by 27 countries world-wide — but Norway, Sweden, Denmark, Switzerland, and the Netherlands still refused to sign because it was in their interest to admit banned German civil aircraft and for their own formative airlines to extend eventually through Germany to Italy and beyond — a matter particularly concerning the Netherlands and its Far East interests. But all things can be circumvented. A Protocol to the Convention was agreed, whereby 'derogations', by which 'exceptions' was meant, could be made if good reason was shown. The wayward signatures followed, and on 17 May KLM Royal Dutch Airlines initiated a thrice-weekly service between Schiphol (Amsterdam) and Croydon, borrowing from A T & T a DH 16 flown by Jerry Shaw for the occasion.

However, it was competition from the French which was proving alarming. 'Their Government', declared Brancker, 'has increased its subsidies to commercial aircraft which has enabled them to reduce the London–Paris fare to £6 6s, and for a year have run a most successful service from Toulouse to Morocco.'

Below: The eight-seat DH 18 with Lion engine was the first post-war design used by A T & T, and made its first flight in March 1920.
Bottom: The Handley Page 0/10 was a ten-seat version of the 0/7 civil adaptation of the 0/400, and G-EATN had an Aveline auto-stabilizer. Fuel tanks were in extended nacelles, unlike the 0/400.

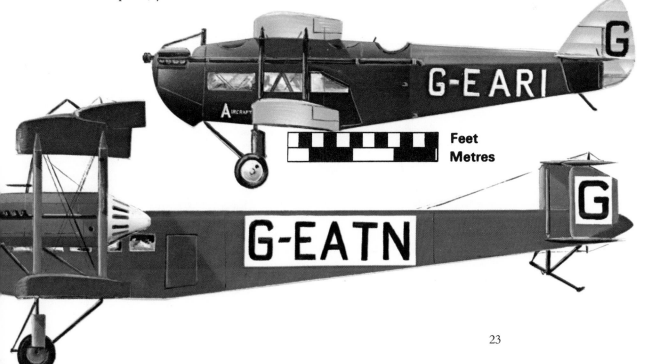

The Civil Aviation Committee, chaired by Lord Weir, recommended direct assistance to the British airlines, and on 26 June a White Paper on *Development of Civil Aviation* hopefully recommended direct subsidies limited to a maximum of £250,000 spread over 1920–21 and 1921–22. Payment was proposed for each three-month period on a basis of 25 per cent of total certified gross revenue of an approved airline, provided that a minimum of 45 days of return flights was made each period — but instead the policy of 'wait and see' was adopted in case the airlines made the grade unassisted, for in the late summer A T & T just managed to break even because every seat was taken on each flight.

Aviation matters were beginning to impinge on the judicial courts. An echo of the crash of a big experimental RAF triplane in May 1919 became a precedential case on the rights of insured persons in aeroplane accidents. The Aviation Insurance Association was sued for £4,000 by the executor of one of the pilots but contended there was no liability because the accident occurred before the machine left the ground, whereas the risk had been accepted 'from time of first flight'. The judge sided with common sense in deciding that the risk of flight began on the ground — but this seemed to yield promise of later legal complexity.

At least it was now clear that civil action was a contingency for which air transport operators must be prepared, so the risks policy on aircraft must be extended to cover passengers. Premiums were generally high, and assured liabilities low. It was unusual to cover pilot or passenger for more than £1,000 because anyone earning that amount was regarded as rich and relatively rare. The greater risk seemed third-party claims for damage to buildings, crashing into a multitude of people, or injury to cattle or crops in a forced landing.

Although Handley Page was uplifted by success in winning the Air Ministry's Civil Aircraft Competition with his W.8, both his airline and that of Holt Thomas's A T & T were rapidly approaching financial disaster. Winter weather and cancelled flights were reducing income, and though both companies sent canvassers to big London firms hoping to persuade them to send goods by air instead of rail and boat, little business was obtained.

On 6 December a brief report in the *Daily Mail* from its Paris correspondent indicated that A T & T Ltd was bankrupt and had stopped operations; that Instone had laid up its aircraft for the winter; and Handley Page, having abandoned the Amsterdam route at the end of October, was sending only an occasional machine across the Channel if there happened to be enough trade or passengers to make it worth while. The eight or nine 0/400s, of which three had been cargo and mail carriers on the Brussels/Amsterdam route and the others ten-seaters, had averaged only 30 minutes flying a day, and there had been about 100 forced landings due to bad weather and frequent engine failure. However 4,000 passengers had been carried without fatality in a total of 320,000 miles.

But on 14 December the worst happened. Robert Bager, chief pilot of the airline, crashed into a tree after taking off in misty conditions on the limited easterly length of Cricklewood. His 0/400 G-EAMA, in use since November 1919, burst into flames on hitting the ground, killing him and two of the six passengers; three survivors escaped through the rear cabin windows, and the fourth was hurled from the nose cockpit, miraculously escaping with concussion, and was discovered next day in Paris. He had absolutely no recollection of travelling there by boat and train.

Only a week earlier Bager had written a typical account of a cross-Channel flight: 'Left Paris 12.35. Messrs Marconi had nothing of interest until crossing the Channel, when Lympne said that because of thick fog we must land at Cricklewood instead of Croydon. Approaching Lympne we met the fog, and Cricklewood Marconi chipped in with "Fog clearing. Carry on". I grunted, and made for Cricklewood via north London. Passing Maidstone, Mr Marconi of Cricklewood said "Thick fog at Cricklewood. Proceed to Croydon". I didn't know exactly where Croydon was, but hoped to see the Crystal Palace — but the fog grew thicker and thicker. We went on, not recognizing a thing, until by my watch we should be somewhere near, so I told the mate to ask Croydon to oblige with a rocket; but instead — what do you think? — they told us where we were! They said change 80° for Croydon. I remembered how we were shot down in the big war when we got triangulated by listening posts, and thinking this must be the same sort of thing, altered course. Five minutes later we came plonk over Croydon. It couldn't have been done better if they had thrown us a line. We landed at 3.10 with five passengers and freight.'

1921

On Christmas Eve 1920, Major Brackley tested G-EATN, an 0/10 civil variant of the 0/400 fitted with the French-designed Aveline Auto-stabilizer which could, if the air was not too rough, hold a steady course and attitude. On the 30th he recorded: 'To Paris for French Government competition with stabilizer. Flew for over an hour without touching controls.' On 7 January he 'landed at Lympne in pouring rain with clouds on ground'. Next day 'flew from Lympne for one hour without touching controls but SE London fogbound; came low to keep on course. Both engines began misfiring. Had to return to Gravesend to find clear air. Landed in rotten field, side of hill.' For the rest of the month there were more demonstrations. One of his passengers was Colonel the Master of Sempill, who invited him to join a Mission to the Imperial Japanese he was leading. Brackley accepted, having proved the value of the stabilizer, and Handley Page received a Ministry contract to install the equipment in fourteen of the RAF's 0/400s.

With the departure of Brackley, Capt McIntosh was made chief pilot of Handley Page Transport. In the next fortnight only six flights out and five return were made, totalling ten and five passengers respectively. Although McIntosh, as spokesman for the pilots, offered to fly, at least for a time, without pay, Handley Page declined, expressing appreciation of this loyalty. On 28 February 1921, all operations ceased, and Instone Air Line followed suit. *The Aeroplane* fumed: 'British civil aviation died on Monday last with the cessation of the Handley Page cross-Channel service killed by the forward policy of the French Government and apathy of our own'.

Two days after closure, Winston Churchill appointed Lord Londonderry as chairman of a 'Committee of Three' empowered to consult representatives of the three British airlines on the burning question of subsidies. Within a fortnight terms proposed by Alfred Instone had been agreed.

Woods Humphrey resigned from Handley Page Transport and joined Col Searle of the Daimler Hire Co Ltd to form Daimler Airway from the ashes of Air Transport & Travel Ltd. In his place Alex Cogni, the publicity manager, was promoted to manage Handley Page Transport, and on 19 March the airline again began flying to Paris, but now charged the same fares as the French, Capt Hope making the opening flight with G-EATM carrying seven passengers. Two days later the Instone Air Line reopened in more splendid fashion, attended by the Press and adorned with dignitaries, including Lord Londonderry, to witness departure at 12.30 p.m. of their Vimy *City of London* flown by Frank Barnard. To make the occasion even more memorable a magnificently attired commissionaire was employed to shepherd passengers to their seats; but so arduous did he find the task that at 2 p.m. he was discovered in a state of utter inebriation and was instantly dismissed — followed by a search for suitable garments with which to send the fallen hero home.

Daimler Airway made a slow start. When A T & T went into liquidation in December the BSA-Daimler Group disposed of every asset including the aircraft, but the DH 18s reserved for them would be loaned by the Air Ministry to Daimler Airway. Only a few months earlier Searle had publicly declared that civil aviation had been handled by optimists, and that aeroplanes must fly ten hours daily, not two, to be profitable. He had cuttingly criticized design features that led to unserviceability. However he regarded the £5,000 DH 18 with 450 hp Napier Lion as a big step forward as it could earn £160 a day on two return journeys to Paris, and 'this showed a profit of £100 a day, so the machine could be written off in three months'.

Pilots found the big biplane pleasant to fly, and despite earlier criticism of being so far behind the wings, the landing view had not proved difficult. An impression of safe solidity was given by the plywood fuselage covering, but there were discreet burstable fabric escape hatches in the roof. 'Cy' Holmes was the first to demonstrate their value, for the engine of his DH 18 failed at take-off, and he crash-landed into a Croydon garden; the machine fell sideways and the door jammed, but the passengers escaped through the roof without too great panic. Impressed by the economics of these machines, Instone Air Line proposed adding three to their fleet, of which two were hired from the Air Ministry.

Departure of Churchill from his post as Secretary of State for the Department of War and Air led to division of these offices and Capt the Hon F.E. 'Freddie' Guest was appointed Secretary of State for Air. Three weeks later he reported a temporary scheme of airline subsidies. 'The Air

Pre-flight preparation of the DH 18 owned by Instone Air Line, which operated five of these machines.

Council guarantee a clear profit of 10 per cent to each firm on gross receipts excluding subsidies, any excess to be returned to the Air Ministry. The subsidy will be £75 for each single scheduled flight, provided the maximum payable does not exceed £25,000 to each firm for the trial period of seven months subject to total liability for the Air Ministry of £88,200 for the financial year ending 31 March 1922.'

Hope sprang anew. Croydon regained its atmosphere of camaraderie. 'English once more can be heard in the Trust House, and Emile Bouderie and his Goliath aircraft are again getting their legs and undercarriages pulled. To make it still more like last summer some of the old pilots are returning in varying capacities', wrote a devotee. Nevertheless Handley Page Transport was far from the end of its troubles. The entire Handley Page empire was bankrupt, and the factory manning was less than 100. Lieut-Col J. Barrett-Lennard was installed as general manager by the Bank of Scotland to take control. Cricklewood was eliminated as a Customs Airport at the end of May and though the 0/400s were still housed there, passengers had to make their own way to Croydon.

The five remaining Handley Page Transport pilots, headed by McIntosh, sometimes found these old machines had a great struggle to take off from Croydon. Capt Wilcockson, with eight passengers aboard an 0/400 overladen with cargo, was the first to experience the down-draught caused by a southeast wind across Purley Valley. Taking off for Paris from

the far northwest corner, he just managed to become airborne, then the machine sank, veering to port, scraped across Coldharbour Lane, and was forced down in a field just long enough to pull up. The passengers were disembarked, the 0/400 flown back to the airfield, lightened, and a new start made. A week later another was unable to clear Purley Ridge and thumped down in a field beset with scrub woodland.

Then came the knock: the Certificate of Airworthiness (C of A) was reduced to permit only five passengers. Investigation showed that several aircraft differed by as much as 500 lb; hence that sinking feeling, as one wit put it! Walter Savage was appointed engineering manager. Engines were checked for power, rigging adjusted, and eventually approval was obtained for eight passengers and Marconi AD 2 radio, for which the Air Ministry planned to set up direction-finding stations at Croydon, Pulham, and Lympne — yet it was still a pilot's personal knowledge of the countryside which counted, because flying still depended on visual balance; artificial horizons and direction indicators remained a dream of the future.

The only sign of Daimler Airway at Croydon was one storekeeper with a shed of oddments and two Airco 16s deteriorating in a Bessoneaux hangar. The pilots had dispersed. Cyril Holmes and Robin Duke, together with Gordon Olley from Handley Page Transport, had joined KLM, where one-eyed Capt Hinchliffe was chief pilot.

By comparison, Instone Air Line had fur-

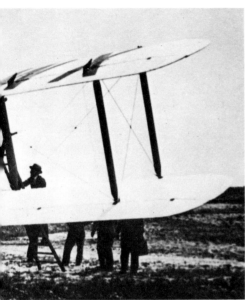

nished one of the white-washed single-storey brick buildings as a waiting room, and the company name was the first which caught the eye after passing the Trust House Hotel, now with a public bar, at the entrance to the narrow aerodrome road. To go one better Handley Page erected a notice twice as big above the roof of their new offices a little farther on, and by the beginning of June were fully established at Croydon.

Instone had lost one of their DH 18s, *City of Paris*, through a forced landing in France. This was partly offset by purchase from the receiver of the British Aerial Transport Co of that air-line's BAT FK 26 five-seater for excursion day flights to Paris, flown by smiling Capt Philip Robins, youngest of the pilots, who had joined Instone when A T & T had closed down, and was destined to become a priest a few years later.

Back from his Empire Tour, the Prince of Wales, charmer of the public, spoke prophetic words at a dinner for the Dominion Premiers: 'There is no doubt that the future of rapid Imperial inter-communication lies in the air, and I trust that the time is not far distant when civil aviation will have built a great air organiza-tion on the same lines as our mercantile marine, and that delegates of the next Imperial confer-ence will travel by the Imperial routes now being worked out. Present ship and rail com-munications are insufficient for a Common-wealth of Nations which extends over all parts of the globe. The British Empire has more to gain from efficient air communication than any other State in the world, and I feel sure no time will be lost in solving the problems connected therewith.'

Churchill, on return from the Middle East, spoke to similar effect: 'Plans are being made for aeroplanes to fly regularly to and fro across the desert between Baghdad and Cairo. Once the route has been marked out the whole Air Force in Mesopotamia could be speedily trans-ported to Palestine or Egypt. Arrangements could also be made to fly a certain number of commercial aeroplanes carrying mails, and possibly passengers, and could afford a valuable link in the chain of Imperial communications, ultimately resulting to great advantage of shortening communication with India and with Australia and New Zealand,'

Between Transjordan and the great rivers of Iraq spread 500 miles of desert. Those who flew across it saw how unmistakable were the wheel tracks of lorries used near military camps. Therefore Sir Hugh Trenchard, Chief of Staff, decided that the best guide for aircraft would be a double furrow ploughed the whole length of the route, with fuel reserves stored in drums at suitable points. Work was immediately started by parties moving centrally from either end to Rutbah Wells, the meeting place of Arab tribes, where two sparse streams gleaned water from the distant rugged hills.

On 15 June the Air Ministry announced new terms of state assistance for commercial flying. Operating firms were to be 'approved', but this implied no intention of discontinuing the Handley Page Transport and the Instone Air Line services under the temporary scheme. Here was the green light for Col Searle and Major Woods Humphery who had completed the metamorphosis of A T & T into Daimler Airway. The Air Ministry stated: 'With approval of the Lords Commissioners of HM Treasury, a sum of approximately £200,000 per annum will be set aside from civil aviation votes for three years'. This included expenditure on the temporary scheme to date, and cost of pur-chasing 'aeroplanes of modern commercial type to be hired out to approved firms at a monthly rental equivalent to 2½ per cent of the cost of the machine. After thirty payments the machines will become the property of the firms.' Operatives, directors, and shareholders of the firms had to be British, and only aircraft and engines of British design and manufacture qualified. Approval having been obtained: 'The Air Ministry will grant subsidies during the same period of three years on the basis of 25 per cent of an approved firm's gross earnings operating on any of the following routes: London–Paris, London–Brussels, London–Amsterdam. Further routes may be approved at a latter date.'

Summer brought a sudden rush for flights to Paris. Handley Page's dapper Alex Cogni was despondently wringing his hands, saying there were more passengers than seats — largely because G-EALX had been scrapped after a heavy landing in April, leaving less than half the original fleet and still no sign that the 0/400s would be replaced by the new W.8. The prototype was 'incessantly expected' at Croydon, but was engineless and quietly accumulating dust at Cricklewood while Handley Page endeavoured to hire Jupiter engines from the Bristol Aeroplane Company. The competitive risk stirred Napier's to provide Lion engines which were promptly installed, and on 29 August H.H. Perry of Aircraft Disposals flight-tested the machine at Cricklewood and then ferried it to Croydon where the Handley Page pilots flew it with glee, finding enormous improvement on their old ex-war bombers in both ease of handling and ability to climb. However, its Public Transport Category C of A had still to be issued.

Four days earlier Daimler Hire Ltd were 'approved' under the new subsidy scheme, and now their long-delayed operations recommenced, using the hired DH 18s. Searle had hoped to replace them with DH 29 cantilever monoplanes, but these proved to have deficiences, so de Havilland returned to biplane design with a machine based on the valiant DH 18 but re-located the crew of two in front of the wings to give better view. Because of low price an ex-war Rolls-Royce Eagle engine was initially selected, but Searle insisted that Napier Lions must be standardized as they were fitted to his DH 18s, and could be run at low power to reduce wear and tear. Thus the DH 34 evolved, with all-up weight increased from 2·56 tons to 3·2 tons, though this gained only 100 lb on the original disposable load of 0·9 tons because of greater fuel requirements; but it also resulted in what was regarded as a frightening landing speed of 60 mph, and that certainly meant disaster if force-landed in the small fields of England. Searle's intention was to use the DH 34s in the spring of 1922, and great pressure was applied to ensure that delivery dates were met.

That late summer and early autumn traffic steadily increased. Some 400 passengers a week were passing through Customs, whereas the previous year there had been only a few score — yet the public at large remained indifferent, nor was the cause of air travel helped by the dramatic catastrophe which overtook the airship R.38, which broke up amid flames and smoke and fell into the Humber.

October passed with no sign of the revised subsidy scheme being put into effect. Traffic began to fall.

That autumn the British pilots with KLM were being replaced by their Dutch colleagues. Gordon Olley left to re-join Handley Page Transport; Hinchliffe became a freelance; and Jerry Shaw retired from active flying and joined Shell in charge of petrol sales at Croydon to counter the rival activities of Anglo-American,

both having recently installed a battery of petrol pumps in the Customs enclosure to replace hand-operated bowser and petrol cans. Not only was the airfield thus enhanced, but it now had an aerial lighthouse controlled from the Tower, and there would soon also be one at Lympne on a 50-ft tower. For the interest of waiting passengers at Croydon a large route map was displayed on which model 'air expresses' moved along the various routes. There was even talk of Instone Air Line ordering uniforms of naval cut for pilots and operational staff instead of their motley civilian suits. It was the joke of the day for the cheerful band of youthful airline and freelance pilots drinking their pints at the Trust Bar, or playing darts, or poker.

Fog on 20 October prevented the first Paris-bound scheduled flight of the new Handley Page W.8, but that same day Capt McIntosh fortuitously found fame though no fortune as 'All Weather Mac'. *The Aeroplane* reported: 'What is considered by those at Croydon to be one of the finest shows yet put up by civil flying was accomplished on Thursday by Mr. R.H. McIntosh. Just before 1400 hours those having lunch looked out of the window and seeing the fog concluded there would be no flying. Soon afterwards the familiar double beat of Rolls-Royce engines could be heard from the SE so the aerodrome firework display began. Col Bristow went to the Control Tower and kept in communication by wireless with Mr McIntosh who could not see the aerodrome. Colonel Bristow told him that he had crossed south of the aerodrome. He then turned and passed low over Wallington, went along the north side, of which he was duly informed, then started to climb above the fog to see if he could spot the rockets and presently saw little puffs which he thought were pieces of cloud until he saw a

Daimler Airway began commercial operations with this scarlet-painted DH 34 on 2 April 1922, only a week after Cobham had made the initial flight of the prototype, which was cleared by Martlesham in one day.

rocket burst. Thereupon he shoved his nose towards whence they came, suddenly caught sight of the ADC sheds through the murk and a moment later we on the aerodrome saw him. He promptly dived for the ground and landed across Plough Lane, disappearing into the fog, out of which he was presently seen taxi-ing to the Customs. He was accorded an ovation and whisky and soda, both well deserved. The feat goes to show that landing through fog can be made quite practicable when wireless methods are more developed, and with improved lighting and pyrotechnics.'

But in fact, as 'Mac' said later, he had lost his trailing aerial in the branches of a tree and the radio set was useless, so he heard nothing of the instructions that Col Bristow was so briskly giving. He had been flying in clear blue above patchy overcast, and not until passing Sevenoaks had low cloud forced him to fly under it at a mere 200 ft, dropping to 50 ft where he lost his aerial. Presently, realizing he had overshot Croydon, he tried approaches from various directions through the mist and fog, saw the twin towers of the Crystal Palace sticking through the low cloud $1\frac{1}{2}$ miles away, and knowing they pointed southwest at Croydon, set course above the overcast and began a gradual let-down using low power ready to open up and climb away at any moment, but glimpsed the glint of the ADC's glass roof, realized he was too high, went round in a left-hand turn, saw the western boundary hedge of Plough Lane, cut engines and touched down. Why did he take that risk? Partly a pilot's pride in overcoming difficulties, but largely because to toil back to Lympne would take 40 minutes and meant sending the passengers on by train, and returning for the machine another day.

But there were greater problems. Sir Eric Geddes, a big man of iron will and strong prejudice, had been appointed chairman of an official committee to recommend drastic reduction of government expenditure. Under his shrewd surveillance there seemed little chance of help for the struggling airlines — and certainly no sign that he might soon be linked with them.

1922

In January 1922 Handley Page Transport Ltd were fortunate that a forced landing of their 0/400 G-EATM piloted by McIntosh did not end in fatality. All the way from Croydon he

had struggled to fly beneath low cloud, but at Beauvais, where the ground was higher, he was forced to turn back and landed on the nearby airfield. On phoning Le Bourget, cloud base was reported at 500 ft with visibility two or three miles; off he went again, this time flying blind. Assuming 30 minutes for the 40-mile flight to Paris, he made a gradual let-down, expecting to break cloud over Le Bourget. Instead there was a resounding crash as the machine hit the hard earth, then a series of bangs and bounces for 100 yards until it tipped on its nose, crushing the structure and twisting the fuselage. An elderly male passenger and a young German girl were flung against the forward bulkhead, relatively unharmed, and the wireless operator despite three cracked ribs managed to extricate McIntosh, who had fractured the bones of his feet and torn a ligament. It was all in the game.

Handley Page at last had sufficient money to lay down two more W.8s, for which he extracted Rolls-Royce Eagle engines from his Aircraft Disposals business, tactfully explaining: 'Practical experience showed that not only is the excess of power provided by the Lions too great, but the speed is greater than necessary for the London–Paris line'. With those engines, cruising speed had been only 100 mph; now it would be 90 mph. His economics also dictated that the engines were uncowled because 'by the time the weight of cowling has been added, and considering the extra complication and difficulty of getting at the engine, the gain would be so small that it is better to leave the engines bare'. Ostensibly as a safety precaution, fuel tanks were placed on the top wing, but these introduced new danger, as Capt Wilcockson found: 'I was operating the evening flight to Paris on the modified G-EAPJ and presently noticed that fuel in one tank was O.K. and the other nearly empty. Some 20 miles from Paris this engine stopped. That was because no provision had been made for petrol interchange between the two tanks, and although there was plenty in the other tank it could not be used. I landed in a cornfield but the aircraft dropped into a sunken road across it and was a complete write-off. I had eleven passengers but luckily no one was hurt: two were thrown through a gap in the fuselage on to the ground and the rest in a heap at the front of the cabin.'

Despite huge slashes resulting from the Report of the Geddes Committe on reduction of every aspect of governmental expenditure,

the deferred 'permanent' subsidy scheme went into effect in April, based on hopeful assumption that traffic would double — but there was a poor start with particularly bad weather seriously limiting the number of flights. However, the new DH 34, carrying a consignment of newspapers, was flown on its inaugural service to Paris by Capt Hinchliffe, but there was some concern about its performance. *Flight* reported: 'After an extraordinarily long run it only just managed to clear the hedge, and was so low that it disappeared from sight in the valley south of the aerodrome. When attempting to leave Le Bourget for the return journey, again with a heavy load, the machine stuck in the mud, and was unable to get away. It will be remembered that this happened with the DH 18s; for a long time their full load was at the most seven passengers, but when pilots and mechanics gained experience, the full load of eight and quantities of baggage could be carried with ease.'

Later that day the second machine, with silver-doped wings and blue fuselage in the livery of Instone Air Line, was flown by Capt Barnard to Paris, but excited less comment because he discovered that it paid to keep the tail down during the take-off run.

There were changes in techniques too at the Air Ministry. On 1 April Sir Frederick Sykes resigned as Controller-General of Civil Aviation, and the department became the Directorate of Civil Aviation, of which Sir Sefton Brancker was appointed Director (DCA) at the beginning of May. At a ceremony on the 16th

he christened the first two Handley Page W.8bs *Princess Mary* and *Prince George*, and commented: 'In the past I have criticized the Air Ministry's aviation policy, but now it becomes my turn to be criticized'. Removing and resecuring his glittering monocle, the dapper 'Brancks' added with richly crisp intonation: 'Unfortunately, as far as the present financial year is concerned, the policy for civil aviation is already settled, but next year I hope to frame the best possible'. Handley Page, towering benignly beside him, was seen to smile with gratification — or was it because he had stolen another march over the Instone Air Line, whose pilots were making familiarization flights between London and Paris with their new, single-engined, deep-bodied Vickers Vulcan biplane which clearly had the same lineage as the now almost ancient twin-engined Vickers Commercial which had been their mainstay?

Disaster now overtook popular Robin Duke of Daimler Airway flying a DH 18 (G-EAWO) on 7 April. It was the first mid-air collision in the history of air transport. There was misty visibility. He was flying at a few hundred feet, following a road through a valley near Grandvilliers, his forward view obliterated by the broad width of the fuselage. A Farman Goliath of Grands Express Aériens by unique coincidence was flying at the same height on the reciprocal course above the same road. They met head-on. All were killed, one being the sixteen-year-old air steward of the DH 18, whose newly instituted job was to serve coffee

Left: Public image: Jack Sanderson of Daimler Airway was the world's first aerial steward, but was victim of a fatal DH 34 crash in 1922.
Right: Public image: Gordon P. Olley, a characterful cockney pilot, with a millionaire passenger ready to embark on a DH 50 of the eventual Imperial Airways Air Taxi service.

out of a vacuum flask to his passengers.

Air Ministry officials, airline representatives, and pilots from all companies immediately met 'to plan routes and rules which would make the chance of air collision practically nil'. But the problem was not so easily solved, for each pilot had his favourite landmarks and none could agree which was the best route for every kind of weather. Though it was recommended that all machines should carry wireless sets it was not feasible to concentrate on them when low down in bad visibility, nor was there a proper system of let-down when a machine had precariously climbed through the opaqueness to the clear skies above.

Nevertheless, on the evening of Duke's crash, 'an aeroplane which carried eight people, including a navigator, wireless officer, and Air Ministry officials responsible for lighting and wireless arrangement of the route, left Biggin Hill about 8.30 p.m., flew to Croydon, and landed there. The very experienced pilot reported that the aerodrome floodlighting of dispersed searchlight beams and an illuminated "L" were the best he had ever seen, and made landing as easy by night as by day.' Thereafter the machine flew to Lympne, guided by temporary aerial lighthouses at Tatsfield and Cranbrook, then over the Channel towards St Inglevert, aided by the marine lighthouse at Cap Gris Nez which was visible from above Biggin Hill, and soon the French aerial lighthouse at St. Inglevert came in sight. The pilot then retraced his course, landed at Lympne, left again for Croydon, re-circled the massed lights, and headed back to Biggin Hill, his landing lit only by wing-tip and ground flares. 'The general impression of those aboard', said one of the passengers, 'was that it is easier to find a course by night than day, and provided the Continental organization is as good as ours there should be no difficulty in commercial night flying over the London–Paris route.' That was splendid if it was clear weather.

The Daimler accident seemed to cause renewed misgivings for traffic build-up proved slow, yet on 2 June one of the DH 34s (G-EBBS) broke all records by making five single journeys between London and Paris in a day. Unfortunately that was tempered with news next morning that a Spad of the French airline *en route* from Croydon to Paris inexplicably dived into the sea off Folkestone; and the pilot, M Morin, and two passengers were killed. Four days later René Labouchère, piloting a

Farman Goliath, made the first commercial night flight from Paris to Croydon, then took off again and arrived at Le Bourget before dawn.

The end of that month marked the first occasion on which a railway company became interested in aviation other than to compete with it — for an agreement was made between Supermarine Aviation Works Ltd and the London & South Western Railway (LSWR) to run a joint airline between Southampton and Le Havre, Cherbourg, and the Channel Islands, though discussions with the Air Ministry would be necessary to ensure a share in the subsidy fund, and the firm still had to be registered as The British Marine Air Navigation Co Ltd.

Whether it could prove profitable seemed doubtful, though between 14 and 20 August 734 paying passengers crossed the Channel in British airlines, of which Handley Page Transport alone carried 260. However the latter's parent firm was again in dire trouble with debts of £800,000, and the £1 preference shares were worth only 6d. The Board had no option other than to retain H.P. as managing director, for it was on his genius and determination that the whole future of the company depended. He had long cultivated the friendship of Sir Sefton Brancker and was preaching the gospel that separate routes should be allocated to each British airline, undoubtedly implying that the most popular should go to the safest airline — which must be the one using twin-engined aircraft exclusively! Backed by Col Searle and Sir Samuel Instone, he argued that the current subsidy scheme was financially unworkable. In the first six months of the year, combined traffic of the three companies had been 5,860 passengers on 1,588 flights, resulting in a gross revenue of only £38,184 plus subsidies of £31,130. As former managing director of A T & T, Brancker fully understood the problem. The result was than on 1 October a revised scheme was introduced giving compensatory payment of £19,108 for the first three months of the current year, £15,931 for the next three months, and £304,000 was allocated from that date to 31 March 1924. Additionally, each company received free equipment to the value of £28,500, and in the following year would be given £15,000 each towards the purchase of new aircraft.

November fogs were beginning to dislocate air services to the Continent, though the London–Manchester route operated by Daimler Airway was attaining considerable regularity. With more cash available, Handley Page became more optimistic of eventual success of his own service, particularly as he had modified the W.8b to the W.8c which could carry sixteen passengers, thus materially improving the economics. *Flight* reported: 'Any one seeing the new W.8 take off must realize that the reserve power is more than ample, the machine literally bouncing into the air after an exceedingly short run and climbing at an angle reminiscent of a Scout'. There could have been no load aboard, for at maximum all-up weight the ground climb was only 370 ft/min, increasing to a mere 425 ft/min if load was reduced by 1,000 lb, and that meant eliminating half the passengers or all the fuel!

1923

Early in 1923, Sir Samuel Hoare appointed a committee 'to consider the present working of the scheme of cross-Channel subsidies, and to advise on the best method of subsidizing cross-Channel air transport in future, on the assumption that HM Government would be prepared to continue to make provision for this service at the rate of £200,000 p.a. for a further term of say three years'. The new Committee of six was chaired by Sir Herbert Hambling, deputy chairman of Barclays Bank. They quickly decided that limitation to three years would prevent proper development of their recommendations, so terms of reference were changed to: 'Advise on the best method of subsidizing air transport in the future'. Deliberations were swift and conclusive, and their Report was published on 20 February as a White Paper which asserted that all three recent subsidy schemes had no effect in assisting civil aviation to 'fly by itself' nor was there hope that any material change could be effected by the time the present scheme expired on 31 March 1924. The Committee was convinced that existing services were on too small a scale to be more than commercial experiments and that new and longer routes must be developed, and came to the broad conclusion that: 'A company be formed to have a capital of £1 million (of which at least one half shall be subscribed before operations begin). The Government shall not exercise direct control over the activities of the company other than by appointment of one or two directors, except for purposes of checking

accounts to determine amounts of subsidy payable, and such general control as may be exercised by the Department of Civil Aviation over all civil flying.

'The profits shall be devoted to:- (i) the payment of a cumulative dividend of 10 per cent p.a. on ordinary shares. (ii) After payment of (i) any balance to be divided equally between shareholders and the Government. (iii) When the Government under (ii) shall have received £1 million (the proposed total amount of subsidy) the Government interest in the company shall cease and the whole profits shall belong to the shareholders.

'No restrictions as to route, types of machine, number of services etc., should be necessary as it would be the company's advantage to manage the business to the best commercial advantage at minimum cost and with the best possible equipment, but provision should also be made for the right of the Government to take over all engines and plant in the event of war, and for termination of the Agreement in case of liquidation of the company or cancellation under stated conditions.'

The burning question was whether sufficient passenger interest could be generated worthy of a £1 million company. The airline outlook remained modest. Even Daimler Airway under the skilled and rigorous control of Searle was operating at a financial loss, though it was very creditable that all their aircraft might be in the air on the same day — one flying from London to Amsterdam, another returning, a third away to Cologne, and the fourth *en route* from Manchester to London. The ailing Holt Thomas, its ancestral founder, was pressing the Government to give 'due and immediate consideration to the foundation of an air mail throughout the Empire'. Brancker gave assurance that not only was that policy under consideration but tenders for three types of airliners would shortly be called for — the first having maximum economy for European routes; the second for the Indian run with non-stop range of 500 miles against head winds; the third to fly non-stop from London to Malta.

Search for methods of landing in fog were being urgently pursued, for pilots could only contact Croydon *en route*; Croydon would then obtain cross-bearings from Pulham and Lympne and within a minute relay a 'fix' back to the pilot, who then had to plot it on his map. Though an experimental acoustic method of location had been tried, the results were indeterminate, so now the Air Ministry was investigating the possibility of an electric cable round the aerodrome detectable by an energy-measuring apparatus in the aeroplane so that the pilot could assess the confines and glide down in hope of locating the landing area. But because of the 'hit or miss' tactics of bad-weather flying, airlines now paid over 30 per cent for insurance per aircraft per annum for hull damage, and third-party claims required special premium and cover. Losses to underwriters had become so serious that only two companies undertook aircraft insurance, and in March they amalgamated as the British Aviation Insurance Group.

The inadequacy of Croydon as the London

there and land towards the Customs House whatever the wind direction.

The Air Estimates introduced on 14 March were primarily concerned with bringing the RAF up to strength, but Sir Samuel Hoare explained and endorsed the findings of the Hambling Committee adding: 'France is spending 100,000,000 francs a year on civil aviation and not less than 50,000,000 on subsidies. Because of that the Committee concluded that one strong company would be better than a number of small companies. The Air Ministry is prepared to negotiate with any one who can fulfil the necessary conditions, and if existing companies can fulfil them so much the better.'

Unfortunately he laid himself open to critic-

Three of these mahogany-hulled Supermarine amphibians were operated by British Marine Air Navigation Co in 1923, but G-EBFK was wrecked in the following year.

The Vickers Vulcan, powered with a war-surplus Rolls-Royce Eagle, aimed at economic operation unaided by government subsidy. First flown in 1922, it achieved 105 mph at a mere 45 hp per passenger and had a range of 360 miles.

terminal was causing concern. Of twelve possible alternatives only Gunnersbury Park or Wormwood Scrubs seemed suitable, but adaption would cost about £350,000, so the Air Ministry decided to improve Croydon at a cost of £225,000 by filling in Plough Lane to incorporate 75 acres of adjacent Beddington, and making a new arterial road from London giving access to the terminal. Pilots were delighted, for this would double the landing area, and even if the hangars and offices were left in the centre it would mean that machines could take off from

ism, and the Socialists pounced: 'Does not the Rt Hon gentleman consider it inadvisable that of this Committee, one should be his brother, another his brother's partner, and the third the late partner of the Rt Hon gentleman himself?' they demanded. For a moment Sir Samuel's even tenor was disturbed. 'No!', he angrily replied.

Holt Thomas, with the aid of the business expert Frederick Szarvasy of the British, Foreign and Colonial Corporation, rescuer of Dunlop Rubber Co from financial difficulties, now submitted plans for an Imperial Air Transport company comprising Daimler Airway, Handley Page Transport and the fledgeling British Marine Air Navigation Co Ltd, employing existing equipment and shared management with £285,000 capital. The Instone Air Line countered with a 58-page printed document for their version of 'a national aerial transport company' costing £250,000, including £150,000 subsidy for the first year and none after 1930, with assurance that by 1933 the company would be making a profit of 20 per cent. Currently the company's DH 34 was engaged for a film, *Out to Win!*

Meanwhile British civil aviation was continuing its erratic course, but though traffic was slowly increasing it had not yet achieved 500 passengers a week, yet was so variable that on occasions there were insufficient machines. Even so, Handley Page Transport was running four a day in each direction, and Daimler Airway was encouraged to open a Monday service to Berlin returning next day, matched by the Germans in the opposite direction. From Wednesday to Saturday, Daimler was running from London to Amsterdam — but the peril of single-engined flights was emphasized when Capt Hinchliffe force-landed a DH 34 with engine failure on the water's edge of a small island of the Netherlands group, but managed to take the machine by barge to Rotterdam aerodrome where a new engine was installed, flown in by another DH 34. By the time work was completed it was dusk, and became dark over the Channel, so both aircraft landed at Lympne, startling everyone because only Hinchliffe's had lights and the other suddenly materialized and touched down. Next day they left at dawn.

Each week one or other airline created its moment of suspense. The French had their share. A Goliath overshot at Croydon and crashed into a shed near the Disposals factory. A few weeks later *en route* to Croydon another caught fire and crashed near Amiens, killing all aboard. A month later a Goliath crashed near Maidstone. In August two more piled up at Croydon. The feeling grew that British airlines were much safer.

All through these months prolonged consideration was given to the proposals of Holt Thomas and the Instones. No conclusion had been reached. Said C.G. Grey: 'Whether it was that the three older firms objected to the predominating Instone influence or whether the issue was mere incompatibility of temperament, the most desirable scheme of all, pooling the four existing interests, has fallen through'.

A letter from Holt Thomas to the *Daily Telegraph* on 23 August revealed the problem: 'Sir Samuel Hoare called together the four existing companies saying he wished them to combine. The first question was raising the large capital of £1 million, but was immediately cleared by the patriotic action of a firm of highest standing who agreed to guarantee the money without remuneration subject to satisfactory agreements between the new company and the Government. Handley Page Transport Company,

The Vickers Vulcan, soon known as the 'Flying Pig', was the first single-engined commercial aeroplane to give adequate headroom. Nine were built, of which Instone Air Line acquired four, but when Imperial Airways absorbed the private airlines in 1924 two were re-engined with the 450 hp Napier Lion (as illustrated).

Daimler Airway, and British Marine Air Navigation agreed to throw in their lot with a national company, and the managing directors of these companies have been most helpful in setting aside all individual and personal interest. The Instone Air Line however would not agree to join without such reservations as were clearly impossible in a company of national importance and aspect.

'The three companies therefore requested me to submit a proposal to the Air Ministry, and this has been done. It simply embodies necessary clauses such as minimum mileage to be flown, zones of operation, provision of capital, limitation of dividends, subsidies to be paid, and method of repayment to the Government etc., and no individual or firm enjoys any special privileges. The proposal embodies as a Board, representation of the operating companies, two directors nominated by the government, and two directors whose names must be approved by the government. Many meetings have taken place at the Air Ministry and it has always been understood that, on the details being approved, the names of two independent directors of eminence would be submitted.

'However Messrs Instone have put in their own proposal on their own behalf, and not submitted it to the other companies; and they have secured the services of Lord Invernairn as chairman even before their scheme is accepted. My sympathies are with the three companies who acted on the Air Ministry's expressed wishes to join a national scheme which is opposed by a scheme put forward by the one company who did not so act. The three firms have always been willing that Messrs Instone should join the new company on similar terms as themselves, and intimated this to the Director of Civil Aviation last Monday.'

The battle continued. Sir Samuel Instone accused Holt Thomas of trying to force the Government's hand. Knowing Szarvasy's interests, he believed a financial group was endeavouring to force Instone's out of business. Similarly the Holt Thomas group was suspicious of Lord Invernairn, better known as Sir William Beardmore, head of the big engineering firm of that name on the Clyde which had aircraft constructional interests.

Handley Page lost no time in giving a luncheon to the Press. Benignly, with mock modesty, he expressed lack of competence to give an opinion on the merits of competing schemes for the £1 million monopoly company, but sug-

gested that the group comprising his, the Daimler, and Supermarine interests plus Mr Holt Thomas, 'combining as it does all the pioneers of British aerial transport, and composed as it is of the concerns which carry nearly 70 per cent of the air traffic in and out of England, has a *prima facie* claim to be the best fitted for the operation of the proposed national service'.

On 20 October *The Times* predicted an announcement might be expected shortly from the Air Ministry concerning the formation of a national air transport company on the lines laid down by the Hambling Committee, and stated that the difficulty of securing complete agreement among the four companies had at last been overcome.

Meanwhile winter brought marked inactivity because of fog. On one week the only aircraft movement was by Capt O.P. Jones with a DH 34 which he flew to Cologne. Geoffrey Dorman hazarded that: 'The state of inactivity is partly due to weather but mostly to

the state of not-knowing-where-one-is-ness which is bound to exist until some definite statement is made with regard to the formation and personnel of the new company. The latest rumour at the aerodrome is that Sir Eric Geddes is to be chairman. It is thought that armed with his famous Axe and aided by his equally famous prenominal motto "Little by Little" he ought to be the one person in the world who can make a real success of the venture.'

His forecast was correct. On 5 December *The Times* reported that an agreement between the Air Ministry and the British, Foreign and Colonial Corporation had been signed. Rumour intensified that Sir Eric Geddes, who was currently chairman of the Dunlop Rubber Co, would be chairman of the new company and that his skilled financial assistant Sir George Beharrell would be one of the directors. On 17 December the Government nominated Sir Herbert Hambling and Major J.W. Hills as its own directors.

Perhaps it was the weather, or it may have been discord created by the forthcoming amalgamation that explained the absence of any pilot or head of a British airline at the third Croydon Aerodrome Annual Dinner at which Sir Sefton Brancker was chief guest. He emphasized to those present that something like permanent employment was assured for ten years ahead, but that the national airline agreement laid down that all airline pilots and 75 per cent of the ground personnel, whether administrative staff or mechanics, must be members of the RAF, the Reserve, or the new Auxiliary Air Force when it came into being. He remarked that the existing firms had a difficult financial problem in preparing their balance sheets, and for the purpose of subsidy had to prove they were making a loss whereas for company-promoting purposes they must show they were making a profit! He regretted there had been so little flying lately, owing to the pervading fog, which he ascribed to the joint efforts of the meteorological department and the politicians.

The Supermarine Sea Eagle, powered with a pusher Rolls-Royce Eagle, carried six passengers in a low cabin in the bows, with access through a folding nose hatch. The pilot's open cockpit was immediately abaft the cabin.

Imperial Beginnings 1924-29

The *City of Birmingham,* the first Argosy Mk.1 to be delivered to Imperial Airways.

The Argosy's first service flight was made by this aircraft on 16 July 1926 when it flew from Croydon to Paris. By 8 December 1928, this aircraft had built up a total of 1,843 hours in just over 28 months. Imperial Airways stated that the Argosy was the first aircraft to pay its way.

On sale early in January 1924, price 6d from HMSO, was the long-awaited *Air Ministry Agreement made with the British, Foreign, and Colonial Corporation Ltd, for the formation of a heavier than air air transport company to be called The Imperial Air Transport Co Ltd.* This guaranteed that no subsidy would be given to any other such firm, but reserved the right to subsidize airship transport. 'The initial share capital will be 1,000,000 shares of £1 and the British, Foreign, and Colonial Corporation Ltd guarantees subscription of half.' Working capital was to be secured by issue of 500,000 ten-shilling shares.

The Government guaranteed an annual subsidy of £137,000 for the first four years subject to minimum yearly mileage of 1,000,000; thereafter the subsidy would be progressively reduced to £32,000 for the tenth. Profits were to be distributed with 10 per cent on paid-up capital to shareholders and the balance divided in thirds for repayment of subsidy, development of the service, and dividend for shareholders. All aircraft must be available for the Government in a national emergency.

As with any commercial amalgamation and change of directorships, every employee

including the pilots became increasingly concerned about his future. Who would be made manager? Who the chief pilot? Who the chief engineer? Organization became chaotic. Traffic dropped to a remarkable degree. There were rumours of Board deadlock and of difficulty in assessing the cash value of the constituent companies. Nor were matters improved by a change of government from Conservative to Labour on 21 January. Never had there been such inexperience as that of the new Labour ministers; not even the Air Minister, tall Brig-Gen C.B. Thomson, had experience of aircraft. There was talk of a levy on capital, and people became chary of new investment. Those concerned with floatation of the new air transport business therefore postponed offering shares until there was reasonable prospect of public support. Meanwhile the airliners retained their old liveries — the Handley Pages had silver fuselages emphasized by blue silhouette lines, Instone's had blue fuselages, and the Daimler DH 34s sported pillar-box red, but all had silver-doped wings.

The prospect of European national airlines operating in conjunction led to a regulatory conference of IATA in mid-January attended by representatives of eight nations, with Woods Humphery on behalf of Great Britain. The Croydon pilots disliked his incisively autocratic manner, and that boded ill when it was discovered that Daimler's had virtually secured control of the combined airline, for Col Frank Searle was confirmed as managing director with Woods Humphery as general manager. The pilots, whose engagements terminated at the end of the month, had not been offered new contracts. Criticism of Woods Humphery became public, with allegations that he coerced pilots into flying on numerous occasions against their judgement — a not uncommon practice in all spheres of flying. Sixteen pilots of Handley Page, Instone, and Daimler, with twelve more self-employed or with ADC and DH Taxis, therefore formed a Federation of Civilian Air Pilots, and the ground personnel formed a Federation of British Aircraft Workers — both registered as trade unions. On 6 March the pilots' Federation wrote to Sir Eric Geddes recommending a manager of their own

31 March 1924: an important day for aviation, when the companies operating between London and the Continent were absorbed by the newly-formed Imperial Airways Ltd. The photograph shows Lieut-Col Bristow presenting Captain Alfred Instone, on behalf of the staff, with a clock inset in the boss of a propeller.

choice as the only one acceptable to them. Sir Eric Geddes was not the man to be intimidated by a group of young men, and to their dissatisfaction confirmed Woods Humphery.

The question of pay and employment conditions became of overriding concern. Each airline had its individual and widely ranging terms. On the assumption of flying 600 hours a year, salaries averaged £800 to £900 per annum, though some pilots earned as much as £1,000. The Federation therefore proposed to Searle a standard basis of pay. Instead he offered a low retaining fee of £100 a year and flying pay 'which was the basis on which the payment to Daimler pilots operated, and under which they have earned bigger salaries than any other pilots employed'. This was indignantly refused.

On 31 March the name of the new company was announced as Imperial Airways Limited, and the directors listed as Sir Eric Campbell Geddes, chairman; Lieut-Col Frank Searle, managing director; Sir George Beharrell; Sir Samuel Instone; Lieut-Col John Barrett-Lennard; and Hubert Scott-Paine, with Sir Herbert Hambling and Major John Waller Hills as government representatives. The statement added: 'In view of the necessity of centralizing the systems of operations, inspection, and control, in connection with the various staffs and aeroplanes of different types as employed until yesterday (Monday) by the four companies, the aerial service to and from Croydon Air Station will be suspended temporarily, as from to-day. Statements are erroneous which suggest that pilots of the Air Station were "On strike" yesterday. Until last night they were still in the employ of the four existing companies, and the new Imperial Company has, as yet, made no appointment of pilots, but the directors have decided that pilots who pass the rigorous medical tests shall be offered an annual retainer and "flying time" which will ensure an annual income of £750 to £850 according to seniority.'

On 1 April a deputation from the Federation of Pilots, led by Lieut-Col G.L.P. Henderson, a freelance pilot, was introduced to the Secretary of State for Air by the Socialist Ben Tillett, with Bob Williams of the Transport Workers Union in advisory attendance. As soon as they left, Sir Eric Geddes and Col Searle were summoned to the Air Ministry.

The position became exacerbated by Woods Humphery's attempt to force the issue by announcing that: 'The company is now prepared to receive applications from pilots for appointments at the rates of remuneration agreed by the directors'. That was a false move, for it would have been the height of folly to engage raw recruits. Subsequently the pilots discussed their criticisms with Col Searle and requested new terms of 10s per flying hour with retainer of £500 a year for pilots of the old companies and £400 a year for any new pilot, plus £25 increase in the retainer after 500 hours flying, and required a contract for twelve months and £1,000 insurance for death or injury.

Meanwhile all operations came to a standstill, with great benefit to the Continental airlines which were running fully loaded with passengers and goods on almost every trip.

On 24 April Imperial Airways Ltd issued a statement recapitulating the position and agreeing that pilots would have a year's contract, thereafter subject to three months' notice, and that all the pilots of the absorbed companies would be employed though in excess of immediate requirements.

Sir Sefton Brancker, as DCA, had been deeply concerned over the impasse, and had worked closely with the directors and Air Ministry to find a solution. It so happened that Major Brackley had completed his advisory task with the Japanese Air Mission, and on returning to England had for some months been seeking employment. To Brancker he seemed the right man at the right moment, and the consequent proposal that he be made Air Superintendent of Imperial Airways was accepted with alacrity by Searle and Woods Humphery.

On 2 May Imperial Airways announced that full agreement had been reached with the pilots, mechanics, and ground staff of the absorbed air transport companies, and services would be resumed on the following Monday.

Operations were quickly in full swing with the Handley Page W.8bs and the DH 34s. There was even a temporary service to Birmingham for the British Industries Fair. Croydon at last was having its face-lift; Plough Lane was in process of vanishing. Buildings at the centre were about to be demolished and new flight sheds and an imposing central office building would be constructed on the eastern boundary where the new main road would be.

One of the first steps in reorganization was to ensure that pilots could be interchanged whatever the route or aircraft type. All pilots began converting from machines of their original airline to those of the others. It was almost hilarious except for the ensuing damage. The DH 34 pilots Barnard, Powell, and 'Scruffy' Robinson readily converted to the W.8, which one of them described as 'a nice confidential old bus', and although the three had no previous experience of twin-engined machines they were sent off on the cross-Channel service after the briefest practice around the aerodrome. But the easy-going Handley Pages must have blunted the finer perception of their pilots when it came to flying the DH 34s, for the first aircraft ran amok when taxi-ing and hit the beacon-lighthouse, and the second, after being bounced around for several hours, suffered collapse of its undercarriage and ploughed into the ground. But even the most experienced could make mistakes, for Robinson, who had flown them throughout the past year, took off with one at Ostend, hit the local War Memorial and crashed, but though the machine caught fire and was totally destroyed he escaped with a few bruises.

Though it was summer, with the knee-high aerodrome grass being laboriously cut by an antique horse-drawn mower, there remained a slightly cynical air at Croydon. One of the pilots ironically wrote:

'The way is long and the morn is cold,
The weather is far from good I'm told.
But up, up, in the "thirty-four"
Ballast and sand provide in good store
For the goods be few and the passengers nil
And the mail is light as a Beecham's pill.
So let us away from the Gallic shore
Just as we did the day before
So fill up with ballast and passengers three
And away with a cargo of subsidy!'

Nevertheless, discipline was vigorously attempted. To ensure that pilots could not use 'lack of knowledge' to excuse misdemeanours they were issued with a printed *Pilot's Handbook and General Instructions 1924* giving Rules and Conditions of Service, International agreement, Aerodrome rules, Forced landing procedure, Customs requirements, AD 6 Wireless operation, Cargo regulations, Routes, and Duties of Air Superintendent. Smoking had been suppressed in the offices, but that did not stop the pilots. Said one: 'Tall hats will soon be compulsory on the aerodrome so that befitting dignity may be maintained while aircraft depart'. Soon the pilots found they must abandon their motley civilian clothes and be outfitted in blue uniforms and peaked hat. To further enhance prestige the aircraft livery was standardized by painting all fuselages blue, with wings still silver-doped. Implementation and expansion was the target.

25 August marked the fifth anniversary of civil flying. Harry Harper wrote: 'In 1919 there were three questions civil aviation had to answer. Can 100 mph air transport be made reliable? Can it be made safe? Can it pay? During the summer our winged expresses have attained 91 per cent reliability. Even with winter fogs the all-the-year round figure is as high as 88 per cent. British planes have carried nearly 50,000 passengers and though six lost their lives, it can be regarded as safe. As to whether air transport can pay, Imperial Airways have 'planes forthcoming which will carry 20 per cent more payload for a given power, so there is every prospect that the speed and safety of flying will be combined with commercial success.' But it still had to be proved. As an expression of confidence Imperial Airways made history by publishing traffic receipts, which in June were £27,398, improving in July to £42,520.

The locals were beginning to protest at the increased traffic, complaining of the low altitude at which machines crossed houses while struggling to gain height. If an engine cut it could be disastrous. That the risk was ever-present was shown by a Goliath which landed at Lympne with the mechanic sitting on the wing alongside the starboard engine; the throttle control had broken five minutes after leaving Croydon, so he crawled from the cockpit to the wing and for 45 minutes hand-operated the throttle. So horrified was one of the eight passengers that he decided to continue to Paris by train.

There was still some unrest among the pilots of Imperial Airways. Several had left. Latest was McIntosh, who accepted the job of chief pilot of newly formed Northern Airlines, only to find that it was even more boring and miserable than the routine of Imperial Airways. Of the original Hounslow pilots there remained only George Powell, Will Rogers, Arthur Wilcockson, Gordon Olley, and Frank Barnard, together with Bill Armstrong and Col Minchin who had just returned to the fold. But on Christmas Eve fate struck at the most recently-joined pilot David Stewart, who had a distinguished record on big bombers. Carrying full load, his DH 34 (G-EBBX) took off up hill

The initial European routes of Imperial Airways were inherited from the original independent companies in 1924.

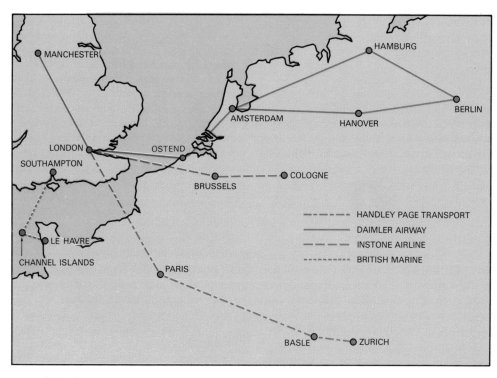

MANCHESTER

HAMBURG

BERLIN

AMSTERDAM

HANOVER

LONDON

OSTEND

SOUTHAMPTON

COLOGNE

BRUSSELS

LE HAVRE

CHANNEL ISLANDS

PARIS

BASLE

ZURICH

- - - - - HANDLEY PAGE TRANSPORT
——————— DAIMLER AIRWAY
– – – – INSTONE AIRLINE
· · · · · · BRITISH MARINE

towards Purley against a gusty wind. Onlookers saw he was having difficulty but the machine surmounted the ridge bounding the north side of the valley, then disappeared and an ominous column of black smoke was seen. Beset with engine trouble, Stewart must have turned back to avoid landing among the houses, stalled, and dived from 200 feet into the ground. The machine burst into flames and all eight were killed.

1925

In the New Year C.G. Grey wrote: 'People are beginning to forget the brief though intense War of 1914–18. By the same token the pilots of Imperial Airways whose experience now seems very considerable have an average age of barely 30.' Stewart at 36 was one of the oldest. There were allegations that Imperial Airways had been negligent in letting him fly with an engine which Hinchliffe had earlier reported faulty. However the official inquiry dismissed this: 'The engineer was fully justified in signing the daily certificate of safety. Facts did not call for more than a ground test. It was in no way negligent or imprudent to embark upon the flight with passengers without making such a flight test.' That remained open to question.

Behind the scenes trouble was brewing, for-

gotten for the moment in the triumph on 17 March of Brancker's return to Croydon aboard the DH 50 on completing an epic 8,000-mile flight to India and back piloted by Alan Cobham. Next day a Whitehall delegation headed by Sir Samuel Hoare and Leo Amery, Secretary for the Colonies, departed on a 3,500-mile sequence of flights encompassing the Near East in a tour that would last two months.

Then came the bombshell. At the beginning of April, newspapers reported that the Imperial Airways' managing director had resigned. The *Evening News* commented: 'Col Searle's aim has always been safety first and then high efficiency, but non-aeronautical members of the Board, notably the chairman, Sir Eric Geddes, are more concerned with attracting revenue and cutting down expenses to show that the business is a commercial success'. Since Imperial's formation a year earlier, about 800,000 miles had been flown — which was regarded as a remarkable attainment, particularly with so few aircraft; but the services had made a considerable loss, causing a split in the Board, resulting in Geddes asking Searle to resign.

Said Searle after leaving: 'The Board consists of very successful men who know the danger of trusting the unknown, but none of them had successfully operated any new form of trans-

port. My experience has in fact been unique, but such men want a lot of convincing, and in such company my rhetoric may have left a lot to be desired, but at least I have the satisfaction of knowing that what has been accomplished has placed the company in a very strong position for its second year of operations.'

Currently the company only had three W.8bs, valued at £10,000 each; three of the four DH 34s from Instone worth £5,000 each and three more from Daimler Hire. There was also the Vickers Vimy valued at £4,500 and a Vickers Vulcan at £3,800, both of which were used solely for freight. As Searle realized, they must get rid of the DH 34s and substitute new multi-engined aircraft of greater economy and capacity. Through his close and friendly contact with Brancker, the Air Ministry had ordered a three-engined version of the W.8, named the Hamilton W.8f, powered with Jaguar radials. An unwanted result was considerable vibration in the passenger cabin caused by the nose engine. De Havilland's and Armstrong Whitworth's were both building three-engined airliners, the Argosy and the Hercules, representing the latest techniques with good performance and economic passenger cost per mile — but they would not be available until spring next year. Major Brackley was also investigating the new and splendid twin Napier-powered Supermarine Swan flying-boat to supplement the Sea Eagles which would be used during the summer for the service from Southampton to the Channel Islands.

Chaired by Sir Sefton Brancker, ICAO opened its eighth session on 3 April, and the members in due course agreed on modified air traffic regulations; adoption of further regulations on minimum requirements for airworthiness certificates; a meteorological annexe to the Convention; unification of terms and symbols used in aeronautical technics; unification of material characteristics used in aeronautical construction; composition of aircraft crews;

Top: The Handley Page W.8b *Prince Henry* was commissioned in June 1922, led Sabena to equip with this type, and was honourably retired in 1931.
Centre: Handley Page W.8f Hamilton, a three-engined development of the W.8. Only one aircraft, the *City of Washington*, served with Imperial Airways, making its maiden flight in November 1924.
Above: Daimler Airway initiated their commercial operations on 2 April 1922 with the DH 34 G-EBBQ, which almost immediately was victim of an air collision on the Paris run.
Far left: Interior of a Handley Page W.10 airliner, with route-map set into the ceiling.

and exclusion of women from any employment in such crews of aircraft engaged on public transport!

A woman transport pilot would have outraged the public. As it was, Imperial Airways had to face frequent criticism. Thus S.F. Edge, famed as an early automobile racer, had no qualms in venting his opinion. Outbound to Paris he had been the only passenger, but there were three on the return. So few, he said, was due to inadequate publicity. Statistics of safety and names of prominent travellers should be published to create confidence. There was lack of smartness at the Terminal, and the interior of the aircraft must be improved. His seat was restrained by a strap, the legs fitting into thimbles, but on leaning back the legs came out of their housing and would have alarmed a nervous person. There should be a pamphlet explaining the normality of the steep angle on take-off, and that when a turn was made the machine banked over, and if 'bumps' were compared to sea waves, it would relieve the impression that the machine was not under proper control. Two pilots should be on board as a reassurance and enable one occasionally to go into the cabin to explain things. As to the appalling noise, passengers should be given ear protectors.

On return from the Near East, Sir Samuel Hoare said at the Royal Academy banquet on 2 May: 'That the air will become a great Imperial highway was shown by the fact that in a few weeks we made a journey which would otherwise have taken twelve months, traversing Iraq from end to end and visiting the mountains of Kurdistan and the Persian plains through which the British pipe line brings oil for use of the Fleet. We stayed in Transjordania, Palestine and Egypt, and inspected every British activity, military and civil, in those distant and largely inaccessible countries. It was a long and varied journey, but British pilots, British machines, and British organization enabled it to be performed without risk, delay, or incident. This spirit of enterprise will drive through the air a new highway for the British Empire and enable ministers and traders and travellers to pass swiftly and easily as a matter of ordinary routine from one end of it to another, united by an aerial line of closer and quicker intercourse.'

The Sabena airline was already exploiting the air route to the Belgian colonies, spearheaded by stage-by-stage flights to Alicante in Spain, then over the Mediterranean to Oran, across the Sahara to Gao in Nigeria, thence circuitously to Lake Chad and eventually to Léopoldville, and on 29 April a regular service was instituted. Britain's Empire air route had to await the new generation of multi-engined airliners.

At Croydon, Air Express Co Ltd had been formed as an air transport agency for passenger and goods on the extensive system of airlines in which every European State participated. Arrangements were made with Imperial Airways to connect at Amsterdam with the Europe-Union system and other services to Switzerland, Austria, Hungary, Germany, Sweden, Denmark, Danzig, Poland, Estonia, Latvia, Lithuania, and Finland. This linked some 30 important European cities with London, and passage for travellers and goods could be booked at each centre by Imperial Airways, Air Express, or Thomas Cook & Sons.

Indicative of Germany's resurgence was a visit to Croydon in August of an impressively futuristic all-metal airliner — the three-engined Junkers G.24 low-wing monoplane. Though all at the aerodrome flocked to see it, few Air Ministry officials bothered, blinkered as they were by the old biplane tradition. True, this machine was no faster, but its engines were of low power, comprising a 195 hp Junkers in the nose and two 100 hp Mercedes on the wings. Napier Lions could be fitted if more speed was required — but Imperial Airways was debarred from buying foreign aircraft, and in any case had not Sir Eric Geddes been assured that the new British machines were of latest type with steel-framed fuselage, even though canvas-covered?

With biting sarcasm Geoffrey Dorman of *The Aeroplane* said: 'One gathers that the present numerical strength of Imperial Airways is "according to plan", and is not, as thought, due to short-sighted policy of the directorate. To qualify for the subsidy their aircraft have to complete a million miles a year. This is all planned so that on about the last day of the financial year the millionth mile is achieved. And then, if as was the case last year, they run it too fine and are short of the million, they make excuses to the Air Ministry that a strike, or a pestilence, or a famine, held them up. If they find they are covering too much mileage a machine can be taken off the service and passengers kept waiting and told no machines available. That is why the French are reaping a reward in the shape of

passengers. Imperial Airways have sold out to the French for a mess of pottage (or any rate a mess) the birthright of British civil aviation, built up so well in the past by the pioneer companies.'

The three-engined Handley Page Hampstead was being tested by Capt Hinchliffe at Cricklewood. Compared with the Junkers and latest Fokker monoplane it looked impressive — but outdated. There were seats for fourteen in the modestly roomy cabin, with toilet room aft. At full load with all three Jaguars running the climb was 700 ft/min, but with one out of action, preferably the nose engine, the ground-level climb was barely 200 ft/min, becoming a descent of 280 ft/min if two engines failed. However, it was an improvement on the W.8, though no less cold and noisy for passengers, and there were still snags, reported Geoffrey Dorman: 'The tail appears to bounce constantly between the slipstream of the wing engines, and unless the pilot works at the rudder the whole time it is uncomfortable for the passengers. The W.8bs behaved much as the original W.8 did, and it looks as though the projected Napier-powered W.10s will have the same trick.'

A month after the Hampstead appeared, Handley Page, a towering figure, sent for his works foreman W.H. MacRostie and told him that Imperial Airways had accepted his W.10 tender. 'They stipulate delivery by the end of March. If we can do that they will order four. This is vital. See that you do it.' MacRostie agreed that he would if the D.O. merely kept track of what he did instead of issuing design drawings. That was November. By the end of the year, relentlessly urged by H.P., the

machines were assembled in the shops and awaiting engines.

No less a zealot was the dashing Sefton Brancker. At the beginning of September he was off again, flying with Lieut-Col Minchin and Imperial's assistant manager Col Burchall on a survey of the proposed air mail route to India. In seven weeks they covered 3,000 adventurous miles. On 12 October Brancker returned in company with Sir Samuel Hoare, whom he met in Brussels where they attended an International Air Congress at which they stated that on signing a suitable contract with Imperial Airways the air route from Egypt to India could be started.

Another survey began in mid-November with the departure from Croydon of Alan Cobham, accompanied by his cheerful engineer Arthur Elliott and B.W.G. Emmott of Gaumont as ciné photographer. Flying the Jaguar-powered Imperial Airways DH 50 G-EBFO he would explore the possibilities of the route across darkest Africa to Cape Town. At the end of the year they were in the Sudan, the newspapers following every stage, for Cobham was regarded as 'a good story'. One reporter described Cobham's departure as being 'pen in

Top: Imperial Airways inaugurated its 'Silver Wing' service with the Argosy I on 1 May 1927. Later versions were used for the first stage to Basle of the Indian run, and also had interim use in 1930 on the South African service.
Above: The DH 66 Hercules, powered by three 425 hp Bristol Jupiter radials, inaugurated in 1927 the Cairo–Baghdad section of the all-British route later extended to India and Australia, and the type remained in service until 1936.

one hand and control stick in the other'.

On the penultimate day of December Imperial Airways Ltd held its first ordinary General Meeting. Sir Eric Geddes explained that important negotiations with the Government to establish an air service from Egypt to India and modification of the subsidy scheme had delayed the trading account. Despite the subsidy of £139,409 18s 5d there was a loss of £16,217 6s 3d after providing an obsolescence reserve of £22,998 1s 3d. Nevertheless, said Geddes, the four original airlines had been welded into an efficient single organization; repair shops and stores had been centralized at considerable expense; new maintenance and overhaul schedules had been prepared and the combined staffs instructed in the new system. The problem of maintenance was receiving earnest attention, and while safety would be maintained costs must be brought down. The solution lay in simplification and standardization of design, use of metal alloys for components hitherto made of wood, research into causes of metal fatigue, and an increase in the payload per horsepower so that greater potential earning power would compensate for the necessarily high costs of inspection, main-

tenance, and overhaul. In thanking the staff it was announced that Major J.W. Hills resigned as a Government director upon election as an MP, and Air Vice-Marshal Sir Vyell Vyvyan had succeeded him. The retiring director, Sir Samuel Instone, was unanimously re-elected.

1926

Gales, rain, and floods played havoc with Continental air services at the beginning of 1926, but in more tropical climes Wolley Dod and Colonel Shelmerdine were making a ground survey of part of the Kantara–Karachi route, and the Imperial Airways team of Col Minchin and Col Burchall was gaining experience of the route to India, selecting every likely-looking landing ground. They had none of the publicity attendant on Cobham's brilliantly organized progress. On 17 February he arrived at Cape Town, the journey of over 8,000 miles having taken three months of careful survey of 27 landing places for Imperial Airways.

That airline's latest purchase, the Handley

Page W.10, had made its first flight a few days earlier, thanks to MacRostie. Growled C.G. Grey: 'The engines are unhoused and uncowled; control cables and pulleys and a species of sheet metal lever stick out all over the machine in war-time fashion. Even the cabin chairs are of old straight up, short-backed type of inflammable wicker which provides about the least comfortable seating imaginable.'

Within a fortnight the W.10 completed the somewhat superficial flight trials, and on 5 March received its C of A. So devoted were those early factory workmen that the other three aircraft were certificated within a few days, and on 30 March all four, resplendent in the new livery of dark blue fuselage with thin white outline, were handed over to Imperial Airways at Croydon, where next day Lady Maud Hoare ceremonially named them *City of Melbourne* (G-EBMA), *City of Pretoria*

(G-EMBR), *City of London* (G-EBMS), and *City of Ottawa* (G-EBMT); for good measure, the prototype three-engined W.9a Hampstead was named *City of New York* (G-EBLE). At the subsequent splendid lunch at the Aerodrome Hotel, Handley Page blandly prompted Sir Eric Geddes to say that Imperial Airways' fleet, after starting with a nondescript collection, now had 75 per cent one type — the good old Handley Page! Certainly it was a personal triumph that a machine designed in 1919 was regarded as the latest airliner in 1926.

Meanwhile on 13 March, Cobham arrived back at Croydon, having beaten the SS *Windsor Castle* which had left Cape Town at the same time on 26 February. Roads to the aerodrome were lined with cars, the public enclosures crammed. His blue-and-silver DH 50J came gliding in and landed. A seething crowd broke

Handley Page's W.10, powered with two 450 hp Napier Lions, was a civil version of the military Hyderabad — typically British with struts and wires and uncowled engines, but it was sound business to develop a proven design rather than risk a revolutionary failure. Two of the four built remained in service with Imperial Airways until March 1933 when they were sold to Sir Alan Cobham.

Alan Cobham poses with his photographer B.W.G. Emmott, and engineer Arther Elliott, before their flight of exploration to Cape Town.

Fares for the summer service on the Paris run, commencing 19 April, were increased both by Imperial Airways and the Air Union to six guineas single and eleven guineas return. Three days earlier the last of the DH 34s made the final flight of that type, and now the new W.10s were in use. Almost immediately Frank Barnard, flying the *City of London*, encountered a new peril when he ran into a thunderstorm near Beauvais. With a report like the firing of a 60-pounder a flash of lightning struck the lower wing, burning through the fabric to scorch one of the main spars, fuse the bonding and damage the adjacent aileron. With the compass out of action and one engine misfiring because of a depolarized magneto he managed to land safely at Lympne, to the relief of his fourteen startled passengers.

Barnard was highly regarded by Sir Eric Geddes, whose Siskin entry for the King's Cup he had flown to victory the previous year. It was therefore understandable that when the new Argosy three-engined airliner was ready he was granted leave to make the first flight for Armstrong's. After a few minutes one of the Jaguars failed; nevertheless his report was enthusiastic — but though very experienced he had no training as a test pilot, consequently the Argosy was accepted with very heavy ailerons, leading to considerable eventual modification of the balance system.

One of the younger technicians, Frank Radcliffe of Gloster's, said: 'I recently flew in both Hampstead and the Argosy. Neither offers the comfort of an old Ford car. The bracing wires came through the woodwork in the Argosy with huge clearance for draughts. As for noise, even cotton wool did little good. Further, the nose engine makes sure you are aware of it by the vibration transmitted to the passenger cabin, especially if there is irregularity in the cylinder firing. "Ripping panels" on top of the cabin ought to be waterproof, so that when it rains they do not become "dripping panels" to the discomfort of the passengers. Then there is design of the chairs: the Hampstead's cause cramped knees, and the Argosy a stiff neck as one's head cannot rest against the back. With the present wide wings of biplanes all that some passengers see is an expanse of fabric, which is a dull sight. A cantilever monoplane seems an absolute necessity; if we place it above the cabin the passengers have a clear view and flying becomes more interesting, but when the novelty goes, flying in a commercial airliner is dull.'

through the barriers. Only with difficulty were the police able to rescue pilot and crew. He was carried shoulder-high to Customs. 'Subsequently, as recorded on all news-sheets of the world', wrote C.G. Grey, 'Mr Cobham was commanded to Buckingham Palace and granted an interview with HM the King.'

Augmenting the expanding vistas was the new agreement with the national airline 'substituting for the maximum annual mileage of one million miles a composite minimum of 425 million "horsepower-miles" and every mile performed by a marine aircraft shall count as a mile and a half'. This was to encourage use of more powerful aircraft. *The Aeroplane* commented: 'One scarcely imagines that even with its new subsidy-monopoly Imperial Airways will be able to afford the luxury of sending off ten or twelve passengers with three engines of 400 hp to carry them. The essence of success is frequency of service.'

Towards the end of March there was an alarming experience for thirteen passengers aboard the Hampstead *en route* from Paris piloted by Dismore, for the starboard engine seized, and the propeller flew off, damaging the wing, though Dismore landed at Littlestone without mishap. Three weeks later the Hampstead had another engine seizure shortly after taking off from Croydon, but again landed safely. Such risks at least led to the decision that all single-engined machines would be scrapped.

The country was now hit by strikes — first the miners, next day the railwaymen, transport workers, and printers. Private and commercial aircraft maintained communications all across the country. Imperial Airways tripled the Paris service. Such was the demand that passengers at Le Bourget tried to force their way without tickets into machines already booked. As a national stoppage, the strike lasted only nine days, but the miners remained out, adding a million to the workless. By the time they returned, six months later, £60 million had been lost in wages. The Government presently passed the Trades Disputes and Trades Union Act making strikes in sympathy with other unions illegal and attacked political use of Union funds. Not until 1946 did the Labour Party succeed in securing its repeal.

The airlines continued to do remarkable business. Every machine in or out was full of passengers and goods. By now the terminal buildings alongside the new arterial road were rapidly growing and the skeleton of an enormous hangar towered above them. Even a licence had been agreed, after long dispute, for the new hotel at Croydon.

But for fliers there were no new safeguards. Herbert Horsey, flying a twin-engined W.8b with eight passengers *en route* from Amsterdam had an engine failure over the Channel when flying at 1,000 ft beneath cloud. With the other at full throttle requiring heavy foot pressure to keep the machine straight, he just managed to reach the coast, but could not clear the cliff tops, so scraped into a valley, touched down in a field, the machine swinging violently round, collapsing the undercarriage and damaging the wings and fuselage, but nobody was hurt.

Two days later a KLM Fokker crossing from Amsterdam in dense fog patches 50 ft above the water, emerged near Hythe only to find the cliffs like a wall, their tops lost, so the pilot instantly put down on the beach where the machine was later submerged. A few days later a Goliath had engine failure when crossing the coast, but the pilot managed to land at the same spot where the Hampstead earlier lost its propeller, though the undercarriage collapsed.

Better things were hoped for with three- or four-engined airliners. On 29 July, the first of the Argosy fleet left Croydon with eighteen passengers on a maiden flight to Paris piloted by Barnard, completing the distance in 1 hr 51 min compared with the 2½ to 3 hours the old 0/400s had taken — but the Press omitted to say

that the flight had been down-wind. The return flight took 2 hr 33 min.

Introduction of any new aircraft type, civil or military, is always complicated by initial faults. The Argosy was no exception. Valve trouble with an engine caused one to land at Lympne, and after disembarking passengers it was flown back to Croydon using nose and port engines only; but instead of regarding this as a demonstration of the machine's ability the Press headlined: 'Yet another airliner in trouble'.

Soon Imperial Airways would have the first of the Jupiter-powered three-engined de Havilland Hercules airliners (G-EBMW) on which success of the Far East route depended. On 30 September it was flown by Hubert Broad, the de Havilland test pilot, with all the works watching. Such was the power that presently he flew on two engines, then skimmed the length of the aerodrome on one, and though lateral control would have to be improved it was confidentially announced: 'She will be handed over to Imperial Airways in about a month's time, and until January 1 she will probably fly on the cross-Channel services'.

Two days later Cobham, flying the Imperial Airways DH 50 seaplane, triumphantly returned from the 24,000-mile survey flight he had begun on 30 June to Australia and back, and alighted on the Thames alongside the Houses of Parliament where the terrace was crowded with watching MPs and friends. Next day the Department of Government Hospitality gave a lunch at the Carlton to Mr and Mrs Cobham — and there Sir Samuel Hoare announced that His Majesty had been pleased to confer a knight-

Following Cobham's triumphant flight to Australia and back in 1926, his well-tried DH 50 was taken to Selfridge's for display, watched by an admiring crowd of Londoners.

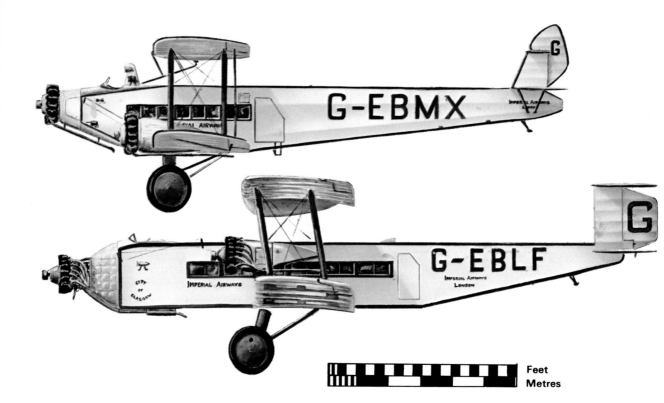

Feet
Metres

Comparison to the same scale of (*top*) the De Havilland DH 66 three-engined Hercules which inaugurated the Imperial route to India in January 1927, and (*above*) the contemporary three-engined Armstrong Whitworth Argosy. In deference to pilots' wishes, both had open cockpits.

hood on this determined pilot.

There was no mention of this epic flight in the Annual Report of Imperial Airways, nor of early intention to open the air route to Australia, but Sir Eric Geddes averred that the Egypt to India service would be initiated in January. Unfortunately, 'owing to the delay in delivery of new aeroplanes, the company was unable to earn the increased revenue which the Board had anticipated and considerable traffic passed to foreign competitors. The Accounts, which show a loss of £20,414 19s 8d reflect this loss in revenue. Your fleet now consists of sixteen aeroplanes, and five three-engined aeroplanes of most modern design are under construction for the Eastern service. Part of the capital for this service has been provided from existing resources, but additional capital will be necessary, and the balance of 10s on the shares will be called up by two calls of 5s.' As a gesture the directors decided that though entitled to a combined £6,500 per annum they would reduce this to £2,500.

With an eye to the future, and a step towards greater safety, the Air Ministry promulgated a requirement that after 1 January 1928 every aircraft carrying more than ten passengers for more than 100 miles must carry a certified second-class navigator. All Imperial Airways pilots were therefore instructed to take the examination. As the company had not yet established a pilots' school every man had to get

down to reading, memorizing, and, if possible, understanding the relevant Air Ministry publications. The examination took place in the first week of December, and to the disguised surprise of Woods Humphery all passed.

Meanwhile Brackley was in trouble. Woods Humphery wrote: 'I do not doubt you have done your best to carry out your duty but regret to say you have not rendered the standard of service which the Company expects from a highly salaried official. Your failings include lack of foresight, tact and leadership; also failure to assist me on policy, or to take advantage of the talent among our pilots to provide well considered and balanced views on matters of importance to the technical development of the Company. I therefore regret to tell you and the Board that it is not in the best interests of the Company for you to continue in your post.' However reprieve followed, and he was given six months to demonstrate his ability. Undoubtedly the pilots thought 'Brackles' too self-important and that rather than mingle with them he preferred more spectacular occasions such as acceptance tests of new types of aircraft — whereas the pilots were more interested that cooking had improved at the Aerodrome Hotel and food was much cheaper, or that a piano had been installed in the lounge so that there could be music and merriment.

More fundamentally, the annual Imperial Conference held in London was emphasizing the great importance from the political and economic angle of bringing the most distant parts of the Empire within a fortnight's journey of London. In that quest Woods Humphery and Col Burchall left for Cairo on 24 November to finalize arrangements for the Karachi route, leaving Sidney Dismore, the hard-working secretary, in charge.

By now traffic was decreasing in the usual seasonal manner. When Sir Harry Brittain in the Commons sought comparison between British and German airline traffic he was informed that in the year ending 31 October Imperial Airways carried 16,655 passengers, but there was no information on the Germans. Spat C.G. Grey: 'Comparing Imperial Airways traffic with German traffic is like comparing traffic out of Penzance railway station with that of Manchester!' In fact Luft Hansa had become the biggest air traffic combine in the world and in its first year transported 56,268 passengers and 950 tons of freight.

Snags with the Jaguar engines were persisting. On 8 December an Argosy piloted by O.P. Jones *en route* for Croydon broke a tappet rod and then oil pressure dropped on another engine, but he landed safely at nearby Pluckley, and sent the twelve passengers on by train to London. Replacing the tappet rod next day he flew to Croydon, arriving at the same time as the first of the triple-engined DH Hercules. It was immediately allocated for familiarization. There was no period of route proving. Next day, with nine passengers aboard, Barnard set off with it for Paris but thick fog forced him to land at Beauvais, and he flew back next morning to Croydon. Within days two more Hercules were received — a remarkable feat by de Havilland's, for in only twelve months the type had been designed, tested, and delivered.

On the 18th Capt Wolley Dod, as chief pilot of the new Eastern route, took off with the prototype to position it at Heliopolis for the Desert Air Mail service; aboard were the indefatigable, monocled Sir Sefton Brancker, Air Commodore J.G. Weir and his wife, and Capt T.A. Gladstone to operate the Cairo–Kisumu sector. Two days later the second Hercules left for Cairo, piloted by one-eyed Capt Hinchliffe with H. Warner and Dudley Travers as second and third pilots. On Boxing Day the third Hercules, piloted by Frank Barnard and navigated by Sqn Ldr E.L. Johnston, with Sir Samuel and Lady Maud Hoare as passengers, inaugurated the official service carrying the Royal Mail.

1927

At Aboukir on New Year's Day, 1927, Wolley Dod took over the Hercules from Barnard and headed for Baghdad, there to be joined by Sir Sefton Brancker — then by stages to Jask, Karachi, and New Delhi where they swept nobly in to land on 8 January, greeted by Lord Irwin the Viceroy and the C-in-C Sir William Birdwood. Next day Lady Irwin ceremonially named the airliner *City of Delhi*. Not until 17 February did Sir Samuel and his wife arrive back in London, after completing the last stage from Paris by train and ship because of fog. Typical of the times was C.G. Grey's comment: 'One tenders congratulations on their happy return. Few in their circumstances, endowed with wealth, social and political power, and with a family of charming children, would risk their lives merely because they consider their duty was to set a good example to the travelling public.'

In contrast to the suffocating heat of the desert route there was snow at Croydon, but that did not deter McIntosh in a W.10 leaving for Paris because passengers hated to stand about waiting; but the weather won and he was forced down in a field and could not complete the trip until next day. Flying certainly remained an art. 'On Friday last Mr Barnard brought off one of the finest landings ever seen at Croydon', wrote a reporter. 'He came from Paris on an Argosy when the south-west gale was at its height, and did an autogyro (helicopter-like) landing, without run, on the tarmac in front of the Customs. Twenty men were needed to hold down the machine, and he found taxi-ing so difficult that he took off again from where he landed and put down in the same fashion outside the hangar doors.' However the problems of pilots, sitting leather-coated, helmeted, and freezingly cold in their open front cockpit, were somewhat ameliorated in bad weather conditions or at night by a cone light at Lympne, a Neon at Croydon, and beacons at Cranbrook, Tatsfield, and the emergency landing grounds of Penshurst and Littlestone. There were also floodlights at Croydon and Lympne switched on at the moment of landing to illuminate a semicircle of 1,500 ft radius. By contrast the thirteen great air mail routes flown by night in the USA had beacons every few miles.

The little that was being done for civil aviation, additional to air defence, was dictated by the Air Estimates for 1927–28 published on 5

The locals flock in their hundreds to inspect and wonder at *City of Arundel* — the first Argosy to land at Khartoum on the England–Central Africa service in March 1931.

March, which allocated only £137,000 to subsidize Imperial Airways for European services and £93,600 for the Cairo–Karachi route; alterations at Croydon would absorb £111,000, with £10,000 for a wireless telegraphy station, and £8,000 for meteorological services. As *The Times* reported: 'Sir Samuel Hoare has all the scrupulous precision which he proudly ascribed to-day to British aeroplane engines, and like them on his great Imperial flight last year, he went through the long journey of his Estimates purring like a kitten'.

1 April marked the third anniversary of the formation of Imperial Airways. Apart from the new Karachi route, only five of the seven services taken over from the original airlines were being operated — Paris, Zurich, Ostend, Brussels, Cologne. Amsterdam and Berlin had been abandoned because the subsidy was insufficient. Difficulties were now encountered on the Eastern route, for though it had been intended to open the Basra–Karachi extension, the Persian Government, dominated by the Russians, revoked the agreement that had been signed in Teheran in October 1925.

Bearing in mind recent criticisms of lack of 'publicity', Imperial Airways not only allocated

a W.8 for joy-rides over London at two guineas per head, including transport to and from London but on 1 May the Argosy *City of Glasgow*, doped silver, with interior in pale blue and silver-grey, inaugurated a luxury 'Silver Wing' service to Paris which coincided with a Congress in London of the International Convention for Air Navigation (ICAN) of whose 22 signatories Persia was a renegade member. Welcoming the guests, Sir Samuel Hoare emphasized the important part ICAN had played in developing civil flying during the seven years of its existence, and particularly in establishing 'rights of flying over foreign states which had brought a measure of order and mutual help where there would otherwise have been anarchy and national suspicions'.

International ties were certainly strengthened when the hitherto unknown lanky young American, Charles Lindbergh, made the first solo flight across the Atlantic, landing at Le Bourget in the late evening of 21 May. A week later enormous crowds watched him arrive at Croydon from France. They swarmed on to the aerodrome in a tidal wave, so that he had to make two attempts at landing. Amid the world-wide enthusiasm it was forgotten that Alcock and Brown made the first non-stop crossing in 1919. But if Lindbergh could do it single-handed, why not Imperial Airways?

Sporting Frank Barnard, as a change from routine airline flying, was again set to compete in the King's Cup Race on August Bank Holiday. Disaster ensued. While he was testing his mount, the Jupiter-powered Badminton biplane racer, the engine seized just after take-off; he tried to turn into wind, stalled, and dived in from 80 ft. That was the end. 'He was one of the best fellows we have ever had in British aviation', said C.G. Grey. 'He had an unusual gift for imparting information. Few have done more to establish the practical side of commercial aviation.'

Meanwhile the summer business was booming. In mid-August 565 passengers were carried in one week in the course of 87 flights. The Silver Wing Service was proving popular because of the innovation of lunch served by a steward. Said a passenger: 'He was a very good lunch but I cannot hold him down'. That was due to the light wing loading of the Argosy, making it susceptible to atmospheric turbulence, sometimes dropping like a lift. Though easy to fly, these machines tended to wallow, and that could be tiring because of heavy controls. What the pilots liked was the splendid long-travel undercarriage which ironed out the many irregularities of the Croydon aerodrome surface.

Imperial Airways was trying to cope with

shortage of aircraft and pilots, for the former had been reduced by accidents and the latter were a changing population, the older pilots departing on private ventures, resulting in infiltration of newcomers with need to secure experience on the several routes. All Imperial machines were being fitted with fixed aerials for Marconi short-wave direction finding (D/F) sets, but still had the standard AD 9 and trailing aerial. The new sets caused new problems such as heterodyne whistling due to interference between ground stations, and some pilots took longer than necessary to follow the Air Ministry procedure for bearings, making it impossible for others to take their turn quickly. As Capt W.H. Sayers of Boulton & Paul said: 'Quite how the unhappy pilots disentangle anything at all from their wireless is distinctly puzzling to anyone who has heard the ethereal noises on the aircraft wave length band on a ground receiving set'.

Fog remained the major enemy, often stopping every service, but gave the pilots opportunity of ragging and baiting the ground crews.

A wildly excited crowd streamed into the aerodrome when Charles Lindbergh, the hero of the hour, attempted to land his trans-Atlantic Ryan monoplane at Croydon.
Inset: Lindbergh at Curtiss Field, Long Island, shortly before his flight from the USA to Paris.

A journalist commented: 'It is as well they should have an occasional morning in which to work off the brilliant but scurrilous invective they have invented, but in any case it is good for the ground staff to be insulted at fairly regular intervals'. That was often extended to the meteorological officers to whom pilots of all nationalities were shepherded as soon as there was sign that fog was abating. Tremendous competition would follow to be first away, and they would be signalled off with minimum pause between each machine.

Commercial aviation seemed at the turn of the tide, for the third annual Accounts of Imperial Airways revealed the first-ever profit, though only £11,000, and it was reported that traffic had increased steadily, achieving 92 per cent of scheduled flights in Europe and 100 per cent in the Middle East where the weather was more favourable. Unfortunately Persia still refused to ratify arrangements for extension to Karachi. Said Sir Eric Geddes: 'Imperial Airways have the knowledge and experience to run these Imperial routes, but a bolder policy by the Government is essential or we shall be left behind by Continental competitors whose governments give much greater financial support'. That led to the resolution: 'This meeting considers the present Government subsidy inadequate for the services rendered and should be substantially increased'. Frederick Handley Page was prompt to second it. Already his chief designer George Volkert had formulated a still larger biplane than the W.10, powered with four engines. 'If there is a limit in size', said H.P., 'it is not yet in sight, but it is more difficult to obtain orders for giant aeroplanes than to execute them when received.'

Indicative of Imperial Airways' forward thinking was an impressive three-engined, metal-hulled flying-boat almost ready at Short Bros alongside the Medway at Rochester. Named Calcutta, it was sister ship to the Ministry-loaned Singapore with which Alan Cobham departed from Hamble on November on the initial stages of another South African tour, but after staying overnight at Bordeaux and then at Marseilles, it was damaged at Malta and was now awaiting repair. The Calcutta derivation was largely the result of Brackley's recommendation to the the ever-willing Sir Sefton Brancker, who in turn induced the Air Council to place a contract for two at £18,000 each. Luxury was the aim, with fifteen passengers spaciously seated in a 17-ft cabin beauti-

fully upholstered. The steward had a buffet cabinet abaft with twin-burner oil cooker to port, and on the other side was the toilet compartment.

By comparison, passengers in the Argosys and W10s were soon complaining of the December cold penetrating the cabins, for the muffs around the engine exhausts failed to provide sufficient heat. The airline engineers therefore devised a system in which warm air entered the cabin at the rear instead of the front, drifting forward because of the low pressure in the open cockpit, effectively warming the entire cabin even when the windows were open. Quickly all Imperial machines were altered to this pattern.

Bitter weather took over and the year ended with great snow storms; the pilots of Air Taxis Ltd dropped hundreds of parcels of food by parachute to snowbound villages and isolated houses.

1928

In January 1928, while snow was falling and gales raging in England, came an emergency in the torrid heat of the Middle East, for Dudley Travers, flying the Hercules City of Cairo, wirelessed that strong head winds across the desert had forced him down short of petrol between landing grounds No 5 and No 6, two hundred miles west of Baghdad. No more messages came. A car laden with cans of petrol was immediately dispatched but failed to find the machine, nor did search by air along the route. Luckily two days later Capt Warner flying the second Hercules spotted the machine well off track surrounded by Arabs, who they found on landing had treated the crew and the four passengers with the utmost courtesy. Mails and passengers were transferred to Warner's machine. Petrol was sent by air, and later that same day the beleagured airliner safely reached Baghdad.

In England, Imperial Airways set up a charter department to obtain additional non-scheduled business instead of awaiting casual inquiries. Cocky little Gordon P. Olley, the pilot allocated for such flights, became manager of this special section.

Meanwhile all the airline staff was moving to the Airport Terminal Buildings scheduled for operation on 30 January. Much of the engineering equipment had already been transferred and special test-beds were being installed for running air-cooled radial engines. All air traffic would be handled directly from the new Control Tower which dominated the main building. On the north was the new Hotel, then came the main block of offices and Customs beneath the Control Tower and on the south were two big aircraft sheds with workshops beyond. A large concrete apron in front of the Terminal building accommodated all arriving and departing aircraft.

On 13 February the Calcutta prototype G-EBVG was launched on the Medway and moored for 24 hours to check watertightness. Late next afternoon Short's test pilot, John Parker, with Brackley as co-pilot, took off for a two-minute straight, but adjustment was required before they made full flight a week later, after which the two pilots shared the test programme for the next five months.

The question of future airline equipment was looming large. In the debate on the Air Estimates the Hon F.E. Guest strongly advocated development of flying-boats because of the Empire's maritime geography and considered that a base for them at Southampton would be required. He emphasized the national need for a permanent, assured, and prosperous aircraft industry, and said that bold expenditure and an elaborate Imperial civil air route could provide it.

By agreement with Sir Sefton Brancker, Imperial Airways that spring invited tenders from all British manufacturers for the separate requirements of 40-seaters with three engines and with four for service in Europe, and for similar types suitable for Eastern operations. Quotations were required for batches of three, four, five, and six aircraft, and manufacturers were offered 'the greatest possible freedom to express their own ideas, coupled with greatest safety, highest possible payload capacity, and lowest cost of operation', but stalling speed must not exceed 52 mph — for aerodromes were small, and in the East high temperatures increased the stalling speed noticeably. A bonus would be paid if delivery date and/or performance exceeded specification, but there would be a penalty for shortfall. Five firms tendered, and after months of deliberation the Handley Page was selected, possibly favoured because he had employed both Woods Humphery and Brackley after the war.

Such big machines seemed a risky venture, for the springtime passengers were barely 100 a day, but with 'summer time' in force on 20 April, Imperial Airways re-started services to Basle and Zurich, and on 2 May Lady Maud Hoare officially opened the new Croydon buildings. She and Sir Samuel were received at the entrance by Sir Sefton Brancker, where she unveiled a commemorative bronze tablet and then unlocked the door. Passengers of all nationalities seemed impressed with the air of solidity and permanence of the new buildings for there was ample room for those waiting. Various airlines had booking offices made attractive with displays of posters, photographs and literature. In the new hotel the dining-room was open to the general public.

Twelve days later, the Secretary of State for Foreign Affairs announced: 'A Treaty regulating the commercial relations between this country and Persia was signed at Teheran on May 10 by his Majesty's ministers . . . and for the proposed air service between Egypt and India, the Persian Government have formally stated their readiness to enter negotiations with a representative of Imperial Airways'. On 1 June Woods Humphery departed by Hercules *City of Cairo* to Teheran for discussions.

The day before he left there was renewed publicity for Cobham when his big Singapore flying-boat completed the 20,000-mile African flight by alighting alongside Cattewater Air Station at Plymouth, and, after a long delay for Customs, was welcomed at the Mayflower Steps by the Mayor and Mayoress and Sir Sefton Brancker. Said a reporter: 'Despite the unfortunate mishap at Malta on the outward journey and long delay on the West Coast of Africa on the return owing to radiator trouble, Sir Alan has proved that airlines using flying-boats can reasonably be maintained through and round the African continent'.

However landplanes were the immediate preoccupation. Three improved Argosys were on order with the new geared-type Jaguar engines giving enhanced performance despite better silencing. Lateral control had been made lighter by an ingenious balancing system operated by vertical surfaces; and the steward and his pantry were now at the fore end of the compartment.

In the Commons Civil Aviation was being debated on the motion that 'A sum not exceeding £450,000 be granted to His Majesty to defray the expenses of Civil Aviation in course of payment during the year ending 31 March

1929'. Sir Robert Lynn took the domestic view that there should be subsidies for internal airlines from Southampton to Manchester and Liverpool, thence to Belfast and Glasgow; and Sir Harry Brittain advocated a subsidy for flying-boat services, and extension to the West Indies, Bahamas, and Florida. In closing the debate Sir Samuel Hoare, with customary lucidity, outlined the Government's view on civil aviation, and particularly consolidation of Imperial Airways 'which is the envy of every country and has a remarkable record of reliability. We are now at the stage where with possibly two or three more changes from present types to more up-to-date, our aeroplanes will cover the expenses and our airline will be self-supporting.'

A special demonstration for the Parliamentarians followed on 1 August when Lankester Parker flew the newly certificated Calcutta from Rochester to alight on the Thames between Vauxhall and Lambeth Bridges and anchor off the Albert Embankment. A week later Brackley officially accepted delivery at Rochester on behalf of Imperial Airways and flew it to Southampton, thence next day to Guernsey and back. Subsequently he gave dual instruction to Drew and Horsey, and it was then used on the Southampton–Guernsey route to study behaviour in every kind of sea conditions.

Thus inspired, Sir Eric Geddes chartered the second Calcutta from the Air Ministry for a cruise to Stranraer and Holy Loch, and subsequently experimental flights were made between Liverpool and Belfast before joining the prototype Calcutta on the Guernsey run. 'I think that in the near future', said Sir Eric, 'we shall be prepared to tackle the long overseas flights which would take us from Singapore to Australia.'

His speech to the shareholders on 7 September was optimistic. Not only did the balance sheet show £72,500 profit compared with £11,000 for 1927, but he was able to announce an increased subsidy of £335,000 a year for the first two years; slightly less for the next four; then steadily reducing from £220,000 to £70,000 for the tenth year — which, he said, gave 'a total of almost £2½ million compared with £600,000 remaining under the existing agreements — so you will see that your company has a greatly extended security of tenure of Government support, representing an extension of five years for the existing European

The first Imperial Airways Short Calcutta flying-boat on the Thames at Westminster in August 1928. During the aircraft's three-day visit, MPs had a chance to inspect this important new link in Empire air services.

56

agreement and over seven years for the Middle East agreement. Further the subsidy for the European services for the current year, which should have been reduced by £25,000 under the existing agreement, is now maintained at its present level.'

After such gratification those not in the know were bewildered when the meeting was asked to accept his resignation. Said C.G. Grey: 'Like all strong men he has great enemies, but has earned the esteem of people who, often against their will, recognize that he has succeeded in every task'. However, circumstances were to change and the resignation would presently be deferred.

Certainly it was very satisfactory that passengers had increased from 11,395 in the first year to 26,479 in the fourth, and in August, for the first time, 1,000 had been carried in the course of seven days. 'Traffic revenue', said Sir Eric, 'is now 60 per cent higher than when we met two years ago, but under existing conditions in this small Island our future lies in long distance Empire routes. The longer the route the more our speed tells in comparison with sea and rail transport, so the public will be prepared to pay extra for the saving of time which that speed gives.'

Imperial Airways planned to extend activities by introducing a combined air and rail transport system for goods, but it failed to gain Ministry approval — possibly because a much-publicized Imperial airliner race against the *Flying Scotsman* from London to Edinburgh was something of a fiasco, for although it won by a few minutes despite circling the wrong train at Berwick, 1 hr 24 min was lost in refuelling at Bircham Newton and at Cramlington near Newcastle.

But there seemed more behind the Air Ministry's refusal, for a short time afterwards several London papers reported that the Great Western, Southern, London & North Eastern, and London, Midland & Scottish railways were applying to Parliament to operate their own air services. This was emphasized by Sir Felix Pole's comment as general manager of the GWR: 'The railway will certainly not make the mistake many canal companies made in adhering slavishly to one form of transport, but will adopt all forms according to circumstance or demands of the future, whether by rail, road, sea, or air'. Was a great air transport combine of railway interests being formed to put Imperial Airways out of business?

1929

On 1 January 1929, that great airline pioneer George Holt Thomas died at Cimiez in his six-tieth year. Though he had been the most influential aircraft constructor in Britain, he remained too remote to be known to the public. C.G. Grey wrote: 'Numbers of prominent men, some of them millionaires, have posed as patrons of aviation; but with the exception of the late Sir George White of Bristol, Holt Thomas was the only man of first-class mental calibre and good position to take personal part in development of aeroplanes from the begin-ning. He was a man who in every way was worthy of a title.'

A different example of enterprise was that great little personage Lady Bailey, who on 14 January landed her Moth at Croydon, having completed 18,000 miles in the longest solo flight made by any woman to date, during which she encompassed Africa by the east and west routes to which Imperial Airways was still aspiring. Perhaps this stirred the airline to announce that the Empire air mail route of 5,000 miles would soon commence, bringing India within six days of Great Britain. More pilots were being engaged. Among the new trainee staff members was eighteen-year-old Keith Granville, employed at the London Office in Charles Street at 10s a week and happy to be in a romantic business.

1 February 1929 heralded the inauguration of the Guild of Air Pilots and Navigators (GAPAN) at Rule's Hostelry of Maiden Lane, London, where 50 commercial and industrial pilots met under the chairmanship of Sqn Ldr E.L. Johnston to establish themselves as a body of unquestionable integrity to safeguard the interests of professional aviators. The 26 pilots of Imperial Airways constituted the largest individual membership. The standard required for a pilot's position in the Company was justi-fiably high, demanding appropriate licences and 900 hours' experience on multi-engined aircraft including night flying. Practical engineering experience was desirable and knowledge of languages an obvious asset. Pre-ferred age was 25 to 30. There was a pro-bationary period of six months, flying as sec-ond pilot in turn to all the senior pilots who reported on his skill and adaptability on any route and every weather condition. Some of the flight engineers with 2,000 to 3,000 hours' crew flying had become capable pilots though not employed for that purpose. Such was the

rapidly extending status of airline pilots that the Air Ministry decided distinction should be drawn between those of highest skills and the less experienced, so a Master Pilot's certificate was established for those with a 'B' licence held for at least five years during which 1,000 hours had been flown under specified conditions. All Imperial Airways senior pilots fulfilled these requirements.

Because of the specialist operational techni-ques of flying-boats, Flt Lieut B.C.H. Cross, late of the MAEE Felixstowe, had been appointed supervisor of the Calcuttas in the Mediterranean, where he organized docking, mooring, refuelling facilities, motor-boats, staff, and handling crews. The Calcuttas were now fully taken over from the Air Ministry and dispatched to Short Bros at Rochester for over-haul and modification. That meant final closure on 28 February of the Channel Island flying-boat service. A third Calcutta was approaching completion. Overhaul was finished only just in time, for the new Mediterranean route was scheduled to open on 30 March.

At 10 a.m. that day the Argosy *City of Glas-gow*, piloted by Wilcockson and Brackley, left Croydon on the first stage of the Empire run, carrying Sir Samuel Hoare, ever ready by per-sonal action to show his confidence in flying, his private secretary Christopher Bullock, Air Vice-Marshal Sir Vyell Vyvyan as Air Ministry representative of Imperial Airways, and about 1,200 letters. There was no ceremony, but a large number gathered to witness the depar-ture, among them Lady Maud Hoare, Sir Philip Sassoon as Under-Secretary for Air, and Marshal of the RAF Sir Hugh Trenchard.

After a short stop at Le Bourget, the Argosy reached Basle seventeen minutes ahead of schedule. The next stage was by train to Genoa, where Brackley and the three passengers embarked on the Calcutta *City of Alexandria* next day for the flight to Naples, thence to Corfu and Athens where the flying-boat aligh-ted in the rough sea off Phaleron Bay, and a wet ride to shore followed in an Imperial Airways speedboat. Next day they flew via Tobruk to Alexandria harbour, from which city Sir Samuel would tour 4,000 miles of the Cairo–Cape air route. Sir Vyell transferred with the mails to the DH Hercules *City of Jerusalem* which flew via Baghdad to Karachi, arriving on 6 April after sandstorm delay. On the following day the Hercules *City of Baghdad* left with reciprocal air mail for England, carrying the vice-chairman of the airline, Lord Chetwynd, and his daughter, Sir Vyell Vyvyan, and Sir Geoffrey Salmond, who were re-joined at Alexandria by Sir Samuel Hoare.

Said Sir Samuel on return to England: 'This last fortnight has been very important in the history of civil aviation. The outward mail reached India on time, and the Indian mail has arrived absolutely on the tick. Few can have any idea of the enormous organization involved. The journey again shows the great regularity and safety not only of British civil aviation but of British military flying, for after I arrived in Africa a Fairey IIIF machine took me to see as much of the projected African route, and we averaged about 750 miles a day, getting almost to Uganda before we turned back. We certainly hope that the service from Egypt to Cape Town may be started on April 1 next year.'

In South Africa, the Union Government had agreed on application of Union Airways Ltd to operate an air mail service between Cape Town and Port Elizabeth, with extensions to East London and Durban and to Bloemfontein and Johannesburg, with intention to link eventually with the Imperial Airways service, and a three-year contract was granted with annual subsidy of £8,000.

May saw Parliamentary changes. Failing to achieve a clear majority, Baldwin resigned, and on 4 June Ramsay MacDonald was invited to form a Labour Government. It seemed a hopeful sign that he was sufficiently air-minded to become the first Premier to use aeroplanes for his journeys.

Imperial Airways was getting more publicity conscious, and now offered opportunity of short flights in airliners by sending one to every major flying meeting, and in June introduced 'Tea flights' on which, for two guineas each, passengers were flown on a sightseeing tour over London while a monkey-jacketed steward served them tea. Currently a third Argosy was delivered to replace the lost W.10 on the Paris service.

On 16 July Britain's seventh International Aero Exhibition was opened by the Prince of Wales amid the Victorian surroundings of Olympia's cast-iron balustrades and domed glass roof, but here the Imperial Airways stand earned the denigration of the aeronautical Press, for the display, comprising one side of an Argosy cabin with seats, openable windows, and cuspidors for those inclined to be air-sick, was usually dirty, the tin receptacles out of place, the seats singularly uncomfortable, and an unreeling panorama of the England–Egypt–India route seen through the windows gave no illusion of actual flight. The saving grace was an ingenious glass map of Europe on which the air route between London and any selected city lit on pressing the appropriate button and an illuminated sign gave times of departure, arrival, and single and return fares.

However, Imperial Airways received a great boost from the Handley Page stand which displayed the impressively long, white-painted cabin mock-up of the recently ordered four-engined HP 42 airliner. The interior was like a railway Pullman of considerable height and width, with accommodation in two sections, each seating twenty in pairs of chintz-covered double seats separated by a central gangway. Never before had there been such luxurious comfort and *décor*. The forward entrance vestibule contained the wireless, and gave central ingress to the pilot's cockpit, which for the first time in the airline's history was a Triplex glass cabin enclosure. After the Show the 'flight deck' was considerably altered to meet the Eastern route requirements of Capt Wolley Dod who had returned from Cairo for three months' change of scene; a somewhat indignant Brackley had been sent there as temporary replacement — though it turned out to be longer and was indicative of continuing strained relations with Woods Humphery.

25 August was the tenth anniversary of the beginning of British airlines. C.G. Grey wrote commemoratively: 'Primitive was hardly the word for the whole business. But now in 1929 we have a fine new £267,000 air station at Croydon with a great domed Booking Hall, luxurious waiting rooms and commodius Hotel, and from the departure platform go great airline expresses carrying not two but twenty passengers.'

Chief Air Traffic Officer was Capt E.H. 'Bill' Lawford, that pioneer pilot of early Air Transport & Travel days. Describing the daily operations, he said: 'A feature of the navigation room is a 6-ft square map of south-east England and the Continent on which the momentary positions of all airliners are pinpointed with small flags showing the registration letters. On a busy day there may be as many as 25 which are moved along every five minutes, checked by D/F wireless and relayed to the Duty Officer so that he can make instant decisions. A cosmopolitan babel of sound issues from the loud speaker and the wireless experts get busy. This is the sort of thing: "Allo Croirdon — Allo Croirdon, gauliat jay pay vous appelle nous faisons route pour Le Bourget — et nous passons Veegin-ill. Je vous écoute." This is duly replied to; then a British, Dutch or German pipes up, and so it goes on all day.'

There were half-concealed smiles at the Annual General Meeting of Imperial Airways on 26 September, not only of gratification at a dividend of 7½ per cent, but of irony, even amusement, when Sir Eric Geddes announced that, despite his public resignation at the previous meeting, he had continued in office because of pending negotiations and pressure from colleagues that he retain chairmanship. Certainly his report showed that Imperial Airways was steadily making good. Over a million miles had been flown during the year carrying nearly 35,000 paying passengrs and over 870 tons of mail and freight, averaging 75 per cent capacity in Europe and 61 per cent in the Near East. 'I am glad to say that company relations with its staff and employees are of the happiest, and the executive of the company is a team full of enthusiasm and determination. To them throughout, and to Mr Woods Humphery, our general manager, in particular, we owe thanks and appreciation.'

But though Brackley had been supervising the Near East operations and the Alexandria junction for two months Woods Humphery had not written a word, not even when disaster came— for on 6 September the Hercules *City of Jerusalem* (G-EBMZ), piloted by Capt Woodbridge, had crashed at Jask while making a night landing and caught fire; the pilot, mechanic, and one passenger perished, two passengers were injured, and the mail from London was destroyed. Few were more experienced than Woodbridge. 'One of the nicest fellows one could possibly meet — a hard working man with high ideals and keen sense of duty and loyalty', wrote Brackley, adding: 'We had been working at high pressure in the heat of summer, with short staff. This accident was not caused through engine or aircraft failure, but no doubt an error of judgement by a tired pilot after a long day's flying in very trying heat.'

Woodbridge had been thrown out unhurt, but realizing the passengers were trapped he dashed unavailingly into the flames, setting his clothes alight. After his burns had been dressed

he appeared normal, but died of heart failure saying 'Tell them I am sorry'.

C.G. Grey justifiably declared: 'That fatal accident is another example of our muddled way of doing things. Had we been using faster machines a night landing would not have been necessary. Whether a wing-tip flare burst in the air and set fire to the wing, or whether in landing on flat featureless desert the pilot misjudged his height and crashed before the flare had gone out and so set the aeroplane alight, is irrelevant. The point is that the thing should never have been landing by its own lights. If there must be night flying it should be over a properly lighted route, with proper floodlights and beacons on the aerodromes, emergency landing grounds, and an automatic flicker light every four or five miles just as they have in America.'

There followed a private letter from Wolley Dod warning Brackley that he would probably have to stay on at Cairo, but this was not confirmed until 16 October when he received a letter from Col Burchall saying: 'It has been found necessary to send Wolley Dod to conduct a survey of the African route, commencing at Cape Town. He is leaving here on the 25th and probably not back in Cairo for three months. The general manager accordingly is anxious that you remain in Cairo as it is difficult to see any other solution, so I trust that having withstood the heat of summer you will rather look forward to remaining in Cairo for part of the season.'

However, from the PMG came a happy report of the success of the air mail service to India which had now been in operation for six months. 'The Eastbound aeroplanes leave Croydon every Saturday morning, and the Westbound service starts from Karachi every Sunday morning; the actual time of transit over the whole route is seven and a half days. During this first six months working, 14,656 lb of mail have been carried from London to various destinations, and 17,529 lb have reached London. There is no regular long-distance service operated from Europe whose traffic figures can compare with these. The service has been operated with remarkable regularity. Outward, apart from the tragic Jask disaster, there have only been two late arrivals in India owing to floods and sand-storms respectively, and homeward there have been three late arrivals of which two were due to missing the train connection at Genoa and the other because of sand-storms.'

But once again disaster struck. Starkly the newspapers reported that on 26 October the Imperial Airways Calcutta *City of Rome* (G-AADN) had been lost and all seven on board were drowned. *The Times* reported: 'The big flying-boat left the Neopolitan airport of Molo Beverello on Saturday morning. The weather was bad and the sea rough, and bulletins predicted that the journey would be dangerous. Other machines flying the same route decided not to make the journey. After alighting at Ostia the machine left for Genoa, but probably owing to breakdown of an engine had to alight off the Tuscan coast on a sea lashed by a south-westerly gale which threatened to swamp it at any moment. SOS signals were sent. Wireless stations broadcast appeals to steamers. Several tugs left Leghorn, and a destroyer from Spezia went out but was forced by the violent sea to return. Eventually the captain of the tug *Famiglia* found the Calcutta. A cable was thrown. The pilot fastened it to the bow. The tug made slowly towards land, the flying-boat crew helping with their engines going. Fifteen minutes later the cable snapped. The tug crew saw the *City Of Rome* for a few more minutes and heard her engines, but then the navigation lights disappeared. Three times the tug circled where the flying-boat was last seen, but nothing was found or heard.'

The accident should have made clear that flights must be cancelled when seas were rough,

for although hulls might be perfect, the metal-framed wings could be buckled by heavy seas and the entire structure collapse — yet ,the Court of Inquiry glossed over the danger. Four days later both the other Calcuttas were damaged in rough seas at Mersa Matruh, one staving in its bottom while taking off and the other damaging the vital chine struts.

Next day the temporary right of British flying-boats to use Italian ports was withdrawn because Imperial Airways refused to pool receipts from the Genoa–Alexandria route with the smaller returns of the Italians using Dornier flying-boats. Immediate re-routing was essential. The Argosy were switched via Vienna, Budapest, Belgrade, Skoplje, and Salonika to Athens where passengers and mail were transhipped to flying-boat — for which purpose a Supermarine Southampton was briefly hired from the Air Ministry while the Calcuttas were being repaired. Wintry weather soon proved the Balkan route unsafe, so when the Calcuttas returned to service it was arranged that passengers travelled by train between Paris and Athens — to Imperial Airways' benefit as it was a cheaper mode of transit! The flying-boat route was also changed to a shortened course from Mirabella, a beautiful hill-surrounded lagoon on the northeast side of Crete where the depot refuelling ship *Imperia* was stationed, thence to Mersa Matruh instead of Tobruk further east, and so to Alexandria.

Croydon airport control tower, offices and reception hall during the heyday of Imperial Airways – but with evidence that monoplanes are beginning to intrude on the conventional biplanes.

Consolidating the Airline 1930-34

An economic blizzard was beginning to hit Britain, triggered by a breakdown of the New York stock exchange in which US shares slumped by $16 million, affecting monetary credits throughout the Western World, though Britain was still dominant in international finance. As yet there was little reduction in the number of American businessmen and tourists travelling by Imperial Airways, but in any case there was rarely much traffic in winter. These days, if Croydon was weatherbound there was the alternative of fog-free Heston Airport near Hounslow, which was now approved as a Customs Aerodrome and far more convenient for London than diversion to one of the Sussex emergency landing grounds.

Speaking at a banquet of the British Chamber of Commerce in Paris on 9 January, Labour's authoritative Lord Thomson, Secretary for Air, said that in commercial aviation it was a case of get on or get out. With M Eynac, the French Minister of Aviation, he had explored Africa, Arabia, and the farthest East, finding everywhere that their airline activities could be profitably combined, so they had planned a web of air communication covering more than half the surface of the globe 'whose civilizing influence would stimulate the growth of Franco-British trade'. That was not the view of tough Sir Eric Geddes. France was a rival, and must be treated so. It was bad enough that Aéropostale flew from Africa across the Atlantic to Port Natal, then extended south to Brazil and the Argentine, and since July 1929 added Buenos Aires to Santiago with intent to carry mails for Bolivia, Peru and North America through Venezuela and the West Indies.

That private efforts could show the way for the world's airlines was again demonstrated when the unknown Francis Chichester, who had left Croydon on 20 December flying a Gypsy Moth, landed at Port Darwin, Australia,

having traversed in seventeen days the route blazed by Ross Smith in 1919 and latterly by Cobham — but it remained a distant target for Imperial Airways.

However progress was being made. Capt Bill Armstrong, one of the ex-A T & T pilots, was appointed manager of the Near East Division and sent out to Cairo. But what of Brackley? *The Aeroplane* commented: 'This business of Air Superintendent is baffling. Major Brackley was and still is really, but for many months Mr Armstrong sternly occupied the official chair; then one morning Mr Wilcockson was there looking like Mussolini with a liver. A few days later, the Air Superintendent was a positively monumentally portentous Mr Walters. Maybe Mr Scruffy Robinson will occupy the sacred seat one day, and then— Oh boy!' Heavily built Capt Wilcockson had been chief pilot since the fatal accident to Barnard.

By the beginning of March Wolley Dod, accompanied by Tony Gladstone and Frederick Tymms, had completed their survey of the northern portion of the Cairo–Cape Town route. Much work was still required to establish landing places and facilities, so although the southern section was practically ready, the service could not meet the Juf target and must be deferred to October or November, and the full route to the Cape opened in April next year. Headquarters of the southern section would be Johannesburg, and of the northern at Alexandria, with a weekly service each way, the

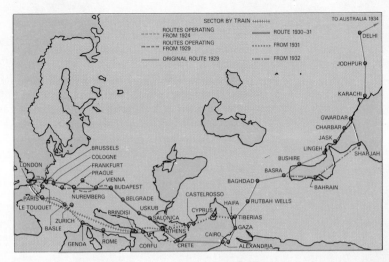

Imperial Airways routes, 1924–34.

machines crossing at Nairobi.

As the Air Ministry's contribution, the current Air Estimates of £21 million allocated an additional £60,000 to Imperial Airways for the South African service. The Commons debate provoked little discussion on civil aviation, though Mr Montague, the ex-newsboy Under-Secretary for Air, stated: 'The Government of India has now extended the service from Karachi to Delhi with aircraft chartered from and operated by Imperial Airways. Ground organization across India is being vigorously pushed forward. The section to Calcutta will be ready by the end of March and by autumn enough progress should have been

A line-up of Imperial Airways biplanes at Le Bourget airport, Paris. *Left to right:* Short L.17 *Syrinx*, HP 42 *Horatius* and Short L.17 *Scylla*.

made for operation to Rangoon. Proposals have been submitted to the Air Ministry for the remaining section between Rangoon and Australia.'

The organizational expansion of the airline to deal with the Indian and African routes involved many crucial problems, among which was the difficulty of finding enough people capable of holding responsible positions overseas in conditions so different from Europe. At least a start was made by establishing a scheme at Airways House for commercial trainees offering a two-year course of practical experience, lectures on every sector of commercial aviation, evening classes, three months overseas, and six months at one of the divisional headquarters. Said the organizer: 'Our man stationed in darkest Africa must know exactly what to do if lions chase his passengers into the bush thus causing a late departure, or if white ants eat the aircraft in the night thus necessitating cancellation of the service'. In the next few years a number of youngsters destined to make their mark joined the school, among them Max Stuart-Shaw, Ian Scott-Hill, Richard Hillary, Edwin Whitfield, and Ross Stainton.

The airline pilots remained a cheery crowd, and had formed a committee to operate the pilots' room in the Aerodrome Hotel at Croydon on club lines, paying an annual subscription for facilities and privacy, with discriminatory powers on membership — for a few undesirable thrusters had sometimes spoilt the congenial atmosphere. At least in public a more dignified air had been introduced by the GAPAN which now ranked among the City Guilds. With due ceremony Sir Sefton Brancker had been installed as first Master, together with Deputy Master, Wardens, and Members of the Court to whom the Reverend Donald Robins, the former Airways pilot, was Honorary Chaplain. The Court had reviewed methods of education and training for commercial pilots, and was requested by the Air Ministry to submit a memorandum thereon.

In the Commons on 5 May Mr Montague moved a resolution on which to found a new Air Transport (Subsidy Agreements) Bill giving the Secretary of State for Air statutory authority to make longterm agreements 'to any persons and to furnish facilities for their aircraft in consideration of those persons maintaining a regular service for carriage by air of passengers, goods and mails, and to authorize payment from monies provided by Parliament of any

sums for fulfilment of any such agreement provided the aggregate for subsidies can not exceed £1 million in any financial year, and no subsidy should be payable under any such agreement after December 31, 1940'. This breached the Imperial Airways monopoly, enabling rival companies to be established and subsidized.

On 12 April the first India air mail to cross Europe by the new route via Nuremberg and thence to Salonika reached Karachi one hour ahead of schedule on 19 April — a record seven days, but despite the hospitable co-operation at the twelve stage-landing points to Athens there was irritation at the number of forms to be filled in and the vast amount of paperwork carried aboard. While this flight was taking place the Duchess of Bedford aboard her Fokker monoplane *The Spider*, piloted by Charles Barnard, was making a swift stage-by-stage flight to the Cape and back. C.G. Grey snatched the opportunity for yet another editorial homily: 'Though Her Grace is not competing with Imperial Airways, she has shown the kind of competition it will have to compete with. She now shows that letters can be sent to the Ćape and the answer back in England inside a fortnight — which is the time letters take for the single journey from England to the Cape by steamer.'

Demonstrating once again that the ordinary man or woman was capable of piloting an aeroplane over long distances was Amy Johnson, who left Croydon on 5 May in her heavily laden second-hand DH Moth, and in stage-by-stage flights achieved Australia on 24 May as the world's new heroine. If a woman can do this, people thought, why not Imperial Airways?

A Civil Aviation debate in the Lords revealed that the Air Ministry was discussing the possibility of initiating airways on the West Atlantic seaboard in co-operation with the Canadian Government. A consultative committee had been set up, but in classic governmental manner there was no representation of Imperial Airways: it comprised shipping, railways, the FBI, and MPs, though they had the aeronautical advice of Colonel O'Gorman. Lord Thomson stated: 'The committee has reported most sympathetically on the Atlantic Airways scheme and I am fairly confident that we should be able to build up something of that sort, on the far side of the Atlantic independent of the monopoly system, but contributions under the Transport Subsidy Bill would be made by the Dominions and Colonies'.

Britain's hopeful solution to trans-Atlantic and long-distance flying was made evident at the RAF Display in June when the monster R.101 floated across the aerodrome, though spectators were unaware that she was steadily losing gas. A month later the rival R.100 successfully flew to Canada and back.

Imperial communications remained the goal. The recent British treaty with Iraq was a hopeful step forward. Said Sir Samuel Hoare: 'Iraq lies midway on the air route between Great Britain and India and the Far East, and is vital for security of our Imperial communications, and particularly our air communications, Iraq is a member of the International Air Convention and therefore under obligation to allow free passage of civil airlines.'

Financial success was attending Imperial Airways. For 1929–30 a profit of £60,138 had been made, but Sir Eric Geddes, still retaining the chair, said the Board considered it inexpedient to give details of subsidies and their effect 'because of erroneous deductions which will inevitably be drawn unjustifiably against fair appraisement of the value of our property. We have the paradox of comparing subsidy with profit. The Air Ministry increases our subsidy on condition that we put by this tremendous obsolescence of 20 per cent and so increase our costs. The Inland Revenue declines to allow the obsolescence in full as a legitimate cost but taxes us on it in part as they say it ought to be a profit. One Government Department says it's a cost and another says it's a profit!'

He also complained that the GPO air mail policy was wrong and that the 'Empire service was being retarded'. The PMG immediately disclaimed the criticism, declaring that air mails were steadily increasing, and over a quarter of the letters were on the India run. 'The uniform combined charge for air fee and postage introduced in June this year and the special blue pillar boxes for air mails have had effect: 30 per cent more letters went by air to European destinations than in the same quarter last year.'

The affairs of Imperial Airways and the Post Office were almost immediately overshadowed by disaster to the R.101. Lord Thomson had said: 'I insist on the programme for the Indian flight being adhered to, as I have made my plans accordingly'. Aiming at dramatic national publicity, his intention was to reach Karachi on 9 October and return in time for an Imperial Conference in London on 20 October. Accordingly at 6.30 in the evening of 4 October the great airship commenced her flight with Thomson and other distinguished passengers aboard. Silence — then a radio rumour of tragedy. Next day *The Times* reported: 'The airship struck the ground and was wrecked and totally destroyed by fire near Beauvais, in the north of France, early in Sunday morning. Of

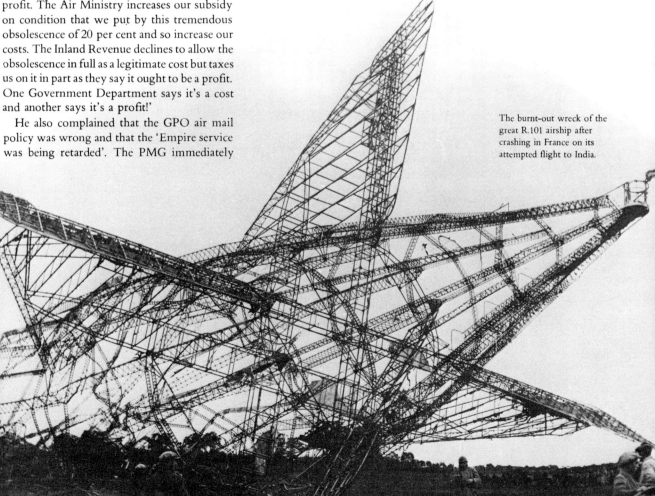

The burnt-out wreck of the great R.101 airship after crashing in France on its attempted flight to India.

An eye-catching advertising poster for Imperial Airways' services.

Bigger and better. The 130-ft span Hannibal-class HP 42, powered with four centrally grouped Bristol Jupiter radials, was the world's first attempt at a large, viable airliner, offering the height of elegance and luxury on its introduction to the travelling public in 1931. The illustration shows *Helena*, the last of these aircraft.

the 54 persons on board, only eight were saved.' Among those killed were Lord Thomson and Sir Sefton Brancker. It was the end of airships. The still airworthy R.100 was broken up and sold for scrap.

Almost every week the RAF, one or other international airline, or a flying club, was victim of a crash. On the foggy morning of 30 October the Imperial Airways *City of Washington* (G-EBIX) — a seven-year-old Handley Page Hampstead converted from three-engined configuration to twin W.8 — flew into the ground near Neufchâtel, killing three passengers and the mechanic, injuring another passenger and the pilot, Paddy Flynn. Absence of appropriate instruments and lack of blind-flying training were the probable cause, for he had no great experience of foggy conditions and for the past ten months was only a reserve pilot, ranking as Flight Officer. Though twin-engined aircraft had been banned for carriage of passengers across the Channel they were exempt on this occasion because the passengers were 'privileged' to travel free as they were on Imperial Airways business.

Imperial Airways could hardly be blamed for the inadequacies of instrument development. Where the administration erred was allowing flights in unsuitable weather, for undoubtedly pilots were under pressure to make an attempt and subject to criticism by inference if they did not. 'Press on regardless' was all very well for the RAF, but not for an airline. Nor could Brackley be wholly blamed, though he had at last been permitted to return from his posting in Cairo. His letters to Woods Humphery were formal in an endeavour to define his duties. 'I feel', he wrote, 'that the Air Superintendent

should be taken into the management's confidence and allowed the same privileges as the consulting and chief engineer and traffic manager by taking part in meetings at which the company's operations and subjects affecting the flight department are discussed — such as development of night flying on the European and Near East routes. To investigate conditions under which pilots are working it is desirable that the Air Superintendent should be allowed to fly these routes at irregular intervals and work in closest co-operation with divisional managers in matters affecting pilotage, wireless, aerodromes, and performance of aircraft.' There was a hint too of the attitude of Woods Humphery: 'In conclusion I submit that with your backing and confidence, I can carry out the duties to your and the Board's entire satisfaction'. It was months before he was firmly re-established, but though he made cautious appeal for 'financial recognition' his salary remained unchanged from the day he had joined Imperial Airways at its inception six years earlier; nor was he selected to accompany Woods Humphery, who arrived in New York aboard the *Mauretania* on 16 November to confer with Juan Trippe, President of Pan American Airways, on the possibilities of an airline from New York to Bermuda, thence by Imperial Airways to London via the Azores.

Meanwhile the Handley Page HP 42 made its initial flight seven months late on 14 November. Losing no time, the Press were invited to view this long-heralded airliner. Said a reporter: 'It is more like a flying-boat than a landplane. The arrangement of engines is notable, with two in the top centre-section, the tips of their airscrews just clear of the fuselage, and the other two in the angle between each outer lower wing and the steep anhedral of the inboard section which slopes above the cabin windows so that passengers get an unimpeded view of the country over which they are flying.' However there were snags to overcome, and months would pass before the machine received its C of A after trials at Martlesham by RAF test pilots. That meant no profit for Hand-

ley Page and considerable loss of estimated revenue for Imperial Airways.

The dream of profitable trans-Atlantic flying was also fading, for *The Times* announced that though the USA Post Office had invited tenders for an air mail service between the USA and Europe, as discussed between Woods Humphery and Juan Trippe a month earlier, it was now stipulated that bidders must be citizens of the USA and any corporation not organized under the laws of that country would be ineligible.

1931

By comparison with Britain's struggling efforts to consolidate the Eastern route and open up the airway to the Cape, Italy startled the world with a triumphant crossing of the South Atlantic by a formation of Savoia-Marchetti tandem-engined flying-boats on 6 January 1931 — but the fact that two of the ten crashed on take-off and two alighted on the open ocean with engine trouble emphasized the fallibility of air transport. Even on the familiar cross-Channel route a trimotor Fokker of Sabena, encountering fog on the Brussels–London night air mail service of 7 January, turned back near Ghent but was so low that a wing-tip struck trees, and the machine turned over, crushing the two occupants under the wreckage. As always, this was headline news; newspapers never bothered with the great background of successful flying going on by night and day.

Commercial aviation was the least of the Labour Government's problems, for the Cabinet was facing massive unemployment and vanishing trade. Speculation on the late Sir Sefton Brancker's successor ceased with the appointment of 50-year-old Colonel Francis Shelmerdine as DCA. Frederick Tymms inherited his difficult task of dealing with an Indian Government determined to operate airlines across that country solely by its own nationals but having suspended all expenditure on civil aviation. Coincident with these appointments

Handley Page HP 42 *Hengist*, which was commissioned by Imperial Airways in December 1931 for the western routes; converted to eastern in 1935; and wrecked at Karachi in 1937.

was Christopher Bullock's as Secretary of the Air Ministry, replacing Sir Walter Nicholson who became a Government director of Imperial Airways.

Lecturing before the Royal Society of Arts on the history of air communications in Africa, Woods Humphery stressed that because nearly all British Dependencies were on the eastern side that must be the side they would fly. 'At the present stage of air travel and human psychology, 700 to 1,000 miles is the maximum comfortable day's travel for the ordinary passenger. That is why the time-table is so slow, for the service initially is only an experimental schedule. From Cairo to Khartoum the Argosy will be used seating only ten or twelve passengers because the great heights and tropical temperatures reduce the payload compared with temperate climates. From Khartoum to Lake Victoria the swamps of Southern Sudan and Uganda will be crossed in Calcutta flying-boats which have been very successful on the Mediterranean, but their capacity will be reduced like the Argosy's. From Kisumu to the Cape the great height and rarified air provide conditions similar to those under which the smaller and faster DH Hercules proved excellent on the India service, and they will cruise at about 100 mph. Growing reliability of engines and improvement in navigation is reducing the

need for intermediate landing grounds, but these have been provided throughout. Where hotels did not exist at the fourteen main stopping places, the company is providing rest houses and accommodation. If the flying-boat stops where moorings are some distance from the rest houses, fast motor boats are provided. Direction-finding wireless will be used. Night flying equipment is provided at Cape Town, Johannesburg, Salisbury, Mbeya, and Cairo so that stages can finish after dark. The fare from London to Cape Town has been fixed at £130.'

The service was confined to air mail for its inauguration on 28 February, when 'an Argosy was ushered off the apron with rather more ceremony and public attention than usually bestowed on these hard-working vehicles, but if the shrinkage of distance be indeed a joyful thing there was no tumultuous evidence that this was realized by the gathering'. Late delivery of the new aircraft made it necessary to open the route with only two Argosys and two Calcuttas. Within three weeks one of the Argosys damaged an undercarriage at Khartoum. Four days later a piston broke in an engine of the Calcutta carrying mails from Mwanza, but it alighted safely at Kisumu. As the local 'wireless' was out of commission a day's delay ensued before the relief Calcutta was dispatched southwards. When it arrived, a petrol tank was

leaking. There were no facilities for repair so both flying-boats lay helpless, and the Argosy waiting at Khartoum was therefore bereft of its mails, completely dislocating the service. Not until 1 April was the Calcutta with repaired tank able to re-commence, loaded with two weeks' mail.

Experience with the Calcuttas in the Mediterranean had demonstrated need for better seaworthiness, greater load-carrying capacity, and improved reliability, so four-engined enlargements were ordered featuring a wide cabin 14 ft long, furnished with fifteen luxurious high-backed seats each side of a gangway in four rows of facing pairs with tables between and large square windows giving a splendid view beneath the wings. Manufacture of these, known as the Kent-class, had begun in October 1930, and by mid-January the first hull was ready for attachment of wing and tail structures. On 24 February it was ready, and after a 30-minute initial flight by John Parker, who was leaving for Japan, completion of testing was handed to Brackley. By 25 March, after minimal testing, *Scipio*, the prototype of the three, was delivered to Felixstowe for official trials. A week later the second, named *Sylvanus*, was launched, and Brackley flew it with Capt Walters and Wilcockson in turn.

Regardless of increasing outlay required for the extending airline operations, the civil section of the heavily RAF-orientated Air Estimates for 1931–32 showed a net decrease of £30,000, despite contributions from Dominion and Colonial governments of £155,000 towards the South African service. Stocky Mr Montague seemed pleased, and said a scheme had been prepared for a weekly air mail service between Calcutta and Australia, assuming the stage between Karachi and Calcutta would be conjointly operated with Imperial Airways as an Indian State service. 'If the extension to Australia gets going, together with the Indian and African services, we shall have cause for congratulation compared with other countries. There would be 29,300 miles of air services in the British Empire against 24,650 for France, 17,000 for Germany, and 10,700 for Holland — though the figure for the USA is larger than ours: 49,550 miles. Development of efficient day and night air mail services to Continental centres is being examined. Electric boundary lights are being tried at Croydon and a new beacon has been installed near Redhill.' But he overlooked the vital blind-flying training. This had been stressed at a RAeS lecture by Capt Florman, managing director of Swedish AB Aerotransport, who said: 'With certain reservations, reliable instruments for blind flying are

The customary rigorous inspection and preparation of a Short Calcutta flying-boat on the Mediterranean sector of the Imperial Airways route to India. These aircraft were the first flying boats with stressed-skin metal hulls to go into commercial service.

Opposite: Imperial Airways poster.

now available. There is no middle way between ordinary flight and flying blind. Many pilots have crashed with fatal results through imagining there was. In this task aeroplanes must have inherent stability and require a horizon indicator, a turn-and-bank indicator, longitudinal inclinometer, variometer, speedometer, compass and reliable altimeter — but even so there are difficulties making a safe landing without seeing the ground practically impossible. It requires tremendous physical and mental qualities on the part of pilots, of whom I am convinced not more than 50 per cent of those employed by European air services are suitable for the task.'

Britain produced the answer with a new type of gyroscopically-controlled turn-and-bank indicator devised by Sqn Ldr Reid. With about six hours' practice, the average pilot in nil visibility could fly straight with an accuracy of about one mile in 60, and safely accomplish any turn manoeuvres. It was to become the standard 'blind flying' instrument — but as Florman indicated, those long used to ordinary visual pilotage found it difficult tó disregard the deep-seated instincts on which they had relied for thousands of hours.

More immediate concentration was on the flying-boats and getting them into service. On 20 April Imperial Airways invited an ecstatic Press to inspect *Scipio* and *Sylvanus* at Rochester. The third Kent, *Satyrus*, was launched on 30 April and flown on 2 May with Sir Samuel

Instone as passenger. Next morning Brackley commenced the Mediterranean delivery flights, piloting *Scipio* from Hythe to Marignane in just under seven hours against a head wind. Capt Bailey then proceeded with it to Genoa, and Brackley flew back to England to check out more pilots in *Satyrus*. On 15 May he delivered it to Genoa via Marignane through blinding rain, then returned to Rochester for final acceptance flights of *Sylvanus* which he delivered on 26 May to Hythe, where the Prince of Wales was given a short flight to see the new Canadian Pacific liner *Empress of Britain* on her maiden voyage down the Solent.

Now that an agreement had been signed between British and Greek Governments permitting Imperial Airways to use the Greek seaplane stations at Salonika, Phaleron for Athens, and Candia and Mirabella in Crete, Imperial Airways initiated an experimental mail service to Australia on 11 April as an extension of the Karachi service. There it was transhipped to Port Darwin by the Hercules *City of Cairo* which reached Singapore on schedule, but thereafter the eastward flight became increasingly difficult because of the unexpectedly early monsoon. Six miles short of its aerodrome 'an unexplained petrol shortage' forced the machine down, but the apparently smooth green field was an area of rocks overgrown by grass, and the undercarriage collapsed. The mails were portaged to Koepang, and to save the situation Kingsford Smith flew there with an Australian National Airways Avro Ten to pick them up and bring them to Port Darwin, thence to Sydney by Qantas. Though the Hercules had to be expensively dismantled, at least tradition was upheld, for the mails got through regardless.

Nor was the African mail without further problems. The southbound service from London on 2 April did not arrive at Nairobi until 17 April owing to engine trouble, and departure of the northbound mail from Kisumu was consequently postponed three days. The Nairobi Chamber of Commerce sarcastically complained that Imperial Airways had not completed the experimental work on the route before causing public inconvenience and loss of money, and asked the Kenya Government to suspend the subsidy pending establishment of a proper service. Nor was the position improved by the company's latest propaganda depicting

Imperial Airways Argosy Captain Percy hands over a mail bag at Croydon airport at the end of an experimental Australia–UK mail flight in April 1931.

IMPERIAL AIRWAYS
EUROPE AFRICA INDIA FAR EAST AUSTRALIA

ONE OF THE 28 NEW 200 MILES AN HOUR TWO·DECKER EMPIRE FLYING·BOATS

The three Short Kent flying-boats *Scipio*, *Sylvanus* and *Satyrus* at moorings in Alexandria harbour. Each aircraft carried fifteen passengers, had a maximum speed of 137 mph and cruised at 105 mph. On the extreme left is a Calcutta.

an elephant with raised trunk and the words 'Where's my mail?' That, a Commerce member said, was what the public wanted to know!

Imperial Airways also had to explain another disastrous incident at Croydon when the latest Argosy *City of Edinburgh* swung heavily across wind on the pilot's seventh take-off for his licence clearance; because Argosys had no brakes he attempted a lift-off, but crashed through the boundary fence. Immediately the machine burst into flames, and though the pilot managed to leap out, it was consumed within five minutes.

Further setback in extending the African route occurred on 5 May when Tony Gladstone, director of Imperial Airways (South Africa) Ltd, was killed with Glen Kidston when their borrowed and overladen Puss Moth crashed in the Drakensberg Mountains in Natal. They had been negotiating for the purchase of Union Airways which ran an air mail service from Cape Town to Durban by way of Port Elizabeth. Kidston had been critical of Imperial Airways. 'There is plenty of demand

for speed, but air mails between England and India average 28 mph. The new fleet of HP 42 aeroplanes is due for service early this year yet still has to pass acceptance tests, but as their cruising speed is 100 mph they will start their career obsolete when finally delivered.'

Some at least of the Imperial Airways problems were being solved with the Kent flying-boats, for they began regular operation on the resumed Italian route from Genoa to Alexandria on 17 May. Near trouble was marginally escaped on the 24th when *Scipio*, alighting on rough seas at Candia, Crete, had a wing-tip float torn off, but the pilot, instantly reacting, opened up and flew round to Mirabella on the other side where the water was comparatively smooth, and on safely touching down, one of the crew walked along the wing to tilt the machine on to the other wing-tip float.

Ever since the New Year tests had been continuing with the Handley Page *Hannibal* in a much more responsible manner than the brief testing of the Kent flying-boats, but there had been a sequence of minor mishaps, so that it was not until 5 June that the full C of A was received, and the prototype delivered to Croydon in heavy rain. Next day Brackley held a briefing meeting with Walters, Jones, Rogers, and Burchall as nominated pilots to operate the marque. That afternoon he and Walters flew *Hannibal* to Hanworth Air Park for Inspection by members from the Commons and Lords, and demonstrated it in flight. Next day Walters began the familiarization and proving flights. Buoyed with optimism, Imperial Airways reduced the London to Cairo single fare from £50 to £45, and out and return to £81; the 5,000 miles to Karachi, taking a little over five days, was cut to £98, which was only £6 more than the first-class fare by surface transport for a journey of seventeen days, and the return fare slashed by £65 10s to £176 10s. To Kisumu the new fare of £95 was £2 less than first-class surface transport and saved 23 days.

However the ribald airline pilots were not taking their new acquisition, *Hannibal*, seriously, even to the extent of christening it 'The Flying Banana'. Certainly it seemed a retrograde device, with its canvased wings and many struts compared with the giant Junkers four-engined G.38 all-metal cantilever monoplane that flew into Croydon on the Berlin–London service of Deutsche Luft Hansa. Like *Hannibal* it accommodated 40, though for the moment the British machine was restricted to freight carrying while the pilots were getting used to it and the engineers determining the maintenance schedules. Martlesham tests showed that *Hannibal* held 10,000 ft at full load with one engine switched off, but with only two going it was tricky to maintain height even at lowest altitude. Cruising petrol consumption was a mere 21 gallons per engine per hour.

New problems came with the HP 42s. *Hadrian*, the second to be delivered, was on its seventh test flight flown by Walters when he detected aileron snatch. Demonstrating this to the firm's pilot, Walters applied full aileron, and this time an outer diagonal wing strut buckled and collapsed. That entailed basic modification to replace the diagonal struts with crossed streamlined steel rods. This delayed carriage of fare-paying passengers until 8 July.

When Frank Bradbrooke of *The Aeroplane* was given a flight in *Hannibal*, piloted by Wilcockson, he reported: 'Admittedly the machine is of the Eastern type seating only eighteen and had no freight, but even so take-off in six seconds is good for so large an aeroplane and the climb astonishing. The décor met with some criticism, for the cushions have too brilliant a pattern and the wall decorations remind one of the drop curtain in a provincial theatre — but furnishings have to be of the lightest, so earthly lavishness cannot be imitated successfully. The seats are at least as comfortable as those in a first-class railway carriage and have as much leg room. The quietness of the cabin is the best yet, and conversation is easier than in a train. The absence of vibration is probably the result of metal construction and large dimensions, giving a resilience which damps out jarring, but there is just enough spring in the fuselage to make a harness necessary for the pilots in the extreme nose when the machine is taxi-ing over rough ground, for it accentuates the effect of the wheel springing and is worse than riding in the back seat of a much overhung charabanc. There were no bumps when airborne. We doubt whether there are more comfortable aeroplanes in the world than the HP 42.'

More ambitiously, the African route was being surveyed for the second time by Sir Alan Cobham for Imperial Airways. On 22 July he and his six-man crew took off from the Medway in the three-engined Short Valetta float seaplane, intending to test alighting places along the Nile and explore a new route from Entebbe to Lake Kivu and possibly along the Congo River to the West coast. Stage by stage, he reached Entebbe on 5 August, and then set out for the high country of the Ruwenzori Range between Lake Albert and Lake Edward, but bad weather and turbulence forced him back, and when he tried again he decided it was impracticable and returned to Entebbe. At the end of the week he headed home, arriving back at Southampton Water on 31 August. 'I gleaned a lot of information' was all he would tell reporters.

While he was away a unique accident attended *Hannibal* when a broken cowling fastener hit the port lower propeller, which disintegrated and the fragments broke the propeller above and set up serious vibration. The Captain, Fred Dismore, had no option but to land immediately in a small field near Tonbridge, but had to approach with his unwieldy machine over houses, found the height insufficient, and turned to avoid them. The starboard lower wing fouled a telegraph pole, but he landed successfully, only to be defeated by a tree stump which caught the tail bracing wires and tore off the rear of the fuselage. Nobody was hurt, but the passengers were astonished to discover how great was the damage — and it meant more financial outlay for the company to dismantle the machine and take it to Croydon for a re-build. It was the old story of the unsinkable ship, for propeller breakage was rare and nobody imagined it might involve the others. Even so the designers had envisaged the possibility of breakage, and therefore placed the luggage and mail compartments in line with the blades to avoid seating passengers in the danger zone. But who would have dreamed this majestic machine could be manoeuvred into quite a small field?

Systemizing airliner take-off procedure at Croydon was the latest move towards efficiency. Stand-by pilots were instructed to post themselves alongside the departing machine so that the aircraft pilot could signal he was ready. The stand-by then turned towards the Control Tower and waved a green flag, whereupon the duty officer displayed the appropriate signal letter of the aircraft if it was cleared to move off. Pilots made rude comment, or affected to ignore the procedure, using the W/T to tell Control that a man was in front of their machine nibbling a lettuce. Matters came to a

head when it was the turn of Rogers the joker. Blowing a whistle, he strutted to the tarmac wearing a porter's hat and under his arm a red railway flag and a green one. It won the day. Responsibility reverted to the aircraft Captains.

Brackley, guardian of the pilots, was in Central Africa while this was going on, and did not arrive back until late August. As a result of his recommendations the schedules of the Indian and African air mail services were being changed to provide independent departures — the Indian service leaving Croydon at midday on Saturday to follow a shortened route by crossing the Mediterranean from Genoa to Haifa on the coast of Palestine, then to Baghdad and on by the old route to Karachi, reached in just under six days. The African mail left Croydon at noon on Wednesday, by way of Brindisi and Athens to Alexandria, and so to the existing route.

Since airline transport was a matter of national prestige, the Air Ministry sought distinction for British aircraft by establishing 'a distinguishing ensign of light blue which may be flown by British aircraft registered in the United Kingdom and at aerodromes in the United Kingdom licensed under the Air Navigation Act 1920'. A little mast was there-

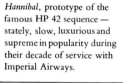

Hannibal, prototype of the famous HP 42 sequence — stately, slow, luxurious and supreme in popularity during their decade of service with Imperial Airways.

fore mounted above the pilot's compartment for a small replica ensign to be hoisted while the aircraft was stationary or taxi-ing to the apron.

Much more emphatically, Great Britain achieved world-wide publicity by gaining the world speed record of 407.5 mph with one of the Supermarine Schneider Trophy Racers — a speed which seemed only possible to a specially designed machine with a short-lived, enormously powered engine. Nobody except a few dreaming scientists thought it had relevance to airliners, whose plodding 100 mph was accepted as satisfactory.

On 8 October Parliament dissolved and a National Government was formed, though MacDonald retained the Premiership. Shortly after the election, Imperial Airways held its seventh AGM, at which Sir Eric Geddes revealed a big drop of £60,000 in net profits to £27,140. Shareholders remained tolerant because the air fleet was alleged to be 41 aeroplanes and flying-boats — but this included three HP 42s approaching completion, eight Atalantas under construction, three obsolete twin-engined W.8s, and two charter machines. However five HP 42s and three Short Kents had been added during the year, but Sir Eric forbore to say that they had only just begun

operating from Brindisi in accordance with the new agreement made with Italy.

In November the HP 42s *Horsa, Hadrian* and *Hanno* were flown to Cairo for the Eastern route. Coinciding with their arrival was the epic flight of Bert Hinkler who had flown his Puss Moth 2,000 miles across the South Atlantic from Natal to Gambia in 22 hours, then headed stage by stage along the West African coast and across the Straits, reaching Hanworth Air Park from Paris on 7 December. There he was greeted by the new Secretary of State for Air, the Marquis of Londonderry.

1932

It was in an atmosphere of disarmament talks that Imperial Airways on 20 January 1932 inaugurated the first through mails from London to Cape Town. The machines for the various sectors made a motley fleet — HP 42s, Kent flying-boats, AW Argosys, Short Calcuttas, and the DH Hercules. The daunting prospect of servicing so many different types created such problems that no passengers were carried for the time being, though on the initial flight, in addition to 20,000 letters and 150 parcels, Francis Bertram as DDCA and AVM Sir Vyell Vyvyan, the Government Director of Imperial Airways, were aboard. After the HP 42 *Helena* left on the initial stage to Paris piloted by Capt Youell, several hundred guests at Croydon were given lunch of distinctive South African flavour, and each presented with a folder of apt quotations and cartoons — *The dream of flying to Africa*. Major Ewart Grogen, who in 1900 had walked from Cape to Cairo, said in toasting Imperial Airways: 'To fly across Africa and back is no longer an adventure but an entrancing experience in which 8,000 miles of Empire unrolls beneath your arm-chair'.

Unfortunately the opening service had its difficulties. The southbound mails arrived at Nairobi aboard the Hercules *City of Baghdad* eighteen hours behind schedule. Next day a violent tropic rainstorm forced the machine to land *en route* so it arrived well behind schedule at Johannesburg, and was two days late in reaching the Cape. The homeward bound *City of Basra* met trouble at Salisbury, sinking into an unmarked rain-washed hole, wrenching the fuselage and damaging the tail. A relief aeroplane arrived and took the mails but was also forced down after 40 miles and tipped on its nose landing on boggy ground, the mails even-

Above: The Captain of the HP 42 *Heracles* with Marconi radio equipment on the flight deck.
Right: A radio operator on board *Heracles.*

tually arriving in England nine days late. 'However', said *Flight* hopefully, 'the new and improved airliners, eight AW Atalantas, will soon be in service and similar comedies should be few and far between.'

At question time in the Commons on 10 February, Capt Harold Balfour was informed by the Under-Secretary for Air that the number of fare-paying passengers travelling from London to India by Imperial Airways was about 75 per annum but it was not practicable to state the cost per passenger incurred by the British taxpayer. A few days later Balfour asked Sir Philip Sassoon 'whether he was aware that the State subsidy for the Cairo–Karachi route amounted to £1,800 per ton of payload, which was equivalent to £180 per passenger yet the passenger fare charged by the company was £58'. Sassoon gravely assented, but thought the question totally irrelevant. Unrepentant, Balfour asked whether the latest agreement with Imperial Airways contained provision for a grant of £20,000 towards flying-boats. Sir Philip explained that this was because the sea mileage of the first Kent on the Mediterranean had to be extended, involving expense not allowed in the original terms. It almost seemed that Balfour, a man of charm and ability on the Board of Saunders-Roe and Spartan Airlines, was gunning for the Under-Secretary, for each week he had another question ready with which to keep the Government on its toes.

In the debate on the Air Estimates in March, he attacked the Imperial Airways monopoly, saying that it retarded civil aviation. 'On the route to Egypt 1,120 miles is by air and 970 miles by foreign railway. The route to Australia

has been flown once and then the machine crashed. Negotiations with India have been so bungled that permission to allow Imperial Airways to run a service across their country has been refused. Nor is the South African service creditable: one can go quicker by car, and mail has arrived earlier by sea. Persian negotiations will probably fail and necessitate a West Arabian route costing the taxpayer another £10,000. The Hambling Committee recommended a 50-50 basis whereby taxpayer and private enterprise should bear equal shares of charges and profits, but Imperial Airways has acquired over £2 million of public money and the shareholder subscribed only £500,000. I propose no fresh agreement be made with Imperial Airways until the House has opportunity of investigating and reporting on the results to date.'

Undeterred, Imperial Airways initiated a series of sixteen-day £80 air cruises including hotel accommodation and first-class sleepers on the Paris–Brindisi train — then by Kent flying-boat to Athens and on to Castelrosso and Galilee, with visits by car for the next three days to Damascus, Jerusalem, and other places, finishing at Tiberias, from there on the eighth day to Cairo with four days to places of interest in Egypt; then on the twelfth day by train to Alexandria, next day flying to Crete and so to Athens, with the remaining three days journeying across Europe to London. At any point a week's stop-over could be made, continuing by next week's airliner. Flying low down, as one did those days, the aerial view of these ancient places was of dramatic interest.

Meanwhile passenger-carrying in both direc-

Passenger accommodation in the eastern type of HP 42 was less than that of the western, in order that a big load of mail and freight could be carried. By using these machines the capacity-ton-mile charges were cut by 50 per cent, resulting in a profit of more than £30 per working hour, and because of the safety of these airliners, insurance rates were substantially reduced.

tions on the London–Cape Town route began on 27 April with simultaneous departure from Croydon and Cape Town at a one-way fare of £130 including meals and hotel accommodation, though there was still that overnight train ride to Brindisi where the journey to Africa really began. On 8 May the first fare-paying passenger to fly from Cape Town to London arrived at Croydon aboard the dignified HP 42 *Heracles*, but though there were 25 passengers from various points on the route only one flew the entire way. Next day the sister airliner *Horatius*, flown by O.P. Jones, with thirteen passengers aboard, was climbing through cloud to reach clear skies above Tonbridge when lightning fused the trailing aerial, burnt out the wireless installation, and dislodged a window which damaged the adjacent propeller, resulting in considerable vibration, so Jones turned back and landed again at Croydon — but five of his passengers refused to continue after that experience, though the other eight left with him soon afterwards in the *Helena*.

By contrast with the majestic HP 42s, Imperial Airways' latest airliner, the four-engined Armstrong Whitworth *Atalanta* AW XV, first of Britain's big cantilever monoplane airliners, seemed the epitome of advanced aerodynamics when it emerged for engine runs in May. The roomy cabin, designed for comfort in tropical Africa, accommodated only nine, though a ton of mail could be carried behind the roomy flight deck. With this machine a new take-off technique was necessary, keeping the tail down instead of level, and at appropriate speed rotating nose-up to lift, whereas biplanes skimmed off the ground.

Though the first flight on 6 June did not make the news, the HP 42 again caught the headlines. Dick Fairey, as president of the RAeS, held a garden party at Hanworth on 19 June, with tickets at 5s including tea and a flight in *Heracles*. 'Emplanement developed into a small riot', went one report. 'The sight of prominent scientists jostling for joy-rides was highly diverting.' But *Heracles* came to grief. A conduit beneath the turf proved unequal to the airliner's weight with 32 passengers aboard. The port wheel broke through, damaging the undercarriage, wing and lowest propeller — and there she stuck for days. 'Immediately after the subsidence a screen of Scouts was thrown round the incapacitated giant and one of the most impressive scenes must have been the rumoured interview between a very diminutive Boy Scout and Mr Handley Page who advanced for closer view and found his progress barred!'

Despite inevitable minor teething problems, the A-W *Atalanta* made its first public appearance at the SBAC Display on 27 June, and flew to Martlesham Heath on 11 July for official airworthiness trials which were completed by the end of the month, and the certificate received in mid-August. By then the second machine, *Amalthea*, was ready. Both flew to Croydon at the beginning of September for acceptance tests and crew training. The wheel brakes were a novelty in British aircraft and were immediately appreciated because they offset the higher landing speed. On 26 September *Atalanta* made its inaugural flight to Brussels and Cologne, and on the same day the third aircraft, *Andromeda*, was handed over at

Croydon. A fortnight later *Atalanta* returned to Coventry for minor modification, but it piled up through fuel starvation when their Alan Campbell Orde, that early pilot of the 1919 Communications Flight, took off for a test and all four engines stopped.

Meanwhile on 18–19 August James Mollison with his Puss Moth *Heart's Content* made the first westward crossing of the Atlantic; but other than emphasizing the rash courage of the pilot did nothing to show the feasibility of such flights for commercial flying. Wisely, he returned by SS *Empress of Britain*. Nevertheless a New York newspaper was predicting that trans-Atlantic flying would become fashionable within three years and cost little more than the first-class steamer fare.

A more important expression of private enterprise was the official debut on 24 September of bulky Edward Hillman as an air transport operator. All the great ones in aviation were invited to lunch in Romford Town Hall, and to his aerodrome at Maylands came massed thousands to cheer the Lord Mayor of London and his lady who arrived by Spartan Cruiser with other distinguished officials, and more in a second machine, and an RAF squadron as escort. There were speeches from on high, followed by Hillman to toast his guests with phrases cribbed by his PRO from that amusing scoundrel Horatio Bottomley: 'Ladies and Gentlemen — I have not the advantages of education which you enjoy. Mine was the great university of life.' Whereupon he stopped. 'Oh Hell! I can't go on with that rubbish. I just wishes you all good 'ealth!' There were cheers and roars of laughter for this endearing, rough tycoon. But little did he guess that this was a stepping-stone towards Britain's ultimate great airline — nor did the directors of Imperial Airways, who on 25 October issued a much more forthcoming Annual Report than previously. Profit for the year ending 31 March was £10,186 15s 10d, representing a decrease of £16,953 6s 1d from the previous year because 'financial results were adversely affected by late delivery of certain of your new aircraft'. Owing to the illness of Sir Eric Geddes, the chair was taken by Sir George Beharrell, whose main activity, like Sir Eric's, was the Dunlop Rubber Company. Beharrell, the financial expert, was a man of great tact and charm and could put over the chairman's policies in incomparable manner.

Coinciding with the Report, Balfour's pre-diction was proved correct, for the Persian Government refused to renew the agreement for Imperial airliners to use Persian aerodromes. The route was therefore expensively changed from the northern side of the Persian Gulf to the southern by way of the British Protectorate of Bahrein, requiring extra fuel tanks to be fitted to the HP 42s. 'The first flight left Croydon on 5 October, and I hope the civilizing effect of civil aviation will eventually have its effect on the local sheikhs', said Col Shelmerdine. Perhaps British tact and diplomacy had not been at its best, for KLM had currently obtained permission from the Persians for their Amsterdam–Batavia service to use the northern route; the company was also negotiating with the Australian Government for route extension from Batavia to Sydney to compete against Imperial Airways.

On 27 December Sir Eric Geddes, accompanied by Woods Humphery, left Croydon by Imperial Airways to visit stations on the London–Cape Town route; they would break their journey to confer with the Italian authorities in Rome.

1933

Sir Eric Geddes was having problems. The Atalanta which took him as far as Cairo had developed snags, and the HP 42 *Helena* with which he continued to Cape Town arrived at its destination four hours late. Possibly unconvinced of the advantages of air travel, Sir Eric left Cape Town by steamship on 27 January. However, he had impressed the Cape Press with prognostications of a regular trans-Atlantic air service very few years hence, but 'co-operation of Canadian and American interests is necessary to ensure an adequate volume of American mail'. The current express mail co-operation between American airline companies, Imperial Airways, and the Cunard and White Star steamship companies was concurrently demonstrated by the safe arrival of a parcel addressed to Mahatma Gandhi which had travelled 12,000 miles in eighteen days, saving fifteen days over surface transport.

At best, aircraft were a compromise. Imperial Airways had been endeavouring to get Handley Page to construct two more HP 42s, but fitted with the more powerful Armstrong Tiger II engines in drag-reducing Townend rings — but because it was more costly to make two instead of a production run he quoted twice the original

By comparison with the three-engined Short Calcutta (*top left*), the four-engined Short Kent (*left*: drawn to the same scale) was a substantially larger development of similar aero-marine form. The cabin was luxuriously furnished and carried fifteen passengers. The freight and mail hold had a capacity of two tons.

Feet
Metres

price. There was argument. He remained adamant. Major Mayo, the airline's professional adviser, therefore recommended the cheaper expedient of substituting an under-slung fuselage to a set of Kent wings and engines. Oswald Short jumped at the idea, undercut the Handley Page price, and achieved an order for two 38-seat Scipio landplanes. Because delivery was required early next year all idea of a beautifully rounded monocoque fuselage was dismissed, and a flat-sided structure skinned with corrugated Alclad was used. To complete them in time would be a miracle — but Short was happy to have scored against the wily Handley Page.

'The possibilities of air transport all over the British Empire', wrote C.G. Grey, 'have been clearly indicated by the development of air transport in this country during the past year. Imperial Airways have been carrying record loads of passengers across the Channel in their big four-engined Handley Page biplanes, and could have carried more if they had more aeroplanes. This is just one sign of the new willingness of people to travel by air if given the opportunity.'

The veteran pilot C.F. Wolley Dod was now manager of the European Division of Imperial Airways and had re-scheduled the Continental services for the forthcoming season, but fares had been raised to various degree although the economic slump was now a thing of the past. With businessmen in mind, early morning and

late evening services to Paris were established giving nearly six hours in either the French or the English capital for a cut fare of £7 12s. Hillman, however, charged only £5 10s from Romford. That was worked out on the back of an envelope, but Imperial Airways had an elaborate costing system of mechanical computing and tabulating equipment to deal with accounts in 25 currencies from the nineteen countries in which the airline operated and the bookings from six others. The routes now totalled over 12,000 miles compared with 1,000 or so in 1924, and on 18 February the ten millionth mile was flown.

The relative safety of air travel was indicated by the latest quotation for insurance of passen-

Sylvanus, one of the three Short Kent-class flying-boats operated by Imperial Airways on Mediterranean routes, was commissioned in May 1931, but was burnt-out at Brindisi in November 1935.

The four-engined Armstrong Whitworth Atalanta was the first big monoplane in the Imperial Airways fleet and intended for the final sectors of the South African route.

inquiry but assured members that 'public confidence has rightly refused to be shaken by this accident and the company's early service to Paris this morning was filled to capacity and had a waiting list of passengers anxious to travel if space had been available'.

gers carried by Imperial Airways Ltd, for the rate was now slightly better than travel by boat and train. Previously 12s per £1,000 per day, it was now reduced to 1s; whereas a £2,000 policy for a passenger flying from London to India used to be £7 4s, the cost was now 14s compared with 16s for surface transport — described by *The Aeroplane* as: 'One of the most striking advances yet made in commercial air transport and should be reflected in the increased popularity of air travel'.

Although Imperial Airways was now accepted as 'about the best organized and best run air transport service for passengers in the world', the air mail service remained subject of criticism. 'The fact that our old passenger-carrying crates fly only a few hours a day because if they went further they would have to camp for the night in the desert or in the marshes or in the sud, cuts the speed of our air mails to something a good deal less than 30 mph', fumed a critic. 'One is forced to the conclusion that the directors do not want to see what can be done with high speed air mail transport.' But in fact Boulton & Paul had been given a contract for a powerful Mailplane with 1,000-mile range and 1,000 lb capacity — and it was now flying, though it was far from satisfactory as well as costly.

Abruptly the fatality-free operations of Imperial Airways for the last 2½ years was shattered. On 28 March their Argosy *City of Liverpool* (G-AACI), flown by Capt Leleu, caught fire in the air and dived vertically into the ground at Dixmude, Belgium; all twelve passengers and crew of three were killed. In the Commons there were anxious questions, and the Under-Secretary for Air promised an

On 11 April the Great Western Railway commenced the first air service to be operated by a British railway under the powers acquired in 1929. Gordon Olley was chief pilot, and a six-seat Westland Wessex (G-AAGW) in GWR livery of brown and cream was used for a route connecting Cardiff, Torquay, and Plymouth, beating the train journey by well over three hours because of the direct flight across the Bristol Channel. Within six weeks fares were cut by 30 per cent, implying that it was difficult to attract passengers. However the PMG now agreed that the service could carry mails handed in at any of the GWR air booking offices, where an air surcharge stamp of 3d would be affixed. Thus encouraged, the service was extended on 21 May from Cardiff to Birmingham.

In July Lord Londonderry appointed an independent committee 'To determine the requirements of the present Air Navigation Regulations'. Lord Gorell was chairman, and Capt Balfour one of the six members. Investigation was directed not only to Air Ministry control of air commerce but also opposition to the international control mooted at Geneva, for Britons still zealously guarded their personal freedom, though Germany, with by far the largest airline coverage in Europe, was heading for totalitarianism. But all the airlines put together barely matched the Americans. A visiting British designer to the USA reported: 'One of the lessons America can teach is that speed is important, and not so expensive after all because their aircraft can do 50 or 100 per cent more in a year than slower types. As a result, careful streamlining and retractable undercarriages are *de rigueur*.' Typical was United Airlines with 60 metal-skinned twin-engined Boeing 247 low-wingers which cruised at 171 mph with crew of two, ten passengers and a stewardess — the nearest British equivalent being the Atalantas — but the lessons were not lost on Imperial Airways. Already their technical department was considering a specification for an 'Empire-route airliner'. This was envisaged as a completely metal-skinned four-engined high-wing monoplane of greater size than anything the Americans were operating.

Relations between Woods Humphery and Brackley were now more in accord, and it was decided to fly the A-W XV *Astraea* (G-ABTL) on a good-will tour to Australia and back, largely to obtain the co-operation of Hudson Fysh, managing director of Qantas. On 29 May Brackley departed from Croydon accompanied by a crew of three and Capt Prendergast as second pilot. *Astraea* toured leisurely across India, down the Malay States, across the Netherlands East Indies to Darwin, and then along the north and east of Australia to Sydney, reached within ten days of England. At every stop local notabilities had been taken for a flight to publicize what a real airliner was like as a transport vehicle. However, there had been a very near go. Between Koepang and Darwin head winds so reduced speed that petrol would be exhausted 100 miles short of destination. Below was the solitary jungle island of Bathurst. Looking down, Brackley was astounded to see an unmapped landing ground. Having safely landed he found that a Franciscan, foreseeing that aircraft on the Timor route might fail to reach the mainland, had induced the aborigines to make the landing ground and had built a mission house and wireless station, so the mission lugger *St Francis* was dispatched on the 30-hour voyage to Darwin to fetch petrol.

On 7 July Hudson Fysh joined Brackley aboard *Astraea* and they began the return journey, reaching Darwin, 2,330 miles away, on 9 July, then the 4,650 miles in stages to Calcutta which was attained on 15 July after two days at Rangoon. The Atalanta running the shuttle air mail from Calcutta had damaged its tail when landing, so *Astraea* took over the mails and left for Karachi on 18 July. There Brackley transferred with the mails to the normal Imperial Airways service for London, leaving *Astraea* to carry on with the Karachi–Singapore service which at last had been established on 1 July as a joint operation with Indian–Transcontinental Airways of which Imperial Airways owned 51 per cent capital and was management contractor. On 24 July Brackley arrived back in London well satisfied that his Atalanta throughout the 23,540 miles had required only routine attention.

Quick turn-round was key to the success of Imperial Airways in keeping their aircraft hard at work. H.L. Hall, the disciplinarian chief engineer, was architect of the system. An HP 42 would arrive at Croydon, taxi to the disembarkation apron, and within fifteen minutes passengers, luggage, and mail were out and the machine was being towed to the hangar apron several hundred yards distant. Two-storey rostrums were wheeled up so that work could be done simultaneously on all four engines. Fuelling pipelines were uncoiled to each tank and petrol pumped electrically at 16 gal/min; meanwhile inspectors were examining undercarriage, tail, and every structural component, while others checked engines and wheel brake compressor system. Simultaneously the cabin was being tidied, the carpet brushed, kitchen stores brought in and mail stowed in the special compartment. Faults reported by pilot and engineer were rectified. In less than 30 minutes the machine was ready for the next flight and dragged backwards to the foot of the Control Tower. The aim was to keep the machines in continuous service for a year with the aid of intermediate inspections every 30 hours — by which time it would have flown 1,500 hours, and then be completely overhauled for the annual C of A.

Arrival and departure at Croydon was akin to sailing ships 100 years earlier, echoing Tennyson's 'argosies of magic sails'. On sunny days many visitors came to watch at Croydon and every other airport in the world. A Calcutta resident wrote: 'Four Air Orient and four KLM machines pass twice through Dum-Dum each month, and four times a week Imperial Airways machines come in and go back again — which means one big airliner every week-day. Many come to look at the big machines just as they still gather to welcome a liner arriving at port.' It was a busy day at Croydon if there was a mixed bag of twelve machines from the British, French, Belgium, German and Dutch airlines standing in the vicinity of the hangars.

The final link of the Empire route was now a prime concern of the Australian Government, which on 23 September, the day on which the Empire service was extended to Rangoon, invited tenders for the Singapore–Darwin section and connecting services in the Commonwealth. They had also issued to de Havilland's a specification for a relatively low priced, four-engined, fast ten-seater biplane which could operate in safety across the Java and Timor Seas yet at a break-even load factor of 70 per cent. Hudson Fysh would base his tender upon this new all-wood machine. The crunch was delivery in four months, during which time a

200 hp engine must be built and type-tested.

At the ninth AGM of Imperial Airways on 30 October, Sir Eric Geddes revealed the year's satisfactory profit of £52,894 1s 10d — a spectacular increase of £42,707 6s 0d, for traffic had gone up by over 75 per cent, and during the year the fleet had flown well over 2 million miles of which 1¾ million were on regular service. To emphasize the attention paid to comfort, the Report pictured a small covered gangway newly employed to protect passengers from the slipstream as they walked to the cabin door of an HP 42 airliner. Tactfully, Sir Eric forbore to mention that a few days earlier the new Boulton & Paul mail-carrier had stalled at

Below: Neatly uniformed stewards added impress to the carefully cultivated Imperial Airways image of perfect attendance to passengers.
Below right: The first covered gangway for passengers, designed to protect them from the slipstream of engines running during embarkation.

low height, begun to spin, recovered, and then hit the ground; it was completely wrecked and the pilot badly injured. Meanwhile the policy had changed, for 'there were signs that the postal administration was now realizing that air mail services were accepted as normal by the public who would soon demand that first-class correspondence should not be segregated for special treatment and for special fees'. If that happened it would be more economic to use the airliner holds than employ special machines.

Before the winter fogs began, the Air Ministry issued a 'Notice to Airmen' defining a new system of air traffic control at Croydon if visibility was less than 1,000 feet vertically or 1,000 yards horizontally. Only aircraft with wireless would be permitted to enter a zone of ten miles around the airport on receiving clearance from Control, and similarly for departure — but it meant flying along incoming and outgoing corridors in blind faith. Although weather all over England and the Channel remained extremely bad, the Imperial Airways Continental service maintained a remarkable record of regularity, though it often had to use Heston or Gravesend as alternatives. There were even days when the cross-Channel steamer had to cancel, yet only on one day was the airline service closed down. But in the end came Nemesis.

On the penultimate day of the year the Imperial Airways Avro Ten *Apollo* (G-ABLU), piloted by Capt Gittens, *en route* from Cologne to Croydon, ran into thick fog, and just after midday hit a stay of the 900-ft wireless mast

near Bruges, and entangled with half the mast, dived into the ground; all were killed. Two minutes later petrol from the burst tanks caught fire, badly burning nine Belgians who had rushed to rescue the occupants. There was an unexpected consequence. Relatives of a Polish passenger, Samuel Halperine, were quick to claim £40,000 damages, though by the Warsaw Pact liability was limited to £1,560 if the carrier proved proper precautions were taken to avoid the accident; but that was unlikely, for *Apollo* was twelve miles off-course and far too low, and the pilot had radioed to ask his position, but there had been no time to answer before the machine crashed.

1934

The New Year 1934 signified a new *rapprochement* between the British and French Governments, for it was mutually agreed that persons flying from London to Paris or *vice versa* between Friday and the following Tuesday could do so without passports.

On 15 January the new DH 86 four-engined biplane, which had been built with astonishing speed, was given its maiden flight by Hubert Broad. All was well. In the following week it went to Martlesham for airworthiness trials, and obtained its C of A on 30 January, satisfying the Australian contract with one day in hand. All now depended on acceptance of the Qantas tender.

Similarly the Dutchmen were edging their way further into England, for the Lord Mayor of Manchester held a conference for the benefit of KLM at which Dr Albert Plesman proposed that this densely populated area must have direct connection with the Continent, so he planned to open an Amsterdam–Hull–Manchester service. Imperial Airways showed no dismay, nor on 28 January when Jersey Airways Ltd inaugurated a London–Jersey air service with a DH Dragon, using Heston Airport for the London terminus and a strip of beach near St Helier as the island base.

But on 21 February the Railway Companies Association announced: 'The four main line railway companies and Imperial Airways Ltd have reached agreement for the formation of a new company with nominal capital of £50,000 to provide and operate air services in the British Isles and elsewhere and to form connecting links with the services of Imperial Airways'.

The Southern Railway was already a large shareholder in Imperial Airways and the latter's new offices were practically on their premises at Victoria. A month later Railway Air Services was registered, and each of the five main railways and Imperial Airways appointed one director; ex-Brig-Gen Sir Harold Hartley of LMS Scientific Research was elected chairman. To keep a grip on the new company Imperial Airways ensured that their assistant chief engineer, Wg Cdr Measures, was made Superintendent. There was no proposal to appoint Gordon Olley as chief pilot despite his relative success with GWR flying, so he formed his own Olley Air Services. To make competition more difficult all railway travel agents were instructed not to handle bookings for rival airlines.

Imperial Airways had already ordered a number of DH 86s and some were clearly intended for Railway Air Services because they were painted in red, green, and silver livery. Croydon would be the main base. Communication facilities there were improving. Not only was there a new D/F mast but Sir Philip Sassoon had recently opened a new microwave (later known as HF) installation matching another at St Inglevert for direct communications by telephone or teleprinter, so that departures and arrivals could be instantly signalled. Said an expert: 'The future development of these rays should be watched with interest. There seems to be a large field of use in aviation for rays which can be focused and reflected like light and can pierce fog, cloud, and darkness.'

Though appreciating that such an aid was required, Imperial Airways' first requirement was more aeroplanes. All through the bitter months of January and February, Short's had been assembling the hybrid *Scylla* airliner in the open air. Compared with the HP 42 it was boxy and inelegant, but at an all-up weight of 15 tons could carry 39 passengers, mainly five abreast, in three commodiously wide cabins. It was ready for flight on 26 March and Lankester Parker, accompanied by the designer, made an initial fifteen-minute trial, then landed for Brackley to try the dual controls. By the 31st the full-load schedule flights were completed and on 20 April the machine (G-ACJJ) was flown to Martlesham for official C of A trials. A week later Parker and Brackley flew it to Croydon so that Capt Youell and other pilots could begin familiarization flights.

By that time the annual Air Estimates had

been promulgated, and the net total of £513,000 for Civil Aviation represented the highest the vote had stood for the past ten years. Although subsidy payments for the Egypt–South Africa service were reduced by £50,000 there was provision for extension of the India service to Singapore, and the New Zealand Government offered an annual £5,000 towards the subsidy for the Australia service. There were increases too for such things as meteorological services, air route lighting, establishment of new wireless stations, and a night–flying beacon in Transjordan for the Cairo–Karachi airway. Sir Philip Sassoon also mentioned provision of £10,000 for a weekly service between New York and Bermuda to be operated by Imperial Airways in co-operation with American interests; this, he explained, was likely to be the first link in a trans-Atlantic service.

In April it became known that the Qantas tender had been accepted for the Australian extension, with a five-year contract at reducing subsidy. The DH 86s ordered by the Australian Government were being built with an elongated nose to seat captain and first officer side by side, and tankage was increased to 183 gallons. The prototype of this Diana-class now reappeared in full Imperial Airways colours named *Delphinus* (G-ACPL).

But things were not so good in South Africa. A takeover of Union Airways Ltd by the Minister of Railways and Harbours was clearly intended to make matters difficult for Imperial Airways on the Pietersburg–Cape Town section because it had failed to employ South African nationals except the four pilots Caspereuthus, Elliott-Wilson, Donald, and Gordon Store. As yet there was no *impasse*, and on 1 April Imperial Airways speeded the England–South Africa service by one day, and similarly accelerated the England–India–Malaya service on 14 April.

Whitsun marked the opening of the summer season and the start of several new air services. Imperial Airways put its reserve machines into operation. The Southern Railway announced that the Heston–Portsmouth–Isle of Wight service operated by Spartan Airlines in conjunction with Railway Air Services would include a stop at Bembridge, and clarified that 'this new Railway Air Service is one of co-operation with existing private enterprise rather than of antagonism'. Railway Air Services also began a daily passenger schedule between Plymouth, Haldon, Cardiff, Birmingham and Liverpool

using an eight-seat DH Dragon (G-ACPX) flown by Imperial Airways pilots. Additional flights were being run by Hillman Airways from its Essex airport for Paris, charging a cut-price £4 5s day return. The LMS Railway-backed Midland & Scottish Air Ferries linked with Hillman so that Paris to England passengers could transfer at Romford and be carried onward to Birmingham, Liverpool, the Isle of Man, and Belfast.

But always tragedy lurked. On 9 May, a day when Imperial Airways HP 42s were flying peacefully in sunshine above the fog came an SOS signal, M'AIDEZ, from the latest Wibault airliner operated by Air France, formerly Air Union. Lifeboats were alerted. A Fokker monoplane was sent to search. Oil was sighted and what looked like wreckage, but there was no sign of life. Three weeks later an Air France freighter hit the D/F mast at Croydon and plunged with it into an adjacent garden, killing pilot and mechanic. At the inquest the Air Ministry agreed that the question of shortening the 100-ft mast had been under consideration for some time.

Though the Press made sensational news of air accidents it was equally ready with stories of derring-do and even about airline pilots. One of the first to feature was Capt Oscar Philip Jones, known as 'O.P.' by his contemporaries but more cautiously by juniors whom he addressed as 'Mister'. He was headlined in May as the air pilot who had flown one million miles and carried 65,000 passengers without accident, but it was his air of command and raking jutting beard which intrigued newspapermen.

The Press also commented on the arrival at

Croydon on 18 June of a Lufthansa Heinkel mail-carrier. But a single-purpose machine was not Imperial Airways' policy, though one of the airline pilots remarked: 'What a jolly good bomber it would make'. In fact it was faster than any fighter. Alongside the 113-ft span, 30-ft high lumbering Short *Scylla* the Heinkel seemed futuristic with its torpedo-shaped fuselage and elliptically tapered cantilever wing — but *Scylla* was the profitable work horse, and that month, together with its sister *Syrinx* (G-ACJK), went into service on runs to Paris, Brussels, Basle and Zurich to supplement the Handley Page 42s. The pilots' opinions were not flattering, for it wallowed in gusty weather and ailerons and rudder were heavy to operate. On 3 August a wheel brake jammed when *Scylla* landed at Le Bourget and the massive machine tipped on its nose and was damaged. As a safety move the C.G. was moved further aft to put more weight on the tail.

These days, at busy times between 60 and 80 tons of goods were carried weekly by air in or out of London. Urgent machinery parts were dispatched to distant places, such as mining equipment to Johannesburg, which reduced transit from twenty days to nine. In particular, transport of bullion from Africa and India to London had increased, for though the cost of air transport was greater the insurance rate was lower than for consignments by train and ship,

and the gold achieved its market three weeks sooner.

The long-awaited report of the Gorell Committee was issued on 20 July, and proposed that administration could be transferred to a purely civil Department of State dealing with certification, airworthiness, supervision of competency, and mandatory third party insurance: formation of an Air Registration Board was therefore recommended.

The idea was welcome to Imperial Airways. Organization had become increasingly complex, stretching across thousands of miles beyond direct supervision of the main management; but up and down the Imperial routes things were going well, thanks to the keenness of overseas staff. At every station improvements were being made. At Singapore a big shed was extended to house two Atalantas; in Siam new runways would be ready before the rains began; at Kuala Lumpur a new runway was being constructed so that the aerodrome could be used at all seasons; at Penang pumping machinery was being installed in hope of making the landing ground suitable for use during

Although a compromise compared with the HP 42s, the Short L.17 *Scylla* proved effective, and the spacious 11-foot-wide cabin seating 38 was appreciated by passengers — but pilots disliked the way the machine yawed and wallowed in rough weather. This aircraft and *Syrinx* were operated by Imperial Airways on the London–Paris service up to the outbreak of World War II.

the rains, and at Margil, Basra, a new aerodrome was being built. The night stop at Luxor was proving popular, for passengers were able to make a quick visit to the Valley of the Kings and the Temples of Luxor and Karnak, for which Imperial Airways provided currency coupons. At Pietersburg in Transvaal a new rest house was almost finished so that 'instead of going by car to an hotel in the town, passengers would have meals at the aerodrome, which will be more restful and probably 'more healthy', and experiments were being made to find suitable grasses for Nairobi aerodrome and Kakamega landing ground. Flying-boats were also having attention. At Alexandria a D/F station had been installed, and moorings rearranged for easier approach to the refuelling base.

That summer Railway Air Services and the many other small independent airlines got into their stride, and Imperial Airways' routes operated busily but uneventfully. Unfortunately both London, Scottish & Provincial Airways' Courier and Hillman Airways suffered fatal accidents. The latter's initial DH 89 Dragon Rapide, after signalling MAYDAY, crashed into the English Channel and the pilot and six passengers were killed. That disaster could be blamed on Hillman himself, for the pilot had never been given a course in blind flying, nor did he hold a navigator's licence, and he was inexperienced in radio communication.

Multiple engines and metal construction were the world-wide themes for new airliners. Outstanding among the entrants for the much-publicized MacRobertson Race to Australia, which started at dawn on 20 October, were a twin-engined, smoothly skinned Boeing 247D airliner and its competitive equivalent, the Douglas DC-2 entered by KLM. At Mildenhall, the starting point, they had been the focus of attention of every British aircraft designer, particularly Gouge of Short's and little John Lloyd of Armstrong Whitworth, engaged as they were on respective designs for Imperial Airways of marine and landplane airliners bigger than anything the Americans had yet produced. The chief British entrant, specially designed for the purpose, was a small out-and-out racer, the twin-engined DH Comet. Exactly 70 hr 54 min 12 sec from take-off, the Comet arrived at Melbourne, made the two stipulated circuits, and landed,

winner of £10,000. Second arrival was the glittering DC-2 with complement of passengers; third was the Boeing. Said the Society of the British Aircraft Constructors (SBAC): 'Two practically standard large airliners of foreign design and construction have just put up a performance little inferior to that miracle of achievement, the Comet. There is no reason whatever technically why the proposed time schedules for the England–Australia service should not be halved. We are told that increased speed is merely a question of cost — but speed, a thing we have to sell, has been proved.'

At the tenth AGM of Imperial Airways on 5 November, Sir Eric Geddes, after announcing the year's financial results in which a gross surplus of £314,661 resulted in a net profit of £78,571, proceeded with a long and informative set speech dealing with every aspect of the company's operations and aspirations. At the end he added impromptu comment on the MacRobertson Race, saying: 'No one must think that a concern of our size can change its policy suddenly because of a very gallant flight which has beaten all records between here and Melbourne, flown under conditions which could not possibly apply to commercial aviation. . . All machines in the Race flew free from such hampering regulations as Customs and Passports which would be applied in the ordinary way to passengers and freight . . . The Douglas DC-2 carried twice the amount of fuel she would normally carry; that saves stops. It flew by night over a route mainly unlighted, and no commercial company would care to do that on a regular passenger service, nor does the Douglas provide comfort for long flying such as given by our Hercules . . . I need hardly say we wish to take advantage of all increase in air speed offered by scientific development, but within economic limits represented by government payments for mail and subsidies. It is only a limited field by which we can provide additional speed: first, if the shareholders decide the company can run at a loss; secondly, if the user will pay more; thirdly, if the government wants higher speeds they must pay for it. We believe our function is best fulfilled by offering the widest public the lowest economic fares — but we can operate any kind of service, and it is for the government and our customers to say and demonstrate which class and which scale of charges they wish to have.'

Soon afterwards the *Morning Post* announced that a 'composite' aeroplane comprising a

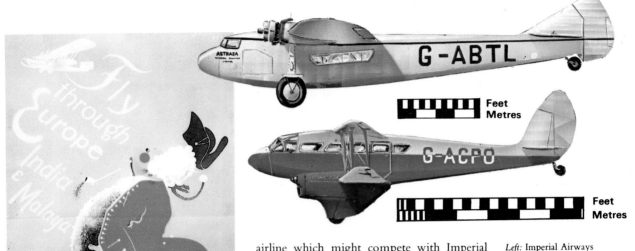

Left: Imperial Airways advertising poster.
Top: Armstrong Whitworth AW 15 *Atalanta* (Instone Air Line, 1932).
Above: Developed from the small twin-engined DH Dragon six-seater biplane, the taper-winged DH 89 Dragon Rapide was sold to several operators, including Hillman Airways, even before its first flight.

highly loaded seaplane mounted on and launched from a lightly loaded flying-boat had been ordered from Short's by the Air Ministry in conjunction with Imperial Airways to carry mails across the North Atlantic at very high speed.

Parliament was more concerned with accelerating the programme for 22 Home Defence squadrons. Nevertheless the daily run of parliamentary sniping on all manner of affairs including the Post Office led the PMG, plumply benign Sir Kingsley Wood, to propose flat rates for air mail anywhere in the Empire. It was also announced that Hillman Airways, in competitive bidding, had won a contract for a daily postal service between London, Liverpool, Belfast and Glasgow. Buoyed with success, and aided by financial advisers now that he was successful, Hillman decided to cash in by forming a new company to acquire his business of Edward Henry Hillman Ltd by recapitalizing it with £150,000 with 5s ordinary shares; the vendor company receiving a consideration of 120,000 fully paid shares. In addition to improving existing operations, air services were contemplated from Essex Airport to Ostend, Brussels, Dieppe, Cherbourg, and increased frequencies to Paris — so here was the genesis of an

airline which might compete with Imperial Airways at any rate in Europe. Sir Charles Harris of Cotton Plantations Ltd was elected chairman, with Hillman as managing director and his son as works manager.

To meet increasing passenger bookings for the two Empire routes, Imperial Airways decided on 20 November to double the services and deploy every available landplane and flying-boat; but in England traffic was often badly held up by heavy fog banks trapping an opaque layer of London's smoke to produce midnight at midday. Despite bad weather, the first scheduled air mail to Australia was duly sent off on 8 December aboard *Hengist*, piloted by Capt Walters. Lord Londonderry, Sir Philip Sassoon, Sir Eric Geddes, Sir Kingsley Wood and other high officials added dignity to the occasion, and letters from the King, Queen, and Prince of Wales were duly franked by Sir Kingsley Wood and handed to a typical London postman who placed them in his blue air mail bag which he then deposited aboard. The engines started, and away went *Hengist* carrying 100,000 letters and 500 lb of parcels — some two tons in all.

The Hillman Airways postal run to Glasgow had also made a difficult start, but at least it was under weigh — but this peak of personal triumph for bulky, ill-educated, tough Edward Henry Hillman ended with his death on 31 December, for his forceful spirit and relentless work inexorably led to high blood pressure resulting in a coronary. Such was his success and thrift that beginning as a farmer's boy living on a few shillings a week he ended with a huge fleet of buses and a vigorous airline, his success marked by acquisition of an outstandingly smart Rolls–Royce car and the plaudits of his contemporaries.

Re-orientation 1935-39

Stylishly gowned mannequins parading the passenger aisle of *Syrinx* flying high in the night sky above the spangled lights of London heralded New Year's Day 1935. Twenty Press photographers, selected to give maximum advertisement for one of the leading London stores, watched as they sipped champagne. Nothing like this had been done before, but though it hardly enhanced the dignity of Imperial Airways it enchanted the public. So did pictures of the recently-wed Duke of Kent and his beautiful Duchess boarding the Imperial *Heracles* on 5 January when they flew from Croydon to Paris on their way to Munich to stay with the Duchess's family before departure on a voyage to the West Indies. Ten days later a barrage of cameras greeted the arrival from Paris of *Horatius* with the Infanta Beatrice of Spain aboard, and her husband and brother. What better advertisement than Royalty?

In Scotland the freezing winter weather brought to light a new cause of accidents. On 8 January one of the Dragons operated by Highland Airways from Inverness was forced into the sea shallows a few minutes after take-off. The pilot reported that at 100 ft altitude his machine began to sink, although carrying only two passengers and several newspaper packages. There seemed no explanation until several weeks' investigation revealed that carburettor icing was the cause, necessitating modification for input of heat. An Air France Farman freighter flying in from Paris became the next example, for ice formed on the wings as well as throttling the carburettor, and the pilot, flying up the valley towards Dorking, found he could not surmount the hills, and landed in a nearby field from which take-off proved impossible and the machine had to be dismantled.

Even more puzzling had been the crash of a

KLM Douglas DC-2 just before Christmas, found wrecked and burnt out in the desert near Rutbah Wells, with no survivors. First assumption was lightning, but there was no previous authentic instance of an aeroplane being set on fire in that manner, so it was thought there might have been structural failure, for there was increasing concern that metal aircraft after considerable flying often showed dark black rings round the rivet heads, indicating they were not bedding, and there had also been cracked sheeting in the tails of some machines and hinge bearings pulling away from control surfaces. The possibility of fatigue failures, hitherto disregarded, began to be taken seriously — though the Dutch designer Fokker had warned of this problem several years earlier.

Just as continuous inspection of aircraft and engines was vital so were constant checks of routes and aerodromes. Thus on 27 January Brackley commenced the year's first survey, taking him to Bangkok and back in the course of the next two months. Two days later the Director of Postal Services, Brig-Gen Sir Frederick Williamson, and the PMG's Parliamentary Secretary boarded the next airliner of the Eastern route so that they could study at first hand the problems of a proposed network of Empire postal services carrying mail without surcharge. Coincidentally Imperial Airways received the two replacement but unwanted twin-engined Mailplane biplanes from Boulton & Paul re-arranged as thirteen-seat passenger-carriers and named *Boadicea* and *Britomart*.

That there were financial problems in running internal air services was evident when the chairman of the Southern Railway told shareholders that air transport receipts for 1934 were £272 but expenses came to £5,042. Nearly as poor were the LMS returns of six months' experimental operation of the air service between London, Liverpool, Belfast and Glasgow, for expenditure had been £10,147 and receipts only £2,904. When Sassoon introduced the Air Estimates in March he confirmed that internal services in Britain on the scale of the USA were impossible, for even America's huge expenditure of £2·8 million between 1927 and 1933 still left American air transport unsound economically. Of the Empire air services he

Economy through speed was the criterion of the beautifully streamlined DH 91 Albatross — but though a breakthrough in design, the advent of war prevented its extended use. First flight was on 20 May 1937. Seven were allocated to Imperial Airways, of which the three earliest were commissioned in the autumn of 1938. The cruising speed of 210 mph, carrying 22 passengers on stages of 1,000 miles, was considered phenomenal.

Right: Though originally produced to meet Air Ministry specifications for aircraft carrying 1,000 lb of mail for 1,000 miles at an average speed of 150 mph, *Boadicea* was used by Imperial Airways mostly for luxury charters and VIP flights.

Below: An advertisement from 1936.

Travel
comfortably
IMPERIAL
AIRWAYS
AND ASSOCIATED COMPANIES

Europe—Africa—India—China—Australia

was confident there had been striking progress, but some £2 million would be required by Imperial Airways fr a new fleet necessitating improved ground and night-flying facilities. He also announced that Italy had ratified a ten-year agreement permitting Imperial Airways to operate freely over its territory for the Empire air services, and that a similar agreement with France had been reached. That would reduce the time to India to just over two days, South Africa to four and seven to Australia. He added: 'No other country in the world has formulated plans for the carriage of its first-class mail by air without surcharge. It will carry letters between the UK and the Empire at about 1½d per ½ oz. We are negotiating with the Dominions about this.' To co-ordinate their own responsibilities in this connection Imperial Airways engaged 31-year-old Aubrey Burke, who had been on airship construction with Vickers and latterly was Works Manager of Airwork Ltd.

More and more Ministerial officials were using chartered aircraft. In March Sir John Simon flew in the DH 86 *Delia* to Berlin and Anthony Eden in *Delphinus* to Paris and Amsterdam. The sister ships *Delia* and *Dorado*, which had dual control, were being used to train probationary First Officers (FO) on sunny days at Croydon. Other probationers were often flying as assistant pilots by day, then studying at night for the essential second-class navigator's certificate, and whenever there was a spare moment, rigged the offices with

makeshift Morse keys and Heath Robinson buzzers wired to Woolworth batteries and vigorously proceeded to disturb the peace. Probably none of them had ever heard of Lieut-Col John Barrett-Lennard, that pioneer director of Handley Page Transport Ltd and initial Imperial Airways days, who died early in March.

On the 21st Brackley, back from his Eastern tour, was summoned to Woods Humphery 'to discuss discipline', and that afternoon attended a Board meeting at which Sir Hardman Lever was elected to replace Barrett-Lennard, and the Hon Esmond Harmsworth and Irvine Geddes, son of Sir Eric, were appointed to fill vacancies. Next day the shortage of aircraft was further aggravated by the loss of *Delia* in a crash at Brindisi.

In April a new company, United Airways, was inaugurated, jointly owned by Whitehall Securities Corporation Ltd (of which Capt Balfour was a director) and W.L. Thurgood of Jersey Airways, with Spartan Airlines Ltd acting as agents; the new company also had financial interest in Northern & Scottish Airways Ltd. With a blare of trumpets on 30 April United opened its London, Blackpool, Isle of Man and Carlisle service with a lavish lunch provided by Blackpool Corporation and attended by Sir Philip Sassoon, Col Shelmerdine, the Mayors of Blackpool and Heston, who were all flown there in the company Dragon Rapide escorted by four RAF aircraft, though directors and other guests including insurance interests arrived in two DH 86s borrowed from Jersey Airways. United Airways proposed charging 72s from London to Blackpool, whereas the cost by Railway Air Services was 105s. The price war was becoming established.

For the moment business matters, the future of airlines, disarmament, and the slow climb from the economic depression of the early 1930s was forgotten in the Empire-wide celebrations on 6 May marking the 25th anniversary of the accession of King George V and Queen Mary. The scene at Croydon Airport each night that week was spectacular. British and foreign aircraft were coming in and going

out along the bright beam of searchlights every few minutes, either on scheduled services or taking parties for tours over London to see the beacons, floodlighting, fireworks, and illuminations. Even Ramsay MacDonald and his family had a flight — but that weekend he resigned as Prime Minister and Stanley Baldwin took office. On 21 May Hitler announced Germany's repudiation of military clauses in the Versailles Treaty. Next day proposals for increasing British front-line aircraft to 1,500 by 1937 were laid before Parliament.

Early in July Woods Humphery's passion for 'discipline' as discussed with Brackley resulted in exclusion of pilots from the buffet in the main Reception Hall of the Air Terminal. Many a visitor used to go there just to see some of the World's most famous pilots hob-nobbing — but apparently that was bad for prestige. The pilots of course fumed at the ban because they now had to walk to the hotel if they wished for a hot drink or sandwich, and this was impossible if there were only a few minutes to spare. More ominously, that month every householder received from the Home Office a circular explaining action to be taken in the event of a bombing war. Bomb-proof shelters, gas attack, action by local authorities and much more were described.

There were other unpleasant reminders of aerial dangers, for on 14 July the two port engines of a KLM Fokker failed while taking off from Schiphol, Amsterdam. The machine struck a high dyke and piled up; fire broke out, and though thirteen escaped when the impact burst open the door, two passengers and five crew were killed. In their blatant way the English newspapers gave as much publicity as to a crash in England, and even *The Times* had 32 lines on a middle page, though only six for an accident in Belgium when a motor-bus with twenty aboard fell into a canal and eleven passengers were drowned. In the next eight days

Above left: This Hillman Airways DH 86 was commissioned in June 1935 and transferred to the newly registered British Airways at the end of the year.
Above: One of the commercial successes of the immediate pre-war years was the four-engined DH 86 low-power Express twelve-seater, originally built for the Qantas Empire route, but also flown by all British airlines, including Imperial Airways, whose *Dorado* is shown at Kai Tak, Hong Kong.

there were four more airline accidents of which three were fatal, but the effect on the air-mindedness of potential travellers was small, though Imperial Airways, KLM, Lufthansa, Sabena, and Air France all experienced a moderate reduction in passengers on the first two or three days of the week following the last accident, but no ill effect after. Each week now there were some 3,500 passengers in and out of Croydon, of which Imperial Airways carried about 250 a day on the Paris, Cologne, Budapest and Zurich services. Co-operation with shipping was becoming profitable, for the French were chartering machines from Imperial Airways to meet the *Ile de France* and *Normandie* in order to take urgent passengers to London.

On 30 July the Government announced: 'The Prime Minister has appointed a committee to consider measures which might be adopted to assist promotion of civil aviation in the UK and requirements of the Post Office for air mails and the relation between aviation and other forms of transport'. Seven members were appointed, with Brig-Gen Sir Henry Maybury in the chair and Col Shelmerdine representing the Air Ministry. Their deliberations would prove important.

Imperial Airways was organizing subsidiaries to take over operations in specific areas. Thus Imperial Airways (Far East) Ltd ran the branch line to Hong Kong from a conve-nient junction on the London–Brisbane route; Imperial Airways (Nigeria and Gold Coast) Ltd was formed for the main branch line from Khartoum across to West Africa; more recently Imperial Airways (Continental) Ltd was registered to take over all European services excluding the Imperial lines. What would happen on the North Atlantic had not been established. However, navigational techniques must first be improved. Even the tricky weather of early September, with dense cloud and quick moving local storms, lightning, and deluges of rain was providing problems at Croydon, for atmospherics gave radio operators little chance of hearing instructions when seeking the aerodrome. 'Taking them all round, the airline pilots of all nations gave a splendid demonstration of the possibilities of air transport in contrast with sea transport', wrote a critic, 'and although passengers by air have been bumped a bit, they did not suffer so badly as those who crossed by sea — if the boats went out at all.'

A significant moment in airline history came on 10 October when Hillman Airways Ltd held an extraordinary general meeting in London to discuss a merger with United Airways Ltd and Spartan Airlines Ltd. Sir Charles Harris, the chairman, said that efforts had been made to discredit the company in the absence of Mr Hillman's guiding hand. Working capital was

down to a dangerously low level, but they had now been offered the support of the other two airlines. Gerard d'Erlanger, who in the spring had bought a large block of the Hillman family shares, had obtained a guarantee for a further £15,000 towards unissued shares of the company. If the amalgamation was approved it would be possible to start the new year with control of funds amounting to £100,000 and might then secure approval of the Government. Agreement for the merger followed, and it was decided to name the new business 'British Airways', commencing operation from Heston Airport on 1 January of next year.

A sequence of accidents followed for Imperial Airways. First the HP 42 *Hanno* swung so violently on landing with a burst tyre at Kampala that it tipped on its nose with considerable damage. A few days later the Avro 652 *Ava*, the first type used by Imperial Airways with retractable undercarriage, set the pattern of forgetting to extend it and smashed the propellers. Then on 10 October, the Short *Syrinx* while being taxied by Wilcockson at Evere, Brussels, swung uncontrollably in a 65 mph gust and turned on its back, injuring one of the four passengers. Only a fortnight later the Boulton Paul *Britomart* undershot at the same airport and was badly damaged and two of the seven passengers slightly injured.

Despite earlier expensive mishaps, Imperial Airways announced that after allocating £192,960 for obsolescence, there was a net profit of £133,769, so the Board recommended a dividend of 6 per cent plus bonus of 1 per cent. At the AGM on 31 October Sir Eric Geddes explained that because the airline carried more passengers on the Continental routes than all foreign companies put together the present terminus at Victoria was inadequate and the Head Office overcrowded, so a new London Terminus and Head Office would be built 'able to deal with all developments that can be foreseen for a long time'. Dealing with developments on the Empire routes he announced that Imperial Airways had joined with Elder–Dempster Lines to form Elders Colonial Airways Ltd which would develop feeder services in Nigeria and other West African Colonies. 'When considering the results we have achieved', he said, 'it should be remembered that we were pioneers of the multi-engine principle for commercial services . . . The new aircraft we have ordered to replace the main line fleet on the Empire routes will have a load-carrying capacity of 3½–5 tons.' These were the 123 ft span Armstrong Whitworth 'Ensign' four-engined monoplane and the comparable 18 ton Short 'Empire' flying-boat.

But devices to increase safety were also essential. The first big step forward was the German-developed Lorenz blind-landing system being installed at Croydon. A main radio beacon transmitted on 9 metres at the end of the

The AW Ensign G-ADSR was the first of fourteen for Imperial Airways, but though ordered in 1935 the initial flight did not take place until 24 January 1938, and after commissioning that June for limited service, engine and other problems caused temporary withdrawal. Spanning 123 ft, of all-metal construction and powered with four 850 hp A-S Tiger engines, the Ensign seated 40 passengers for day flights or 20 by night in sleeper berths.

longest landing run, with a vertical fan signal beacon three kilometres from the aerodrome and another on the approach boundary. The aircraft received signals as impulses in a neon-tube instrument. The pilot heard a string of dots and and then turned starboard until the dots merged into dashes, at which point he kept to the approach course denoted by a steady note, maintaining level flight at 2,000 ft until the neon flickered on his dashboard as he passed the first beacon. For the next few seconds he watched a meter indicating rapidly mounting values of radio intensity, and when the neon went out, the same reading must be maintained to touch-down. As pilots soon found, the initial tendency was to overshoot, then put the nose down and over-correct, resulting in a switch-back bringing the machine uncomfortably near the ground, but though the system required great concentration, pilots managed quite successfully after a few hours' practice.

Of the training course for pilots, Capt S.T.B. Cripps, an ex-war pilot who had flown 6,000 hours commercially in Canada, recorded: 'After an interview with Air Vice-Marshal Webb-Bowen, the staff manager, I was told to report to the new Airways School a short distance from Croydon Airport. The fellows there were mostly ex-RAF. I recall meeting Don Bennett and Kelly Rogers who were soon allocated to the flying-boats at Alexandria. We were given supernumerary First Officer trips. On Friday August 21, I set sail on the HP 42 *Horatius* with Bert Perry as captain. I said "set sail" because after the slick American Vultee I had been flying, the HP 42 seemed so slow and cumbersome. All communications between ground and air were carried out by W/T on the "Q" code designed to overcome language difficulties. Whereas in the USA we flew down one of the legs of the radio ranges leading automatically to one's destination, in Europe the pilot had to navigate, flying in or above the overcast, and his radio officer obtained true bearings known as QTE from the ground stations. To make a let-down in bad visibility the operator would ask for a sequence of QDM's giving the magnetic course to steer to the airport. A most important term was QBI meaning clouds below 300 metres and/or visibility one kilometre or less. No aircraft could then enter the airport zone and would be given QGP and position number in the queue, landing only when QGP One was given. In all there were 30 three-letter codes. I had not been long in the school before I realized that all was not well with the pilots in general, and there seemed a lot of uneasiness about rates of pay which we were told was 10s an hour in Europe and 15s overseas, but there were higher rates for senior pilots. Matters reached a stage where several pilots resigned after absorbing sufficient knowledge at Imperial Airways' expense to sit for their 2nd-class navigator's exam and some were later taken over to form British Airways.'

There was contention too in Parliament over sanctions and rearmament, with the result that Baldwin 'went to the country' and overwhelmingly won, though MacDonald continued as Lord President. There was even contention among aeronautical pundits, for aerodynamic research showed that if aircraft ever attained 700 mph there would be a shock wave which some said would prevent going faster, and even the Director of Research considered it was useless to achieve stratospheric flying 'which when done is of no practical use'. Safety and luxury comfort remained the immediate target.

But there could be no guarantee of safety. On 2 November the Imperial Airways *Astraea* overshot when landing at Rangoon and the scrub damaged the starboard wing-tip and floor of the flight deck, slightly injuring the pilot, though the two passengers were unhurt and the damage was repairable locally. Next day *Atalanta* on leaving Kisumu aerodrome before dawn hit a tree in the darkness and was badly damaged on striking the ground, injuring the crew, though the passengers, including Lord Balfour of Burleigh, were unhurt.

That month, Sir Charles Kingsford Smith, hero of many a long-distance flight, in attempting to beat the England to Australia record with his American-built Lockheed Altair was reported missing after being seen crossing the Bay of Bengal, and was never heard of again.

During this time Woods Humphery was at Ottawa where British, Canadian, Newfoundland and Irish delegates agreed proposals for a North Atlantic air service. A meeting followed with USA interests on 4 December at which the prohibition of American air services to Bermuda was removed. As a result Woods Humphery and Juan Trippe, the Pan American Airways president, for whom he had great respect, were able to agree on co-operation between their airlines for Atlantic flying.

So to the year's end and more dismay. The Imperial Airways flying-boat *City of Khartoum* was an hour late on its evening haul to Alexan-

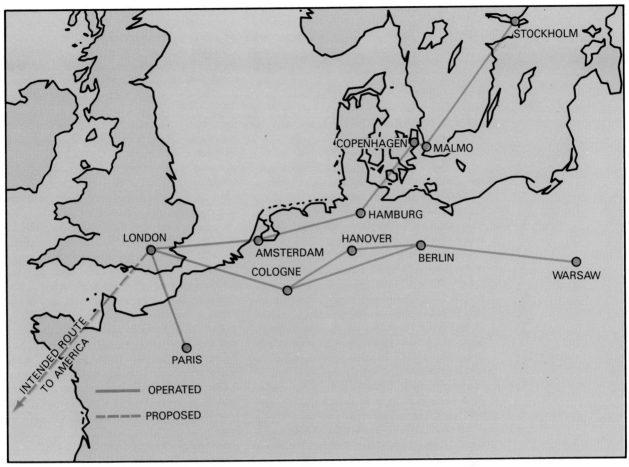

COPENHAGEN ○ ● MALMO

STOCKHOLM

○ HAMBURG

HANOVER
○

LONDON
●

AMSTERDAM
○
COLOGNE
○

BERLIN
○

WARSAW
○

PARIS
○

INTENDED ROUTE
TO AMERICA

——— OPERATED
– – – PROPOSED

The original British Airways routes, 1936–39.

dria from Crete where it had refuelled. While approaching the flare path set out in the harbour, all three engines stopped. None saw the machine crash in the dark, but when it failed to appear naval vessels began a search, and after five hours found the pilot swimming and then discovered wreckage containing the bodies of all nine passengers and three crew. At the accident investigation some weeks later there was wrangling as to whether the carburettor jets had been altered or the tanks inadequately filled, but the Consul-General decided it was impossible to deduce the cause of the stoppage.

1936

The portents of war overwhelmed the minor news value of the beginning of British Airways' operations on 1 January 1936. Armament was the world theme. Priority orders for Armstrong Whitley bombers were slowing design and construction of the Ensigns. However the Empire flying-boats were well advanced, and so were the components for the Short–Mayo seaplane mailplane and its flying-boat launcher.

But on the 20th the entire Empire was plunged in mourning, for the venerated King George V died at Sandringham. World respect was obvious even at Croydon where many air travellers wore an armlet or rosette of black, and all aircraft hoisted the little flags and pennants at half-mast. As Edward VIII, the popular, air-minded Prince of Wales succeeded to the throne.

An important step in February was the Air Ministry decision to give British Airways a subsidy of £20,000 for their service from Croydon to Sweden, and the Post Office granted a contract to carry air mails on the northbound journey. Because the airline in previous guise as Hillman Airways already had three contracts for air mails within England, there was immediate outcry from many of the small operators who would have liked to cash in on contract or subsidy. Certainly subsidies remained the life blood of Imperial Airways, and the Air Estimates in March included £204,000 additional provision 'for improving the ground facilities along existing air routes, to permit speeding up services and organizing modified routes to be followed by the flying-boats'. To that was added £75,000 'towards the cost of constructing the requisite flying-boat and landplane bases'. There was also £20,000 for 'experimental flights next summer with a view to the organization of a regular service across the North Atlantic'. The Imperial subsidies were £65,000 for the European services, £105,000 for England–India, and £18,300 for the projected air service between Bermuda and New York, one-fifth being provided by the Bermudian Government.

With Easter the air traffic at Croydon began to build up with every indication of a record season. These days more than 50 per cent of the aircraft complement were long-distance travellers. To ensure their road transport was worthy of the luxury standard of the big airliners, Imperial Airways purchased resplendent, smoothly running coaches painted silver and grey and beautifully upholstered — for an air journey begins and ends at city centres and to get to Croydon took 45 minutes. An earlier traveller, asked to give his impression of flying exclaimed: 'Air travel! Just a lot of noise sandwiched between two bus rides!' But these days even the relatively small DH 86 Express airliners were reasonably quiet and comfortable. On 20 April they began the Imperial Airways summer service on the London–Basle–Zurich route carrying the inevitable party of journalists in the cause of publicity. That month also saw departure of Major Brackley for yet another inspection of operations on the Australian run. 'There is so much organization required for a scheme of the magnitude of ours', he recorded, 'and as that is my responsibility I ought to be the first to do it and do it thoroughly.'

Racing back from Cape Town on 7 May came Amy Mollison at the end of another record flight. Thousands of fans were at Croydon to welcome her, but the airport these days was far too busy for such events. In future there should be some traffic relief from the new London airport of Gatwick, where a splendid rotunda Terminal Building replaced the original club house, and aprons and taxi strips had been built, though the extended airfield was still grass-surfaced. From 17 May British Airways, which had just increased its capital to £300,000,

switched their Continental services from Heston to Gatwick, which had the advantage of adjacent electric trains to Victoria.

British Airways had become a force to be reckoned with. The managing director was shrewd Major Ronald McCrindle. Added to their fleet were four DH 86 Express airliners which were the most completely equipped in the country, for they had an APB three-axis automatic pilot, a Lorenz blind-approach receiver and Marconi directional finder, and two-way radio equipment. Because of the Scandinavian service, they had chemical de-icing, ice-proofed airspeed pitot heads, and carburettors specially heated. The cabins were air conditioned and fire-proofed. Significantly, on 30 June British Airways, by agreement with the Secretary of State, absorbed its nearest rival, British Continental Airways, which was the personal venture of Sir Percy MacKinnon, the chairman of Lloyd's, and had been one of the happiest and most enthusiastic of airlines.

The end of June also saw completion in bare hull condition of the imposing Short Empire flying-boat *Canopus* (G-ADHL) and after engine tests it was launched on the Medway on 2 July. Next day John Parker found it handled so well on fast taxi-ing runs that he took off for fourteen minutes, and after adjustments continued with flights throughout the month, though once an engine failed at take-off but he circuited and alighted without difficulty.

On 27 July, British Airways initiated their night air mail to Hanover via Cologne using the first of their DH 86 Express airliners, but after several further successful flights it crashed on 12 August at Altenkirchen, southeast of Cologne, 30 miles off course due to incorrect radio bearings, and in the ensuing fire both crew members met their death. Only two days earlier the Vickers *Velox* operated by Imperial Airways for freight-carrying and tests of the Lorenz approach system, crashed at Croydon just after taking off, struck houses and burst into flames, and pilot and two crew lost their lives. But that was not all. On 22 August disaster came to Imperial Airways' flying-boat *Scipio* on alighting at Mirabella Bay in an abnormally rough sea. The wireless operator had inadvertently set the tailplane at maximum incidence, making the machine nose-heavy. Realizing something was wrong, Capt Wilcockson opened up the engines to make another attempt, but the high thrust line increased the nose-down pitch and the machine dived in. The Imperial Airways yacht *Imperia* rushed to the rescue, but two passengers had been killed and the other nine occupants injured. Because of the weather *Imperia* was unable to land anyone until morning.

In an attempt to make up lost time because of that accident, the HP 42 *Horsa* made a night flight to Bahrein, but overshot in the darkness and at dawn the pilot radioed he was landing and could not communicate further. RAF aeroplanes searched throughout next day and eventually found the airliner undamaged 100 miles south of Bahrein, so the eight passengers were rescued by an RAF Vickers Valencia transport. Though the cause of the miscarriage was not divulged, it was known that the D/F wireless set was subject to night error, and as the moon had set and primitive Bahrein was unlit, it was all too easy to fly past in the dark. With such a succession of accidents, how could people be induced to believe it was safe to fly in airlines? Yet fatal accidents with cars and buses and even shipping far exceeded those of aeroplanes.

An extraordinary affair was now revealed in *The Times* of 6 August in which George Woods Humphery, Sir Eric Geddes, and the Permanent Secretary to the Air Ministry Sir Christopher Bullock were involved, and the latter dismissed from office. Bullock had reached the pinnacle of achievement in the Civil Service and thought that in the near future he might be still more useful as head of Imperial Airways. Openly he lunched with Sir Eric and discussed becoming a government director, but 'this topic was distasteful to Sir Eric because he considered Sir Christopher's aspirations to be hopeless and he did not intend to support them'. That attitude arose because at the beginning of negotiations the previous year on carriage of first-class Empire mail, Bullock had suggested to Lord Londonderry that Sir Eric's services should be recognized by conferring an honour — but nothing had eventuated. Woods Humphery had become involved in June when Sir Christopher referred to Sir Eric's recent indisposition and said that a good working combination would be himself as chairman and Woods Humphery as deputy chairman and managing director. Looming behind the affair was Lord Swinton, who did not like Bullock. A Government committee of inquiry reported: 'In 1928 principles were formulated regulating conduct of civil servants in relations with the public. We cannot escape the conclusions that Sir Christopher Bullock's conduct was comp-

letely at variance with the spirit of this code, which clearly precludes a civil servant interlacing public negotiations with the advancement of personal interest.' Sir Christopher said: 'I do not seek to burke responsibility — but it is easy to be wise after the event, and fortunate is he who can honestly say that if every private and informal conversation he had held was sifted and re-sifted in the rarified atmosphere of a solemn and formal inquisition, no passing phrase uttered in an unguarded moment could be held injudicious, no word or deed be called in question in some degree by absolute standards of taste or propriety'. But that was the end of Sir Christopher Bullock as a public figure, so Col Donald Banks, the current Director-General of the Post Office, was appointed in his place.

Meanwhile *Canopus* had completed full-load trials on 9 September and was moved into the works for fitting out and furnishing. *Caledonia* had already been launched, and two days later Parker flew it for an initial twenty minutes. After only two more flights he took it to Felixstowe for C of A trials on the 15th, though a modern airliner would have had hundreds of hours' development flying before reaching that stage. By then *Canopus* had been re-launched, and was flown jointly by Parker and Brackley on the 18th and 19th. On 25 September Medway Town Council officially celebrated the success of *Canopus* — but that day there came another disaster for Imperial Airways when the twin-engined Boulton & Paul *Boadicea* disappeared over the Channel; although aircraft and shipping searched extensively nothing was found until the body of the pilot was washed ashore a month later.

On 29 September there was a slight flicker of public interest when an air race to Johannesburg started from Portsmouth for a prize of £10,000, but one by one the competitors force–landed or crashed, and only the Vega Gull owned and navigated by 25-year-old Sir Giles Conup Guthrie, piloted by Charles Scott, completed the course and collected the major prize. The fiasco seemed to underline the Imperial Airways policy that it was better to fly slowly and arrive, though the airline was widely advertising: 'IMPERIAL AIRWAYS THE KEY TO THE WORLD: To Africa in days instead of weeks; India in five days; China in ten days; Australia in ten and a half days; the principle capitals of Western Europe in a few hours.'

In that cause the now certificated *Canopus* was being demonstrated to Lord Swinton, Sir

Eric Geddes and his friend Sir John Reith, and many officials. Landing flaps and two-speed propellers contributed to its outstanding success, and top speed of 199½ mph made it the fastest flying-boat in the world. On 7 October Brackley began checking out pilots, making a brief pause on 12 October when the Duke of Kent presented him with the Cumberbatch Trophy for Reliability at a GAPAN ceremony. As the programme explained: 'The claims of over 50 pilots were narrowed to the "skippers" of our oldest airline, Imperial Airways. Of that great company the award is given to Sqn Ldr Brackley both for his own record and on behalf of the other eight who joined in 1924 whose names will also be engraved upon the Trophy.'

Brackley now commenced route-proving with *Canopus*, flying to Rome on 22 October, where it was taken over by Capt Bailey who continued to Alexandria, and from there to Brindisi on the 30th. To pilots, passengers, ground crew, and onlookers, this great machine, with its wide and luxurious cabin, seemed the epitome of all that an airliner should be. Meanwhile 27-year-old Jean Batten almost halved the time scheduled by Imperial Airways for the England to Australia run, by flying a Percival Gull to Darwin in 5 days 21 hours.

Imperial Airways' profits had mounted to

£140,705 for 1935–36. Therefore in addition to the 6 per cent dividend the bonus was doubled as a sign of increasing prosperity, leading Sir Eric Geddes to say: 'For some time the directors have been quite inadequately remunerated, so I feel sure you will desire to pass a resolution increasing the fees from £6,500 to £12,000 a year' — yet he also warned that: 'For the purpose of carrying out our various developments, and particularly the Empire mail scheme and the Atlantic services, we shall before our next annual general meeting have to issue fresh capital'.

British Airways was also planning ahead, and on 11 November ordered a small fleet of the latest American metal-skinned twin-engined Lockheed Electras. A week later one of their Fokkers on the night mail run from Scandinavia crashed near Gatwick after attempting to approach in bad weather under low cloud and flew into trees, wrecking the machine and killing the two pilots and injuring two crewmen. Decision had already been made to establish an operational manager, and to that end 38-year-old Alan Campbell Orde, the ex-AT & T pilot who had joined Armstrong Whitworth's in 1924 and became chief test pilot, was appointed on 1 December, for he was shrewd and efficient, and a good judge of aeroplanes, engines,

Advertising poster, 1937–39, showing roomy internal arrangement of the Empire flying-boats.

and pilots. In effect he was the equivalent of Brackley, though the two were very different in character and temperament.

Brackley had allocated *Caledonia* for training flights on the North Atlantic techniques of long-distance radio and navigation; but Newfoundland was ice-bound, so *Caledonia* was used for Christmas mail, and piloted by Capt Cumming departed on 13 December with 5½ tons of letters for India, and was back on 22 December. But these inaugural flights passed unnoticed by the Press, for the whole nation had been moved by the dramatic announcement on 10 December that King Edward VIII had renounced the throne in favour of his brother, who now became King George VI, Marshal-in-Chief of the RAF.

1937

At Short's the tempo of production was resulting in a steady flow of Empire boats. Regular service flights from Marseilles to Alexandria via Rome, Brindisi and Athens began on 4 January 1937 with *Castor* (G-ADUN) flown by Capts Powell and Store, and in the following week *Centaurus*, piloted by Capt Egglesfield, initiated the reciprocal service from Alexandria to Southampton, making an overnight stop at Brindisi. Enthusiastically Imperial Airways advertised the Empire boats with the description: 'COMFORT! Two decks: smoking room: promenade saloon: 3,000 horse power: 200 miles an hour: 28 being built.'

Encouraged, Imperial Airways in their next advertisement stated: 'We have under construction a fleet of 40 high speed airliners with a total horse power of 125,860, with accommodation for over 1,000 passengers and space for over nine million ½ oz letters.'

Creaking implementation of the Gorell Report published in 1934 had led to the Air Navigation Bill passing into law in June 1936—and now at last the resultant Air Registration Board was established comprising four expert groups on construction and maintenance; insurance; knowledgeable viewpoints such as piloting; and commercial operators represented by George Woods Humphery on behalf of Imperial Airways, L.T.H. Greig of Jersey Airways, and E.L. Gander Dower of Aberdeen Airways. Revenue would be obtained from the SBAC, Imperial Airways, unsubsidized operators, and from C of A services, licences, surveys. For once, professionals had overcome

bureaucracy and become bureaucrats.

Currently the 1935 Maybury Committee Report was issued in the form of historical background, situation survey, and eleven major recommendations focusing on a proposed central airway junction between Liverpool and Manchester from which internal services would radiate. 'A prerequisite is that cut-throat competition must be eliminated, so operations should be entrusted to a single company or closely co-ordinated group and a Licensing Authority should be appointed to make selection.' That gave C.G. Grey opportunity for a homily in which he described the Report as: 'A gigantic blinding flash of the obvious analogous to the statement that if you don't stand up you'll fall down'. However he conceded: 'The idea of Maybury junction is a perfectly gorgeous idea'. In fact it was most rational, but would it ever be implemented?

The *Daily Express* attempted to cash in by sending a DH Dragonfly over the Junction routes with the paper's aviation editor, so that he could comment 'in a manner which would best satisfy the editorial attitude towards the Maybury suggestion'. They had visited Speke, Ards, and Renfrew, leaving on 2 February. A radio message came a few minutes later; then nothing more. After searching by land, sea, and air for two days the burnt-out wreckage of the machine and the bodies of those aboard were found near the crest of Darnaw, a 1,500-ft hill in Kirkcudbrightshire. Here was grim evidence that the Report's criticism of the unsuitability

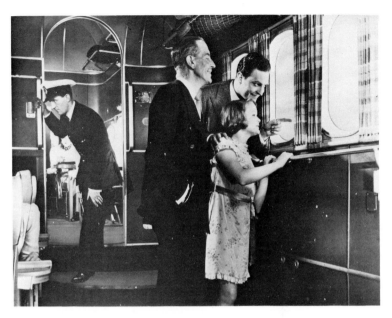

Ensigns provided passengers with a promenade deck to view the scene below on the long stages of the flight to Africa, India and Australia.

of present equipment for bad-weather flying was all too true.

On the following day the regular Empire air service effectively began when the flying-boat *Castor*, piloted by Capts Alger and Stone, arrived from Alexandria with fifteen passengers, two of whom had come from Sydney. Their first question on reaching shore was 'who has won the Test match?'

The last landplane Empire service arrived at Croydon on 4 March from Africa. All future flights would start from Hythe. Each Sunday the inward Australian service would arrive; Tuesday the outward African service would depart; on Wednesday the outward Australian and inward African and inward Australian services made a busy day; on Friday the outward African service departed; and Saturday had the outward Australian and inward African services. Many of the ground staff were happy to work a seven-day week, such was the peaceful fascination of flying-boats.

However the Air Estimates for the current year, despite a civil aviation vote of £2½ million, were almost wholly concerned with preparation for war; but Sassoon announced that from the beginning of 1938 all first-class mail from the UK to Empire countries would be carried by air at a flat rate of 1½d per ½ oz using 'flying-boat services to South Africa, India, and Australia, with certain additional landplane services to India — all flown by new Empire aircraft of Imperial Airways'. Unconsciously defying fate he assured the Commons that routes would be thoroughly organized with wireless and other equipment so that regular and punctual operations would be possible by day and night in all weathers and with due precautions against collision. Next day, 16 March, Wolley Dod, the up-and-coming European manager and ex-pilot of Imperial Airways, was killed in an experimental night flight from Croydon to Cologne when the DH 86 *Jupiter* crashed and was burnt out shortly after midnight amid driving sleet and snow. The cause of the accident was not fully established, but it was assumed that ice forced the machine down on trees. Then, on the day of his funeral fate struck again, for *Capricornus* (G-ADVA) set out with the first through air mail to Australia but crashed into a 2,000-ft mountain in the French Alps shortly after radioing Lyons Airport that it was lost in snowstorms. The crew were killed, and the

Below: Cambria and *Caledonia* were the two long-range Short Empire flying-boats used for the trail-blazing trans-Atlantic experimental flights in the summer of 1937.
Bottom: Local inhabitants watching the Empire flying-boat *Challenger* taxi-ing on the Sea of Galilee.

only passenger, a young woman, died in Mâcon hospital that evening; the sole survivor was the radio operator who despite injuries struggled through snow for two miles to a farmhouse to summon help.

As always, success and failure were close attendants. Several Empire flying-boats, with the aid of 'George' the automatic pilot, made non-stop runs from Alexandria, and *Caledonia* achieved the 2,300 miles in a record 13½ hours. The Short production flying-boats were emerging with timetable regularity, but the Armstrong Ensign prototype remained far behind schedule, the company alleging that this was due to innumerable changes demanded by Imperial Airways at every stage of design and construction. For more concentrated attention it was now transferred to the ATS hangar at Hamble. Meanwhile the HP 42s were flying valiantly and profitably — but in May *Hengist* was destroyed by fire in the great airship hangar at Karachi. On the Paris run, *Scylla* and *Syrinx* were manfully carrying their daily load of passengers. Of the ubiquitous DH 86 Express, Capt Cripps said: 'Being a biplane with struts and flying wires it was a sitting duck to pick up ice. They did not even have a heated pitot head, and the gyro instruments were operated by a venturi system which could freeze up. The official answer to lack of de-icing equipment was "political paste" — a heavy yellow grease daubed all over the leading edges, struts and flying wires. Luckily passengers seemed unaware they were flying at risk.'

The up-dated successor of the DH 86, the newly finished elegant four-engined DH 91 Albatross monoplane, had its first flight on 20 May, having been designed and built in the remarkable time of sixteen months. Watched by the entire company personnel, young Bob Waight, who had succeeded Hubert Broad as chief pilot, made several exploratory runs then climbed steadily away, reporting at the end of the flight that all was promising.

This was the month of the King's Coronation. A fortnight after that stately event Baldwin resigned in favour of Neville Chamberlain. Changes followed. Sir Philip Sasoon was replaced as Under-Secretary for Air by Lieu-Col A.J. Muirhead, and as part of the process of up-grading Sir Francis Shelmerdine's title was changed from Director to Director-General of Civil Aviation (DGCA). The Government's impartiality towards technical matters was indicated by the appointment of Sir Francis

L'Estrange Joseph, a man of business experience but no knowledge of aircraft, as Government director on the Board of Imperial Airways in succession to Sir Walter Nicholson.

On 22 June, eleven days after the Spitfire designer Reggie Mitchell succumbed to cancer, the great Sir Eric Geddes died after a short illness. As C.G. Grey said: 'He was a driver of men. Those who worked closely with him developed an intense admiration for his ability, his foresight, but they feared rather than loved him. However, in spite of multiplicity of employments, official and commercial, the establishment of Imperial air communications by sea-going flying-boats may remain for future generations a lasting monument of Eric Geddes.' He was succeeded by that charming financial expert, his close supporter Sir George Beharrell, even though Woods Humphery was assessed as having 'more influence on the Continent of Europe to-day than any man in air transport, and probably more than any but a few of our political people'.

For months Humphery and Juan Trippe had been planning simultaneous American and British trans-Atlantic flights. *The Aeroplane* presently briefly commented: 'The first of the two Short Empire boats especially for experimental crossings of the North Atlantic, the *Caledonia*, commanded by Capt Wilcockson, left the new base on the River Shannon at Foynes at 1955 hours on July 6 for Botwood, Newfoundland. *Caledonia* differs from other boats only in the amount of fuel carried and in having no furnishing in the passengers' apartment, and in carrying special radio equipment.' Though a dozen people by now had crossed the Atlantic in small aircraft, this was nevertheless a great occasion — matched by the equivalent Pan American departure of their Clipper III Sikorsky flying-boat which left Botwood eastward bound. 'Early in the morning of July 6 two aerial merchantmen spoke to each other in mid-Atlantic, thereby making a significant piece of history, the more so as one was British, the other American, and both running to a mutually agreed schedule', reported the *Daily Mail*. Both reached their destinations uneventfully and were greeted ecstatically. Endorsement of the Pan American–Imperial Airways flights soon followed. The return journeys of the two airliners were made simultaneously on 15–16 July by the same crews. Five more double flights were planned to take place before the end of the year, of which *Cambria*'s on 29 July would be the next.

Significant though these flights were, much more interest was taken of a 50,000-mile encirclement of the world by Mrs Walker-Sinclair using regular airline services and crossing the equator four times. At a dinner in her honour at the Forum Club she gave the details of her expensive air tour which started from Croydon with a flight to Brussels and Cologne in a Sabena machine, then from Frankfurt across the Atlantic to Lakehurst USA in the *Hindenburg* airship; thence to South America in a Pan American DC-2; across the Pacific in a Martin Clipper to China where she spent a month touring by air; finally Australia — returning by Imperial Airways across India and Arabia, and so to Crydon having been away five months. 'For a traveller like myself, whose time is of no value, and who is interested in the constantly changing sky and the countries and seas flown over, may I plead with aircraft designers to let us see out and watch the view. I think we should marvel, while it is still marvellous, that it is possible to fly round the world as ordinary fare-paying passengers not only in safety but mostly in considerable comfort.' Of all the airliners, the Atalanta was her favourite because it was the easiest to board and alight, and the high wing gave shade and did not obstruct the view. Woods Humphery was the advocate of cabins below the wings, as first exemplified by *Hannibal*, and now with the massive, shoulder-wing AW 27 Ensign.

Though Mrs Walker-Sinclair's flight was splendid advertisement for the regular air services, the risks of long oceanic flights were emphasized by the disappearance of the famous Amelia Earhart (Mrs Putman) who set forth on a much publicized round–the–world flight in her twin-engined Lockheed Electra accompanied by a navigator; but of their fate nothing was ever heard.

A new milestone was reached on 23 July when G-AAXC *Heracles*, oldest of the seven HP 42s, achieved her millionth mile. A splendid party was given aboard as she droned onward in brilliant sunshine above the overcast. 'At 1415 hours in the middle of a well served lunch, Capt Dismore emerged from for'd through a forbidden door, glass in hands, and announced that the millionth mile had just been passed. We drank his health and the health of the ship, while a steward perambulated with a

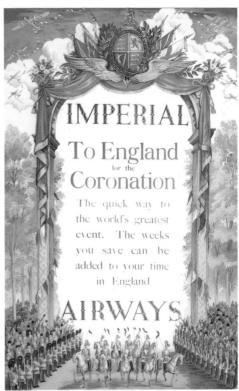

Birthday cake. The pilots of Imperial Airways, despite the jibes of foreigners when the seven HP sisters put on their poke bonnets and crinolines to take the air at Croydon, will start a riot if the girls are forcibly removed when their day is done. They have carried some 300,000 passengers in safety, and bred confidence in air travel. Passengers seem to prefer spacious comfort to vicarious speed, so they can hold their own for years to come.'

A few days later the Short-Mayo lower flying-boat component *Maia* was launched, Parker flying it for 20 minutes. Then it was taken ashore to have the pylon structure attached. On 12 August it was demonstrated to the Press. *Mercury* the pick-a-back four-engined seaplane emerged from the Short factory at the end of August and on 5 September was launched for a first flight by Parker.

At Croydon winter timetables were coming into force, for the weather was generally unpleasant and there was plenty of rain — yet it was the glittering sun of the Mediterranean and a glassy sea which brought the next catastrophe to Imperial Airways, for Capt Poole, flying the Empire flying-boat *Courtier*, misjudged his height on final approach to alight in Phaleron

The Captain talking to passengers on board an AW 27 Ensign-class aircraft of Imperial Airways.

Bay off Athens, impacting hard on a surface which blended with the sky, and the hull burst open, drowning three passengers and slightly injuring four, but four others and the crew of four were unhurt. An Air Ministry regulation followed, making lap straps for passenger seats compulsory in British aeroplanes. On that same day young Waight, who had tested the Albatross fitted with a new tail, was killed when flying a small racing aeroplane built by students of the de Havilland Technical School.

There were pilot problems at Imperial Airways, for several had been summarily dismissed. Their newly formed British Airline Pilots Association (BALPA), more a trade union than the GAPAN, met on 9 October to consider what action might be taken. The help of Robert Perkins, MP, a critic of Government aircraft policy, was invoked. On 28 October he told the House: 'I want to draw attention to the grave dissatisfaction among pilots employed by Imperial Airways. Their Association has been refused the right to collective bargaining. There have been curious dismissals. Capt Wilson, pilot of the *City of Khartoum* which crashed two years ago in the Mediterranean, was dismissed and no reason given. I feel it was because he opened his mouth too wide when the inquiry took place. Similarly when the Association

wrote to Imperial Airways suggesting the Budapest service be suspended for the winter, as it was not properly equipped, the two who signed the letter, Capt Rogers and Capt Lane-Burslem, were dismissed. That is victimization. Imperial Airways have done everything to break the Association and refuse to recognize it or discuss with the pilots at all. Another grievance is the question of wages: while directors' fees have been increased, they have cut pilots' wages. Then again, the majority of the pilots regard the equipment provided by Imperial Airways as not good enough. Machines with one or two exceptions are not equipped to effect blind landings; few are equipped with de-icing, and very few, if any, with a spare wireless set. Finally, machines on the London–Paris route are obsolete and certain others on European routes are definitely unsuitable for winter service. We have no alternative but to ask for an impartial inquiry into the whole position of pilots engaged by Imperial Airways, and in fact into the whole organization.'

On the day following the death on 9 November of Sir Samuel Instone — founder of the pioneer airline which in 1924 had been involved in the similar fracas — matters were worsened by the AGM of Imperial Airways. Although it was financially satisfactory to know that the net profit had increased by £24,000 to £164,735 it was a bad moment to reveal that in addition to £12,000 previously allocated for directors' fees they were granting themselves another £5,000, and £42,126 was used to pay a 7 per cent dividend plus 2 per cent bonus at a time when Government Bonds yielded only 2¾ per cent. The pilots were therefore further ruffled, nor were matters helped by Sir George Beharrell's attempt to justify the dismissals.

Robert Perkins had forewarned the Commons that he intended to raise all the issues in a motion on civil aviation. On 17 November he held the House in a sweeping polemic dealing with airports, safety in the air, stranglehold of railways on internal air transport, lack of blind-approach equipment, and castigation of Imperial Airways, speculating 'whether nationalization of British air services is not preferable to their control by two financial houses — d'Erlanger's and Whitehall Securities. Imperial Airways are not sacrosanct. They are heavily subsidized and to all intents are a public service utility company. Criticism of guardians of the public purse is essential, for there are grounds for inquiry into the affairs of the company.'

Seconding the motion, that historic pioneer Moore-Brabazon said he had seldom heard a more terrific and sustained onslaught. He thought Mr Perkins had great courage because criticism of Imperial Airways had been hitherto regarded rather as something against the Government. He would not like the House to think that Imperial Airways was a nefarious organization; further they had to operate Engl-

ish machines, which was a grave difficulty considering the rearmament position. He hoped that the House would accord the inquiry because civil aviation should be taken right away from any idea of party politics. In due course Lieut-Col Muirhead announced that the Secretary of State authorized him to say that in view of the specific allegations a departmental inquiry into charges of inefficiency would be set up, but there would be no inquiry into matters already dealt with by the Maybury Committee. The Secretary of State would also discuss with the Imperial Airways' Government directors the system employed for dealing with staff, including methods by which pilots and others had their grievances considered, but the Government would not go into specific grievances nor dictate to the company on the recognition of any particular union.

There followed the resignation 'on personal grounds' of AV-M Sir Tom Webb-Bowen who for some four years had been staff manager of Imperial Airways. He was succeeded by R.E. Richardson, but Major Brackley, as air superintendent, remained responsible for the pilots though he found it difficult to do so when one

Mr and Mrs Whitney Straight are received at a Royal Aeronautical Society garden party by Lord Brabazon.

of them on hearing that Perkins had described Croydon as a 'second-rate Balkan State' exchanged his uniform for a bulging skirt and green hat!

On 24 November the Under-Secretary announced the formation of the promised committee, but it only consisted of two Permanent Secretaries, chaired by Lord Cadman of the Anglo–Iranian Oil Company, with W.W. Burkett of th Air Ministry as secretary. There was immediate opposition from Clement Attlee which led to replacement of the officials by the economist Sir Frederick Marquis (later Lord Woolton); T. Harrison Hughes of the Suez Canal Company; John W. Bowen of the Post Office trade union. Wider terms of reference were permitted including the Maybury Report. Interviews with many witnesses began *in camera*. Imperial Airways presented a statement of 32 printed pages and 32 pages of appendices. Theirs was a spirited and factual defence, but the Board, and Woods Humphery in particular, were convinced that the Cadman Committee was not basically concerned with BALPA at all, but designed to force a merger with British Airways which by this time had

involved the stockholders in losses of some £20,000.

Appropriately the Cadman Committee was launched in a period of continuing fogs at Croydon and many services had to be cancelled. Several aircraft from the Continent were unable to land and flew back. Then on the foggy night of 26 November a Lufthansa Junkers Ju 52 in attempting to land hit a hangar head on, caught fire, and the three occupants died. That was followed by more tragedy. Taking off from Brindisi outer harbour in a choppy sea, Capt Mollard, an experienced landplane pilot, inadvertently set the flaps of the Empire flying-boat *Cygnus* fully down, causing the machine to bounce off, drop with a splash, rebound, and after rising 20 or 30 feet, nose down for the second time, staving in the bow. One passenger and the steward were drowned, and all four crew and the six other passengers were injured, among them Marshal of the RAF Sir John Salmond the Government director of Imperial Airways. In the official inquiry Imperial Airways was censured for inadequate escape hatches and insufficient push-out windows. Ssequently Short's test pilot demonstrated to the Air Ministry, Imperial Airways, and the insurers, that an Empire flying-boat could be taken off with full flap though porpoising 'developed frighteningly fast'.

1938

On the first day of January 1938 taxi-ing trials began of the Mayo composite with *Mercury* mounted on its launching crutch above the

Centre: The Short-Mayo composite aircraft *Mercury* and *Maia* climb to their separation altitude. *Mercury* captured the long-distance record for seaplanes with a 6,045-mile flight from Dundee to the Orange River, South Africa, in October 1938.
Below: Major Mayo, designer of the Mayo composite plane, congratulating Mr Lancaster Parker and Mr Piper (*left*) after the first flight on the Medway on 20 January 1938.

The first type of American aircraft purchased by the original British Airways was the Lockheed 10A Electra — a speedy, all-metal eight-seater representing the 'new-look' in monoplanes. Commissioned in March 1937, this particular aircraft crashed at Almaza in 1944.

broad wings of the flying-boat *Maia* which Lankester Parker manoeuvred on the Medway for an hour, and again on the 3rd. Then on the 20th the first combined flight of 20 minutes was made with Parker at the controls of *Maia* and his assistant Harold Piper operating *Mercury's* throttles, though the controls were locked.

During this time, Pan American Airways, whose flying-boat fleet had flown more than 1,300,000 miles, carrying over 2,000 passengers without incident, sustained its first loss on the trans-Pacific air service. The *Samoan Clipper*, flown by Edwin Musick, radioed on 11 January that one engine had developed an oil leak and petrol was being dumped in readiness to alight at Pago Pago in the Samoan Islands. A fire in the air must have followed. Next day the burnt wreckage was found by a minesweeper fourteen miles from the island, and the crew of seven had perished — the first fatal accident with a PAA flying-boat. That was a sad beginning for the first trial separation of the Mayo composite on 6 February, for Musick, the American expert on flying-boats, was a friend of Lankester Parker, the expert on British flying-boats. However separation proved uneventful. On 23 February, with Capt Wilcockson as co-pilot, separation was repeated at low altitude for the Press. Asked to comment on the flight, Parker typically said: 'The chief thing we discovered was that it wasn't a fluke the first time'.

No less important were the refuelling experiments. On 20 January, with Parker at the controls of *Cambria* and Geoffrey Tyson lying the flight-refuelling twin-engined ex-bomber AW 23, the first successful contact had been made, and a series of all-weather trials commenced in which transfers were made even in fog.

Two years late, the Armstrong Whitworth Ensign was also ready. Brackley rushed to Hamble on the 23rd to see the big airliner fly, but it only taxied across the road separating erecting shop from aerodrome, so he continued to the Imperial flying base at Hythe to check that all was going well. Next day, while he was busy in the London Office, the Ensign made its first brief flight, piloted by Turner-Hughes and Eric Greenwood, but the rudder control required the combined foot pressure of both pilots to move it. Two days later, after rudder adjustments, Turner-Hughes flew it to Baginton Aerodrome near Coventry where the maker's tests would be conducted. That same day Brackley went to Hatfield and flew the Albatross for an hour with Geoffrey de Havilland junior, delighted with its performance and handling. There was, however, a disquieting rumour that British Airways would also be equipped with the Albatross.

That company had now transferred to Heston Airport, which had been taken over from Airwork by the Air Ministry on 25 November. Farey-Jones and J.R. Bryans had resigned, and Campbell Orde was in active command. The

60,000 sq ft main hangar afforded extensive maintenance facilities for the smart Lockheed Electras, Junkers Ju 52s and stand-by Fokker. The Electras left Heston for Paris on a 95-minute flight simultaneously with those from Le Bourget, maintaining a two-hour frequency from 8.35 in the morning to 9.25 at night, and a single fare of £4 10s or £6 6s return was charged. For the night mail to Germany, the Junkers took off at 10 p.m., returning the same night. Lockheed 14s had been ordered for the route planned via West Africa to South America.

·The destinies of British Airways and Imperial Airways now became governed by the Cadman Report which Colonel Muirhead on 9 February announced was in the hands of the Secretary of State for Air and would be published in March; but first the Air Estimates of nearly £74 million intervened. The net vote for civil aviation was some £3 million of which

£250,000 was for equipment and accommodation proposed by the Maybury Committee — but air traffic control, radio, and meteorological facilities for fifteen area stations and twenty aerodromes remained Air Ministry responsibility. An Order in Council set up a Licensing Authority for internal air routes as recommended by the Committee, and the Air Registration Board was allocated £16,000 towards expenses of its airworthiness certification work.

The Cadman Committee Report followed immediately and was forthright, boldly stating: 'There is not a medium-sized airliner of British construction comparable to leading foreign types'. Had the Committee been more aeronautically knowledgeable it might have praised the Empire flying-boats, the Ensign and the Albatross, and given commendation for British aero engines. C.G. Grey commented that the Report was 'the most sensible official

British Airways, unlike Imperial Airways, had no government-imposed ban against purchase of non-British aircraft, as shown by this Junkers JU 52 at Gatwick, but on formation of BOAC it was taken over with two others and a number of Lockheeds.

Initially operating from Heston in 1936, British Airways added a Fokker F.VIII and F.XII (shown here) to its fleet.

document that has yet been issued on civil aviation'. Certainly it emphasized that at least two companies should operate external airlines — Imperial Airways on the Empire routes and British Airways to Europe and South America, and on the London–Paris run a new company should be formed with Imperial Airways and British Airways as co-owners.

But there was strong criticism of Imperial Airways: 'Although carriage of passengers in safety and comfort and conveyance of mails and freight have been achieved with considerable efficiency, we cannot avoid the conclusion that the management has been defective in other respects. In particular it has failed to co-operate fully with the Air Ministry and has been intolerant of suggestions and unyielding in negotiations. Internally its attitude in staff matters has left much to be desired.'

Below: The Captain and First Officer on the flight deck of an Imperial Airways DH 91 Albatross Frobisher-class aircraft.
Bottom: To enable easy slipping of the Empire flying-boats for hull maintenance and general overhaul, a self-floating set of wheeled legs was used which were readily detachable when the hull was afloat.

'It seems that the managing director — presumably with the acquiescence of the Board — has taken a commercial view of his responsibilities that was too narrow, and has failed to give the government departments with which he has been concerned the co-operation we should have expected from a company heavily subsidized and having such important international and Imperial contacts. There should therefore be an immediate improvement in these respects, and this may well involve some change in directing personnel.

'We further consider that the responsibilities which now confront the company have increased to the point where they can no longer be borne for practicable purposes by a managing director. In our view the chairman of the company should be in a position to give his whole time to the business and should do so. We think the chairman should personally control the management of the company, and he should be aided by one or more other whole time directors.'

Not untypically what had been missing was any personal touch between Board and staff, particularly the pilots. The Report stressed this: 'In our view, contact must now be supplemented by collective representation of employees. The desire for such change has been expressed by representatives of the pilots. Imperial Airways has stated that it has no objection to "collective bargaining". However, any organization with those objects should be in a position to negotiate authoritatively on behalf of a substantial proportion of the class it claims to represent.'

The company immediately defended their general manager and their own record in a circular to shareholders: 'Mr Woods Humphery

has been condemned by the Committee without opportunity of saying a word in his defence on the matters in question'. To refute the assertion that it had been 'intolerant of suggestion and unyielding in negotiation' Imperial Airways documented *Criticisms of the Company* to show that the Air Ministry had procrastinated in many matters, whether letters, contracts or subsidies, and that the Empire air mail negotiations had dragged on for four years, and for two years over proposals to use Langston Harbour as the Empire flying-boat base.

The chairman of the Captains Committee wrote to Sir George Beharrell: 'My Committee and the Captains express their unanimous satisfaction in the management of Imperial Airways, with particular reference to the managing director, who has been subject, in their opinion, to unwarranted criticism by the Committee of Inquiry. Indeed they are glad if there have been times when the management have been intolerant of suggestion and unyielding in negotiations with the Air Ministry.'

C.G. Grey recommended: 'The best thing would be to make George Woods Humphery full time chairman and then find a couple of other full time directors. Quite definitely, his resignation would be the very worst thing that could happen for Imperial Airways and for British civil aviation. Besides being a good engineer, Woods Humphery was a competent pilot in the war and kept his licence until recently. Consequently he can talk to his pilots as one pilot to another and to his engineering staff as an engineer.'

Repercussions continued. Imperial Airways refused to accept BALPA, and the Government began to investigate possible candidates for chairmanship, though Air Marshal Sir John Salmond, the Government director, was quick to decline.

Meanwhile there had been problems with the two prototype Imperial Airways airliners. While Turner-Hughes was flying the Ensign on 8 March all four engines simultaneously stopped; but the pilot was an artist of fine judgement and despite the strangeness of forced-landing an eight-ton machine of limited manoeuvrability, he put it down safely on the RAF aerodrome at Bicester. At the end of that month the Albatross in the hands of young de Havilland developed trouble in the undercarriage operating system and he had to make a belly landing at Hatfield to the detriment of propellers, engine nacelles, and under side of wings.

Major Tryon (*left*) and Sir Kingsley Wood make the governmental gesture of posting letters to Australia.

G.P.O.
GREAT BRITAIN
TO
AUSTRALIA
FIRST THROUGH SERVICE
EMPIRE AIR MAIL SCHEME

With both aircraft it would take time to discover and correct the causes.

For airlines the weather remained the chief hazard. Early in April a foggy night flight caused an Imperial Airways machine from Paris to land at Heston, and when a British Airways machine tried to get into Croydon without using the Lorenz, the ilot overshot and went through the fence and damaged his Electra. Soon afterwards an incoming German freighter landed blind using the Lorenz, but the pilot imagined he was too near the boundary, slammed on the brakes, swung round with open starboard engine, skidded on the grass, and the undercarriage was wiped off sideways. After that nobody tried.

Early in May Lord Swinton resigned as Secretary of State for Air and was succeeded by Sir Kingsley Wood, a small plump man with sparkling spectacles, who had been Minister of Health since 1935 and previously PMG, but had no knowledge of aircraft. His immediate task was to implement the Cadman recommendations and decide the chairmanship of Imperial Airways. On the short list was Sir John Reith, the earliest organizer of broadcasting, and now Director-General of that new public corporation the BBC. By extraordinary coincidence he and Woods Humphery were trainee draughtsmen before the war at the Yarrow Torpedo Works, so knew each other well;

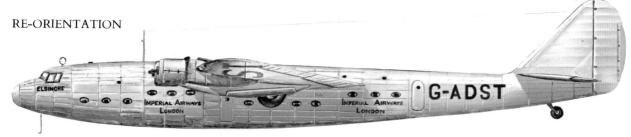

Top: Armstrong Whitworth AW 27 Ensign 1 (Imperial Airways, 1938).
Centre: Lockheed 14 (British Airways, 1937).
Above: De Havilland DH 91 Albatross (Imperial Airways, 1938).

further, Sir John's father, the Reverend J. Reith, had officiated at the marriage of Woods Humphery, with John junior as best man. Throughout their careers the two had lunched together from time to time, exchanging views about their work.

Woods Humphery soon heard rumours of the possible appointment of Reith and went to see him. The latter recorded: 'He went so far as to tell me that he could not possibly have a full time chairman; there would not be nearly enough work for him. He was in fact booming me off. But it was unnecessary. I had no desire to go there. Even had the idea been attractive we were not likely to get on; his ideas and mine were radically different, nor could I have contemplated putting an old friend out of a concern which was largely his own creation.' Nor was the Corporation Board willing to let Woods Humphery go.

Nevertheless on 14 June Sir Kingsley Wood

told the Commons that the Board of Imperial Airways had decided upon Sir John Reith as chairman, and that Sir James Price, the Deputy Secretary at the Ministry of Labour, would be appointed to the Board to look into accusations of management malfeasance.

At that Woods Humphery resigned, though he agreed to stay long enough to initiate Reith in all aspects of the management. Col Burchall expressed the widespread feeling: 'We have intense indignation at the campaign of calumny waged against the company and our chief for whom we have respectful affection and loyalty. We know his immense drive, his vast ability, and his everlasting energy. Under his guidance the finest commercial aviation service in the world has been produced.'

Hudson Fysh cabled: 'Resignation Woods Humphery at this stage inauguration Empire air services fantastic and unacceptable to all interested in Australia. Do hope British stability will prevail.' It did not. Nor did Sir John Reith think much of the new job. 'I was brought to the door of an old furniture depository behind Victoria Station. It was Imperial Airways: a plate on the wall said so. Inside were counters, luggage on the floor, a few people standing about — a booking office evidently. I inquired where the head office was. A young man pointed to a dark and narrow staircase; up there, he said. The managing director's office: second floor he thought. Having ascended thither I went along a dark passage between wooden partitions, peering at the doors and wondering which to try first. Here it was — a bit of paper with "Managing Director" written thereon. From Broadcasting House to this!'

That the disciplinarian Woods Humphery had friends was shown by their signatures on a silver salver presented to him at a testimonial dinner two days before the first through flying-boat service to Australia was inaugurated on 26 June. Capt Wilcockson spoke of the resignation as 'a dirty political move'. A few days later Sidney Dismore, the resolute supporter of Woods Humphery, wrote to the Prime Minister quoting his Board's *Comments on the Cadman Report* and challenging the critics to plan ten years in advance — a letter eagerly

Below: Lockheed 10A Electra (Hillman Airways, 1937).
Bottom: De Havilland DH95 Flamingo (BOAC, 1940).

seized upon by London papers. The *Observer* commented: 'Mr Woods Humphery was charged with making commercial aviation pay, and he came nearer to succeeding than anybody else in the world. The new executive chairman, Sir John Reith, is charged with making British aviation technically advanced, no matter whether it pays or not.'

Under the new management the Corporation agreed to pay Capt Rogers, the cause of it all, a retaining fee and ensure re-employment when the London–Paris joint company was established, but there was nothing for other pilots sacked as 'redundant' because they did not meet the requisite standard. In all this Brackley was strangely quiet, though on 19 July he attended the first Board meeting chaired by the darkly formidable Reith. The attitude towards BALPA remained indeterminate, though a ballot by the pilots confirmed it as their bargaining agent. The daily round continued, though not uneventfully, for on 14 July *Mercury*, piloted by Capt Don Bennett, was launched over Southampton from *Maia*, piloted by Capt Wilcockson, and flew 2,000 miles to Foynes and back. A week later it was launched over Foynes and Bennett set forth across the Atlantic, reaching Montreal in 20 hr 20 mins against head winds of some 25 mph, the four engines having consumed less than 54 gal/hr and 80 gallons remained. After refuelling, *Mercury* continued to Long Island, USA, then headed home in stages via Botwood, Horta in the Azores, and Lisbon, having averaged 160 mph for the outward and return journeys — but while the flight showed the feasibility of carrying mails long distances non-stop it was still a far cry to carrying a payload of passengers.

The USA were a big jump ahead. Their impressive four-engined, 29-ton Douglas DC-4 had flown, and already there were orders from United Airlines, Trans-Continental and Western Air, American Airlines, Pan American and Eastern Airlines. Imperial Airways was not permitted to buy American airliners, though the Air Ministry had placed orders for American military aircraft to reinforce the rearmament programme. Hope was therefore pinned on the 20-ton Ensign under test at Martlesham Heath for its C of A. The ailerons were criticized as too heavy; tail trimming too sensitive; the engine for slinging oil and tending to cut at take-off because of oiled up sparking plugs — and that could be dangerous because

the machine could hardly climb until flaps and undercarriage were retracted. However the C of A was granted at the end of June subject to modifications which would take at least three months, though during July a quick visit was made to Croydon for confirmatory handling by Imperial Airways pilots and a run was made to Paris and back.

The Ensign's smaller sisters of the eight-ton Atalanta-class also had their problems but so far had been repairable, except for *Athena* which was destroyed by fire when a bottle of compressed oxygen instead of air had carelessly been used to start the engines. But now in August came the first fatal accident. *Amalthea* on its way north to Alexandria crashed into a Kenyshillside near Kisumu a few minutes after taking off, and the four crew were killed, though luckily there were no passengers.

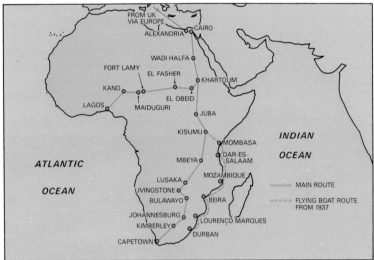

Imperial Airways routes in Africa up to 1937.

The second DH Albatross was the next in trouble, for the fuselage suddenly sagged abaft the wings and broke in two when landing during overload trials on 27 August. This renewed fears that wooden construction was not only outdated but dangerous. However de Havilland's had already turned to metal stressed skin construction for their next design, the DH 95 Flamingo, a twelve- to seventeen-seater shoulder-wing monoplane powered with two 890 hp Bristol Perseus sleeve valve radials intended for Jersey Airways as a rival to the Lockheed 14s of British Airways. Nevertheless fears over the Albatross proved groundless, and it was readily repaired with light wooden stiffeners.

But now the threat of war was looming. On

15 September, Neville Chamberlain flew in a British Airways Electra to Munich in a bid for peace between Hitler and the Czechoslovak Government. He returned empty-handed. On the 22nd he flew to Germany again. A dispirited Prime Minister returned to Heston two days later. The King signed a State of Emergency. The Navy was mobilized. Trainloads of children were evacuated to the country. An invitation came from Hitler to participate in a conference at Munich with Daladier and Mussolini. On 29 September Chamberlain flew there by British Airways. On the afternoon of 30 September he was back at Heston, and stepping from the cabin doorway of the shining Lockheed he triumphantly waved a small piece of paper. From the windows of Downing Street he told the cheering crowd, 'I believe it is peace in our time'. But was it?

While the Prime Minister was shuttling to and fro, Woods Humphery was finally pushed out of his life's work with severance pay of £15,000. The new reign was under weigh. Bookings and freight were so great that flights on the India–Australia route had to be duplicated; a third service was added on the Singapore–Sydney section; in Africa not only had the Johannesburg to Salisbury services been increased to six a week, but the routes from

Khartoum to Lagos, Lagos to Accra, and Bathurst to Freetown were put in operation although not listed in the original plan.

In England the airlines were told to be ready to move from Croydon before possible hostilities began. Imperial Airways pilots were issued with a new list of prohibited areas on Germany's frontier through which specific corridors were allocated — yet crews of the airliners from potentially hostile countries were mingling in no less friendly fashion with their British equivalents, though refugees were moving both into England and out according to nationality, among them many Czechs. Slowly the panic died down, and cool consideration followed of Empire routes in the contingency of war.

On 7 October British Airways dispatched two Lockheed 14s, flown by Capts Robinson and Flowerday, on a trial run carrying Clive Pearson and directors to Portugal as a first stage to West Africa and across the South Atlantic. After their return, Major Brackley on behalf of Imperial Airways and E.P. Hessey of British Airways jointly began planning a more extended survey: 'To examine and report on the practicability of operating Lockheed 14 and

On 30 September 1938, Neville Chamberlain arrived back at Heston from Munich in a British Airways Lockheed 14 (piloted by Captain Nigel Pelly) after signing the 'peace in our time' agreement with Hitler.

Albatross "F"-class on a reserve air route from England to North Africa, across the Sahara, Sudan and Belgian Congo to Central Africa, with the object of maintaining services with Egypt and the East, Central and South Africa in the event of war'.

The prototype AW Ensign was now handed over to Imperial Airways, and on 11 October some 50 guests were invited to take tea over London, though in two parties because this machine could then accommodate only 27. One of the passengers reported: 'The key note is spaciousness. The spacious Airways chairs are the main furniture, each with plenty of room and a fair sized table. The windows are not so large as the old HP 42's or Empire boats, so passengers with no window seat may feel the outlook restricted. The noise is subdued, though speed and power are nearly double that of the HP 42. Retracting the wheels is fascinating seen at close quarters beneath the wing. The huge balloon wheels and attendant ironmongery lift ponderously like the Tower Bridge in action. The fairings click shut and the view of the landscape becomes uninterrupted. Capts O.P. Jones and Horsey made the smoothest of landings.'

De Havilland's also came into the news — first with the maiden flight of their twin-engined, all-metal Flamingo, and then a few days later when the first 22-seater Albatross was delivered and named *Frobisher* as flag ship of the new 'F'-class. A wit suggested it should have been 'Furbisher' as it would brighten up the Imperial performance.

Early in November Sir John Reith chaired his first AGM. 'The Year under review ended before my advent, but I gave them the usual statistics; explained that the company was hampered by shockingly late deliveries, and was operating aircraft that should long have been replaced. I questioned the policy of using only aircraft and engines designed and built by British manufacturers. Actuated by considerations of efficiency, I felt the present position was neither commercial nor constitutionally satisfactory: the company was neither wholly free nor wholly secure.' However the net profit was £97,267, permitting a 7 per cent dividend.

On 11 November Sir Kingsley Wood, in answer to a private notice from the Opposition leader Clement Attlee on future relations of British Airways and Imperial Airways, said: 'The Government have this question under consideration with a view to creation of a suit-

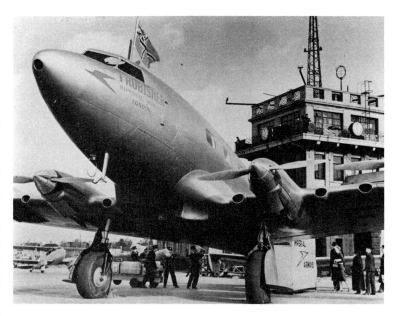

able instrument for our overseas civil aviation communications . . . In the circumstances the Government are of the opinion that this would be provided by the association of the two chosen instruments — Imperial Airways Ltd and British Airways Ltd — in a single public Corporation. The Government therefore proposes to recommend to Parliament legislation which will acquire the existing undertakings of these airways. The Government hopes to fix with the directors of the two companies a fair and reasonable price for each undertaking and it is proposed that the new Corporation shall obtain funds for the purchase of two undertakings and capital requirements by issue of fixed interest stock guaranteed by the Government.'

Because the British Airways capital of £363,204 was insignificant compared with the £1,648,869 of Imperial Airways, its chairman, Clive Pearson, had qualms and proposed that two separate companies be established within the corporation — but the Minister remained adamant, influenced by Sir John Reith's insistence that he would resign unless the company was nationalized though he welcomed Pearson as deputy chairman. Who decided to bring in Leslie Runciman, a keen amateur flier and director of Lloyd's and the LNER, is not known, but the intention was to establish this heir of Lord Runciman as chief executive next April.

But once again there were set-backs for Imperial Airways, for the Empire flying-boat *Calpurnia* (G-AETW) was wrecked at night on Lake Habbaniyah, Iraq, on 27 November;

Four specially-developed DH Gipsy Twelve air-cooled engines powered the elegant Frobisher-class DH Albatross airliner, shown here with passengers entering the shielded embarkation steps.

long-serving Capt E.W. Attwood, his First Officer and two crew were killed, and three supernumeraries were injured, though there were no paying passengers. Nor were the new Ensign-class without problems, for in December they were pressed into service as relief aircraft to carry the heavy Christmas mails to Australia: *Egeria* was grounded at Athens for an engine change, *Euterpe* failed to reach India, and *Elsinore* was grounded at Karachi with another engine failure. It was a fiasco. They were withdrawn and returned to Armstrong Whitworth's. However two DH Albatrosses were successful on an experimental Christmas mail service to Cairo, averaging very high speeds.

But Imperial Airways had been looking beyond these machines to the next stage, and the Air Ministry agreed to issue two specifications for 32-ton four-engined airliners equivalent to the Douglas DC-4 for the Empire and European routes. Operational use in 1940 was the target. Short's successfully tendered for the long-range version and Fairey Aircraft for the other. Both were designed to achieve 275 mph, and alternatively 330 mph at 25,000 ft if built with pressure cabin. Dryly C.G. Grey commented: 'People who have most say on the subject in the States have no belief in the present usefulness of stratospheric flying, whatever use it may be to those who want to fly 7,000 miles non-stop'.

1939

The euphoria of Chamberlain's success at Munich had given place to sombre realization that only a breathing space was secured in which to rearm with utmost speed. Every manufacturer by January 1939 was engaged in drastic expansion of production. Possibly it was that same threat which prompted Harold Balfour, the new Under-Secretary for Air, to say that Croydon must soon undergo major reconstruction. Spring was the target for a new Lorenz-guided fog-line runway — but the faster landing speeds of the projected Short and Fairey airliners would soon necessitate a new airport and Lullingstone in Kent was being considered.

At Hythe, docking arrangements had already been extended. Two flying-boats could now be dealt with simultaneously instead of leaving one moored until the other cleared. That flying-boats were safer than landplanes was

mistakenly believed by many travellers, particularly after *Calypso* was forced down with engine trouble in the open sea north of the Channel Islands and the crew of six and two passengers were rescued by a tug which towed the flying-boat into Cherbourg Harbour. Certainly the confidence of the management was increased by the fourteen Atlantic crossings to date by *Caledonia* and *Cambria*. The improved S.30 flying-boats *Cabot*, *Caribou* and *Connemara* had been cleared for flight refuelling to a weight two tons greater than take-off load. *Clyde*, fitted with propellers of the new constant-speed type, arrived at Hythe on 24 January — preceding by a day the loss of *Cavalier* on the New York-Bermuda run when icing stopped two engines and the other two began to fail. Within fifteen minutes of touch-down the seas broke her in two. Ten hours later ten of her thirteen people were rescued, two having died from exposure and one having drowned. A long inquiry followed during which an intensive flight programme with *Champion* was begun at Hythe to improve de-icing of the Perseus engines.

The planned expansion of Imperial Airways was suffering for additional reasons. The Frobisher-class were grounded because the undercarriage of one collapsed when the machine slid sideways through the mud on to the tarmac while taxi-ing in a strong side wind. Even more irksome was the absence of the Ensigns, for they were being fitted with more powerful Tiger engines and constant-speed propellers to improve reliability and performance.

Petty criticism of Imperial Airways during the Debate on the £200 million Air Estimates was brushed aside by Capt Balfour. As to new aircraft, he mentioned the Short and Fairey machines, and that 'to help Imperial and British Airways the Air Ministry had placed orders for two prototypes and a further twelve production machines'. There was also the almost completed Short G-class flying boat. This enlargement of the Empire boat with 20 ft greater span and an all-up weight of 33 tons, made it the nearest rival to the USA's new Boeing 314 flying-boat. That sheer size was becoming important was indicated by Sir Kingsley Wood's statement that in the past six years the annual carriage of mails had increased from 190 to 2,000 tons.

Shortly after these Air Estimates, Brackley was told that Campbell Orde would be appointed as Operations manager. A private letter followed from the latter explaining the circumstance and expressing friendly co-operation. Brackley was devastated. His diary for 1 April read: 'Campbell-Orde arived and reported'. *The Times* stated: 'This change releases Major Brackley for other and special duties for which his experience fits him well. In future he will undertake, among other things, the survey and development of new routes.' His immediate task was the projected survey of the 'reserve route', for over Europe the war clouds were gathering. Forty German divisions had mobilized, and Hitler announced that Czechoslovakia had become a German Protectorate.

By now most of the Empire-class boats had been delivered, but in two years eight had been lost, apart from several major accidents where the aircraft had been salvaged. Retrieving *Corsair* was still in process, for she had run short of fuel on 14 March, necessitating a forced landing on the relatively narrow River Dangu in the Belgian Congo, and sank in shallow water when the hull stove in. Short's and Imperial Airways had flown a rescue team to Juba, the nearest point though 150 miles away over roadless, broken country. Brackley flew there a few days later to cheer them on, and reported on the terrible conditions of heat, humidity and mosquitoes under which they were working.

From the USA came news that on 18 March the new Boeing 307 Stratoliner, which had a pioneering pressure cabin accommodating 33 passengers and crew of five, had crashed through explosive decompression, all being killed, including the technical director and chief engineer of KLM who had been sent from the Netherlands to assess this very advanced aircraft.

In England a glorious Easter produced a record number of air travellers, 40 machines leaving for Paris and 30 for Le Touquet during Thursday and Friday, and extra aircraft were required on the Scandinavian and Austrian routes. *Heracles*, returning at midnight, encountered a phenomenal bump over Croydon which put Capt O.P. Jones through the roof and injured the crew, so that all appeared in bandages next day; luckily the steward and stewardess had insisted on the passengers securing their belts. From 16 April the London–Paris service was operated jointly by British Airways and Imperial Airways, with eight return services every week-day. On the following day British Airways inaugurated its new European services with the dispatch from Heston of a Lockheed to Budapest. An hour later another Lockheed 14 left for Berlin and Warsaw, and among the passengers were Sir Francis Shelmerdine, Major McCrindle and members of the Polish Embassy.

Ten days later the Government's plans for compulsory military service and limitation of arms profits was announced in the Commons. But there were still expanding horizons. Next day the Imperial Airways Britain–West Africa service was extended to Takoradi on the Gold Coast. By that time Brackley and his team from Imperial Airways and British Airways were *en route* for Equatorial Africa to survey an alternative route from Algiers in case the Mediterranean became closed. He found Hessey of British Airways good company. 'Hessey, by the way', he wrote, 'used to be a cowboy in Australia and has done the trek with thousands of head of cattle from Darwin to Queensland; any one who can do that must be tough.'

Because of the threat to Empire communications the Australian Government was organizing, in conjunction with the United Kingdom, a special survey across the 4,700 miles of Indian Ocean between Australia and India, using the Consolidated PB 2Y flying-boat *Guba* piloted by Capt P.G. Taylor, who had made a name not only for his airline work but as a long-distance flier. The flight was a tremendous challenge, for the difficulties of flying-boat operations were yet again emphasized on 1 May, when *Challenger* (G-ADVD) on taking off at Mozambique struck a small boat, swerved and ran hard ashore, the impact killing the flight clerk; the radio operator was drowned, though the remaining three crew and two passengers were unhurt.

That same week Imperial Airways opened its splendid new Terminal Offices of Airways House, Buckingham Palace Road, London — yet the occasion attracted little publicity. A week later Sir Kingsley Wood announced that negotiations between the Government and the two major airlines had been successfully concluded, subject to approval by Parliament. Imperial Airways shareholders would be paid 32s 9d for each £1 ordinary share, and British Airways shareholders 15s 9d per £1 share. If payments were approved the sum paid to Imperial Airways would be £2,659,086, and British Airways would receive £262,500 together with £311,000 as repayment to the principal shareholders for advances made. On

22 May Imperial Airways stockholders agreed to sell their company and a fortnight later British Airways followed suit.

Two days after the Imperial Airways agreement, trans-Atlantic passenger flying was brought a stage nearer when Short's test pilot successfully flight-refuelled Imperial Airways' flying-boat *Cabot* from a Handley Page Harrow bomber converted to a 900-gallon tanker. Two Harrow tankers were shipped to Hattie's Camp, the big aerodrome later known as Gander, which had been cleared from the forest near the Newfoundland coast. The third Harrow was flown to Rineanna, later known as Shannon Airport, as the outward-bound refuelling point. Further practices were taking place over the Solent while awaiting delivery of *Caribou*. Meanwhile on 20 May Pan American inaugurated its first 'commercial' crossing with the departure of *Yankee Clipper* carrying 200,000 letters, freight, and twelve 'crew', arriving at Southampton on 23 May.

Losses of Empire flying-boats continued. On 12 June *Centurion* stalled while alighting at Calcutta and nosed like a submarine into the Hooghly River, but luckily only one passenger was injured. That was followed by a night-time burn-up of *Connemara* when a refuelling barge came alongside her moorings at Hythe and caught fire with so furious a blaze that the flying-boat's wings fell off and she sank within twenty minutes. *The Times* pronounced that these two losses cost the underwriters £150,000

and warned that the insurance market was finding aviation so expensive that higher rates would follow.

Nor were things better with *Corsair*, remotely distant in the Belgian Congo. A wonderful job had been made of repairs, and with advent of the rainy season she was launched with the river in full spate — but it was only 12 ft wider than the wings, and though Kelly Rogers attempted to take off it was impossible in the available distance, so he was turned round by the ground crew pushing the wings from the bank but hit a rock and once again the hull was holed. Petrol drums were lashed under the wings and the engines removed to increase buoyancy; then the long task of repairs started again, but this time gangs of tribesmen were recruited to make a lake by damming the river so that take-off could be made at the next rains.

On 12 June Sir Kingsley Wood presented to Parliament the British Overseas Airways Corporation Bill which gave a monopoly of subsidy for overseas air services but no monopoly of flying, and a sum not exceeding £4 million, less £100,000 for assistance to internal airlines, was allocated until December 1953. The new Corporation (BOAC) would not officially take over from the older companies until 1 April 1940, but between that day and the end of March 1941 it would be paid a subsidy on any deficiency resulting from continued operations, but after that would be based on three-year periods to enable the Corporation to plan

Below: The *Golden Hind* was one of the three Imperial Airways Short S.26 flying-boats intended as non-stop trans-Atlantic mail carriers. The outbreak of war prevented this service from being established, and the aircraft were used on other routes by the RAF and BOAC.

ahead. Despite the crowded Parliamentary calendar and war's alarms, the Bill was pushed through, reaching the third reading on 26 July. Except for a few details the Lords agreed, and the Bill was returned from them on 3 August. Next day it received the Royal Assent.

On the following day Capt Kelly Rogers, flying *Caribou*, began the first scheduled Atlantic service from Southampton, was flight-refuelled above Foynes, and headed for Botwood, Montreal and New York, seen off by *Maia* carrying Sir Francis Shelmerdine, Sir John Salmond, Leslie Runciman, Major McCrindle, Capt Wilcockson, and J. Durante the High Commissioner for South Ireland. *Caribou* alighted next day at Botwood after a flight of

16 hr 22 min, delayed by strong head winds and subsequently rain and fog off Newfoundland. She was quickly refuelled and then took off for Montreal, thence to Port Washington where she alighted 36¼ hrs from leaving Ireland. On 9 August the return was commenced. Three days later *Cabot*, piloted by Capt Bennett, took off on the second outbound service.

At Short's, the first of the big G-class flying-boats, *Golden Hind*, after a month of flotation tests, engine runs and adjustments, had made its first flight piloted by Parker on 21 July, flew again on the 25th for 72 minutes, and after two further short tests this impressive flying-boat was handed over to Imperial Airways with the onus on them for adequate proving trials.

Left: Cabot refuelling.
Above: Imperial Airways C-class flying-boat *Caledonia* over Manhattan after the first east-west experimental survey flight across the Atlantic in July 1937.

That month the modified Ensigns at last began to be re-delivered, and by the end of August, eleven had been received — but though the engines were more reliable there was trouble with overheating oil and problems with the constant speed propellers, and it became evident that these crucial airliners were unsuited for the hottest conditions in the Middle East. For the moment they were used on European routes.

Events in Europe were moving towards a crisis. On 9 August, while 1,300 aircraft were participating in air and ground defence exercises in southeast England, Imperial Airways announced curtailment of passenger bookings on the Empire routes, explaining this was caused by increased mail loads and insufficient aircraft, and that 'the situation will not be much better until January 1940'. Nevertheless all the principal British civil aerodromes and Croydon in particular were reporting heavy traffic. More and more licences were being granted for further operators on routes within the British Isles. The Air Transport Licensing Authority published each month a list of new approvals; thus at the beginning of August 32 were issued shared between eleven firms.

British Airways had a bad setback on the London–Zurich service on 11 August when one of the Lockheed 14s had engine trouble and the machine was unable to hold height. While descending, the carburettor caught fire and the flames spread, so landing was attempted in a field near Luxeuil, but the undercarriage collapsed, and though passengers and crew managed to escape, the machine was burnt out. Four days later British Airways had a repeat with an Electra (G-AESY) on the Stockholm run which caught fire and was ditched by the pilot in the Störstroem Straits south of Copenhagen, nosing over and sinking in nine fathoms with loss of all four passengers and radio officer, though the pilot was found floating unconscious.

Costly, but less distressing in human terms was the loss on delivery flight to Tasman Empire Airways, for the air mail extension to New Zealand, of the Empire flying-boat *Australia* which hit a submerged sandbank at Basra and was badly damaged, though the ten passengers, crew and mails were rescued by boat.

On the credit side, Capt Taylor with the flying-boat *Guba* had arrived back in Sydney, having pioneered almost without incident the reserve route from Australia to Mombasa and back. His detailed report fully proved the feasibility of the route as 'an invaluable auxiliary and eventually alternative means of communication between Australia and the outside world'. Meanwhile Brackley had completed his extensive study and resulting report entitled 'WAR BOOK. Reserve route to Central Africa. Secret'.

At Croydon, airliners to and from the Continent were running with full loads carrying many notabilities. 'Mr Winston Churchill, still with his scowl, returned in an Ensign after having given the Maginot Line the once over and his blessing. Capt Harold Balfour returned from Paris in *Fortuna*, having driven hurriedly from the Riviera in a baby car. Mr Hore-Belisha came in an Ensign from Paris — and a party of twelve German school girls on holiday in England arrived to catch the first plane back to Germany.'

On 24 August Parliament was summoned to enact an Emergency Powers (Defence) Bill, and Reserves of Army, Navy, and Air Force were called up. All ARP services were alerted. Poland was being threatened. Chamberlain wrote persuasively to Hitler warning that British intervention on behalf of Poland could not be ignored. At midnight on 30 August the British ambassador in Germany was summoned by Ribbentrop, the German Foreign Minister, who tersely defined Germany's offer to Poland; but next morning Germany invaded Poland and simultaneously bombed Polish cities, including Warsaw. Complete mobilization of the British Forces followed, and a 'black out' throughout Britain from sunset to dawn was ordered. At midnight the eastern half of England became a prohibited area for civil aircraft. Imperial Airways and other operators were instructed to evacuate Croydon. Within 24 hours all Imperial Airways airliners except three which were unserviceable had been transferred to Whitchurch near Bristol — their predetermined but secret destination.

On 3 September, in a broadcast to the nation at 11.15 a.m., Prime Minister Neville Chamberlain said: 'This morning the British ambassador in Berlin handed the German Government a final note stating that unless we heard from them by 11 o'clock that they were prepared at once to withdraw their troops from Poland a state of war would exist between us. I have to tell you now that no such undertaking has been received, and that consequently this

IMPERIAL AIRWAYS ➤ LE 'FROBISHER' LE PLUS RAPIDE DES AVIONS DE LIGNE ANGLAIS
4 MOTEURS · RAPIDITÉ ET CONFORT
EUROPE-AFRIQUE-INDES-EXTREME ORIENT-AUSTRALIE-ETATS UNIS D'AMERIQUE-LES BERMUDES

country is at war with Germany.' Every European air service was now suspended.

Capt Cripps recorded: 'August 31 should go down in British civil aviation history as the end of the pioneering era 1919–39. This period had seen the start of air transportation at a time when flying was considered a very precarious pastime. The years have seen the gradual change from contact flying and map reading to air navigation by D/F bearings when flying above or in the overcast. Great development in use of wireless had taken place, from the time when the pilot had no communication with the ground to eventual use of the "Q" code which overcame language difficulties and enabled aircraft of any nationality to fly on any route in adequate safety.

'By the introduction of the E-class Ensigns and F-class Albatrosses during the last nine months, cruising speed had gone up from 100 mph to 200 mph, and the time from London to Paris cut from 2 hours 30 minutes to 1 hour 15 minutes.

'This had been the hey-day of pilot individuality and independence. For twenty years he had been Captain in the real meaning of the word, operating to his own ideas whatever the weather or circumstances. For pilots such as Wilcockson, Jones, Perry, Horsey, Walters, and Youell, and those senior members of the maintenance and traffic staffs who pioneered the European routes and whose whole careers had been established on the Croydon operations, the evacuation to Bristol must have produced many nostalgic thoughts. This was a sad day. It was the end of Croydon as the airport for London, and the name Imperial Airways began to fade into history.'

Imperial Airways' poster showing internal accommodation of the DH 91 *Frobisher* was published in several languages for world-wide distribution.

World War II and BOAC 1939-45

One of the Mosquitos with which BOAC operated a war-time freight and passenger civil air service between Britain and Sweden. They had war-time camouflage but retained civil registration augmented with tricolour marking.

Ten minutes after Chamberlain announced that Great Britain was at war with Germany, the air raid sirens began their ominous wailing — but it was a false alarm, significant of the country's state of mind. War could not have come at a worse time for the embryonic BOAC, for integration of Imperial Airways and British Airways was presenting involved and extensive problems of staffing, policy, and implementation. The subsidy agreements for the two com-

panies stipulated that all their aircraft on the advent of war must be placed under direct control of the Air Ministry's National Air Communications Centre whose initial action was to dispatch an Ensign from Croydon loaded with the first batch of RAF officers and men to be sent to France. All flying crews and the mixed bag of airliners were kept standing-by at Whitchurch, but on the 9th the HP 42s and DH 89s were transferred to Exeter Airport.

Meanwhile a number of RAF Reserve pilots and aircrew were called up for military service.

Publication on 17 November of the Chartered and other Bodies (Temporary Provisions) Act gave authority for emergency statutes governing operation of British Overseas Airways, and on the 24th the Corporation was formally established by the Secretary of State's direction that Sir John Reith be chairman, the Hon Clive Pearson deputy chairman, and the Hon W.L. Runciman and Harold Brown members of the Board, which then elected Runciman as chief executive with title of director-general. On that same day the new *Golden Hind* Short G-class flying-boat was flown to Hythe and handed over to the Corporation for crew training, but was soon commandeered by the RAF together with the other two G-boats for long-range maritime reconnaissance, and so were *Cabot* and *Caribou* for ASV radar trials as they had completed their eight flight-refuelled trans-Atlantic crossings.

BOAC was instructed to vacate Southampton Water and establish war-time flying-boat headquarters at Poole — a big task, for there were over 400 marine, maintenance, and office staff. Sailing club buildings were commandeered and moorings laid in the main channel. Empire boats were converted to maximum cargo capacity with austerity seating limited to 29, and time-expired engines replaced with more powerful Pegasus XXIIs enabling take-off weight to be increased by 4,000 lb.

In October Sir John Reith conducted his first meeting as nominee chairman of British Overseas Airways though the Corporation could not take over the two constituent companies until the 'appointed day' on 1 April 1940, but the Air Ministry permitted a twice-daily service between Heston and Le Bourget to be resumed with Ensigns. Major Brackley concurrently severed his connection with the embryonic Corporation and reported for duty as a squadron leader to Headquarters of Coastal Command at Northwood, Middlesex. After the Parliamentary fuss of 1937 the BALPA-orientated pilots had regarded him as hostile to their trade union though his intent had been moderation of their views, but since the appointment of Campbell Orde as Operations manager he had been an embittered man for this had virtually demoted him from high position to mere membership of that department.

BOAC's immediate problem was to avoid impressment of every airliner as a transport, but erosion was occurring in other ways. On 7 November, the HP 42 *Horatius*, returning after carrying troops to France, was wrecked in attempting an emergency landing on the golf course at Tiverton, Devon, and in the following month one of the Ensigns, *Euterpe*, over-ran the small airfield of Chipping Warden near Banbury and was so damaged that she had to be taken to Hamble for a re-build.

Throughout the ensuing bitter winter not only were the limited services from Heston to

This photograph illustrates the way in which a passenger was carried in the bomb-bay of a Mosquito. Although physically cut off from the crew in the cabin above, he could speak to the pilot on the intercommunication telephone.

The Armstrong Whitworth
AW 27 E-class, of which *Euterpe*
was the fourth (delivered in
December 1938), suffered
operational problems resulting
in withdrawal for modification
after limited use, and eventual
clearance was too late for them
to resume flying before the
outbreak of war.

ter'. But to his delight on 5 January, Neville
Chamberlain appointed him Minister of
Information. He took office within a few days,
leaving Runciman to carry on the business.

At a special General Meeting on 6 March
Reith finally vacated the chair and was succeeded by Clive Pearson. The Board was
strengthened at instigation of the Minister by
the appointment of I.C. Geddes, son of the late
chairman of Imperial Airways, as deputy
chairman, and Gerard d'Erlanger also became a
director.

Meanwhile the airline fleet was dwindling.
On 1 March, *Hannibal*, the luxurious trend-
setter of the early 1930s, vanished without trace
while flying with a crew of four and four passengers over the Gulf of Oman *en route* from
Jask to Sharjah. This prompted recall from
Cairo of the three remaining HP 42s of the
Middle East run, and Empire boats were substituted, of which *Aotearoa* and *Awarua* reached
Sydney during the month to establish a weekly
service to Auckland, New Zealand.

A fortnight later a gale of wind at Whitchurch caused all hands to rush to the score of
dispersed aircraft and hang on grimly. *Heracles*
was lifting first one side and then the other and
finally heaved backwards through a barbed-
wire fence and was wrecked. Within minutes
Hanno lifted bodily, drifting backwards into the
same field and was wrecked beyond repair. The
Short *Scylla* suffered a similar fate at Drem in
April, and *Syrinx* earlier had been condemned
as unairworthy at Exeter.

On 9 April the German *blitzkrieg* over-ran
Denmark, followed by seaborne landings at
Norwegian ports and attacks on Oslo and Kris-
tiansand. However, nine days later British
troops landed unopposed at Vaags Fjord for
operations against Narvik. Radar scanners were
essential to detect enemy aircraft, so *Caribou*
and *Cabot* were diverted from their Shetland
patrols, and on 4 May, commanded by the
former Imperial Airways pilots Capt S.G. Long
and Capt Gordon Store, who were now RAF
officers, flew the radar gear and technicians to
Harstad on the Norwegian coast where British,
French, and Norwegian troops thronged the
streets, and the port was crammed with naval
vessels. All night the two flying boats lay at
moorings, captains and crews sleeping uncomfortably aboard. Next day they were instructed
to fly to Bodø, a little south of Narvik, to
unload, but the moment that was completed the
church bells pealed an air raid alert. The two

Le Bourget maintained, but also the far more
difficult run from Perth to Oslo and thence
Stockholm using two Ju 52s or an occasional
Lockheed 14. More often than not they arrived
over complete overcast with clouds 6,000 feet
thick and mountains a major hazard at the back
of Stavanger Airport.

1940

For those in England these early months of war
seemed uncannily quiet. A few bombs had been
dropped on shipping in the Shetlands — but our
Whitley bombers were showering leaflets on
German cities, and more and more British
troops were pouring into France.

The nation's Budget for 1940 provided
£2,000 million for war purposes. Factories were
turning out ever increasing quantities of guns,
bombs, vehicles, aeroplanes, and there was
utmost concentration on ships to replace inevitable losses from U-boats. That Germany was
withdrawing all troops from the Eastern front
to re-equip and expand for invasion of the West
was known from decoded messages and confirmed in February when bad weather forced
down a German aeroplane in Belgium and the
plans fell into Belgian hands.

Reith still felt he merited a better job and had
not been slow in complaints to the Minister and
Warren Fisher at the Treasury. To fill in time he
decided on a world tour of all routes 'which
would take some months to accomplish, and
get me away from the exasperations of idleness,
of continued waiting, and the sooner the bet-

captains dashed from shore to their flying-boats. The crews manned their guns. Store managed to start his engines and taxied out. Long had trouble getting his going, but was moving. Glinting in the sunlight a diving Heinkel attacked *Cabot*, which vigorously replied. Round came the Heinkel again and yet again in a storm of mutual gun-fire. To get airborne would be useless, for the German could then attack from below and astern, so Store ran *Cabot* on to the mud, whereupon the Heinkel fired a parting burst at *Caribou*, wounding four of the crew.

Both flying-boats needed repair so were left high and dry for that purpose, stripped of equipment and armament, but soon afterwards *Caribou* was bombed and burnt out. For the moment *Cabot* was saved by towing her several miles up the coast to a sheltered spot between a high cliff and a tall rock, but though her wings were disguised with blankets and bushes she was discovered next day by a marauding Dornier flying-boat, and from ashore her crew saw her go up in flames from incendiary bombs. In due course the Navy brought home the two captains, their crews, and the wounded.

The successful German onslaught in Scandinavia and stagnating military situation in the West provoked bitter debate in the Commons on 8 May. Chamberlain resigned. On 10 May, Winston Churchill became Prime Minister, and on that day Hitler began invasion of Holland, Belgium, and Luxembourg, his Panzer Divisions unstoppable, backed by heavy air raids. Within a week a bridgehead was established across the lower Somme between Amiens and Abbeville, isolating the British forces from the remainder of France. The desperate situation brought Churchill to Paris on 16 May for crucial discussions with the French Prime Minister, Paul Reynaud. But by the 23rd even Boulogne had been occupied. Every available BOAC airliner was plying between England and France with food and ammunition for the troops. Typically, five Ensigns, two Savoia–Marchettis, and a DC-2, escorted by six Hurricanes, were sent through pouring skies to relieve troops at Merville, though official communication was so lacking that the pilots were unaware that Germans held all the area west of St. Omer to Calais, and that Merville was the only advance airfield left in Northern France, but had been evacuated by the RAF the previous day.

Ten minutes after they landed a tremendous

battle began between the Hurricanes and fifteen Messerschmitt 109s, of which five were shot down with loss of one Hurricane. 'I shouted to the crew to hurry up with unloading for they were watching the show', recorded one of the Ensign pilots. 'A lull followed and the Hurricanes flew off, probably out of ammunition. A lone Me 109 reappeared, made two runs, concentrating on Sam Hoare's Ensign at the end of the line. Everybody ran for cover under the machines. Bullets were tearing into the ground fifteen yards away. Hoare was killed and his machine began to burn vigorously. Most of the other aircraft were holed. Everybody got airborne as soon as the Messerschmitt had gone. I found Alan Andrew in the cockpit of my machine and shouted "You're in the wrong aeroplane" as I rushed to get in.'

Flying at tree-top level they twice encoun-

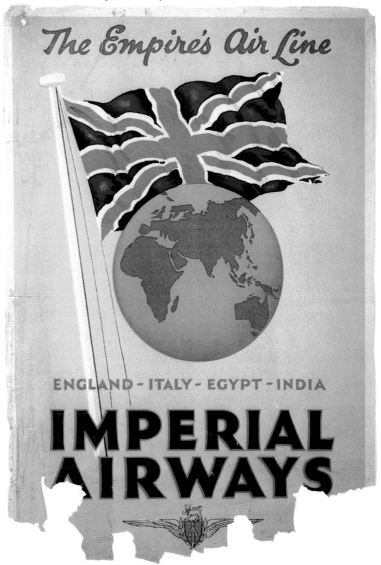

Imperial Airways advertising poster.

The Empire's Air Line

ENGLAND · ITALY · EGYPT · INDIA

IMPERIAL AIRWAYS

tered furious gunfire, and then brief attack by a fighter. The DC-2 was forced down and the crew taken prisoner. One of the Ensigns had a bad oil leak which necessitated throttling the port inner engine, but it managed to cross the Channel at 50 feet, whereupon the starboard inner engine failed. The pilot scraped over the cliffs and made for Lympne, but failing hydraulic power prevented extension of the starboard undercarriage, so on touch-down the machine slowly dropped on to the starboard wing, skidded on its belly through a wire fence, and never flew again.

Events were reaching the final stage before total collapse of France. Complete annihilation of the French army and most of the British army seemed probable. Since 20 May the Admiralty had been assembling a huge fleet of shallow-draught pleasure cruisers, lifeboats, tugs, fishing vessels and two paddle steamers in hope of rescuing some of the trapped soldiers. On the evening of the 26th the Admiralty signalled that Operation Dynamo, the evacuation of forces from the shores of Dunkirk, should begin. By 3 June over 338,000 British and French troops had been brought to England despite dive-bomber attacks, many casualties, loss of three destroyers and several transports, and destruction of numerous British aircraft — but the Battle of France dragged on, and amidst the dangers BOAC continued the Ensign run to Le Bourget until the bombing made so many craters that Ensign G-ADSX was badly damaged and had to abandoned.

The service continued, using other French airfields, and on 10 June BOAC's Le Bourget maintenance staff moved to Tours, the new headquarters of the French Government. On that day Italy declared war against Britain and France, thus closing the Mediterranean to BOAC's operations. Three days later Churchill, looking haggard and worn, flew to France for a last discussion with the French Government, who thereafter retreated to Bordeaux, which became BOAC's operational centre. As the Germans advanced their rumbling tanks across France, the slow undefended airliners continued bringing home RAF air crews and technicians: then they turned to evacuation of Guernsey and Jersey.

Even before the last civil aircraft landed in Britain from the Continent and the last ships steamed from the French coast, the external and internal British air routes were re-organized. The National Air Communications set-up, having served its purpose, ceased to exist. Many airline captains transferred temporarily or permanently to the civilian Air Transport Auxiliary (ATA) which had been organized early in the war by Gerard d'Erlanger to ferry RAF aircraft from factories to squadrons and storage centres. All internal companies, except Allied Airways operating the Orkneys and Shetlands route, were now grouped together with headquarters at Speke, Liverpool, managed by an Associated Airways joint committee chaired by Sir Harold Hartley, operating a combined fleet of twenty DH 86s and 89s on regular services to Eire and Northern Ireland, the Scilly Isles, Isle of Man, Islay, Tiree, the Hebrides, Orkneys and Shetlands. Concurrently BOAC began a twice-weekly service to Lisbon with the Empire boats.

On 17 June Marshal Pétain, who had succeeded Reynaud as Premier, sought armistice terms from Germany, which he accepted in the Forest of Compiègne on the 22nd, and two days later also capitulated to Italy. Said Churchill: 'What General Weygand called the Battle of France is over. I expect that the Battle of Britain is about to begin. The whole fury and might of the enemy must soon be turned on us . . . Let us therefore brace ourselves to our duties, and so bear ourselves that if the British Empire and its Commonwealth lasts for a thousand years, men will still say "This was their finest hour." ' Henceforth every night for months on end would be disturbed by wailing air raid sirens and the thump of exploding bombs, while by day massive dog-fights against armadas of bombers and their escorts took place in the skies of England.

One of the essentials was to re-establish communications between London and Cairo whence mail and dispatches could flow along the still functioning routes to Africa, India, and Australia.

Another was to re-open the trans-Atlantic route to the USA. To that end BOAC had modified the flying-boats *Clare* and *Clyde* with long-distance tanks as replacements for the two long-range flying-boats lost at Narvik. On 3 August *Clare,* carrying three passengers, mails and newspapers, took off from Poole piloted by Capt Kelly Rogers, refuelled at Foynes, and reached Botwood in an uneventful 15½ hours; then the same day proceeded to Montreal and on to New York, arriving there at dusk to a rousing welcome and extensive newspaper reportage.

The day after *Clare* reached New York *Clyde* was at moorings in Poole Harbour, and her captain A.C. Loraine was ashore making final preparations to fly her across the Atlantic when he was told that instead he was to carry a Colonel de Larminet and seven Free French officers to Lagos by the hitherto untried African coastal route which it had been Major Brackley's last task to survey in 1939.

There were no pre-arrangements for mooring and refuelling. French Colonial territory must be avoided. Everything depended on the initiative of Loraine and his co-pilot Capt W.S. May. At Lisbon the flight nearly ended, for in taking off in the dark, part of one aileron was torn off by a ship's mast. Flying all night, and in daylight down the dull coast of Africa, they reached Bathurst for refuelling, and repaired the aileron. Then on to Freetown where a heavy refuelling barge nearly hit them, causing Loraine to move *Clyde* upstream to a bay where fuel drums could be brought alongside by canoe; but it took all day in the tropical rain to hoist them up and pour the petrol in. Next morning a flight of 1,300 miles brought *Clyde* to the big port of Lagos. The reason for Colonel de Larminet's journey was now revealed. It was to persuade the French Equatorial Africa authorities to change allegiance from Vichy to the Gaullists. His destination was their capital Brazzaville on the far side of the dangerous, fast-flowing Congo River, opposite Belgium's Léopoldville where a mooring would be available. Urgent messages from London urged Loraine to risk the flight non-stop rather than alight for *en route* refuelling in French waters. On 19 August he took off.

It was a journey that made history, for Ian Scott-Hill, of the BOAC staff at Nairobi, was fortuitously staying at Léopoldville after surveying a possible flying-boat route from there to Lake Victoria. He happened to be acquainted with Colonel Carretier, commanding the French Air Force at Brazzaville, and invited him to cross the river to inspect the flying-boat which had made such a remarkable journey from Britain. There he met de Larminet, and in *Clyde*'s saloon they worked out a plan for a *coup d'état* which was to suceed in bringing over to the Allies the great colony of French Equatorial Africa and the possibility of a safe air route across the equatorial belt to a juncture with the Durban–Cairo service and onward to India.

BOAC employed stewardesses on its airliners for the first time during the war. Here are two of them, carrying down a case of thermos flasks to provision a long flight. The girl on the left is working as a member of a BOAC flying-boat launch crew.

To co-ordinate the vast programme of production Churchill appointed Lord Beaverbrook as Minister of Aircraft Production. Every kind of manufacturing and repair facility was diverted to war work, among them BOAC, whose long experience of aero-engine overhaul was now directed to military aircraft. Croydon and Hythe had made an immediate start in May. The Treforest Trading Estate factories near Cardiff were taken over in June and within six days the overhaul department at Croydon had been transferred and was quickly in full operation. Another group at Speke was assembling freighted RAF American aircraft, but soon this was transferred to Americans and BOAC established a similar factory at Exeter, and then two at Bath to re-build damaged propellers. Employees came from every profession and trade, including hundreds of women, and were trained under the skilled surveillance of BOAC engineers.

The Battle of Britain was raging in the summer skies. Intercepts by the electronic Ultra of Goering's instruction to the Luftwaffe revealed that on 'Eagle Day', 15 September, they would mount a mighty, final onslaught on Britain. If successful, Hitler would invade. Tides, moon, and weather were favourable for a Channel crossing. By one o'clock the heights were spider-webbed with the vapour trails of 25 squadrons of Spitfires and Hurricanes fighting the massed Luftwaffe, ending in a crushing defeat of Goering's bomber forces. Two days later a decrypted signal revealed Hitler's instruction to dismantle paratroop air-loading equipment at Dutch airfields. England had been saved. 'Never in the field of human conflict was so much owed by so many to so few', declaimed Churchill to the world.

Meanwhile Marshal Graziani and his Italian troops invaded Egypt from Libya. The West African coastal route to Lagos, thence to Khartoum and Cairo was now vital. BOAC dispatched three successive flying-boats to check the practicability of operating this spur to the curving 'Horseshoe' route that ran from Congello (Durban) to Australia. In turn each boat achieved the Congo River as *Clyde* had done in the previous month, then flew northeast over bush and jungle country to Stanleyville and so to Lake Victoria — an epic pathfinding journey of self-dependence amidst great hazards that established a vital lifeline from Lagos, where convoys dumped urgent stores for an airlift to the Middle East forces.

A few days after their departure the BOAC Albatross *Fortuna*, flown by Capt A.C.P. Johnstone, initiated an emergency courier service from Shoreham direct to Egypt and on to India. The two mail-carrying versions were commandeered by the RAF for the Iceland shuttle, but when *Fingal* soon after was wrecked in a forced landing in Gloucestershire the BOAC fleet received seven DH Flamingoes as reinforcements for the trans-Africa route, but they proved disappointing under tropical conditions and eventually were superseded by Lockheed Lodestars shipped to Cape Town direct from the USA.

Ice closing Botwood Harbour put temporary end in mid-October to BOAC's trans-Atlantic flying-boat service, but a new epic began. Lord Beaverbrook had been appointed Minister of Aircraft Production (MAP). To send by sea the many aircraft the USA was building for the RAF would lead to enormous losses because of the submarine warfare. Prompted by the Purchasing Commission, he contacted his friend, Sir Edward Beatty of Canadian Pacific Railways who had Woods Humphery, that valiant pioneer of Imperial Airways, as chief assistant, and it was agreed they would organize an Atlantic ferry service in co-operation with BOAC. Lieut-Cl Burchall was made general manager, and with Capt Wilcockson as operations manager, Capt Bennett as flying superintendent, and Capts Ross and Page in charge of training, sailed for Canada in August. On 21 September, thirteen more pilots, ten radio officers and several ground engineers arrived, and American and Canadian bush pilots began to join them. The great gamble was the Atlantic winter weather of which no airman had experience, but navigation was the major problem because radio aids in the area were negligible.

Bennett therefore decided the initial flights would be in formation, flying at night so that star bearings could be taken. As the most experienced navigator, he would lead. On 10 November the forecast was favourable. Seven Hudson bombers and crews were ready. Bennett took off from Gander and the others followed at half-minute intervals, easily locating him in the brilliant moonlight. Flying three each side at 15,700 feet, breathing oxygen from a tube, all went well until halfway when they entered cloud and lost sight of each other. With dawn the overcast became lighter. Separately they made landfall and headed on radio bearings to Aldergrove, N. Ireland. Bennett arrived first, closely followed by Capt S.T.B. Cripps, who clocked his 10,000th hour of flying with this flight. Some minutes later the third aircraft,

Below: De Havilland DH 98 Mosquito VI (BOAC, 1944).
Centre: Consolidated Liberator II (BOAC, 1945).
Bottom: Boeing 314 A (BOAC, 1941).

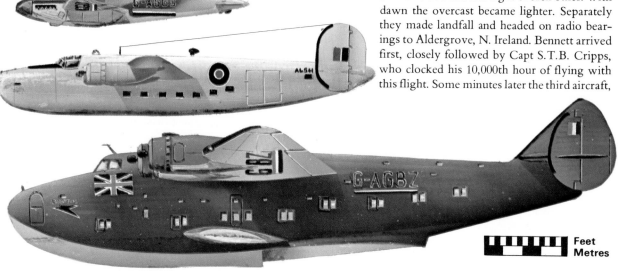

Feet
Metres

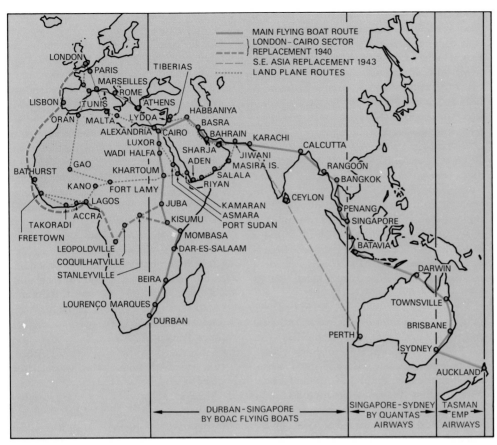

Map legend:

MAIN FLYING BOAT ROUTE
LONDON – CAIRO SECTOR
REPLACEMENT 1940
S.E. ASIA REPLACEMENT 1943
LAND PLANE ROUTES

DURBAN – SINGAPORE
BY BOAC FLYING BOATS

SINGAPORE – SYDNEY
BY QUANTAS
AIRWAYS

TASMAN
EMP
AIRWAYS

flown by Capt R.E. Adams, arrived. Within an hour the others came safely in. They had achieved what the experts had declared impossible.

In fortnightly succession other flights followed, but the fourth, again led by Bennett, had problems: one machine turned back with engine trouble, another crashed on take-off and its wreckage prevented the third starting at all. Because all formations had difficulty in maintaining contact, it was agreed that each aircraft in future must have a navigator and flights be made individually. The risks remained enormous but were considered acceptable even if losses were three in seven, though a higher rate would entail shipping aircraft by sea.

The Luftwaffe was persisting night after night with raids on British cities, and in one of the November daylight sorties three of BOAC's Ensigns were damaged by bomb splinters. Some thought this no loss, for the Tiger engines were giving a lot of trouble. In the next raid on Whitchurch the Albatross fleet was reduced to three when *Frobisher* was destroyed. Then on 6 December *Hadrian* broke

loose in a gust at Doncaster and cartwheeled on to the railway. That was the last lap of the HP 42s — for *Helena* had been condemned after a heavy landing in August and a week later *Horsa* had caught fire in a forced landing — but they had paid their way at a fraction of the operating cost of later airliners and had ensured world-wide reputation for luxurious travel by Imperial Airways.

1941

Early in 1941 BOAC was instructed to recommence the Stockholm service which had been cancelled when Germany invaded Norway and Denmark. Instead of the former Ju 52s an ex-Polish Lockheed 14 was used for swiftest passage through the brief Northern night, flying unarmed by way of the Skagerrak despite searchlights and 'flak', and began a service vital to industry by air-freighting ball-bearings which the Swedes made available in steadily increasing quantity.

Supplies to beleaguered Malta were also a priority. The island was under constant air attack and had only one squadron of outdated Gladiator fighters to defend it, yet BOAC aircraft continued to land and take off at Luqa airfield under cover of darkness and the Empire flying-boats maintained a regular service between Alexandria and Kalafrana harbour. A Lisbon–Gibraltar–Malta link was being organized, but it was necessary to await reinforcement from *Cathay* and *Champion*.

With the German invasion of Jugoslavia and Greece, *Coorong* and *Cambria* of the Horseshoe route were hastily camouflaged to look like Sunderlands and flown to Suda Bay, Crete, to evacuate British troops. Day by day they alighted at dusk, loaded men at dawn and flew away, airlifting 469 between 22 April and 5 May. Meanwhile *Imperia*, the renowned Imperial Airways base ship at Mirabella, up-anchored and eluding the hostile patrols sailed to Port Said.

But now the Horseshoe route was imperilled. Crucial to operations was the BOAC base on Lake Habbaniya 60 miles west of Baghdad. On 3 May, Iraqi forces, at German instigation, laid siege to the adjacent RAF Flying Training Base, and interned the BOAC ground crews. With refuelling impossible the route had to be temporarily suspended until a new base could be established southwestward at Akaba on the Palestine shore of the Red Sea, where *Imperia* was next stationed as depôt ship. Meanwhile two C-class flying-boats fitted with extra tanks

were able to overfly Iraq on a direct shuttle between Cairo and Bahrein.

On the Poole–Lisbon–Lagos route only *Clare* was left after *Clyde* had foundered in the Tagus on 15 February, but among the flying-boats at the Felixstowe RAF test establishment was *Guba*, the twin-engined Catalina flying-boat with which Capt Taylor's team made pre-war survey flights across the Indian Ocean to Mombasa, thence Dakar and across the Atlantic to New York. Beaverbrook ordered her to be handed to BOAC, and in March *Guba* began to supplement *Clare*'s flights. Two more Empire flying-boats were soon added, and then another Catalina. They were still insufficient to meet the demand, so friendly Juan Trippe of Pan American was approached and three big Boeing 314A flying-boats, *Bangor*, *Berwick* and *Bristol*, were purchased for $1,000,000 each, and a maintenance base was set up at Baltimore, USA, to which they returned across the Atlantic for servicing at the end of every round flight between Britain and Africa.

Changes were under weigh in the Atlantic ferry service. Hitherto pilots had returned from England by ship, but in April under the auspices of MAP's Atlantic Ferry Organization (ATFERO) seven Consolidated Liberator bombers were allocated so that crews could be brought back by air. Known as the Return Ferry Service (RFS), the first eastbound flight was by Capt Bennett on 4 May carrying Air Chief Marshal Sir Hugh Dowding. Though the return flight to Canada carrying seven ferry

Passengers disembark from the Boeing flying-boat *Bangor* at the BOAC marine terminal in Britain after an Atlantic flight. *Inset:* Captain T.T. Percy of Newcastle-on-Tyne, flight captain of the BOAC Return Ferry Service.

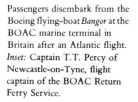

pilots was delayed, the saving in time had been very considerable and set the pattern — though the real test lay ahead with the ice, snow, and gales of winter.

RAF Transport Command was formed on 18 July and immediately took over the Return Ferry, but handed control back to BOAC early in September with the addition of three Liberators, the Corporation taking full responsibility for all maintenance, operation, and provision of crews.

Beaverbrook never knew that he narrowly escaped being victim of one of three major crashes which occurred that August on the ferry run. Early in the month Capt Cripps during a five-day London respite learned that his return flight allocation was the special Liberator used for VIP passengers, but on returning to Prestwick was told that Capt E.R.B. White was taking it and that the passenger was Beaverbrook. Not to be outdone, he induced White to relinquish that flight so that he could take over. White transferred to Liberator 261, scheduled to take off at 2000 hours, and Cripps with Beaverbrook aboard Liberator 915 was due to depart half an hour later. They heard the roar of 261's engines on the take-off run and saw the big machine enter the 300-foot cloud base; nobody knew what happened until two days later. Ten minutes later it had crashed into the mountain on the Isle of Arran, killing everybody — but Beaverbrook in Cripps's machine flew an uneventful voyage to his native Canada.

BOAC's world commitments were resulting in serious shortage of aircrews, so a number of internationally famous pilots such as Clyde Pangbourn, Scott, and Mollison were recruited and RAF pilots were seconded to RFS. In October Qantas magnificently contributed by extending their Darwin to Singapore route onward across Malaysia to Siam, Burma, and so to Calcutta and the long run across Northern India to the BOAC terminal at Karachi.

Because of the disappointing performance of the Ensigns, BOAC was replacing their Tiger engines with the USA's well-proved Wright Cyclones, giving 1,000 hp more for take-off, making them operable in hot climates. They were therefore allocated to the vital supply service from Lagos to Cairo, but on 9 November an enemy aircraft attacked the Ensign *Everest* which was crossing the Bay of Biscay on its first outbound flight, forcing it to return to England for repair. Two months later *Enterprise* made a

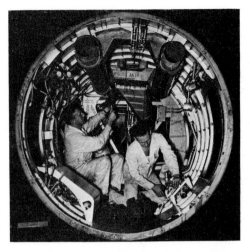

The size of the Boeing flying-boats which BOAC operated between Britain, the USA and West Africa is shown by this photograph of two mechanics at work inside the nacelle of one of the four engines of a flying-boat being serviced at the BOAC base in Baltimore.

wheels-up landing 300 miles north of Bathurst when three of the four engines failed through faulty manipulation of the supplementary oil system, but a Sunderland flying-boat rescued the crew. The French salvaged the airliner and flew it to France, where it was seized by the Germans who substituted Daimler-Benz engines and used it as a transport.

But now Japan entered the war. On 7 December two waves of Japanese fighters and bombers put the entire US Pacific Fleet's battleship force in Pearl Harbour out of action, and that same evening Japan declared war against Britain and the USA. Within a fortnight the Japanese were attacking the Philippines, Burma, Borneo, and the British base at Hong Kong. When the invasion began, BOAC's director-general and the Indian regional director were almost trapped in Bangkok but escaped by chartering a Siamese aeroplane.

The contingency of the Japanese cutting the Horseshoe route had been foreseen. A reserve route through the Dutch East Indies was immediately initiated, but *Cassiopeia*, piloted by Capt C.E. Madge, was wrecked at Sabang in Sumatra on 29 December while taking off after refuelling and the four passengers were drowned. Next day the DCA in Burma suspended all flying-boat services pending use of a route avoiding Malaya by taking them further west and south through Sumatra and Java — but within a month the route proved impossible. Meanwhile Singapore was being increasingly bombed, and the stand-by staff at Airways headquarters were moved to Batavia from which Singapore was then served by a Qantas shuttle service, despite marauding Japanese fighter aircraft.

1942

January 1942 saw the mercantile pilots flying the most dangerous skies in the world. On the 30th, seven Zero fighters caught *Corio*, which had left Darwin at dawn. Its pilot, Capt A.A. Koch, dived to sea-level but the Zeros followed, maintaining accurate fire, killing most of the passengers. Wounded, and with two engines ablaze, Koch attempted to alight, but the sea rushed in through bullet holes and the flying-boat plunged nose down. Only by the determination of Capt Koch and one of the surviving passengers, who swam ashore, and reached Koepang to get help, were the other survivors saved.

For the time being the Horseshoe route was broken. The flying-boats were flown back to Broome, Australia, the last leaving Singapore in the bright moonlight of 4 February carrying 40 passengers. Four days later the first Japanese troops landed on the island, and on 15 February Singapore surrendered, its buildings blazing, a pall of smoke obliterating the sun.

For twelve more days the Australian pilots flew a supply shuttle between Broome and Tjilatjap in Java until the advancing Japanese made it impossible, and on 28 February the last two flying-boats, *Circe* and *Coriolanus*, left at dawn. They kept in radio touch for the first two hours — then nothing more was ever heard of *Circe*. Three days later while *Corinna* was being refuelled at Broome, where *Centaurus* and a dozen more RAAF flying-boats were moored, squadrons of Zeros dived down, and flying back and forth destroyed them all. Next, *Corinthian* crashed at Darwin, killing the pilot and two of the three passengers.

Such details were not revealed to the public. Reassuringly the Minister of Information said: 'Japanese successes in the Pacific can only be a flash in the pan. Mr, Churchill and Mr Roosevelt have been together in Washington to decide how the combined strengths of the British Empire and the United States can be brought to bear on this enemy.'

Certainly Churchill's return by BOAC flying-boat *Berwick* gained maximum publicity, though prior to the flight every subterfuge had kept it secret. Capt Kelly Rogers only learned the identity of his passenger at the last minute when instructed to fly the Boeing from Baltimore to Norfolk harbour, Virginia, accompanied by two Consolidated Clippers to carry the balance of the 90-strong retinue. Churchill arrived by special train from Washington and was installed in a private cabin, and his personal party of 25, which included Air Marshal Sir Charles Portal and LORD Beaverbrook, were disposed in the main cabin. Kelly Rogers lifted off into a light surface haze beneath a cloudless winter sky. Later the Prime Minister lit a cigar and tried the controls, and commented on the vast differences between this great flying-boat and the first aeroplane he had flown in 1913. Their destination was Bermuda for a conference with Admiral Sir Dudley Pound. At its conclusion Churchill said: 'Outside lies the *Duke of York* to take me to England which I can reach in seven days, but Kelly Rogers assures me that he can fly there in not more than twenty-two hours. Such a flight cannot be regarded as a war necessity, but it is a war convenience.' So he decided that if weather permitted he would fly next morning, if not, he would go by battleship.

Meteorological forecasts proved satisfactory. They took off for England with Kelly Rogers very much aware that this was the most important load of passengers he had ever carried and that disaster to the flying-boat would materially affect the course of war. But all went well. That evening Churchill and Beaverbrook again visited the control deck. 'We were riding through a brilliant starlit sky, with the outline of the cloud tops just visible below', Kelly Rogers later wrote. 'The Prime Minister surprised me by saying he envied me my job. All passengers went to bed that night except Beaverbrook, who sat reading the whole time. At dawn Churchill came to the flight deck to watch the sun rise, which seen from an aircraft is comparable to no other in the world.'

At this point Kelly Rogers began the long descent from 10,000 feet until 50 minutes later he was at 1,000 and approaching Land's End. Weather was closing in. Co-pilot Capt Shakespeare made the final approach to Plymouth using the automatic direction-finder. They crossed the breakwater at 50 feet and alighted at the RAF Station in the Cattewater. Before disembarking, Churchill had a statement prepared 'so that the world might be told I have been brought safely home by the British erchant Air Service'.

To supplement BOAC's dwindling fleet of Empire flying-boats, the two remaining G-class, *Golden Hind* and *Golden Horn*, were restored to the civil register, and on 18 July began service from Poole to Foynes, thence to Lisbon without refuelling, and so to the West

The Prime Minister, Winston Churchill, chatting with Captain Shakespseare, of BOAC's Boeing flying-boat *Berwick*.

African route at Bathurst for Freetown, Accra, and Lagos, carrying priority passengers and returning with European refugees from Lisbon.

By now the US Navy had fought the great sea battle of Midway Island, but could not prevent continuance of Japanese attacks in the Pacific, so it remained impossible to re-bridge the Horseshoe route. Meanwhile Qantas pilots began ferrying Catalinas across the Pacific to Australia where they plied by night, often through appalling weather, to New Guinea, ever at peril from Zero fighters.

Meanwhile BOAC's organization of the Atlantic RFS was expanding, and it was announced that 995 of every 1,000 aircraft had reached Great Britain. The Liberators, though heavy on the controls, noisy, cramped, and deadly cold, had proved splendidly reliable despite their nerve-racking long and laden take-off run. Experience with them in every kind of weather led BOAC to consider the prospects of post-war trans-Atlantic flying. Clive Pearson was endeavouring to induce Sir Archibald Sinclair, the Air Minister, to indicate official policy. That led to establishing a committee, chaired by Colonel Moore-Brabazon, to consider future types of airliners for trans-Atlantic, Empire, and internal routes — echoing the action initiated by Holt Thomas in the Great War of 1914–18. The nearest British approach to an airliner was a private venture development of the RAF's most successful bomber, the Avro Lancaster, fitted with a fully-windowed deep cabin fuselage designed and built in a mere five months. First flown on 5 July and named the York, it had a maximum speed of 298 mph and range of 2,700 miles.

BOAC hoped to obtain production machines but they were unlikely to be available for a year or more because Lancasters had priority. As always, the Corporation's financial affairs were hidden under a smokescreen. In the current Annual Report, Runciman merely disclosed that: 'The gross cost for services rendered to the Air Ministry and Ministry of Production is £6,199,064. After crediting revenue receivable, the net cost was £4,589,626. If the traffic revenue of £722,728 (which by agreement with the Air Ministry has been waived) and the £1,374,011 revenue for carriage of mail had accrued to the Corporation, the net cost of activities for the year would have been £2,492,887.'

Adding to the growing toll of BOAC aircraft lost by accident or enemy action *Calypso* was destroyed at Daru Harbour, New Guinea on 8 August. However *Coriolanus, Camilla,* and *Clifton*, marooned in Australia, were transferred to Qantas in exchange for *Carpentaria, Coorong,* and *Cooee,* still in India.

The D.H.86 *Delia* had been wrecked in a forced landing in Nigeria; the Lockheed *Livingstone* similarly at Khartoum; the Ensign *Enterprise* had forced-landed in Vichy French African territory, and *Euryalus* was wrecked at Lympne after attack by a Messerschmitt; a Liberator had been accidently shot down on the English coast; *Maia*, lower component of the *Mayo* composite, sank at moorings in Poole.

Two ex-British Airways Junker 52s had been sold to Sabena for use in Africa, and the 1932 vintage Armstrong Atalantas had been drafted to the Indian Air Force, but in April *Aurora*

force-landed in a swamp near Calcutta and could not be salvaged. On 28 August the prototype *Atalanta* swung off the runway at Madras, caught fire and was destroyed. To keep *Arethusa* and *Artemis* in service, *Astraea* was cannibalized for spares.

When the famous *Clare* failed to reach Bathurst after departure on 14 September the S.30 Empire boats were transferred from the West African route to the Durban–Congo route and replaced by six Sunderland IIIs converted to civil use, backed by Liberators on the UK–Lagos run.

In October the decisive Battle of El Alamein was being fought, and General Montgomery, Commander of the British Eighth Army, routed the Afrika Korps with a mighty combined operation in which the Germans lost 60,000 men, 1,000 guns and 500 tanks. 'Up to Alamein we survived', Churchill said. 'After Alamein we conquered.' While Rommel was carrying out his evacuation of Egypt, 'Operation Torch' began at the other end of North Africa with ship-borne landings of American forces attacking Casablanca and Oran, and the British

took Algiers. There was fierce fighting both by land and sea but France's anti-British Admiral Darlan surrendered on 11 November, and the capitulation led to German troops advancing into southern France to take over the powerful French Mediterranean Fleet in Toulon.

In Russia's bitter winter a pincer movement planned by Stalin and his generals trapped the German Sixth Army between Stalingrad and the Volga. Churchill deemed an air communications route to Moscow was essential, and Capt Percy of BOAC was delegated to make a survey using one of the Atlantic RFS Liberators. Taking off from Prestwick on the evening of 21 October, he headed in bright moonlight towards the Arctic Circle and northern Norway, then south across Finland to the Gulf of Bothnia and east again from Riga to cross the Russo-German lines in the dark and land at Moscow — a flight of thirteen hours and equivalent to an Atlantic crossing. Throughout that winter this direct north-about route was flown nine times, but after that first freezing flight the crews at least made certain they had electrically heated clothes!

But disasters continued with the flying-boats. On 1 December *Ceres* exploded and sank when being refuelled at her Durban moorings. A month later, *Golden Horn* crashed at Lisbon after a piston seized and fire broke out, resulting in steep descent to the Tagus which split the hull, and of the thirteen BOAC crew only the radio officer survived.

1943

The new dispositions of German forces necessitated another meeting between Churchill and Roosevelt in January 1943. On the 12th the Prime Minister, accompanied by Air Chief Marshal Sir Charles Portal, Chief of Air Staff, flew in his personal Liberator to Casablanca, where the American President, with Chiefs of Staff, arrived next day, having flown the Atlantic in a pressurized DC-4. They decided there could be no invasion of Europe for a considerable time, but invasion of Sicily was agreed. At a Press conference on 24 January Roosevelt caused a stir by stating that world peace could only be ensured by 'unconditional surrender' of

When BOAC took over the Atlantic Return Ferry Service from the RAF in 1941, seven fast ex-bomber Liberators proved invaluable in taking back to Dorval, Canada, the crews who had delivered American and Canadian-built aircraft to the UK.

Taken over from the RAF by Imperial Airways were 38 Lockheed Lodestars, which played their part in the great supplies back-up for the army in North Africa and the Middle East.

The pre-war Armstrong Whitworth Atalantas, built for the Middle East and African routes, played their war-time part initially with BOAC and then with the Indian Air Force.

Germany, Italy, and Japan. Next day he flew back to Washington via Lagos and Dakar, and afterwards Churchill flew via Egypt to the Turkish President at Adana, near the Turkish–Syrian frontier, hoping to persuade him to join the Allies, returning to Egypt from Cyprus on 2 February. Three days later he flew to Algiers to confer with Generals Eisenhower, Giraud, and de Gaulle, and on 7 February flew back to England.

What transpired remained a Cabinet secret, but Air Chief Marshal Sir Arthur Tedder was appointed Air C-in-C Mediterranean Command, with Middle East activities delegated to Air Chief Marshal Sir Sholto Douglas, with the RAF in Malta under Air Vice-Marshal Sir Keith Park, and an amalgamation of units from the Eastern and Middle East Command under Major-General Carl Spaatz USAAF, designated the North-West African Air Forces. A consequent outcome was what became known as 'The Tedder Plan' whereby all BOAC air-

craft in that area were made available to him at any time for any purpose not only on the trans-Africa route but throughout the Levant to Iraq. The organization devolved on R.H. Maxwell, BOAC's Near East regional director who set up an engineering base at Asmara, Eritrea, upon which the whole system of routes radiating from Cairo depended. Supplementing the long-haul Ensigns were RAF pilots flying Lockheed Lodestars to Turkey, Saudi Arabia, and Ethiopia.

There had been increasing signs of discord between BOAC and the Air Ministry in the early part of the year. Clive Pearson wrote to Sir Archibald Sinclair: 'As your appointed members, we are in an anomalous situation. Not being an independent concern, we have not the discretion in directing policy such as would rest with a commercial undertaking; while on the other hand, not being a branch of the public service, we have not the defined and regulated authority of a service of the Crown. The Board should be strengthened, and in particular the chairman should be one who at least informally would have access to the Ministers of the many government departments with which the activities of the Corporation are concerned. Can we be informed whether it is intended that the Corporation should remain the sole British instrument for overseas air transport, or if not what limitations are intended?'

A meeting followed on 1 March where Pearson was told that all BOAC operations would in future be subservient to Transport Command. Useless for Pearson to point out that the

RAF had not the Corporation's knowledge of airline work: the Minister at the behest of the RAF was adamant. Discussion reached an impasse. On 24 March Pearson threw in his hand and resigned, together with Walter Runciman, Harold Brown, and I.C. Geddes, but not Gerard d'Erlanger, who was away in connection with his duties as Commanding Officer of the Air Transport Auxiliary for which BOAC had responsibility for general administration, and it is possible that he was unaware of the crisis.

Bereft of directors, the departmental heads held a meeting and proposed that Reith, now a peer but out of office, should be reappointed chairman. The Air Minister brushed this aside 'whereupon the Secretary of State for Air, in exercise of the powers vested in him by the British Overseas Airways Act, appointed Sir Harold Howitt and Mr Simon Marks to be members of the Corporation and temporarily to be chairman and deputy chairman thereof respectively, and appointed Mr John Marchbank to be a member of the Corporation, such appointment taking effect as from 24 March 1943'. There was outcry in the Commons. Howitt was a financial expert without knowledge of aircraft, Marks was from the Marks family of Marks & Spencer, and Marchbank a former general secretary of the National Union of Railwaymen. Aubrey Burke, who had been loaned to the MoA since 1939, currently returned to BOAC and was appointed assistant director-general (technical).

The report of the Brabazon Committee was now revealed to the House by Lord Sherwood. The members, helped by BOAC, industrial, and Air Ministry technicians, had formulated not only aircraft matching the USA's current four-engined Douglas DC-4 and the recently tested Lockheed Constellation, but went far beyond with a 'giant' airliner of 100 tons all-up weight based on Air Staff specifications B.8/41 for a heavy bomber with top speed of 300 mph, and it was envisaged that 150 passengers would be accommodated by day or 75 in sleeping accommodation overnight. The project was allocated to the Bristol Aeroplane Co, and chief designer Leslie Frise, immediately set to work on what became the 230-ft span Brabazon 1. Even more breathtaking was a smaller multi-jet airliner capable of carrying sixty or more passengers for 3,000 miles cruising at 500 mph. As Geoffrey de Havilland was the chief instigator, the task was handed to his company. Of the

Left: Sir Geoffrey de Havilland. *Above:* Pauline Gower, pioneer British airwoman, shown in uniform during her service with the Air Transport Auxiliary.

other three recommended types, the first was an airliner of 50 tons weight, but no immediate order was placed though eventually it became the Bristol Britannia. Next was a twin-engined 36-seater to replace the Douglas DC-3, and this was handed to Arthur Hagg the pre-war de Havilland designer who had joined the DH Airspeed subsidiary in 1942 in charge of their design office. Last, there was a small twin-engined transport for which both Miles Aircraft Ltd and de Havilland's eventually initiated project designs.

BOAC was still suffering uneasy changes. Sir Harold Howitt had been chairing the Corporation less than two months when on 20 May he and Simon Marks vacated office and the Secretary of State for Air announced that 48-year-old ex-RAF pilot Viscount Knollys, DFC, managing director of the Employers Liability Assurance Corporation, had been appointed chairman, and that Howitt would be deputy chairman. Brig-Gen A.C. Critchley, DSO, ex-RFC and war-time organizer of preliminary training for RAF crews, but better known for greyhound racing, was designated director-general. Gerard d'Erlanger, Simon Marks, and John Marchbank remained members of the Board, which was now joined by Pauline Gower, whom d'Erlanger had earlier appointed Commandant of the women's section of ATA.

The Aeroplane of 28 May commented: 'One concludes that the Air Ministry discounts experience of air route operation and believes air transport will thrive on business management. Banker, accountant, multiple shop proprietor, trade union organizer, and a woman pilot now comprise the Board. Its policy will be carried into effect by an officer who in civil life was leader in a popular sport but may be a subtle method of obtaining startling results without appearing to plan them. The Air Ministry has no guarantee that the best things would be done or that things would be done in the best way. The difficulties which led to the resignation of the former directors still remain to be resolved.' They remained unresolved.

The Corporation's operations were becoming still more complex. The Atlantic ferry service increased from three return flights a week to four. To the Ensigns operating the Cairo to Lagos and Takoradi route were added Hudsons, soon replaced by five Dakotas, and the frequency increased to six services a week. The UK–Lagos run with Sunderlands increased from two return flights a week to three, and the *Golden Hind* resumed the Poole–Foynes shuttle service on 27 May, soon reinforced by Hudsons withdrawn from the Scandinavian run, which connected not only with BOAC's Boeing flying-boats but also the trans-Atlantic flights of Pan American Airways and American Export Air Lines.

A once-weekly service was operating between Cairo and Karachi using Ensigns transferred from the trans-African route, where they had become unnecessary because of the opening of the Mediterranean to Allied shipping. The ends of the Horseshoe route were about to be re-linked using four Catalina flying-boats fitted with auxiliary tanks. In April the first two were flown from Lagos to Australia for Qantas to operate direct from Perth in a 3,500-mile stage across the Indian Ocean to Ceylon, enabling a service to be commenced in July with a view to extension in November to Karachi with three services each fortnight.

The route to Russia was also changed, for the hazards had become too great, and it was agreed that BOAC should fly direct to Moscow by a Mediterranean route which Capt O.P. Jones pioneered with Mr Maisky, the Russian ambassador, aboard. From Cairo they flew to Habbaniya near Baghdad, then skirted the Caspian Sea to Kuibyshev, but on his return flight Capt Jones made for Teheran, and this became the adopted route flown by Liberators.

All air services continued to suffer a toll. On 1 June a KLM airliner, flying from Lisbon to Britain, was shot down by an enemy fighter after German Intelligence received erroneous information from Lisbon that Churchill, *en route* from Washington, was aboard. There were no survivors from the crew of four and thirteen passengers who included Leslie Howard, the famous actor. Nevertheless perils

did not deter King George VI flying on 10 June to north-west Africa and Malta in a bomber piloted by the Captain of the King's Flight, and flying back a fortnight later.

That was the prelude to airborne and seaborne landings on Sicily as the stepping-stone to Italy. On 19 July the first air raid on Rome was made by 158 Flying Fortresses of the American Strategic Air Force. Six days later the Fascist Grand Council placed King Victor Emmanuel in command of the Italian Armed Forces. Mussolini was arrested and Marshal Badoglio became Prime Minister. By 17 August all Sicily was occupied. Meanwhile Churchill sailed to Quebec aboard the *Queen Mary* to decide with Roosevelt that Operation Overlord, the projected invasion of France in 1944, should be under an American commander, and that Lord Louis Mountbatten would command the Burmese operations. Final plans seemed sealed when Italy unconditionally surrendered on 8 September and five days later declared war on Germany.

Despite the accelerated tempo of war, Britain's world of commercial aviation remained a priority. A memorandum to the Prime Minister from the SBAC defined three development stages: the immediate post-war period 'using aircraft derived from Service counterparts'; an interim phase 'four or five years hence with aircraft projected with some regard to the needs of actual airline operators'; and a period ten years distant 'using jet-propelled aircraft and related aerodynamic improvements', and the Society boldly stated that it was 'convinced that monopoly is inconsistent with the advancement of British civil aviation'.

Even the British Colour Council jumped on the band wagon with an exhibition featuring a mock-up interior of a wide-bodied air-conditioned airliner incorporating their own recommendations for restful colours giving a pleasing atmosphere whether in the tropics or cold northern latitudes, and intended to eliminate boredom, reduce the psychological tendency towards air sickness, and be easy to clean. In almost every aspect it foreshadowed the luxurious accommodation of the next generation of aircraft. The public crowded into this free entertainment.

The future requirements of air terminals were also being considered. Graham Dawbarn, architect of Gatwick, for which he proposed 6,000-ft runways, forecast that London would require airport facilities accommodating 10,000 passengers daily at traffic density of one aircraft every five minutes, and considered a single terminal would be insufficient. The DGCA, William Hildred, agreed that Croydon could never be developed into a superairport because there was insufficient space for the biggest transport aircraft which the post-war period would bring. Accordingly an area of 2,800 acres had been acquired which embraced Fairey's Great West aerodrome at Heathrow adjacent to Hounslow Heath of old.

By comparison, New York was building a huge airport on the outskirts of Idlewild, planned to handle 360 aircraft an hour on a complex of 10,000-ft runways. Meanwhile the USA Office of War Information was reviewing post-war use of available aircraft such as the Douglas DC-3 and DC-4, and particularly the Lockheed Constellation troop carrier. Already BOAC had conjectured on those possibilities and hoped the Government would abandon its obdurate pre-war policy that only indigenous British aircraft be used for the State airline. The Corporation was awaiting its Avro Yorks, but more immediately likely were Lancaster bomber freighters with faired noses, the first of which had recently flown from Montreal to Prestwick in a record 12½ hours. To gain experience of operational problems, Lord Knollys, accompanied by Campbell Orde, made an air tour of the Corporation's stations in the Middle East where he had discussions with the AOC-in-C, Air Marshal Sir Sholto Douglas, and Air Commodore Whitney Straight, the C.O. of RAF Transport Group, before proceeding to Palestine, the Sudan and Eritrea.

At an Empire Air conference in London chaired by Lord Beaverbrook and attended by representatives of the Dominions and India, it was agreed that a new International Convention was necessary to regulate air commerce between nations. In the Lords the Marquis of Londonderry demanded a Government statement of post-war civil aviation policy, to which Beaverbrook, as Lord Privy Seal, replied with veiled assurances. Advising him on aviation technicalities he now had a keen young journalist, Peter Masefield, lately of *The Aeroplane*. What with Sholto Douglas, Whitney Straight, and now Masefield, the auguries were mounting.

Air movements were now on a colossal scale, whether directly or indirectly for war purposes. Important officials were able to travel to distant places swiftly and relatively safely. When Lord

Wavell went to India it was by BOAC Sunderland, and Lord Linlithgow returned by the same means. In these adapted flying-boats, compartment 'B', formerly the crews' quarters, was now a pleasant cabin lined in grey hide and seating six in comfortable chairs convertible into two curtained bunks. The bomb compartment 'D' was similar but had three seats each side convertible into four bunks. Between the two cabins compartment 'C', originally pantry and drogue storage, had become a toilet and washroom with white doors. Next came a stateroom with two bunks, a desk and adjustable chair, curtained wardrobe and washbowl. Further aft was a complete pantry with electric kettle and refrigerator.

Meanwhile the bombs were raining down on Germany, and squadrons of Boeing B-29 Superfortresses were being organized to bomb Japan.

In preparation for the final great offensive Churchill arrived at Alexandria in HMS *Renown* on 21 November for a Cairo conference with Roosevelt and the Combined Chiefs of Staff. Six days later they flew by different routes from Egypt to meet Marshal Stalin at Teheran. On 1 December the three national leaders initialled a document stating that Operation Overlord would begin in May 1944.

1944

On the first day of 1944 monocled John Brancker, son of Sir Sefton, took over from Dennis Handover as traffic director of BOAC. He had joined Imperial Airways in 1929, became manager of the Continental section at the age of 27, and with the outbreak of war was in charge of BOAC's India and Burma regions, and latterly regional director for West Africa.

Later that month the BOAC development flight at Hurn received the first of its warpainted civil Lancasters (G-AGJI) with little enthusiasm because the fuselage capacity was even less than the Liberator and performance no better — but matters improved when five York twelve-seaters were delivered. 'I am convinced', said Lord Knollys, 'they will stand us in good stead as transports for post-war aviation.'

Once again Lord Londonderry returned to the attack in the Lords. 'British Overseas Airways Corporation is entitled to a testimony for the remarkably good work it has accomplished', he said, 'but I feel that the usefulness of this monopoly instrument is coming to an end. If we adopt a policy of one "chosen instrument" we shall be placing a restrictive influence on all private enterprise, so the Act of 1939 must be repealed.'

There was due discussion in which Viscount St Davids favoured an international company with all countries as shareholders; Lord Mottistone urged separation of civil aviation from the Air Ministry; the Duke of Sutherland revealed that not only two prototype airliners but a big flying-boat had been ordered; Viscount Rothermere hoped questions of ideology would not decide whether airlines should be public or private; and Lord Strabolgi emphasized that there could not be an independent Empire air service linking all the Colonies and Dominions without the collaboration of other nations — thus the quickest way to Australia was not the existing route but required Russian collaboration for a Great Circle course through Moscow to Chungking. Recalling how the Persian Government compelled the Imperial air route to be transferred to the other side of the Persian Gulf, his lordship said: 'We are not going to tolerate any nonsense of that kind in the future'.

The Lord Privy Seal denied that BOAC was

a monopoly. It had a monopoly of subsidies for overseas traffic but nothing else. If other companies, air or shipping, wanted to run air services overseas without subsidies BOAC had no statutory rights to prevent them. He added: 'The design of the Bristol Brabazon has begun and the prototypes are on order — but do not expect a swift conclusion because years must pass before a type so completely new can be brought from the drawing board to the traffic route. For that reason a project for another type with all-up weight of 32 tons has been launched. It will have a cruising speed of 220 mph and will be fitted with de-icing means and constructed suitably for pressurization carrying twelve passengers. This aircraft is the Avro Tudor.'

Beaverbrook concluded: 'I am asked to make a statement about the operations of BOAC. I cannot do so; I am not entirely familiar with the operation of BOAC; but I can say it is under able and competent management. I have spoken to Lord Knollys, and I am convinced that wise and able direction will be obtained under is care.'

Coincidentally Knollys broadcast a talk on BOAC's activities, pointing out that it had 50,000 miles of air routes on which their aircraft

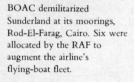

BOAC demilitarized Sunderland at its moorings, Rod-El-Farag, Cairo. Six were allocated by the RAF to augment the airline's flying-boat fleet.

flew 12½ million miles in the past year, and a staff of 15,000 were employed. After describing wartime operations he pictured a typical post-war journey flown at 20,000 to 30,000 feet cruising at 240 mph, and stressed there must be international machinery 'to settle where aircraft shall fly and where passengers may be picked up and set down'. As to being the 'chosen instrument', the British instinct for making apparently illogical schemes work would find a practical solution. BOAC looked upon itself as trustee for British air services abroad and had 'no excessive ambitions to run all air services ourselves — or by ourselves'.

That there was interest beyond that of BOAC in establishing commercial air routes was indicated in February when British Latin-American Air Lines Ltd (BLAAL) was registered with the backing of five British shipping companies operating sea routes to South America who intended to inaugurate air services across the equatorial Atlantic 'as soon as the necessary consents and aircraft can be obtained'. BOAC retaliated by announcing its readiness to start a South Atlantic air service. BLAAL retorted that it regarded that sea as the time-honoured field of the shipping companies, to which General Critchley replied: 'Well, perhaps they have had it too long'. There were current rumours that Don Bennett, now Air Vice-Marshal, intended to retire from the RAF to take up an appointment with the new airline, but he tactfully denied this.

With five Avro Yorks available, BOAC inaugurated the first UK–Cairo route via Morocco on 22 April, and after withdrawal of Sunderlands from the West African route initiated a weekly service from the UK to Lagos using Dakotas. Two months later the Dakota service to Algiers was extended to Cairo with up to fifteen journeys a week. On the Middle East operations nine Ensigns were operating twice-weekly from Cairo to Calcutta via the Persian Gulf, and a Sunderland shuttle service to Karachi was temporarily helping to carry the great load of stores accumulating at Cairo.

After the fall of Singapore, BOAC's seven consolidated Catalina 'lease-lend' flying-boats gave yeoman service in maintaining the eastern end of the 'Horseshoe' route to Australia by flying non-stop across the Indian Ocean between Perth and Ceylon, successfully making 271 crossings.

There was also a weekly passenger mail service from Cairo to Karachi via the Hadramaut coast, using Lodestars from a pool of nineteen which were operating regular services to Gwelo, Nairobi, and Cairo, Teheran, Aden, Addis Ababa, and Asmara. On the Qantas Perth to Karachi route across the Indian Ocean two Liberators were being used because of their greater capacity, and until more became available they were augmented by one Catalina service a week.

The European war was nearing its conclusion. 6 June was D-Day when Operation Overlord, leading to the liberation of Occupied Europe, began. A mighty armada of 4,000 Allied ships converged upon the beaches of Normandy under cover of huge naval and RAF support. By evening 145,000 soldiers were ashore, and by the end of the week 300,000 held a bridgehead 50 miles wide. At the beginning of July nearly a million troops were in France, and within the next month the number doubled. Against them Germany was mustering a quarter of its entire army, led by Field Marshal von Rundstedt.

Soon after D-Day, London experienced a new form of attack when the first V.1 flying bombs were launched from the Pas-de-Calais. Their continuation did not prevent a BOAC luncheon on 25 August to celebrate the 25th anniversary of the beginning of British airline services. Knollys read a congratulatory telegram from the King; then the Secretary of State for Air 'indulged in some of his rhetoric without getting beyond clichés and generalities'. Star of the occasion was Lord Brabazon of Tara who jovially advised the Minister to visit America to see what was being done there. 'You are being manoeuvred off the earth', he said.

In September there was some surprise at the resignation of Aubrey Burke — but it soon transpired that he had accepted chairmanship of the newly formed de Havilland Engine Co which was designing a new jet-turbine for the proposed jet airliner.

That month came larger V.2 rocket bombs of great destructive power — but by now the Germans had been driven back to the old Siegfried Line in the Rhineland. On 1 October the Germans in Calais surrendered. A week later Churchill flew to Moscow by the BOAC Mediterranean route for discussions with Stalin on the conduct of the war and the future of Poland.

Viscount Swinton had just been appointed Minister for Civil Aviation. This was regarded as a clever move, for it defeated critics of the Government's alleged neglect of civil aviation. Nevertheless there was a flurry of questioning in the Commons and the Lords, during which Lord Balfour of Burleigh revealed that the combined British railway companies had delivered to the Government an airline scheme conditionally operated without subsidy if no others were subsidized in competition. Maps and timetables showed a network covering not only Great Britain but extending across all Europe to the Baltic, the entire Mediterranean, and to Moscow. Their war-time services had certainly been effective for they had operated 80 per cent of the total mileage of internal British air communications, flying six million miles carrying a quarter-million passengers.

Within a few days came the first intimation of British Government policy in the form of a White Paper on post-war Civil Aviation, but provoked further contention because it was virtually an irrevocable brief outlining the action British delegates must take at the forthcoming Chicago Conference in November when proposing a new Air Convention to replace those of 1919 and 1928. However Sir Arthur Sinclair, the Secretary of State for Air, admitted that Lord Swinton had not even been consulted about the policy that was now his duty to argue at the Conference.

12 November saw the reinstatement of Railway Air Services' civilian role in the guise of Olley Air Services, operating DH 86 four-engined airliners between Croydon, Liverpool (Speke), the Isle of Man, and Belfast — the first to be resumed since war began. Concurrently Jersey Airways Ltd announced that they were opening a London office, and Scottish Aviation Ltd were equally quick to argue for establishment of their own unsubsidized global air service based on Prestwick Airport, even quoting £80 return fare to New York.

1945

BOAC's maintenance problems were certainly complex. Currently 169 aircraft of nineteen different types fitted with nineteen different types of engine were in use. The Armstrong Atalantas, two DH 91 Frobishers and the prototype Ensign had been scrapped and the other Ensigns were causing big problems of routine maintenance and overhaul, and Cyclone engine spares for them were almost unobtainable. At the beginning of 1945 the Cairo representative of the Air Registration Board recommended that the fleet be withdrawn, and a long wrangle began between the Air Ministry and BOAC in London and the pilots and engineers in Egypt— so the much-criticized Ensigns soldiered on while BOAC tried to obtain replacement Liberators.

By late January Eisenhower had pushed the Germans from the bulge in the Allied line and the Russians had moved deep into Eastern Germany, so the British aircraft industry felt freer to concentrate on the Brabazon designs; but in America the 141-ft span Boeing 377 Stratocruiser was far larger, more commodious and powerful than the British Tudor and Hermes bomber-descendants which still had to be built. Pre-war American research on pressurization had been put to good effect in the spacious two-deck layout of the Stratocruiser which cruised at 310 mph and had a range of 4,000 miles. Nevertheless the British were not lacking in knowledge of pressurization, for Westland Aircraft Ltd had developed a successful system for their secret Welkin fighters which was applicable to airliners.

In the Commons, Lord Swinton reported on the Chicago Conference, but its involved details were essentially affirmation of the doctrine of sovereignty of air space. A week later Clement Attlee, Lord President of the Council, stated: 'Pending the passage of the necessary legislation, the powers necessary for the control of civil aviation and the BOAC will be delegated by the Secretary of State for Air to the Minister for Civil Aviation, subject to a proviso that in matters affecting the conduct of the war the Secretary of State for Air will continue to have the right to give directions'.

A few days later Churchill flew from Northolt to Malta where he met Roosevelt, who arrived by sea on 2 February, and the two leaders, with 700 Chiefs of Staff and advisers, then flew to Yalta in the Crimea for a conference with Stalin to decide the future of Europe and world peace.

On 13 March the White Paper confirming the Government's policy for Civil Aviation was issued and defined three national airline bodies, of which the North Atlantic and Commonwealth routes including trunk lines to China and the Far East would be operated by BOAC in association with shipping lines. An agreed schedule of European and internal routes would be assigned to a new company comprising railways, short-haul shipping, travel agencies, and BOAC together with pre-war operators wishing to participate. 'The European and internal air routes are likely to be more lucrative than some of the Commonwealth routes assigned to BOAC as the direct operating Corporation. The Government therefore think it right that the financial interest of BOAC in the new Corporation should be assessed in the light of this as well as the technical contribution it can make. While it is not proposed that BOAC should have a majority holding in the new Corporation, it is intended that its interests should be substantial.' The South American route would be assigned to the British shipping lines associated as British Latin-American Air Lines Ltd in which BOAC would participate in the capital and management, 'but its share in the capital will be smaller than that for the Corporation responsible for the European and internal services'.

The White Paper made clear that once the Corporation and subsidiary companies were established and the Boards appointed or approved by the Minister, the cardinal principle was that each would be responsible for the operation and management of the air service under its individual control, but the Minister would have general control over broad aviation policy.

There would be tremendous spadework for the two new companies, but BOAC had the overwhelming advantage of established engineering and operational bases across the world run by men who gave outstanding service. The number of administrative, operational, and maintenance staff now totalled nearly 22,000. The biggest overseas engineering concentration, employing 2,000, was the Alamaza landplane base 60 miles from the Sunderland base at Kasfareit on the Suez Canal. The Heliopolis workshop, originally a maintenance depôt for the African route, had become a main aircraft repair centre, and in one month alone put into service 250 overhauled RAF aircraft. In England the BOAC factories at Bath had overhauled 22,500 RAF propellers including variable-pitch units, and the Treforest factories in Wales had rebuilt 8,250 twin-row Bristol radial engines and salvaged many spares.

The BOAC operational set-up comprised four main departments: technical, administration, commercial, and finance — all based in London. Each route had its own superintendent responsible to a local director supervised by the director-general of each region, of which there were six: European with H.Q. in London; India and Burma with Karachi as H.Q.; Middle East based on Cairo; Central Africa at Nairobi; South Africa at Durban, and West Atlantic centred on Baltimore for the entire North and South American continents, Greenland, and the West Indies.

Nevertheless war-time BOAC did not operate as a commercial enterprise. The Secretary of State for Air had directed that the net cost of transport services was chargeable to the Air Ministry, and currently amounted to £5,700,000 in a total expenditure of £9,400,000, excluding £3,600,000 for fleet obsolescence. As an offset it was estimated that £10,900,000 was nominally earned for carriage of mails, but in any case the British Overseas Airways Act of 1939 provided for a yearly subsidy up to £4,000,000 for fifteen years if expenditure exceeded revenue.

But what did it matter now that the war was almost won? The last bombs and rockets had fallen on England, and the Prime Minister had flown to Montgomery's headquarters at Venlo, near the Dutch frontier, to witness the triumphant first crossing of the Rhine by the Allies. On 12 April Roosevelt died, and Harry Truman became President. Meanwhile bombs were raining down on the principal cities of Japan. Amid the chaos Sir Stafford Cripps moved the second reading of a Bill setting up the Ministry of Civil Aviation. Concurrently BOAC's Atlantic Return Ferry Service completed the 1,500th flight.

On 28 April Mussolini was captured by Communist partisans. Next day he was murdered by them, and in an air-raid shelter under the Berlin Chancellory Hitler committed suicide.

On 8 May came unconditional surrender of the German Forces. At enormous cost, victory at last!

By the end of hostilities BOAC had flown more than 57 million miles, uplifted nearly 50 million lbs of cargo and mail, and carried 280,000 passengers. Its fleet numbered 160 of many different kinds of aircraft and the route network spanned 54,000 miles.

But there was still Japan to defeat. The Socialists refused to continue the Coalition any longer, and on 23 May Churchill tendered resignation of the Cabinet he had led since 10 May, 1940. For the time being he agreed to a

'caretaker' government until the General Election in July.

The prospect of continued flying-boat use seemed established by successful flights of the 150-ft span, 56-ton Short Shetland which dwarfed the now commonplace Sunderlands. The production version would have two decks accommodating 50 passengers in a double-bubble pressurized hull. As an example of British aeronautical engineering this marine monoplane was magnificent — but would post-war BOAC be able to afford it?

Meanwhile *Golden Hind* was withdrawn from the Kisumu–Madagascar service for overhaul at Poole, but more than a dozen Empire boats were in use augmented by the Sunderlands.

The Brabazon Committee also approved a Vickers rival to the ubiquitous Douglas DC-3 using Wellington bomber wings and a metal-skinned commodious fuselage, seating six passengers in a fore cabin and fifteen in the aft. 'The Vickers Viking is an aircraft of which we are likely to see a great deal on the Continental air routes in the coming years of peace', prognosticated *Flight*. Even more interesting was a Vickers follow-up project for a 24-seater powered with four propeller-turbines, and a meeting on 14 March between the Ministries of Aircraft Production and Civil Aviation with representa-

tives of BOAC and Railway Air Services led to an MoS order for prototypes known as the Brabazon IIB and later named Viscount.

Pending Parliamentary approval of the new Corporations Bill, BOAC and its partner Qantas were reorganizing the England to Australia route. A weekly service, at last open to the public, was inaugurated at the end of May using adapted Avro Lancastrians which covered the 12,000 miles between Hurn and Sydney in 63 hours instead of the pre-war nine days, thus being the fastest as well as the longest route in the world.

The House of Commons now went into committee on the Civil Aviation White Paper and finally agreed that the Government's newly created 'instrument', British European Airways Corporation, would operate the European services, and those to South America were assigned to British Latin-American Air Lines.

The first formal conference of the Commonwealth Air Transport Council, which had originated in Montreal, held its opening session in London in July, attended by massed representatives including Lord Knollys and Major McCrindle on behalf of BOC. Lord Swinton, as Minister of Civil Aviation, was elected President. A week of debate led to agreement on Empire partnership operating the trunk routes. Each route required separate treatment

because different partners were involved, but the UK was concerned on every route. Because the Chicago Conference had failed to agree on some form of control to prevent unfair competition, every nation would have to negotiate separately with the countries whose territory they wished to use, so each international air route would be subject to bi-lateral agreements. Said Lord Swinton: 'The same kind of agreement we of the Commonwealth make together we will gladly make with other countries and, in so doing, make the highways of the air the ways of peace and friendship for all nations'.

But now the most devastating event of world history took place. On 6 August an atomic bomb was dropped on Hiroshima in Japan, destroying half the city and causing 80,000 deaths. Three days later a second bomb dropped on the naval base at Nagasaki. On 10 August Tokyo radio broadcast that the Japanese Government would accept peace terms provided the Emperor's prerogatives were not prejudiced. There was qualified reply from the USA, Britain, Russia and China. British and American carrier-borne aircraft continued to attack military targets, and the Russians bombed railways in Manchuria. On 14 August the Japanese accepted unconditional surrender, and on 2 September the terms were signed aboard the American battleship *Missouri* in Tokyo Bay.

Avro Type 691 was a 'civil' converted Lancaster bomber given the name Lancastrian C. Mk 1. Twenty-three were initially built for the RAF, 21 of which were transferred to BOAC in 1945. Of 33 Mk 2s, three went to BOAC and five to Skyways.

Picking up
the Pieces
1945-49

It was Clement Attlee who faced the problems of peace, for Labour ousted Churchill in the July election. In the following month Lord Winster succeeded Lord Swinton as Minister, and began modifying the draft Civil Aviation Act. Faced with controversial legislation and chaotic finance BOAC was attempting to rationalize its fleet, now totalling 207 British and American aircraft of which ten types were landplanes and seven were flying–boats. The DC–3 Dakotas would be used for the European services until the Vickers Viking airliner version of the Wellington bomber became available. The prototype had flown on 22 June, a week before the pressurized Avro Tudor of which twenty were under construction for BOAC.

September celebrated the fourth anniversary of the Corporation's supremely successful Atlantic Return Ferry Service. Some 1,750

Inset: One of the many types of military aircraft that were converted for civil use at the end of the war was the Halifax bomber, which became the ten-passenger Halton.

trans-Atlantic crossings had been made carrying 20,000 priority passengers, 600 tons of freight and 1,000 tons of mail, and the long haul was still a vital requirement.

Back to BOAC on 15 October came a familiar figure of pre-war Imperial Airways days — Herbert Brackley, now Air Commodore. He had been outstanding as Air Marshall Bowhill's chief organizer in Coastal Command, and then became his senior Air Staff Officer in RAF Transport Command, organizing many flights abroad of VIP officials, including Churchill, and in that capacity kept in close touch with Knollys to whom he now became transport adviser. Within a day he was sent on a mission to Baghdad, and on return became fully immersed in BOAC's activities.

Air services began re-opening to the public. The Chancellor of the Exchequer, Dr Hugh Dalton, announced on the 18th that a foreign currency allowance of £100 per adult and £50 for children would be permitted for travel outside the sterling area. Imperial Airways and Air France restored the Paris–London service; American overseas airlines inaugurated their North Atlantic route with four-engined Douglas DC-4s. To match them, pending development of the Tudor, BOAC applied for authority to purchase Lockheed Constellations from the USA.

For those in the British air transport business 1 November was crucial, for Lord Winster announced that the Socialist Government had decided public ownership would be the over-ruling principle for the inherited Coalition plan of two additional airline Corporations to operate internal and European routes in one case, and services to South America for the other. BOAC was allocated the Commonwealth, North Atlantic, and Far East services, but would handle all routes until the New Corporations were respectively formed as British Euro-

An aerial view of Heathrow airport, London, under construction.

Accompanied by Lord Winster, Minister of Civil Aviation, Lady Winster christens the first Halton conversion for BOAC with the name *Falkirk*. Twelve were used for the UK–Cairo/Karachi and UK–West Africa and trans-Sahara services.

pean Airways and South American Airways (the offspring of British Latin-American Airlines). It was disquieting that legislation would take a long time, for that gave competitors opportunity to become established.

This did not debar agreement with South Africa, and on 10 November, BOAC, in conjunction with South African Airways (SAA), opened its first post-war Empire service with the Johannesburg 'Springbok' route. Bi-lateral agreements followed between Britain and Greece, Portugal, New Zealand, Canada— and to control matters the International Air Transport Association (IATA) was re-established in December to promote safe and economical operations, rate-fixing, collaboration on international services, and co-operation with the International Civil Aviation Organization (ICAO) formed late in 1944 to ensure strict regulation of airworthiness, airfield and navigational standards, and similar international adjuncts of air transport.

In Britain the process of demobilization and restoration of normal civilian life was proceeding with far fewer problems than after the First World War — but food and clothes remained rationed, and there were frustrating restrictions on many supplies.

1946

On New Year's day 1946 the war-time ban on civilian flying was lifted. Every one could take to the skies again, but with improved facilities, for 21 radio stations were available, and 35 airfields had the war-time Beam Approach

system, lights and beacons. A simple airway zoning pattern reduced risk of collision in bad weather. Every aspect of civil aviation was now the responsibility of Sir Henry Self, who became DGCA when William Hildred resigned to become director-general of IATA.

Heathrow, now transferred to the MCA, was a sea of mud slowly being transformed into London's civil airport but required £25 million to complete and as yet had only one runway as long as 3,000 yds, superimposed on the unfinished RAF triangle of shorter runways. The European Division of BOAC running the Paris, Brussels and Amsterdam services was therefore based at the nearby RAF aerodrome of Northolt, and BOAC's Empire and Atlantic services operated from war-time Hurn in the heathlands east of Bournemouth.

As an expression of disbelief in the Government's plans, Brig-Gen Critchley resigned on 10 January as director-general of BOAC. *Flight* commented: 'It would be idle to pretend that we feel his departure spells ruin. However we are greatly intrigued by his claim that during his three years of office the financial affairs of the Corporation changed from a deficit of £2,300,000 to a surplus of £1,500,000. If these figures mean what they seem, critics have done him great wrong, and he has well earned his salary and expenses.' Two months after resigning, Critchley became the effective owner of Skyways Ltd, registered in 1929 but dormant until revived on 12 March by Sir Alan Cobham with £1,000, increased by £49,000 from Critchley as managing director with expectation of making this a large transport business.

Lord Knollys remained chairman of BOAC, the Board comprising financial expert Sir Harold Howitt as deputy chairman; Lord Burghley, the Olympic hurdler and war-time MAP controller of aircraft repairs; Brig-Gen Sir Harold Hartley, the chairman of Railway Air Services; Gerard d'Erlanger, whose valiant ATA had just been disbanded; Major J.R. McCrindle, formerly managing director of British Airways Ltd and for the past five years deputy director-general of BOAC; the Hon John Marchbank; T.M. Garro-Jones, a barrister and chairman of the television advisory committee; Clement Wakefield Jones, director of Alfred Booth & Co Ltd; and Major Roland H. Thornton, member of the Brabazon committee and director of a shipping firm.

At the end of January, when British Latin-American Airlines was taken over by BOAC, its originator John Booth became chairman, with Air Vice-Marshal Don Bennett as chief executive. Organization of the embryonic British European Airways was allocated to BOAC directors Sir Harold Hartley and Gerard d'Erlanger as future chairman and chief executive. Concurrently the Government lifted the ban on purchase of foreign aircraft and also announced that the BEA division of BOAC would take over the Douglas DC-3s and crews of No 110 Wing, RAF Transport Command, which had operated services to Europe. On 31 January BOAC re-opened the flying-boat service to Singapore with Short Sunderlands operating from Poole via Biscarosse, France; Augusta, Sicily; Cairo; Habbaniya, Iraq; Bahrein; Karachi; Calcutta; Rangoon.

Lecturing to the Institute of Transport, Lord Knollys reviewed the vital airline requirements of safety, regularity, comfort, cost, frequency, and service, emphasizing that aircraft only earned money when in the air and that air transport was on the threshold of dramatic speed increase whereby New York would be reached in six hours and Johannesburg in fourteen. That would bring new problems such as pressurization for flying at great heights and even the confusion of space and time whereby passengers leaving London at lunchtime arrived at lunchtime the same day in New York. As to frequency: 'Passengers do not always want to book, but want to arrive at an airport and catch the next service'. An IATA conference at Bermuda that month established that all countries would have the right to pick up and set down passengers anywhere on international routes in accordance with defined principles of bilateral agreements. An initial schedule was established of routes with mutual interest for the UK and USA to be operated at fares established by IATA to prevent a price war. Agreement was next reached with France, and others were in process with Scandinavia, Australia, and New Zealand.

At this stage BOAC on 10 March withdrew their three famous war-time Boeing 314 flying-boats, each of which had made some 200 trans-Atlantic flights and flown over one million miles in the course of $4\frac{1}{2}$ years. They would be replaced by Constellations, for the Tudor had problems. At an Avro conference on 12 March the Corporation insisted on nearly 350 changes of layout and décor, completely disordering production. The new British South American Airways also expected to operate Tudors, but meanwhile inaugurated a twice-weekly service to Buenos Aires on 15 March with their fourteen-seat Lancastrian *Star Trail*, and when their 21-passenger Yorks were delivered six weeks later, the service flew three times a week.

However none of the British Corporations managed to be first to use Heathrow, officially London Airport, when it opened to international traffic on 31 May, for they were pipped at the post by two Constellations from Pan American and American Overseas Airlines carrying their respective senior executives, who seemed undismayed by the encampment of tents and caravans provided for passengers and offices. However, next day a BOAC Lancastrian arrived from Sydney, two hours ahead of schedule, having flown 12,000 miles in $63\frac{1}{4}$ hours. A fortnight later, BOAC's first Constellation, *Balmoral*, piloted by Capt W.S. May, flew from New York to London in a record 11 hr 24 min for the 3,520-mile Atlantic crossing.

A glance at the flight deck of a Constellation revealed that pilots were dealing with far more

Star Trail, which crashed at Bathurst, Gambia in September 1947. Though uneconomic to operate, eighteen Lancastrian 3s were ordered by BSAAC for the South Atlantic route, but six encountered disaster and the others were sold by BOAC after absorbing BSAAC.

involved techniques than in pre-war days, though they were well acquainted with American control and instrument layouts through their war experience with Liberators. The war-trained newcomers seemed almost a class apart from the old-timers engaged with flying-boats or operating in the tropics. All would now have to conform to new procedures of cockpit drill, precise engine cruise control to obtain maximum range; instead of dead-reckoning and radio loop bearings there was accurate indication in a single instrument of the radio beacons, and exact location in space was obtained by the hyperbolic Loran navigation system based on time interval between two radio signals. On the horizon of the future there was a phase comparison system of Decca and the advanced Doppler which would indicate drift, ground speed, and distance flown. To ensure the requisite standard, BOAC and BEA formed Airways Training Ltd at Aldermaston, Berks. Meanwhile pilots of the Atlantic Ferry were allocated to the Constellations, and on 1 July the London–New York service was opened by Capt J.G. Percy flying from London, and on the 3rd Capt O.P. Jones flew the reverse run from New York. Almost immediately the US Civil Aeronautics Board grounded the Constellations for 30 days while investigating a fatal accident to a TWA machine in the USA because of a Cyclone engine fire. The hold-up hardly affected the Americans because Douglas DC-4s could be substituted, but BOAC could only resort to Lancastrians. (Three weeks later BEA had its first fatal accident when a Dakota on the Oslo run crashed into a hill in fog, killing four of the crew and injuring one, and three passengers.) To replace the Dakotas, particularly for the Karachi and West Africa routes twelve civil Halton versions of the Handley Page Halifax were ordered, and on 15 April the contract was signed for 50 Vickers Vikings already in advanced production.

Change from regional organization to divisional was now introduced by BOAC because each route employed a specific type of aircraft based on England whereas previously several types had been used over various sections of any given route. Three divisions were therefore established: Africa and Middle East managed by Keith G. Granville who had joined Imperial Airways in 1929; the Atlantic and North American continent by Vernon G. Crudge who

joined in 1924; and the Eastern route from UK to New Zealand by John Wood of the original British Airways Ltd. Lord Knollys had explained that the Civil Aviation Bill would in no way limit freedom of management and that there was provision for joint consultation between staff and management, but almost immediate dispute followed when the British Aeronautical Engineers Association sought recognition in a move to forestall the Amalgamated Engineering Union declaring the airline a 'closed shop' with employment conditional upon membership of a union affiliated to the TUC.

On 26 July Sir Harold Hartley outlined BEA's departmental reorganization, He had been joined by wealthy 35-year-old Air Commodore Whitney Straight as deputy chairman, thus acquiring a dynamic man whose pre-war experience of operating domestic airlines, flying clubs, and aerodromes was unique, and his wartime activities courageous and exemplary. Under d'Erlanger departments had been formed to deal with policy, planning, trading, research and development, the latter under N.E. Rowe, former DGTD at the MAP. Operations had been organized into two divisions — a UK group managed by Lieut-Cdr G.O. Waters of pre-war Railway Air Services and Jersey

Airways; for Continental services an equivalent section was managed by Lieut-Cdr Anthony Milward, latterly of wartime MAP. There was difficulty in housing the staff but Bourne School adjoining Northolt aerodrome was acquired as offices, though some departments had to be housed in RAF caravan trailers. The fleet became a mixed bag of Vikings, Dakotas, Ju 52s, and Rapides with the intention of operating 50 routes.

By contrast, BOAC in addition to the Empire routes expected to operate Avro Tudors across the North Atlantic, though Knollys publicly said: 'We shall require a subsidy on every flight. The bigger the share of the North Atlantic business we win, the bigger the bill the British taxpayer must pay. If it were a straight commercial undertaking, the Tudor would not be a good proposition.'

Some wondered whether that also applied to the gigantic six-engined Saunders-Roe Princess flying-boat airliner weighing more than 100 tons. The Corporation still had Hythe civil versions of the Short Sunderland, and the MCA had ordered twelve civil variants of the RAF's Seaford, known as the Solent-class, intended for the UK/Far East and East Africa routes. The Poole base would soon be abandoned and operations revert to the old slipway at Hythe where

docking facilities were being modernized to accommodate two flying-boats at the end of a 1,000-ft pier. In August the Hythes extended the Empire route to Hong Kong.

Key to the future was the Civil Aviation Bill explicitly stating: 'It shall not be lawful for any person, other than the three Corporations and their associates to carry passengers or goods by air for hire or reward upon any scheduled journey between two places of which one is in the United Kingdom'. Of these, British Overseas Airways (BOAC) was allocated £50 million capital; £20 million for British European Airways (BEA); and £10 million for British South American Airways (BSAA). Despite amendments and debates the Bill was steered through the report stage on 11 July, and the third reading completed two hours later, leaving only the final procedure for enactment 'by the King's Most Excellent Majesty' on 1 August.

The new Boards were immediately announced. That of BOAC was reduced to seven with the retirement of Sir Harold Hartley, Gerard d'Erlanger, John Marchbank and Wakefield Jones, while that of BEA was affirmed as Sir Harold Hartley the chairman, Whitney Straight, Gerard d'Erlanger, I.J. Hayward, and that of BSSA was John Booth, J. Stevenson the MAP Labour adviser, Air Vice-Marshal Don Bennett, Sir Edwin Plowden the ex-chief executive of MAP, and G.M. Shepherd, an executive in South America.

The Aeroplane commented: 'No scheme of private enterprise could carry the whole heavy burden of aviation as successfully as an enterprise financed by the State — but we have to be persuaded that the enormous edifice, pyramidical in conception, is going to travel at supersonic speeds which are the target of every aircraft designer'.

Paramount among such designers was the de Havilland technical team to whom the 500 mph jet airliner Brabazon project had been allocated during the war. Several configurations had been investigated, leading to a swept-wing, tail-less design with four Ghost engines but resolved into a more orthodox aeroplane with slight sweep-back and conventional tail — the basic Comet. But now in August the project crystallized, and on 4 September the MOS placed an order for two prototypes. BOAC still had some queries, but on 26 September Sir Geoffrey de Havilland and his chief engineer C.C. Walker clarified by telephone the final points so that detail design could proceed.

Elegantly indicative of economically viable airliners was the splendid Lockheed 049E Constellation, of which BOAC bought five to inaugurate the first regular British post-war service to New York in July 1946.

Feet
Metres

Top: Avro 691 Lancastrian 1, to the same scale as its derivative (*right*) the Avro 685 York.

Above: Limited production of the Avro Type 685 York as a VIP transport began in 1943, and large-scale production followed in 1945–48 for RAF/BOAC joint services, BSAA and others. The last BOAC Yorks were withdrawn in November 1957 but in thirteen years the fleet had flown 44 million miles and carried 90,000 passengers.

Next evening de Havilland's eldest son paid the toll of research when the DH 108 tail-less jet-aircraft he was flying broke up while exploring high-speed effects. Presently research continued with a second prototype to pave the way for the Comet of which fourteen were ordered by BOAC at a fixed price.

But there were other setbacks. On 7 August, BEA had its first post-war fatal accident when a Dakota on the Oslo run forced landed in fog. Nor was BOAC immune. On 23 August the BOAC Sandringham *Bahrein* crashed while alighting at night after a flight from Karachi, the machine bouncing nose down, then swung violently to port and tore off the starboard planing bottom, drowning three of the crew and seven passengers, though the captain survived to take the blame.

At the beginning of September the ban on Constellations was lifted, permitting restoration of the thrice-weekly BOAC New York service coincident with the introduction of BEA's Vickers Viking on the Scandinavian service when Capt James flew *Valerie* to Copenhagen. This type marked the beginning of a new safety aspect, for the Viking was the first to comply with the recently agreed ICAO requirement for take-off ability with one engine stopped. On

3 September the London–Stavanger–Oslo thrice-weekly service with Vikings commenced and also a twice-daily service to Amsterdam for which the fare was £14 8s return.

Two days later BOAC at last received the first of the twenty Avro Tudor Is which had been delayed some sixteen months by aerodynamic deficiencies, though the Lancaster bomber from which the type was evolved had been one of the outstanding aircraft of the war.

Then on 7 September came disaster for BSAA with that other Lancaster-derived transport, the York, for *Star Leader* crashed soon after take-off from Bathurst, Gambia, killing nineteen passengers and four crew. That unfortunately was to become the sporadic pattern of every airline, British or foreign, though the overwhelming majority of flights were made in safety.

September also saw the return of the famous *Golden Hind* to Poole, luxuriously refurbished by Short & Harland of Belfast as a 24-seater, and on the 30th she made her first civilian essay flown by Capt Dudley Travers on the Cairo run.

Autumn brought political changes. On 5 October Attlee appointed Lord Nathan as Minister of Civil Aviation, with dour George Lindgren as Parliamentary Secretary. 'Here are two men who haven't a clue on the theory or practice of aerial transport', fumed *The Aeroplane*. 'If they were not previously interested in the subject why suddenly put them in the driving seat?' However, popular interest focused much more readily on BOAC's pictorial publicity for the new-style 'streamlined' uniform for their stewardesses. Of more direct concern to the Minister was the war of bi-lateral agreements. Thus KLM was operating a trans-Atlantic service from Prestwick because Britain would not grant Fifth Freedom rights to use London Heathrow. The Dutch countered by denying British rights in the East Indies on the Australian route, whereupon Britain withdrew

Feet
Metres

Drawn to the same scale, (top)
BEA's Vickers 610 Viking 1B
airliner derivative of the
Wellington bomber, and (left)
BSAA's eventual Avro Tudor
IV *Star Leopard* derivative of the
smaller Tudor I.

permission to use Singapore and qualified Fifth Freedom use of Indian ports and Bermuda. Only things which could be twisted in dramatic news interested the Press. With huge headlines 'PLANE EXPLOSION OVER OCEAN: 13,000 feet dive saves 34 in airliner' *The Star* on 28 October managed to make the most of loss of pressurization when the plastic astrodome of the BOAC Constellation *Balmoral* cracked at 20,000 ft — a not too dangerous height from which a minute's descent would reach more oxygenated safe breathing air.

Introduction of Vikings for several more BEA routes took place early in November, notably on the Prague, Lisbon, and Gibraltar routes, but BOAC's rumoured decision to relinquish Durban as a flying-boat base and terminate the Horseshoe route at the end of the year was creating outcry in South Africa. It seemed a confirmatory sign when *Cleopatra* became the first of a procession of war-worn Empire boats to the breaker's yard, the other twelve following next year. There were urgent discussions with BOAC, but assurances were given that flying-boats would still be used on the African route, and in implementation the first of the twelve Solent flying-boats, *Salisbury*, which had triple cabins seating 34, was launched on 11 November. Eleven days later the Tudor I received its C of A, but it was

ominous that the still-air range and speed were down on the estimates on which its use had been based.

The Vikings also revealed a snag. In the bitter winter weather ice was accreting on the tail and the machine became unstable. All were withdrawn until this defect could be overcome, so Dakotas again came back into service.

Growth of the world's scheduled airlines in 1946 had been swift and extensive: over 18,000,000 passengers had been carried according to ICAO, each aircraft flying an average of sixteen people.

1947

At the beginning of January 1947 the MCA reorganized air traffic control of Britain's ingoing and outgoing airliners into four geographical divisions: London and South-Eastern England; Southern England; Northern England and Northern Ireland; and Scotland. Plans for Heathrow as London Airport were also complete. Covering more than 6¼ square miles, it would have nine runways in three parallel sets in three directions. Construction would be in three stages, of which the first had been completed, the second was in progress, and the third would not begin until 1950.

London Airport, in all its muddy state, was

Above: The twelve-seater Avro Type 688 Tudor I first flew in June 1945, and fourteen were ordered by the Minister of Supply for BOAC but became the victim of protracted modifications and re-design eventuating in the Tudor IV which seated 32 passengers and the Tudor V accommodating 44 by day or 36 by night.

Above: A policeman stands at the entrance of the passenger reception tent at Heathrow airport, London. Tents were used before the erection of temporary buildings.

Above right: The original control tower at Heathrow airport.

the scene of colourful ceremony on 21 January in which Princess Elizabeth named the fourth production Tudor *Elizabeth of England* as flag ship of the future Tudor fleet. But these machines were still in big trouble despite the air of festivity, and on 30 January BOAC wrote to the MCA stating that it did not regard the Tudor as airworthy at present, and deficiency in performance effectively prevented it operating over the North Atlantic.

On 1 February BEA formally took over the Associated Airways Joint Committee Companies comprising Railway Air Services, Scottish Airways, Channel Islands Airways, Isle of Man Air Services, Great Western & Southern Airlines. Establishment of a Scottish division followed, operating Junkers Ju 52/3m aircraft, of which eleven were from Germany's war reparations. At the end of that month the Air

Navigation Act 1947 received the Royal Assent giving effect to the ICAO Convention signed at Chicago on 7 December, 1944, and also extended the powers of the Air Navigation Acts 1920 and 1936 and provided for Orders in Council on such matters as prevention of interference with air navigation radio apparatus, protection of aerodrome owners against actions for nuisance caused by noise or vibration of aircraft using the aerodromes, and application of Customs legislation to aircraft and airports. A few days later Hong Kong Airways Ltd, a subsidiary of BOAC, was registered, and on 21 March the Australian Government acquired the BOAC shareholding in Qantas Empire Airways (QEA), previously jointly owned by BOAC and Queensland & North Territory Aerial Services Ltd (Qantas) which was also in the throes of purchase by the Australian

Right: The Avro Tudor I *Elizabeth of England* en route from Woodford to Heathrow for the naming ceremony by HRH Princess Elizabeth, 21 June 1947.

Government — but policy was unchanged and the partnership of BOAC and QEA on the London–Sydney route continued.

For months there had been rumours that BOAC had a big deficit, although the accounts had not been published. Eager MPs picked up the story, and criticism in the Commons led to appointment of a Select Committee to inquire into the administration of Civil Aviation. Lord Knollys was called to give evidence. Apparently he considered this a reflection on his chairmanship, and therefore resigned on 1 April with effect from 30 June, the end of the period for which he had been appointed. Next day George Lindgren announced that Sir Harold Hartley, whom Brackley 'recognized as a man of ripe experience in transport', would be switched from BEA to succeed Knollys. Whitney Straight would become managing director and chief executive of BOAC and Major McCrindle be BOAC's managing director for external affairs. Gerard d'Erlanger was appointed BEA's new chairman, and John Wood became managing director. That was followed by the resignation on 8 April of Sir Edwin Plowden on appointment as the Government's Chief Planning Officer.

BOAC now wrote to the Minister: 'The Corporation has concluded that, irrespective of whether the flying qualities of the Tudor I can be rectified, and whether its deficiency and performance can be fully recovered, there is no longer any justification for including Tudor I's in the Corporation's operating programme'. Opportunity was taken to stress that: 'Our main handicap to-day is having to use obsolete and uncommercial aircraft'. That opened the door to a Government decision permitting BOAC to purchase six Boeing Stratocruisers from the USA at a cost of $12 million.

BSAA did not agree with BOAC's findings on the Tudor, and earlier reported to the MCA that they considered it a normal four-engined aircraft suitable for their routes. Accordingly four had been ordered with fuselages extended forward by six feet, and on 9 April the prototype *Star Panther* made its first flight, subsequently receiving full approval of Don Bennett after personally testing it under tropical conditions. The calculated range was 3,350 nautical miles using 3,300 gallons, so there was ample range for the longest BSAA route of 2,260 miles from Santa Maria to Bermuda.

The other customer, BOAC, was pursuing alternatives, and on 4 February ordered two equivalent Handley Page Hermes MK Vs, supplemented on 19 March by an order for 25 MK IVs. But something better was required as eventual replacement for the Lockheed Constellation. Handley Page tendered a revised Hermes but was defeated by the Bristol Aeroplane Co's Type 175 project — later known as the Britannia.

At Filton the great Bristol Brabazon 1, of which the first manufacturing drawings had been issued in April 1945, was now taking form in the huge fuselage jig; before it could be assembled an eight-acre, three-bay erection shop had to be built; but the winter weather was delaying construction. There was delay also in extending the runway, for it involved planning permission to close a dual carriageway and abolish part of a village. In the engine sheds the coupled double-Proteus turbines were being evolved for both the Brabazon and Saunders-Roe Princess, though it might take two years before either aircraft was ready. Few realized the complexity of the new generation of all-metal airliners and consequent time measured in years taken to design and fabricate them — yet only a decade earlier the four-engined de Havilland Albatross had required little over one year. The trail-blazing DH 106 Comet employing jet engines for the first time in the world was a different matter. At half the size of the Brabazon the problems looked less — but they were not. Just as much time had to be spent on design and detail testing, but the priority was completion of the first cabin for intensive pressure testing.

Everywhere there was increasing activity. BEA took over Allied Airways (Gander Dower) Ltd who operated the Orkneys and Shetlands run. On 15 May the Corporation formed Gibraltar Airways with a 51 per cent holding and balance subscribed by Gibraltar shippers. In turn, BOAC opened a service between London and Montreal using Constellations, and at the end of May BSAA made trial flights for the MCA between London and Bermuda during which the Tudor was flight-refuelled.

At the end of May Lord Knollys made his farewell. At a dinner in the ex-chairman's honour Lord Nathan referred to the charm of Lord Knollys 'of which we have all been witness — and some the victims'.

Ten days later the first wholly newly de-

signed British airliner, the handsome, twin-engined, 34-seat, shoulder-wing Airspeed Ambassador, had its initial flight but, though promising, the usual minor modifications were necessary. As yet there were no orders. BEA considered that the somewhat smaller four-engined turbo-prop Vickers Viscount might be more viable even though the Centaurus engines of the Ambassador would be changed to Proteus turbines. Nevertheless BEA was quick to appreciate new developments and saw the advantage of using helicopters for short-distance hauls. An experimental unit was established at Northolt with a Westland S.51 and two Bell helicopters, managed by Reggie Brie of earlier Autogiro fame, assisted by Alan McClements late of MAP as experimental engineer. There were unkind comments that it would be better if BEA turned to the frustrations of passengers as there were many complaints of departure delays on scheduled air routes, for problems arose when there was no spare aircraft available if the intended machine suffered a temporary fault, sometimes resulting in cancellation of a service without notice.

Worse could happen. Bad visibility due to dust led to four unsuccessful approaches at Basra by a BOAC York, on 16 July, then diversion to Shaibah and three more attempts, but finally the machine hit the side of a hill, bounced over a tamarisk wood, and crashed, killing the six crew and injuring all twelve passengers.

With the partitioning of India and Pakistan on 15 August came grave civil commotion, riots and mass bloodshed. Air Commodore Brackley was put in charge of a great air evacua-tion programme with which BOAC was entrusted, initially to remove 7,000 govern-ment employees from Pakistan, using two Yorks, one Lancastrian, and a fleet of 23 Dakotas of which twelve were owned by BOAC and the others by Scottish Airways, Silver City Airways, and Westminster Air-ways. By 15 September the operation was completed, and nearly 42,000 had been inter-changed between India and Pakistan, during which the aircraft flew the equivalent of thir-teen times round the world.

A great setback followed on 23 August, for the 'stretched' Tudor, intended to meet BOAC's requirements for a 60-seater, crashed in an ever-steepening banked turn during take-off, killing its very experienced pilot Bill Thorne, the radio operator, and the famous Avro chief designer Roy Chadwick who typi-cally was aboard to study its faults. Inspection revealed that aileron control cables had been crossed and thus gave reverse response. The Press stated that the Tudor was unlikely ever to carry passengers. Controversy raged. Sir Roy Dobson, managing director of A.V. Roe Ltd, blamed BOAC for delays in bringing the Tudor into service. BOAC on 24 September replied: 'The Board regrets that Sir Roy has seen fit to make this and other serious allega-tions against the Corporation, the accuracy of which it emphatically denies'. A Board of Inquiry was demanded, and the Minister of Supply appointed a committee of four chaired by Air Marshal Sir Christopher Courtney. Undeterred, Air Vice-Marshal Bennett took off for South America with *Star Lion* on 30 Sep-

Opposite: The Speedbird route with wings 'across the world'.

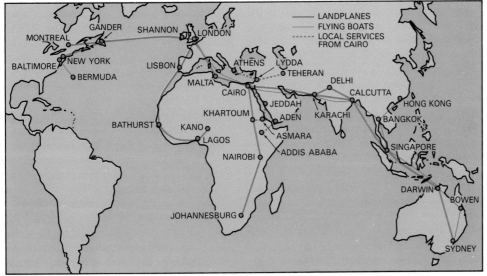

BOAC routes in 1947.

Sir Alan Cobham (*left*) before the first major trial of his flight-refuelling system in which Air Vice Marshal D.C.T. Bennett (*right*) flew non-stop to Bermuda in 20 hours in a Lancaster III. Twenty-one further trans-Atlantic flights followed between May and August 1947.

tember, unprecedentally carrying 32 passengers overseas in an aircraft which had been delivered only the day before. But all went well, and they flew the wartime West African route to Dakar, then across the wide seas to Natal, Rio de Janeiro, Buenos Aires and Santiago — returning on schedule to England on 9 October having completed 16,500 miles without incident. On 31 October BSSA started its first weekly service to the Caribbean via Lisbon, Azores, Bermuda and Nassau to Cuba, and then made a non-commercial flight to Mexico City where Bennett discussed extension to that metropolis.

Meanwhile at Filton on 4 October the 177-ft fuselage of the Brabazon 1, complete with 100-ft integral inner wing and 55-ft tail-plane, was removed from its jig and towed half a mile to the still partially constructed vast assembly shop further down the aerodrome. The problems of piloting such big airliners in all weathers were receiving widespread attention. What the future might hold was indicated when a four-engined Douglas C-54-A of the US Army All Weather Flying Centre landed at the RAF aerodrome Brize Norton having flown the Atlantic solely by automation. In the USA it had only been necessary to switch on the servo-motors for engines and controls. From that point nothing was touched, and still 'flying on the beam' the machine had automatically regulated engine speed and descent, accurately touched down, then compression of the shock-absorber throttled the engines, whereupon the pilot took over and taxied to the hangar.

In the closing months of 1947 BOAC began withdrawing unprofitable aircraft such as the Haltons on the Cairo and West African runs, the Boeing 314s on the Bermuda–Baltimore run, and even the cherished *Golden Hind*, which for a year had made the weekly run to Cairo and back, was withdrawn and a few months later sold — yet it survived another six years. There were also rumours that BOAC had told the MoS that it did not want the Saunders-Roe Princess and might reach the same decision about the Bristol Brabazon and DH Comet in order to cut capital expenditure. Interest centred on aircraft of Constellation type which permitted high utilization approaching 3,000 hours a year. Even so they could only be profitable if traffic greatly increased, but that was hampered by the Government's imposition of still tighter limits on travel allowances. Conversely in the USA there were no problems of

dollar exchange, so of the seven national companies flying the Atlantic, Pan American World Airways took the lead with some 20,000 passengers in a world total of 60,000 carried in the past year.

When the Report of the Committee investigating the Tudor affair was presented, BOAC was strongly criticized for its insistence on non-vital modification which led not only to delays but to deteriorating relations between A.V. Roe Ltd and the Corporation, whereas BSAA had impressed every one with its interest in getting the Tudor IV quickly into service. Though admitting the Tudor had directional control problems, longitudinal instability, buffeting at maximum speed, faulty undercarriage springing, and a deficiency in range, the Report stated: 'We should make it clear there is no suggestion of any unsoundness in the basic design'. Consequently it was recommended that provided the original specification performance was realized, a London–Montreal service should, in the national interest, begin as early as possible with the Tudor I, and the resulting financial deficiency be made good to the operators. But that was not the end of the story.

1948

On 6 January 1948, the BEA Viking *Veracity* crashed into ploughed fields at Northolt after first attempting to land by the beam, unaware of incorrect altimeter barometric setting, and then tried visually with a timed approach, but hit a row of trees, killing the pilot and injuring the eight other occupants.

Nor were the long-overdue 1946–47 Annual Reports of two of the three Corporations encouraging when issued that month. BOAC's confirmed a loss of over £8 million. The *Daily Telegraph* cynically commented: 'It is a moving thought that we should have been in pocket if all the passengers travelling by air had been paid £50 not to go'. The Corporation blamed 'the delay of the Tudors and consequent changes of plans, with their financial repercussions'. The Report bemoaned that provision of marine airports and their accommodation for overnight passengers was costing £1,150,000 a year, but conceded that 'the flying-boat services are popular because of their comfort'. The Sunderland version, known as the Hythe-class, despite night stops, had averaged 2,000 hours each on the long Empire routes. That was very satisfactory, for they required only 4·5 man-hours maintenance per flying hour, whereas the Yorks, with utilization of only 1,350 hours, required 10 man-hours. But above all the Corporation had expected expanding operations, but instead it had been a year of unproductive expenditure because of the variety of uneconomic ex-war converted bombers in use.

Publication of the first balance sheet of BEA seemed to confirm that nationalized aviation had made a bad start, for there was a loss of £2,160,000 — but it had been a difficult initiation, for the Corporation was initially handicapped by using Dakotas and four months' experience with Vikings had been lost because of teething problems. Both at home and abroad there had been delay in providing ground facilities which with unserviceabilities and bad weather cancelled 1,566 flights in a total of 10,191 scheduled services, and a further 208 were not completed. Like BOAC, initial planning had been too optimistic for there was no rapid expansion of European air traffic, and now the slow economic recovery, restrictions

on foreign travel, and limitations on imports necessitated elimination of operations which had no hope of financial success. Because absence of universal radio traffic control often forced aircraft to operate at low altitude, BEA reversed its proposal to use Ambassadors with propeller-turbines which were only economic at height, and on 15 March ordered unpressurized 36-seaters powered with Bristol Centaurus piston engines. Vickers were delighted as this gave a clear go-ahead for their turbine-powered Viscount for use in the 1950s.

By comparison BSAA achieved success with a net surplus of £73,000 from the beginning of their operations on 1 August 1946 to 31 March 1947. BSAA policy was to fix fares and rates as low as possible, though the airline was not a free agent because it was largely bound by IATA. However the Board was confident that services could be run on a commercial basis provided it had control over ordering its own aircraft and that restrictions were not placed on routes, nor competitors given preferential treatment in tax-free subsidies.

But disaster followed. On 30 January their Tudor IV *Star Tiger*, with crew of six and 25 passengers, vanished without trace after being held up by bad weather at the Azores and was last seen flying low to avoid strong head winds. Though a signal had been sent and a D/R position fixed, no distress call came, so the crash must have been without warning. The MCA grounded all Tudors. There were questions in Parliament. An Inquiry was instituted.

Don Bennett, a Board member and a man of vast practical experience whom pilots rated highly, decided as chief executive to challenge the grounding, but did so through a *Daily Express* interview. Booth and his directors were outraged. Lord Nathan stated in the Lords that he was told by the BSAA chairman that Bennett refused to tender his resignation and was dismissed. Said *Flight*: 'It was Bennett's drive and strong personality which was largely responsible for the good results the Corporation was able to show in its first report. It was his long practical experience as a pilot which enabled him to say unequivocally that the Tudor was suitable for its routes, and it must have been galling for him to see the type grounded because one machine disappeared with no evidence that it was due to any fault in the aircraft. The whole unfortunate affair boils down to the fact that Don Bennett would have been the bright man in the right job if the Cor-

Top: Mail being loaded on a BEA S.51 helicopter.

Above: The Sikorsky S.51 operated by BEA carried three passengers side by side behind the pilot.

sued their use, and on 14 April Lord Nathan opened a new Marine Terminal in Southampton Docks where the latest Solent-class flying-boat was ceremonially named *Southampton* by the Mayoress, and left on a long-distance proving flight with 34 journalists in the luxurious two-deck accommodation which had a dining saloon, cocktail bar, and promenade.

April also saw the conclusion of BEA's initial helicopter experiment of a dummy postal run in a 120-mile circuit of Somerset and Devon, landing at villages and town outskirts with a regularity factor of 96 per cent despite adverse weather. In the following months mails were carried to towns in East Anglia with equal success. There had been hope that the PMG would agree to a permanent helicopter mail scheme, but at £28 an hour it was considered too expensive, though it might be applicable to more isolated locations. In charge of operations was Jock Cameron, a keen ex-RAF helicopter pilot.

The loss of 25 lives in the crash of a Pan American Airways Constellation at Shannon using the instrument landing system (ILS) in visibility of only 250 yards drew renewed attention to safety in general. Only a fortnight earlier a Sabena DC-3 had crashed in similar circumstances at London Airport and only two of the nineteen passengers and four crew survived.

Information provided by the MCA of notifiable accidents to British landplanes between 1 January 1946 and 30 April 1948 showed that on BOAC's scheduled flights there were ten and six on non-scheduled flights — all except three ascribed to errors of judgement. BEA had nine accidents on scheduled services of which three were errors of judgement and two due to mechanical failure. BSAA had eight accidents of which six were due to errors of judgement. Of fatal accidents BOAC had two; BEA had three, one of which was a collision with a Russian fighter; and BSAA had four. Perhaps it was memory of huge war-time losses that made this total seem acceptable in relation to the enormous mileage the three Corporations were flying. Traffic statistics revealed impressive figures. From April to December 1947 BEA carried 442,374 passengers in the course of 10½ million miles; from April to October BOAC carried 66,359 in just over 16 million miles; and in the same period BSAA carried 7,507 in just under 3 million miles. Much more was expected in the current year. In expectation, BOAC bought, for £315,000 each, the five Constellations which Aer Lingus had for the

poration had not happened to be a Socialized concern.'

At this point Herbert Brackley returned from a month's mission to Ceylon. There had been earlier discussion with Sir Harold Hartley and Whitney Straight in which he requested consideration as a full-time director of BOAC, but nothing transpired. On 6 March BSAA, not the reluctant BOAC, offered the post of chief executive, and he immediately accepted. Mrs Brackley recorded: 'Mr Booth was to prove not only the ablest chairman with whom my husband worked, but a fine business man devoted to the highest ideals for successful post-war aviation'.

Following a preliminary report from the recently constituted Air Safety Board, the Minister agreed that Tudor, IVs could be immediately ued by BSAA as freighters but not as passenger-carriers. Since the latter were crucial to the airline, the BSAA chairman, accompanied by Brackley and a technician, visited A.V. Roe Ltd to inspect the 44-seater Tudor V of which six had been ordered while Bennett was in office. As the result of his maritime experience with Imperial Airways, Brackley preferred flying-boats for the South American route, but it was BOAC, not BSAA, who pur-

proposed trans-Atlantic service abandoned by the Irish Government because estimated losses would be £647,000. BOAC had a 30 per cent holding in the Irish company and BEA a 10 per cent interest. BOAC intended the Constellations for the Australian run in conjunction with Qantas Empire Airways, the journey to Sydney taking 4½ days compared with 10½ for the flying-boats. The Short Solents would therefore operate the Springbok service to South Africa via Sicily for the first night stop, then via Cairo to Luxor for the second night, and on the next stage across the Sudan to Port Bell on the north shore of Lake Victoria for the third night stop at Kampala, thence Tanganyika and Northern Rhodesia for the River Zambezi, and on the next day to Vaaldam, the terminal for Johannesburg.

Meanwhile the MCA gave permission for the Tudor IV to carry passengers, but until trials of range and consumption were made, they must not fly between the Azores and Bermuda. *Star Leopard* was therefore immediately dispatched with observers from Boscombe Down to carry out the appropriate trials on the route to Nairobi.

In June the Minister, Lord Nathan, resigned to return to his practice as a solicitor, and 44-year-old Lord Pakenham succeeded him. Such changes were always disconcerting to the aviation industry because they often heralded a new slant in policy. One of Pakenham's early exercises was to visit London Airport which now had the full set of runways almost ready, though it still seemed a vast sea of mud. He was particularly interested in the manner in which the stream of airliners was rigorously directed by the Metropolitan Control Zone using three points of entry and exit. Through the Gravesend gate went KLM services to Amsterdam; Sabena to Brussels and Antwerp; American Overseas Airlines to Frankfurt; Scandinavian Air Lines to Stockholm; Pan American Airways to Germany; BEA and Air France to Paris. Through the Dunsfold gate went BOAC Yorks to South Africa and the East; BSAA to South America through Lisbon; Pan American Airways to Istanbul; South African Airways to Johannesburg; Panair through Paris to Brazil; and Qantas, Swissair, Air India heading across Staines Reservoir and the Surrey hills to fan out from Dunsfold. Through the Woodley gate the Atlantic traffic went close to Windsor.

The system of vertical 'stacking' was subject to much criticism, particularly because of danger to aircraft in a layer where icing conditions prevailed, but in any case height separation was considered inadequate. The problem was drastically highlighted on 4 July when four aircraft were circling above a floor of low cloud — a Scandinavian DC-6 lowest at 2,500 ft, a York of Transport Command at 3,000 ft, and two others at 500-ft intervals above. The DC-6 signalled it would return to Amsterdam. To leave the stack a pilot must obtain permission from Approach Control, who contacted the Metropolitan Zone for height, route, and exit gate. If altimeters were set correctly there should be no problem. Instead the York, which had been circling for an hour, and the DC-6 collided, and all 39 participants were killed when the machines crashed to the ground near Northolt.

Despite such bad publicity BEA was experiencing substantial increase in passenger traffic, and freight. Following the PMG's agreement that air mail letter rates would be the same as surface mail to all European countries except Germany, Poland, and Iceland, mail loads had increased from 8½ tons per week to some 27 tons, mainly carried in the regular passenger Vikings. Even more encouraging was Lord Pakenham's statement of Government airline policy, for he announced that instead of adding more Constellations to the BOAC Stratocruisers coming from the USA, an order would be placed for 22 Douglas DC-4M-4s of the latest type built in Canada (known as Argonauts) which were pressurized, air-conditioned, and refrigerated, and carried 40 passengers. Fifteen would operate to India and the Middle East, and seven be allocated for the North Atlantic route to Canada. As a result of Brackley's advocacy the three Saunders-Roe Princess flying-boats would be increased to seven for BSAA's South Atlantic service in five yearss' time. The Tudor II would be abandoned, but the Tudor IV was proven, so nineteen would go to BSAA. In all some hundred new aircraft would be purchased, including the Hermes, at a cost of £25 million. Pakenham indicated that losses would exceed the amount payable in subsidies, but there would be a deficiency grant.

Now that BOAC knew the general policy, Whitney Straight as chief executive lost no time in announcing reorganization. An all-out drive would be made for dollar traffic on Atlantic and

Empire routes. Decentralization would be the new aim, though close co-operation would be maintained between the three Corporations to pool experience and avoid overlapping. Sir Miles Thomas, an ex-RFC pilot and engineer journalist who became vice-chairman of Morris Motors, had earlier been appointed deputy chairman of BOAC, and was assigned responsibility for implementing the reorganization. Sir Victor Tait, the Air Ministry ex-director-general of Signals who had recently joined the Board, became deputy chief executive. The

machine I have ever flown'.

A fortnight later the prototype Bristol Brabazon was cautiously towed from its vast shed and stood like a mammoth outside while the fuel flow from her 27 tanks was calibrated — but though she looked complete except for rudder and propellers, a year might pass before first flight.

Progress was quicker with the simpler Hermes for BOAC, the first of which flew on 5 September. Whitney Straight cabled Handley Page: 'We look forward with keenest anticipa-

Western division would be operated by Vernon Crudge and the Eastern by John Brancker. All UK mails, traffic, and catering would be the responsibility of Keith Granville in London. The personnel subdivision was regarded as particularly important, so its manager, Blair-Cunynghame, was added to the management committee. Alan Campbell Orde became manager of technical development, and the repair division was John Robson's. A significant appointment was Sir Harold Whittingham, previously director-general of RAF Medical services, as BOAC's medical director. Commercial development was under Robert Dunlop Stewart, but like technical development, was an advisory, non-executive section. To advise on gas turbine engines, Sir Frank Whittle was appointed, coinciding with the first flight of the four-engined turbo-prop Vickers Viscount, described by 'Mutt' Summers, the Vickers chief pilot as 'the smoothest and best

tion and confidence to using Hermes on our trunk routes and feel sure will be a winner' — but the usual modifications were required, and on one flight there was nearly disaster due to tailplane flutter.

In Occupied Germany the attempt by the USA, Soviet Union, Britain and France to administer the country collectively was collapsing into a partition between the Western half and the Eastern half, and in June the Soviet Union began to make the West's position untenable by blockading surface communications to Berlin — but three air corridors remained open from Gatow in the British sector and Tempelhof in the American giving access to the frontiers of their zones in Western Germany. On 28 June the RAF commenced a great airlift to Berlin using Dakotas which in the next two days carried 75 tons of food to the British Forces; but there were also two million nationals dependent on supplies from the West. Steadily the operation mounted. Civilian companies were brought into the operation, the first being Flight Refuelling Ltd with two Lancastrian tankers which on each shuttle brought in 3,000 gallons of much-needed fuel. Next came BEA who chartered from nine firms to make a fleet of ten Dakotas, a Halifax, a Liberator, and even a Hythe flying-boat. In charge of operations was E.P. Whitfield, the BEA manager in Germany. The London–Hamburg–Berlin service was maintained, and Germans with a zone pass could buy tickets. Between 5 August and 25 September there were 172 schedule and charter flights to Berlin, let alone the ever-increasing airlift known as Whitfield's Circus, to which still more British firms, includ-

ing BSAA, began contributing. By the end of September 7,000 tons of petrol, food, flour, and freight had been up-lifted in a total of 1,760 sorties. Steadily increasing, it would continue into next year.

Meanwhile Lord Douglas of Kirtleside, who as Colonel Sholto Douglas had been chief pilot of Handley Page Transport in 1919, was appointed to the Board of BOAC, Lord Rothschild having resigned to accept chairmanship of the Agricultural Research Council. Since July, Douglas, at the invitation of the Minister, had been investigating aspects of the Civil Aviation Act in relation to the Corporations. Because reorganization of BOAC entailed pruning staff at home and abroad, Lord Douglas and part-time directors Lord Burghley, Major Thornton, and Clement Jones volunteered to serve at fees reduced from £1,000 to £500 a year. Major McCrindle, previously managing director of external affairs, was now appointed adviser on international affairs to all three Corporations but remained on the BOAC Board.

Despite financial and technical setbacks BSAA was in full operation, for the Tudor IV

had been granted a C of A for still greater load, and though passengers were not permitted on the Azores–Bermuda route, the northern route via Iceland and Newfoundland had begun, but limited to 25 passengers on west-bound flights. Then out of the blue came news that Air Commodore Brackley in the course of a tour of BSAA bases in Brazil, had been drowned on 15 November whilst swimming off Copacabana Beach, Rio de Janeiro. At his Memorial Service in St Margaret's, Westminster, at the end of the month there were representatives from every ministerial and industrial organization connected with aviation.

That all three Corporations were doing badly was apparent from the annual Reports and Accounts at the end of November with £11 million combined losses of which BOAC's had increased by one million, those of BEA by two million, and BSAA had lost nearly half a million. *Flight* cynically commented: 'In BOAC it requires an employee to work for a year to carry five passengers at a loss of £345'.

However BOAC had flown almost 297 million passenger miles with its 126 aircraft of seven different types, most of which were obso-

Left: The famous Douglas C47A Dakota saw extensive service with BOAC during and after the war. The aircraft was used on the European, African and Middle Eastern services until 1950.

The Handley Page Hermes 4 *Hero*, in BOAC livery, was one of twenty ordered in 1948 and commissioned in mid-1950.

lescent. During the year there were two accidents fatal to seven passengers and injuries to nineteen — but that ratio of one fatality for every 43 million miles flown showed it was twice as safe as all international airlines put together. BEA had three serious accidents during the year involving injuries to passengers and crew, resulting in one death in the course of 12 million miles during which half a million passengers were carried. BSAA had the loss of the York *Star Speed*, resulting in the death of seven passengers; the Lancastrian *Star Dust*, lost without trace in the Andes with six passengers and five crew aboard; and the Tudor IV *Star Tiger*, which disappeared between the Azores and Bermuda with 25 passengers and six crew. Because of such losses Lord Nathan had set up a Committee on Accident Investigation Procedure, but Lord Pakenham refused to establish a Board of that kind and decided to end investigations held publicly.

The year ended with a not-unexpected announcement that Peter Masefield had joined the Board of BEA, for it transpired that John Wood, the managing director, was on sick leave and d'Erlanger had added management to his own task of chairman.

1949

In January 1949 BSAA acquired the share capital of Bahama Airways operating flying-boats between Nassau and the islands. However the misfortunes of BSAA continued. On 5 January their Avro York *Star Venture* piled-up 400 miles north of Rio and was burnt out, killing three of the nine passengers and injuring the pilot and two crew. Within a fortnight the Avro Tudor *Star Ariel*, with thirteen passengers and four crew, vanished without trace between Bermuda and Jamaica. On 19 January the Minister announced that it must be presumed lost and

suspended all Tudor IVs pending further investigation. There were fears that sudden structural failure had prevented a MAYDAY signal. It was all too reminiscent of *Star Tiger*. There were rumours that Tudors were finished and of proposals to merge BSAA with BOAC.

Coinciding with an announcement from 10 Downing Street that BOAC in future would be permitted to place direct contracts with aircraft manufacturers came news that 70-year-old Sir Harold Hartley would resign chairmanship of BOAC at the end of June and be succeeded by Sir Miles Thomas, with Whitney Straight as deputy chairman and chief executive.

When the Lords debated Civil Aviation on 2 February there were sweeping disclosures that the three Corporations were costing the nation £26 million of expenditure if the MCA was included. Pakenham, far from giving assurances, agreed that airline losses might be £15 million for the current year, and indicated that overheads were too high — a factor fully recognized by BOAC who had been reducing staff from 25,500 in April 1947 to 19,000 by December 1948. BEA was still cutting its staff and in five months had reduced it from 7,500 to 6,000 but was facing union opposition. The directive to cut expenditure led to revision of BEA's maintenance system by using block period inspections to extend time between overhauls; but gloom was cast by another tragic accident when an RAF Anson on 19 February collided with a BEA DC–3 on the London–Glasgow run, and the crews and four passengers were killed.

For some time a change in BEA's chairmanship had been expected, and at the behest of Lord Pakenham, Gerard d'Erlanger willingly acquiesced. On 27 February Marshal of the

Drawn to the same scale: *Centre top:* The Hermes 4s were given names which included those of the historic HP 42s. *Bottom:* An initial ten Boeing 377 Stratocruisers were acquired in 1949, and seven more were added in 1954–55.

RAF Lord Douglas, now a portly 55, accepted the post. There was immediate criticism in the Commons by Air Commodore Harvey, who said it was most regrettable that Mr d'Erlanger should leave BEA at this stage, and though he had great admiration for Lord Douglas's ability as a war leader, the appointment could only be regarded as political. He doubted whether John Wood could return, so the Corporation would have lost both managing director and chairman in a matter of weeks, and while he regarded Mr Masefield as a great planner it would be better to have a managing director with transport experience and knowledge of operating aircraft.

On 15 March Lord Pakenham officially announced that BOAC and BSAA would be merged to keep the South American routes in operation. John Booth would join the BOAC Board as joint deputy chairman with Whitney Straight. Passengers for the Caribbean area would be carried to Bermuda via New York by BOAC, and the freighter service would be operated on an *ad hoc* basis by two Lancastrians on the UK–Dakar–Natal–Trinidad route. Until the merger Bill was passed Sir Francis Brake of Standard Telephones would be deputy chairman of BSAA.

By purchasing from Scandinavian Air Lines four of their Boeing Stratocruisers and spares for £3 million, BOAC made a flying start in April with the latest type of airliner. Everybody had been impressed by its design a few days earlier when Pan American flew their *Flying Cloud* of this type to London Airport. On the ground there was no immediate impression of size, for the stalky Constellations seemed much bigger than the 60-ton stubby Boeing with deep 'double-bubble' fuselage accommodating 61 on the upper deck and 40 on the lower, which on the Atlantic run became a ten-seat cocktail lounge. A few BOAG pilots were given a 'joy-ride' and discerned a slight swaying of the tail thought to be due to slight hunting in the automatic pilot; but what attracted was that though touchdown speed was 90 mph the inboard propellers were put into reverse to act as a powerful brake as soon as the wheels touched. On the flight deck an 'engine analyser' detected any malfunctioning such as fuel and ignition faults. The flight path to the future was expanding!

Concurrently came an end to the prosperity the Berlin airlift had brought — for on 11 May the blockade ceased. In these ten months, British and American aircraft had made nearly 200,000 flights with a daily load of almost 5,000 short tons, of which the British contributed a quarter and had master-minded the bulk of the organization because six of the eight dispatching fields were in the British zone. An immediate repercussion was that all contributory air transport firms had surplus aircraft and crews left on their hands.

But now another great milestone was passed. In the early evening of 27 July, the beautiful de Havilland Comet made its first flight in the hands of John Cunningham with John Wilson assisting. It was Cunningham's thirtieth birthday. With a high-pitched shriek characterizing the new sound of jet power away went the Comet, climbing to 10,000ft where it was tried over a range of speeds; then descending, flew along the runway at 100ft in salute to the handful of experimental 'hands' and technical staff, and sweeping wide, came to the runway, touching down with an exemplary landing after being airborne for 31 minutes. The new era had started.

Of more immediate value to BOAC was the

Drawn to the same scale:
Top left: Based on the DC-4, the Canadair C-4 Argonaut had Merlin engines and a pressurized cabin.
Centre: Douglas Dakota, of which 60 of various marks were used over the years.
Bottom: Lockheed 049E Constellation, the first of which were acquired in 1946 and the last of 25 in 1955.

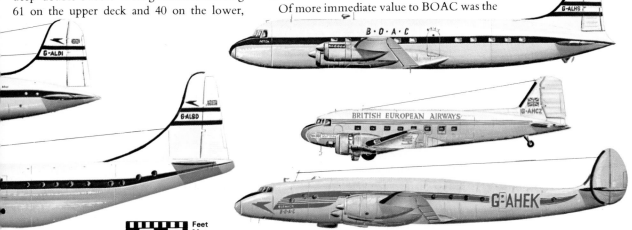

early delivery of the Canadair DC-4M Argonauts — the most cost-effective purchase yet made. The first, *Ajax*, had won its spurs a month earlier with a gruelling 25-day proving flight flown by Capt Crane, one of the Constellation pilots, who established operational procedures under every condition of weather, including midsummer in the Persian Gulf. On **23** August the Argonauts commenced the scheduled landplane service to Hong Kong, covering the route in only three days compared with five for Plymouth-class Short Sandringham. Four days later the service was extended to Tokyo, making that sector two days less than the flying-boats now being withdrawn to effect substantial saving by closing the expensive marine bases.

BEA had been equally engrossed with the 'new look' — this time the Vickers turbo-prop VC 10 Viscount which was flown for ten minutes at Wisley on 16 July by 'Mutt' Summers with Gabe Bryce as co-pilot. Such brevity indicated a probable Dart turbine problem, but the machine was soon on test again, and within a month other pilots were permitted to try it. 'The smoothness of flight might be likened to the penetrating, liquid smoothness of a great liner in sheltered water rather than to the light butterfly movement of a sailplane', said one; but compared with the silent Comet there was a faintly audible mixture of remote noises. The machine was remarkably stable 'and boasts as nice a pair of ailerons as one could wish'.

The Viscount and Ambassador were displayed at Northolt at a ceremony marking the thirtieth birthday of the first commercial London–Paris air service. At a celebratory lunch for the pioneer commercial pilots, executives, and MCA officials, Lord Douglas announced that BEA in the previous month had made a profit for the first time in its existence. Orders, he said, would now be placed for the Viscount. Sir Miles Thomas explained in detail: 'About a dozen Viscounts will be used in the Caribbean area by the BSAA subsidiary, British West Indian Airways'. That was music of the future. Present demands must be met by BEA's 41 Vikings, twenty Dakotas, and twenty DH Rapides; but the whole fleet would be written off the books by the end of 1953. From 1951 the Corporation would have the Ambassador, and looking ahead to 1955 and 1956 it was estimated that 90 million capacity-tonne-kilometres must be provided, but until the Viscount was added in 1952 there would be a 47 million

capacity-tonne-kilometre deficit. By that was meant the VC 700 stretched version with higher-density seating, though only a prototype as yet, had been ordered by the MoS.

But there were bigger things to come. On Sunday 4 September, the mighty Brabazon was towed from its shed, and the newly appointed chief test pilot, A.J. 'Bill' Pegg, with nine crew, started the multi-engines, and in half the length of the 2,700-yard runway lifted the machine and climbed away, flying for 25 minutes, then brought it back in a long flat powered approach and set it gently down. Said modest Pegg: 'It was a very comfortable ride. Every thing went just as we had hoped for so many years.' As usual there was a long way to go, for the fuselage was an unfurnished shell two-thirds filled with a thousand instruments mostly recording photographically. But was this a white elephant, too big for commercial use?

More immediately practicable was its 142-ft-span smaller relative the Bristol 175 Britannia, intended for the Atlantic route and carrying 83 passengers. BOAC was reluctant to order until it had flown, whereas the MoS would not order a prototype until BOAC agreed to purchase 25; but the technical risk was too much for the Corporation, so the MoS gave way and had ordered three a year ago. That meant at least two more years before the first flight. BOAC therefore depended heavily on the Stratocruisers and Argonauts.

BEA was still discovering the reluctance of people to fly on the internal services. After six months' experimental operation between Cardiff, Liverpool, and Anglesey the service was withdrawn, for only 603 passengers had been carried in the Rapides, yielding a total revenue of £1,740, whereas it had cost £9,755. Peter Masefield was hopeful that future aircraft would enable the present fare of 7½d per passenger mile to be reduced to 4d by 1955 but the bread-and-butter machine, he said, was the Viking. There had however been trouble with the Hercules engines just as with the Wright Cyclones of the Canadair Argonauts which were by far the noisiest of current airliners.

October brought the accounts of the three Corporations for the year ending 31 March. It was hopeful that the aggregate loss was 12 per cent less than before, though it totalled £9¾ million. BOAC's deficit was £5·8 million, a reduction of 38 per cent; BEA lost £2·75 million, a reduction of 42 per cent; BSAA had a deficit of £1·13 million compared with £0·42 million the previous year. The accumulated loss since the war exceeded £31 million. At least it was encouraging that the overall cost of combined operations showed a reduction of 14 per cent, and output per employee had risen by 45 per cent.

Yet another new administrative organization for BOAC had been planned for progressive introduction by Sir Miles Thomas, for the merger with BSAA necessitated adjustment to the decentralization plan of the previous year. The first phase would be governed by introduction of the Stratocruiser, Argonaut, and Hermes; thereafter there would be devolution of operating responsibility for a five-fleet system classified according to the type of aircraft, each line having its own divisional headquarters. No 1 with Canadair would be based at London Airport; No 2 with Yorks, Lancastrians, and Hermes at Hurn; No 3 with Stratocruisers and Constellations at Filton; No 4 with flying-boats based at Hythe; No 5 with ex-BSAA Yorks and Lancasters would be at Langley near Slough.

Sir Miles said: 'An economical and well-balanced structure is being achieved in the new pattern, and in the development of the organization at all levels the principle of clear-cut objectives and more precise definition of duties is being followed'. That meant direct assault against over-staffing, and it was estimated that 1,000 redundancies would result, including fourteen senior managers. Executive control of operational and commercial activities was allocated to Whitney Straight and John Booth. Sir Victor Tait became operations director and John Brancker general manager of commercial activities. Administration of Home and Overseas stations was in the hands of P. G. Porter, and world-wide sales was the responsibility of Keith Granville. 'Detailed implementation', said Sir Miles, 'was the result of discussions between the MCA, industrial consultants, and appropriate trade union consultative bodies.' He added that 'the policy expresses the industrial spirit of to-day which demands efficiency above all else'. A commentator murmured that

this realization was heartening even if a little overdue.

BEA was also indicating the new spirit of things, for 35-year-old Peter Masefield, whose advancement had been spectacular thanks to his shrewd comprehension, was made chief executive. People liked him. An initial success was a six-month contract for a regular helicopter night mail service between Peterborough and Norwich. Another move was to reduce family fares on the main UK routes during the off-peak season, with even bigger concessions for members of the Forces and their families privately travelling between London and principal cities of Europe. However, devaluation of the pound in October resulted in complexities for international airlines, the problems of which were being urgently dealt with by IATA. For BEA it meant an increase of £450,000 in the year's operating costs, so efforts concentrated on dollar traffic of the Paris service. As part of the stringent economy programme Masefield introduced a departmental budget control of planned expenditure and estimated income.

BOAC's immediate task was the substitution in three weeks of Argonauts for the Yorks on the twice-weekly Eastern services. *Arion*, last of the Argonauts, arrived at London Airport on 11 November, marking fulfilment of the order eight months ahead of contract date — a feature almost unparalleled in aviation history. The Stratocruisers were also being delivered; the first, *Cathay*, piloted by Capt May, a Canadian who joined Imperial Airways in 1936, arrived at London Airport on 15 October after a 2,600-mile non-stop flight from New York averaging 355 mph at 28,000 ft. At La Guardia Field 36 BOAC crew members had been taking a Stratocruiser training course in which the Captains and First Officers spent 30 hours 'flying' the PAA electronic flight simulator comprising a convincing dummy cockpit with full controls, electrics and radio. BOAC therefore ordered an identical model from the British firm of Redifon Ltd, for though it cost £100,000 it would save an annual £90,000 in training costs.

Trail of the Comet 1950-54

Caledonia, flagship of the Stratocruisers, was officially named by Lord Pakenham at Prestwick at the beginning of January 1950 as a special tribute to Scotland and in memory of the historic *Caledonia* flying-boat. In fact the fleet had been in operation on the thrice-weekly London–New York service via Prestwick since December, but soon would be increased to five times a week, and ultimately daily when the Constellations were transferred from the New York–Bermuda routes to the London–Montreal run.

The second stage of London Airport was now well advanced, though still there were only three runways in use, but work on four others was nearing completion, and terminal buildings at least had been planned for the central area with access from the Bath Road by a main entrance tunnel. Four hangars had been built and four more were under construction, but Pan American Airways had triumphed with a huge hangar shipped from the USA. Radio and telecommunication facilities, beacons and runway lights were operational and seventeen companies were now using the unfinished airport for regular services.

Long-range radar monitoring was centred at London Airport — the first of its kind in the world, as befitted its invention by the British. Air space over the country was now divided into five flight information regions, within which were control zones subject to the quadrangle rule relating height and flight direction, and a Ground Control Approach system (GCA) was the current method of bringing aircraft in to land in poor visibility. Initial identification was by requesting a turn to a heading at right angles to the one being flown and confirmed by VHF D/F. The pilot was given the altimeter setting, requisite speed, cockpit check, and headings to bring the aircraft some eight miles down-wind of the runway for Ground Controlto hand over to the talk-down Controller who every few seconds gave the pilot his distance from touchdown point and height in relation to glide path. When the aircraft was $2\frac{1}{2}$ miles from the runway the Controller reminded the pilot to check undercarriage and flaps, and from then on made a running commentary ending 400 yards from touchdown with the instruction 'Look ahead for landing'. It was an act of faith.

On 26 January Sir Miles Thomas left London Airport by scheduled Stratocruiser on a four-week visit to Australia and New Zealand. 'My mission is threefold', he said. 'First, I intend to make an on-the-spot check that all possible economies are being made on the Far East routes where we have substituted Argonauts for the old, slower flying-boats; secondly, we

BOAC was the first airline in the world to operate jet services. The first Comet 1 was delivered in 1951, and the following year it came into service, cutting flight times by up to 50 per cent. The Comet 1 carried 36 passengers and four crew at a cruising speed of 490 mph. There was appreciative comment on its 'whispering silence' and absence of vibration.

shall talk to officials of other Commonwealth
airlines with a view to strengthening joint operations between Britain and Australia, including
the westbound route across the Pacific and
Canada; thirdly, I am in a sense blazing the trail
for the Comet. Problems of aerodrome length,
high altitude, weather and wind studies, the
effect of humidity and tropical heat on jet performance, especially at take-off with full load,
have all to be investigated.'

To commemorate the famous
C-class Empire flying boats, the
Stratocruisers were given their
names. Here is *Caledonia*
wearing the new BOAC livery
with the blue median line and
the speedbird symbol on the fin.

To ensure the efficiency of BOAC's future operations, Airspeed, Bristol, De Havilland, and Vickers were conducting intensive trials with their vital new airliners. The Viscount 630 had flown 400 hours of pressurization, testing the thermal de-icing system and effect on the aircraft if ice was permitted to form. Similarly the Ambassador had intensively tested pressurization, but found that it noticeably raised the noise level by two to three decibels in the high-frequency range, and reached 90 in the low-frequency band compared with 80 decibels for the Viscount.

The Comet had fared further, and in the latter part of the previous year flew in half a day to Castel Benito in Tripoli and back, and on 21 February the first flight was made with cabin pressurized for $5\frac{1}{2}$ hours at 41,500 feet.

The Brabazon was also plugging away, although there had been apprehensive moments on 16 January when a hydraulic pipe failed during Walter Gibb's first flight as pilot in charge, necessitating a high-speed landing with flaps up, but thanks to reversing propellers the big machine pulled up before the end of the runway, and on 15 February made its longest flight of nearly five hours and reached 12,000 feet.

At Handley Page's there had been problems. BOAC technicians had required weight-saving modification for the Hermes, and the MCA agreed, but the first six were still over weight and BOAC declined to accept them until reductions were achieved — though on 22 February one was borrowed for crew training despite a C of A limited to temperate conditions. As the Hermes were intended for Africa, tropical trials were urgently proceeding at Khartoum. At least the Hermes was easy to fly, for the tab-balanced controls in cruising flight were lighter and more effective than any comparable aircraft and there was automatic compensation for trim change when operating the flaps, but full negative tail and a strong pull was required to get the tail down for landing.

As though substantiating BOAC's criticisms of the Avro Tudor V, one of them owned by Fairflight Ltd crashed on 12 March while approaching to land, killing the crew of five and 75 of the 78 passengers.

By agreement with IATA, airliner travel had been luxurious single class, but now Air France became the first to introduce tourist class, and did so by using a 44-seat Skymaster for first class at existing fare, and another for tourist with seat spacing below that specified by IATA so that 55 passengers could be accommodated. The experiment was closely watched by all other airlines. Meanwhile devaluation increased the cost of fuel, maintenance, and services. Consideration at an IATA Traffic Conference in Mexico City on 22 March led to agreement that fares to Africa, Middle East, and Far East would be increased by 10 per cent, but would remain unchanged on the North American routes, and on the trans-Atlantic services there would be a reduction during seven of the twelve months, making the New York to London round trip $630 in the peak season and $466 in the off season.

A hint of the future was indicated on 24 April when John Cunningham flew the Comet from Hatfield to Khartoum and Nairobi for tropical trials, setting an official record by flying the London–Cairo section in 5 hours 7 minutes at 429 mph. The Comet returned on 11 May having flown a further 40 hours, bringing the total air time to 287 hours. Tests at Khartoum and Nairobi confirmed that gas turbines were more sensitive than piston engines in tropical conditions, though serviceability of airframe and power units had been remarkably good. But there was sad news. While Cunningham was away the last of three tail-less DH 108s had crashed on 1 May, killing its RAE test pilot. There was renewed concern as to whether the accident was due to high-speed effects or explosion of the jet engine. That same day the first lightened Handley Page Hermes crashed when it took off from Hurn during crew training.

The slow-speed end of the flight regime remained one of BEA's interests. Their night mail Peterborough–Norwich helicopter run ended in April, having achieved 80 per cent regularity for six months. BEA was content to continue for the present with the three S.51s and two Bells, the fleet having already amassed over 2,000 hours, and now inaugurated a service between Liverpool and Cardiff which was opened on 1 June by Lord Pakenham, who with Lord and Lady Douglas flew in the first S.51 to leave Speke that day.

In the contemporary *BEA Magazine* describing the occasion, Peter Masefield referred to the Corporation handling over the Lisbon route to BOAC, but denied current rumours that this indicated amalgamation of the two Corporations: 'In fact BEA's progress to date shows clearly the advantage of having two separate Corporations to deal with the very different problems of short and long haul transport'. In the equivalent *BOAC News Letter* Sir Miles Thomas referred to the drastic 'streamlining' of the administrative staff, and that the merged BOAC and BSAA currently employed 17,200 compared with the 24,000 alone for BOAC in 1947 — as a result the capacity tonmileage figure per employee had increased from 3,000 in 1947–48 to 3,800 in 1949–50. One way to increase it further was by using bigger airliners, and to that end Sir Miles Thomas arranged for the giant Brabazon to visit London Airport on 5 June for inspection by Mr Strauss as Minister of Supply, Lord Addison, and Lord Pakenham. The great talking point was its ability to fly regularly non-stop between London and New York in short time and with exceptional comfort for the passengers, yet with direct operating cost of £400 per hour.

With Sir Frederick Handley Page's flair for publicity added to that of BOAC, London Air-port became well advertised on 11 July when Lord Pakenham gave the famous name *Hannibal* to the flagship of the Hermes IV fleet as the first British modern post-war airliner to operate. Appropriately the Fleet Superintendent was Capt A.S.M. Rendall who had flown as First Officer on the original *Hannibal*. At the ensuing luncheon Sir Frederick, referring to Pakenham's description of him as 'The Dean' of civil aviation, beamingly remarked that he was not considering Holy Orders but was more interested in other kinds. With benign praise he advocated the merits of his aircraft, adding that the latest form of Hermes would achieve the impossible — an even finer record of safety, reliability, and comfortable service than the original HP 42s. He hoped it would turn the target deficit into a target profit. When that happened he would begin to believe in nationalization.

The prototype Vickers Viscount Type 630 was also well on its way to finalization, for it landed back at Blackbushe on 10 July after completing tropical and high-altitude trials at Khartoum and Nairobi — the first turbo-prop aircraft to undergo such tests. As an indication of intent it was granted a C of A, and piloted by Capt Rymer operated the world's first turbine-powered passenger service, carrying Sir Alec Coryton representing the MoS, Peter Masefield, Sir Frank Whittle, Vickers designer George Edwards, and other senior officials. This led to BEA's signature on 3 August for twenty Type 701 Viscounts in addition to those ordered by BOAC. The Paris service continued for two weeks followed by a week's Lon-

The first turbine-driven aircraft for fare-paying passengers left Northolt Aerodrome on 29 July 1950 to inaugurate a temporary London–Paris service. The photograph shows Sir Frank Whittle (*fifth from left, front row*), the jet pioneer, with a group of passengers, and the BEA Viscount G-AHRF in the background.

Captain and crew of *Hengist,* the first BOAC Hermes to operate the UK-West Africa service, on 6 August 1950.

radar sets constructed by E.K. Cole Ltd had been ordered for regular operational use in the new aircraft, and three were being tried in Hermes IVs. Cliff coastlines and mountains, or clouds which might produce severe turbulence, could be detected up to 40 miles away, and airliners could be 'seen' at 10 to 12 miles, or smaller aircraft at half that distance.

The new apparatus gave reasonable safeguards, but the phenomena of clear-air turbulence was also causing concern as it was not detectable before entry. Pilots described the effect as 'cobble-stone' bumps, but they ranged in size from one foot to several hundred, and their frequency could be as high as three per second at 350 mph, and that could coincide with the natural wing vibration of aircraft with a span of 130 feet. Pilots were warned to avoid flying in what had become known as the jet-stream which swept across the Atlantic at great altitudes. If heavy turbulence was encountered the aircraft must climb or descend or fly at right angles to the local wind direction, and speed, surprisingly, should be increased.

BOAC also decided to standardize Zero Reader equipment as a priority for the Comet. Pilots were unanimous that this was a valuable aid to instrument flying by increasing accuracy and reducing fatigue, though it did not replace the standard blind-flying panel. Instead, its single dial with cross pointers gave a natural indication of the action required by the pilot to maintain attitude for all normal flying, and eliminated the usual mental effort of co-ordination and translation entailed when several instruments were observed together. The pilot simply steered a fixed centre spot on to the intersection of the crossed pointers.

don–Edinburgh service, totalling 1,815 passengers carried in what was described as 'extraordinary silence and freedom from vibration', but more tersely by a US Navy passenger as 'just swell'.

That the day-to-day risk of accidents was ever-present in poor weather was again evident when a BEA Viking diverted from Northolt because of dense fog, made a GCA at Heathrow, bounced off-track, hit a pile of drain pipes, and burst into flames. Only the stewardess and one passenger survived of the 30 occupants because the fog hampered fire and rescue teams, and that led to demands for installation of the war-time 'Fido' fog-dispersal system burning oil under high pressure.

Every possible step was being made to ensure that aircraft travel would soon become safer. Because of the very high speed of future aircraft, such as the Comet, old dangers were becoming more dangerous. Risk of collision was greater with relative closing speeds of 1,000 mph, and the impact of heavy gusts, particularly the tremendous vertical movements in monsoon weather, could induce structural stresses near the limit of safety factors which normally afforded a big margin of strength. The BOAC Development Unit had therefore been conducting cloud-and-collision warning radar experiments using Vikings at Hurn and Hythe flying-boats in the Far East. So promising were their results that a number of special

It was a calm, clear evening on 27 July when the second Comet was flown, exactly a year after the first. In that interval some 320 hours had been flown. This was regarded as rapid progress 'due to extremely thorough pre-testing of components on the ground' — but considerable flying was still necessary to prove the cabin pressurization and air conditioning at height. A fortnight later *Hengist,* the first Hermes to fly commercially to Africa and back, landed at London Airport. From mid-October the Hermes would operate the Springbok service three times weekly in each direction, and SAA would fly a similar service with Constellations.

However it was in America that BOAC was

getting such valuable returns for Britain, earning $2 million in the first six months of the year. Yet from the statistical morass of the annual Reports and Accounts of the two Corporations a £9 million deficit loomed, although both airlines had made substantial progress amid ever-growing competition of foreign services. Under the vigorous regime of Sir Miles Thomas a tremendous sales onslaught was being made. Luxury was still the star attraction. Competitively Pan American had named their trans-Atlantic run the 'President' service, offering sleeping berths, seven-course dinners, champagne, perfume for the ladies and cigars for the men. In pre-war days Imperial Airways secured similar prestige with their 'Silver Wing' service, but now with a touch of genius, BOAC scored by advertising their forthcoming London–New York service as the 'Monarch Line', with similar elaborate meals.

BEA's annual Report drew attention to its fundamental problem that in August traffic was at its zenith but in November fell to almost half. Least productive were the internal services, particularly the social services to isolated places which caused 20 per cent deficit. Perhaps that was why BEA now agreed to recommend to the Air Transport Advisory Council that 73 out of 92 applications for internal services made by 21 companies should be approved with BEA agreements embracing an integrated network. This caused strong protest from the British Air Charter Association, and Eric Rylands, the chairman, said 'apparently BEA intends to take over 80 per cent of the charter companies business. It is clear that if independent operators are to survive, a proportion of their work must come from the Government. Only speedy appreciation of this fact will preserve this valuable asset of a reserve of trained aircrews and ground staffs which will always be available in an emergency.'

Economy-class was becoming a probability. Juan Trippe of PAA followed the French lead by ordering eighteen Douglas D.6Bs, a much-revised version of the DC-4 with fuselage lengthened by 34 feet and all-up weight increased from 32·5 tons to 66 tons, adding considerably to the already high landing speed, though takeoff remained satisfactory because of considerably higher power. By arranging five abreast the seating was increased from 52 to 82. Lavish meals were abandoned and a simple tray service substituted.

Most of the world's airlines were planning to reduce crews, whether stewards and stewardesses or pilots and navigators. Elimination of one man per aircraft was expected to save £100,000 annually. Meantime some of the BOAC pilots would be transferred to BEA whose need was likely to be urgent in the spring.

Another setback for BEA occurred on 17 October when one of the DC-3s crashed with loss of 28 lives after the starboard engine failed while climbing away from Northolt in foggy weather. The pilot tried to turn back, but hit beech trees on Mill Hill; a wing was sheared off and the machine dived into a road, bounced 40 feet, crashed inverted, and burst into flames. Contributory to the accident was a mix-up in monitoring by the telecommunications staff at Northolt when the pilot requested GCA facilities. Few situations can be more difficult than a twin-engined aircraft with only one engine going.

The first production Ambassador now encountered trouble. In a heavy landing on 13 November the port undercarriage took the initial impact, causing the port engine to break away, immediately followed by the starboard as the load redistributed. Freed of the weight, the Ambassador zoomed up before dropping some 450 yards further down the runway. Anxious calculation showed that the first bump had been $2\frac{1}{2}$ times the design maximum — so to the relief of the technicians it was ascribed to pilot's error, though in fact the extremely forward C.G. demanded by BEA meant that the elevator had insufficient power to hold the nose up when flattening for the landing.

Whatever BEA's worries, at least they were tempered at the end of December when finances revealed that in the seven months since publishing the annual accounts a profit of £¼

Drawn to the same scale:
Top: BOAC's DH 106 Comet of 115 ft wing span.
Above: BEA's turbo-prop Vickers Type 701 Discovery-class Viscount of 94 ft span.

million had been made compared with a loss of £163,000 in the same period in 1949.

1951

Echoing the sentiments of Peter Masefield for BEA, Sir Miles Thomas, in his 1951 New Year message to BOAC staff, announced figures showing that the revenue earned per employee had increased from £900 to £1,100 in the past year, and passenger traffic from 150,000 to 180,000, with the result that the rate of annual deficit had reduced from £8·4 million to £5·7 million and the future had never been brighter — but he warned of the financial damage of the strikes they had recently experienced. Changes in the commercial side followed. Keith Granville was promoted to sales director, and John Brancker became general manager of international affairs, though Major McCrindle remained his director and in the hunt for dollars had ensured that seats on the DC-3s of BOAC's subsidiary Bahama Airways Ltd would be increased from 21 to 32 on the Florida service, and had also helped to bring to successful conclusion the long-drawn-out negotiations between the UK and Government of India in which Indian Air Lines were granted reciprocal rights.

On 9 January the third Comet, which was the first of BOAC's order, made its maiden flight at Hatfield. The second had been allocated by the MoS to BOAC for proving trials in the near future on the Corporation's main routes.

For the ninth Sefton Brancker Memorial Lecture, Peter Masefield produced one of his masterpieces. Said *The Aeroplane*: 'He is a phenomenon in the airline industry of this country. It is not an exaggeration to say that no one has got down to the analysis of estimating, costing, and budget control so thoroughly as he.' Nevertheless there was immediate *riposte* from that pioneer manager of Imperial Airways, George Woods Humphery, who rather cuttingly said: 'BEA is progressing, there is little doubt, and Mr Masefield and his team are to be congratulated. The progress could have been illustrated more clearly in fewer words; the lecture is unnecessarily complicated.' But the imperturbable Masefield in turn took him to task in what seemed a knock-out.

On 15 February the second phase of the UK airways system was instituted, with the addition of five new airway corridors added to the existing Green Airway 1 connecting London

with Shannon which had been instituted six months earlier. Under the new airways system the existing Metropolitan inner control zone would be replaced by the London control zone, extending from ground level to 11,000 feet, and the Metropolitan outer control zone would be replaced by the London control area — all as heretofore operated by the Air Traffic Control Centre at Uxbridge. Three sectors, of 120 degrees each, controlled the airways in and around the London area. At London Airport, extension of the constructional programme was under weigh, and a new two-storey reinforced concrete building was becoming visible at the Bath Road Terminal area which would house airline offices and a new departure lounge to prevent overcrowding when BEA transferred from Northolt to Heathrow. There was still no sign of the buildings for the central area, though excavations for a 2,000-ft tunnel to carry traffic under No 1 runway were well advanced. Strikes had been holding up work, including a new public enclosure; watching the airliners take off and land had become a popular public pastime, and 340,000 visited for that purpose in 1950.

As a pointer to BEA's progress a huge prestressed concrete five-bay hangar, 1,000 feet long, was being constructed on the east side of the airport as maintenance base for the Viscounts and Ambassadors at a cost of £2 million. Nearby another great hangar was being built for BOAC.

The much advertised BOAC 'Monarch' service from London to New York opened with a blare of trumpets on 1 March. There was a surcharge for this luxury service, but passengers had free cocktails and lashings of champagne followed by a gourmet dinner of caviare, turtle soup, salmon, chicken, strawberries and cream. However the airliner's range was insufficient for a non-stop flight to New York, so re-fuelling was necessary at Gander on the outbound flight. Meanwhile in East Africa BOAC were offering low concessionary fares limited to residents to encourage them to fly.

There were increasing doubts over the viability of flying-boat services. In the Commons on 14 March the Air Minister, Mr Henderson, announced that the three Saunders-Roe flying-boats would be completed for the RAF and not for BOAC. That led to increasing belief that the equally large Brabazon would not be wanted.

At the end of March BEA withdrew its Cardiff–Liverpool helicopter passenger service, having gained such valuable experience that plans were made for a London to Birmingham service. The Corporation had now ordered 26 DC-3s to be converted to 32-seaters by Scottish Aviation at Prestwick. Known as the 'Pionair', five had been delivered and on 23 March inaugurated a service to the Channel Islands as a preliminary to using them on all the internal routes. Two DC-3 airframes fitted with Rolls-Royce Dart engines had also been ordered by BEA for experimental use on cargo services.

By now BOAC was proceeding with familiarization flying of their second Comet. Although it was not fully furnished nor sound-proofed, the intention was to try it on routes passing through tropical climates, in expectation of using it for the UK to Calcutta service. On 24 May it flew to Rome, where thousands invaded the aerodrome to see it, and thence to Cairo. On 28 May it was back after a 5,500-mile tour of the Mediterranean. Four days later it left for further tests in the Middle East piloted by Capt Majendie, accompanied by Capt Alderson, manager of the BOAC Comet development unit.

There were changes at the Ministry of Civil Aviation. Lord Pakenham resigned, and early in June was succeeded by Lord Ogmore of the Commonwealth Relations Office. Pakenham's term of office had been crucial. He had seen flaws in the management of BOAC, 'so he changed them quickly and uncompromisingly', commented *The Aeroplane*. 'Unquestionably Lord Pakenham qualifies for the title of the most successful civil aviation minister of the four that have held the post since the war.' Signs were not wanting that the Socialist Government's policy was now to mark time until a general election later in the year.

With 81-seater Stratocruisers now available, BOAC on 1 June re-opened the New York to Bermuda dollar-earning service which they had had to close in March 1950 because of the shortage of aircraft. Initially running three services a week, the steadily increasing demand soon led to an additional service, and then to a fifth.

Meanwhile BEA launched its new helicopter venture of a regular service between London and Birmingham on 1 June at a single fare of £2 10s. Westland S.51s were used in which 'the three passengers and pilot sit intimately

Breakfast in bed for a 'Monarch'-class passenger on board a BOAC Stratocruiser.

together in a cabin about the size of an 8 hp car and have a superb view all round. Cruising at 90 mph, the countryside can be studied at leisure and points of interest explained by the pilot, though the vibration might be expected to cause some apprehension.' But there was also cancellation of BEA services on the Oslo, Amsterdam, and Scottish routes because of delivery delays of Pionairs and Ambassadors; services inside Germany were cut, and those planned between London and Paris could not yet be introduced.

Round-the-clock at London Airport: replenishing the drinking-water supply of a BOAC Argonaut.

To facilitate future navigation BEA proposed to fit the Viscounts and helicopters with the new Decca radio-fixing device giving instantaneous, comprehensive, and permanently recorded information on a map on which a dot was automatically made every six minutes to show the exact track. The system operated from a master station at Puckeridge, Hertfordshire, but there were only two chains of stations working as yet, though others were being erected in Great Britain and France and nine chains in all would eventually give complete coverage of Europe.

Pionair Dart-powered freighter experimentally used by BEA.

BEA had recently carried its millionth passenger, but was suffering not only from the cramping effect of delays in delivering the Pionairs and Ambassadors, but also from a 'go-slow' strike by 500 technicians at Northolt. Service after service had to be cut. These men seemed uncaring that such stoppages were a dangerous financial loss to the struggling Corporation. The Minister of Labour intervened, but by the time the men returned the dispute had cost £75,000, and it took three or four days before normal services could be resumed.

Pilots were the next problem. For some time negotiations had been conducted between the BALPA and the two Corporations because pay was far below that of American transport pilots. This led to a new scale on 2 August increasing remuneration of senior captains first-class from £1,500 to £2,150; senior captains second-class from £1,200 to £1,585 with annual increments of £55 to a maximum £1,915. Junior captains increased from £1,000 to £1,335 with annual increment of £50 to a maximum of £1,535; first officers, the soubriquet of budding pilots under surveillance in the right-hand seat, increased from £750 to £1,035 with annual increments of £30 to a maximum of £1,305.

Probably Miles Thomas acceded to these increases with lighter heart because the Annual Reports of the two Corporations published in September confirmed that the gross deficiency had been reduced by approximately £3¼ million to a current £4,565,428. Biggest contributor to

Airspeed AS 57 Ambassador 2 (Elizabethan, BEA, 1952). The Ambassador became one of the legendary airliners but it had more than a fair share of development delay. The first flight was in December 1947 but the Elizabethan class, as it was named by BEA, was not in full service until June 1952.

Feet
Metres

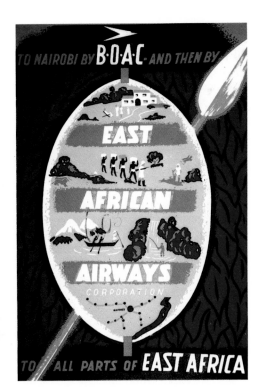

the operating loss was £3·3 million on the South American route. BEA losses had reduced by 28 per cent but amounted to almost £1 million — all incurred in the four winter months.

BEA urgently needed the new advanced types to replace the Vikings and converted Dakotas, but so far only the first Ambassador, known as the Elizabethan-class, had been received, and on 3 September it was put in service on the Paris run, carrying Lord and Lady Douglas, Mr and Mrs Peter Masefield, and other members of BEA as hosts to senior officials of interested Ministries. On 21 October, after receipt of the second machine, regular scheduled services commenced drawing high commendation for the large and tastefully furnished cabin which had rows of three seats to left and two to right of the aisle.

On 10 September that parliament of the world's airlines, IATA, had met for its seventh annual general meeting, and Sir Miles Thomas took office as president. Main topic was mass air travel and its economics. There was pressure from Sir Miles for a tourist rate 'which would not merely provide a cheap cut price or austerity means of travel, but must be made attractive and saleable. Introduction of a second-class rate, devoid of all extraneous luxuries, offers the most obvious means of cheapening and

further popularizing air travel.' Eleven trans-Atlantic operators subsequently proposed rates, subject to confirmation, for an experimental period beginning October 1952.

In parallel with the IATA, a Commonwealth Government Conference chaired by Air Chief Marshall Sir Frederick Bowhill, discussed problems of a traffic control arising from introduction of turbo-prop and turbo-jet aircraft. Though proceedings were held *in camera*, the general conclusions were published confirming that the Comets could fit into existing traffic patterns, but control methods and high-altitude weather forecasts would have to be improved when jets were operating in larger numbers. Despite the stacking problems of jets with high fuel consumption it was agreed that no priority could be given over other commercial users, but it was realized that vertical separation was no longer practicable *en route* because jets must make a long flat climb to altitude and a similar long descent.

Highlight of BOAC's activities in October was the midnight flood-lit departure to Montreal of Princess Elizabeth and the Duke of Edinburgh aboard the Stratocruiser flagship *Canopus* commanded by that distinctively bearded personality Capt O.P. Jones. As this was the first occasion Royalty had crossed the Atlantic by air, a special lounge had been made in the aft section furnished with divans convertible to beds, easy chairs, writing table, intercommunication telephones, and a private washroom; walls and ceilings were in pale-grey gaberdine carpeted in maroon, and in honour of the Princess the curtains were tartan. The Queen and Princess Margaret, together with the Minister of Civil Aviation and numerous BOAC officials, were on the tarmac to see *Canopus* take off. Gander was reached at breakfast-time after a slight diversion to avoid a storm, and at 1700 hours GMT they landed at Dorval, the airport of Montreal.

To increase efficiency by more effective employment of personnel and more economical use of its fleet, BEA was extensively reorganizing the administrative structure on the principle of functional rather than geographical responsibility and thus eliminate the artificial divisions of 'British' and 'Continental' services. There would be seven main departments: commercial under Philip Lawton; traffic under Lieut-Cdr Gilbert Waters; flight operations controlled by Capt 'Jimmy' James; aircraft movements and schedules by Anthony Milward; engineering under Beverley Shenstone; finance controlled by the accountant R.L. Weir; and administrative services under James Tyzack. All would be directors instead of general managers. Administration would be decentralized to the various stations controlled by the traffic department who also dealt with all staff at out-stations except flying personnel.

1952

The Comet's 500 hours of route proving and crew training culminated in January 1952 with simulated passenger schedules to Johannesburg carrying freight, but it was evident that the ten 36-seater Comets were unlikely to prove very remunerative. A Series 2 was therefore proposed with greater seating and range, and the lower specific fuel consumption of its more

Princess Elizabeth and the Duke of Edinburgh on the steps of the aircraft which was to take them to Nairobi for the start of their South African tour.

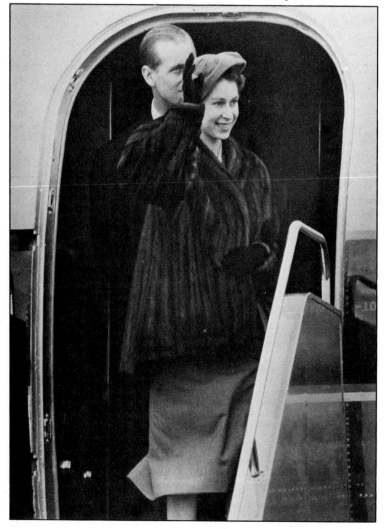

powerful Rolls-Royce engine would enable the ton-mile costs to be materially reduced. Even more economic was the four-engined Proteus turbo-prop Bristol 175 as the next urgent requirement for trans-Atlantic operations. BOAC therefore 'decided to exercise its contractual right' to take all 26 in production instead of the provisional fifteen ordered. At a gross of 58 tons it would carry 5,790 Imperial gallons yet have excellent take-off performance and carry up to 83 passengers.

On the last day of the month, Princess Elizabeth and the Duke of Edinburgh, who had returned just before Christmas, again resorted to air travel by flying to South Africa in the BOAC Argonaut *Atalanta* which had been slightly modified for the occasion to provide a private compartment. The King and Queen and other members of the Royal Family, together with Sir Miles Thomas and Sir John d'Albiac, were present at London Airport to see them take off at midday. A sequence of radio reports marked its continuing safe passage, and, after a stop at El Adem to change crew, the Royal airliner arrived at Nairobi at 7.15 next morning.

But now came high drama. The Princess's father, King George VI, having partially recovered from a grave illness, unexpectedly died on 6 February. Within an hour all the complex arrangements to fly her back to England had been completed, and an East African Airways DC-3 carried the new Queen of England, Elizabeth II, 500 miles from Nanyuki to re-embark on *Atalanta*. At 4.30 p.m. on 7 February the airliner touched down at London Airport, having flown the 4,127 miles from Entebbe in 19 hours 43 minutes, and Her Majesty set foot on her new realm.

A less historic but nevertheless important flight took place nine days later when the Comet 1 with trial Avon installation flew from Hatfield as the Comet 2X, returning at dusk after a two-hour flight. All who flew in the Comet were delighted not only with the vast vista from the heights, but by the entire lack of vibration and almost complete absence of noise except for a light hoovering sound from the jets. Said one: 'The Comet will put existing airliners in the shade; passengers will be wholly dissatisfied with other types once they have experienced this kind of travel'.

BEA had recently taken delivery, on loan, of four Elizabethan-class Ambassadors with appropriate names such as *William Shakespeare, Lord Howard,* and *Sir Walter Raleigh,* and they were being used for crew training with intention of integrating with the Viking flights on the London–Paris run. On 3 March *William Shakespeare*, commanded by Capt Riley, made the first of the *ad hoc* London–Paris services, but not until 27 March were two put into twice-daily scheduled operation.

On 9 April the BEA experimental London–Birmingham helicopter service was withdrawn. The operation had only been feasible because of an experimental grant of £80,000 from the MCA and MoS, for until larger machines were available they were too costly to operate because revenue amounted to only 5 per cent of expenditure.

Both Corporations remained hampered by delayed delivery of new aircraft, but for the first time in several years BOAC was advertising 50 Second Officer vacancies for pilots in their early twenties with an instrument rating. A more plaintive advertisement was for stewardesses because 'they got engaged or married at the rate of one a week': the romance, if not the pay of £5 17s 6d a week plus £2 a week when flying, attracted 800 applicants but only 3 per cent were accepted.

The operational staff of BOAC was busy preparing for the first pure-jet service in the world. They were encouraged by cheering news on 1 April that not only had the Treasury provided a grant of £1 million for the forthcoming year but the Corporation was 'at last able to fly on its own wings', for finally a profit had been made. Said Sir Miles: 'This has been done in the face of intense international competition and against a flood-tide of rising world costs. It is the outcome of a combination of airmanship, craftmanship, courtesy, and comradeship that rebounds to the credit of everyone in the Corporation.' On the following day, for the first time in British civil air transport, BOAC initiated a service through Germany to India, Hong Kong and Japan using Canadair Argonauts, bringing Tokyo within five days of London.

At last came the great day on 2 May when the Comet service was inaugurated between London and Johannesburg. That sunlit afternoon at London Airport: 'Airliners of many nations crowd the apron, their cabin tops white against the sky. Among them, out of sight of those watching at windows and on the terraces, is BOAC's Comet G-ALYP. To-day it carries for the first time fare-paying passengers. With a full complement of 36, and his initial cockpit checks completed, Capt Majendie, Flight Captain of

Members of the royal party which had come to see Princess Elizabeth and her husband take off on the Argonaut *Atalanta* walk out to the airliner.

the Comet fleet, is ready to start the four Ghost turbo-jets. Watching nearby are Sir Geoffrey de Havilland, the Comet's designers R.E. Bishop and R.M. Clarkson, with the engine designer Major Frank Halford and test pilot John Cunningham. BOAC's representatives include Mr Whitney Straight, Mr John Booth, and Capt Campbell Orde. Now the shrill jet-song drowns the background hum of piston engines, and heat-haze floats away from the machine. Promptly at 3 p.m. chocks are pulled away and the Comet turns towards the taxi track. Twelve minutes later, climbing swiftly away from No 5 runway in a wake of thundrous sound, the Comet is airborne for Rome.' A great crowd awaited at Johannesburg, where the Comet arrived 23½ hours later — two minutes ahead of schedule. 'It went without a hitch', said Sir Miles Thomas, who had joined the aircraft at Livingstone. 'This flight has put British civil aviation on the map of the world.'

Meanwhile BEA had inaugurated a new daily service with Elizabethans on two routes formerly operated by the Vikings, saving 1 hour 20 minutes to Vienna and just over two hours to Milan. On every route traffic was steadily increasing, and on the Paris run on 9 June BEA reinstituted the 'Silver Wing' service inaugurated 25 years earlier with Argosys. Simultaneously services would leave London and Paris at lunch-time every day carrying 40 passengers who would be served, without supplementary charge, a hot luncheon and champagne during the 1½-hour flight.

Almost immediately civil aviation slowed nearly to a halt because of a strike involving

90,000 American oil workers. There was world-wide dependence on the USA for aviation spirit. The MoS promptly issued The Control of Aviation Spirit Order barring operators from acquiring more than 65 per cent of the amount of the previous month's supply. BEA had just sufficient to cope with the Whitsun rush, and BOAC managed to maintain their Mayflower service to New York and the Comet to Johannesburg. On 8 June restrictions were lifted, but by then BEA's scheduled services had been reduced by 50 per cent and BOAC's by 40 per cent, and that would knock the finances of both Corporations.

BOAC had suffered the additional misfortune of having one of its Hermes wrecked through a navigational error, for *Horus*, after leaving Tripoli for Kano, had to land short of fuel in the Sahara sands after flying eleven hours on too westerly a course. A wing was torn off and the ten passengers and eight crew slightly injured, but First Officer Haslam died from exhaustion five days later.

Because the two Corporations had monopolistic rights for all scheduled services, special consideration had to be given to independent commercial operators who could establish a case. For that purpose A. Lennox-Boyd, the new Minister of Civil Aviation, announced that applications would be considered by The Air Transport Advisory Council chaired by Lord Terrington of the Industrial Disputes Court, assisted by those familiar figures Viscount Runciman and Gerard d'Erlanger, together with Sir John Primrose of

the Aerodrome Owners' Association and Scottish Advisory Council for Civil Aviation, and Joseph Taylor the treasurer of the Air Registration Board and manager of the Workers' Travel Association.

BEA was keeping ahead of the rival independents by establishing the new 'tourist Viking' in which the number of seats could be varied from 27 to 38 depending on the length of route. The Scottish-route Rapides were also about to be replaced by Pionairs. To control and coordinate commercial, traffic, and flight operation departments Milward was given a new post with direct responsibility to Peter Masefield, who currently flew to Cyprus and back in the Elizabethan *Earl of Leicester* on the inaugural service from London.

On 16 August the long-awaited 140-ft-span Britannia made its first flight in the hands of A.J. Pegg, but there was an immediate problem of over-balanced elevator, and the undercarriage was so slow to lock down that the crew

thought a belly landing might be necessary, but the pilot diplomatically told the Press: 'The flight was completely satisfactory and the aircraft handled well'.

Three days after the Britannia flight, the huge Princess flying-boat was launched at Cowes. Three days were spent in final checks, and conditions being favourable on 22 August, with Geoffrey Tyson as pilot and eleven crew, she slipped moorings and motored into the Solent. After waiting for waves from RMS *Mauretania* to subdue, Tyson opened up and in 25 seconds was airborne. Sir Miles Thomas flew alongside in his DH Dove, and reported: 'She looked beautiful — perfectly steady and very much in her element. The powered controls were obviously perfectly smooth in operation, and she glided along — a lovely sight in the sunshine.' But it was ominous that the two uncompleted sister ships were being cocooned.

In a speech at the conclusion of the SBAC Show, where the Princess made a triumphant circuit, Sir Miles said that BOAC was now making continuous profit. Two weeks later,

publication of the Accounts showed that the £4½ million loss had turned into £1 million gross surplus, though reduced to £250,000 profit after payment of dividends. Such was the efficiency which Sir Miles had inspired from his much-reduced staff of 16,600, that the revenue per employee had risen from £550 in 1948 to £2,000, and operating costs per ton-mile were halved.

BEA's results, despite considerable recent improvement, showed a loss of £1·4 million. That was magically explained away by Peter Masefield in a typical compendium of 73 pages, ten appendices, and five financial statements, revealing such unsuspected facts as one-fifth of BEA's deficit comprised fuel tax which found its way back to the Exchequer. Said Lord Douglas: 'If all British people flying over the route network served by BEA had flown on this, their own national airline, the deficit would have been eliminated two years ago'. As traffic was expected to double by 1960 the MCA planned to treble the area of Gatwick and make two 7,000-ft runways, running from east to west, necessitating diversion of the main London to Brighton road. The new generation of jets could then use it.

Despite predictions to the contrary the Series 1 Comets on the London–Johannesburg route had already shown they could operate at a profit, and on 11 August a service was opened between London and Colombo, Ceylon, via Rome, Beirut, Bahrein, Karachi and Bombay. Then on 14 October a third Comet route was opened to Singapore bringing it within 27

BOAC Comet 1 against a dramatic cloud background at Heathrow airport, London.

Jerry Shaw, who joined De Havilland's in 1953 after long service as Shell's aviation manager, found early fame when chief pilot of the pioneer A T & T by making the first charter flight to Paris on 15 July 1919.

hours of London instead of the 2½ days by Argonaut. But once again the fallibility of man's efforts was demonstrated by a mishap to BOAC's Comet on the London to Johannesburg run, for the pilot lifted the nose too high during take-off at Rome on 26 October, thought the port engine was losing power when the machine was partly airborne, and attempted an immediate landing on soft ground beyond the runway end, damaging the machine and puncturing the tanks, but it did not catch fire because of the low flashpoint of paraffin fuel. All 35 passengers and crew of six were able to walk from the aircraft. Because of national presige both De Havilland's and the MCA drew a veil across the incident. Three weeks later the Press was much more interested in the retirement from Shell Petroleum of the famous Capt 'Jerry' Shaw, the old chief pilot of BOAC's precursor Aircraft Travel & Transport Ltd of 1919, who since 1922 had managed Shell's aviation department. His latest task had been the establishment of kerosene refuelling points for the Comet and Britannia routes, but it was his flow of aviation anecdotes and his camaraderie which was remembered.

Maybe that was because the romance of flying was submerged by economics. At last fares for European tourist services had been agreed by representatives of 50 member airliners at an IATA Traffic Conference at Cannes. Those for the North Atlantic routes had already been reduced by 30 per cent on condition that passengers flew in more densely packed aircraft and were not offered meals or souvenirs. Traffic swiftly increased by 50 per cent. In December Peter Masefield stated that provided currency restrictions did not affect travel too stringently, BEA cut fares would be introduced on 1 April, 1953. Meanwhile over 100 additional flights were allocated from London to the Continent in expectation of a record number of Christmas passengers.

1953

To make the airlines pay, the new airliners were essential. At the beginning of January 1953 the new Conservative Government gave fresh impetus by according highest priority for the Britannia, Comet, and Viscount. Even so, BEA and BOAC viewed the early versions with an eye to future 'stretching' so that a type could be kept in service by progressive improvements and thus save money on training, specialized

equipment, and continuity of spares. Thus a more capacious Comet 2 would be a stepping-stone to the proposed Comet 3 for North Atlantic travel.

But there were always setbacks. On 5 January, one of the Admiral-class Vikings on the London–Belfast run crashed at night 'on finals' at Belfast Airport, hitting a post supporting an approach light 400 yards from the runway, fell into a field, hit a substantial building, and disintegrated; 27, including crew, lost their lives and eight survivors suffered injuries.

The initial Viscount 700s for BEA were now being delivered month by month. The first was named *Discovery* by Lady Douglas at a ceremony at Weybridge aerodrome on February 11. At the subsequent luncheon it was announced that the Corporation had placed an order for twelve stretched versions, the Viscount 800, which had a fuselage twelve feet longer and accommodated twenty more passengers. To cope with the load the Dart engines would have increased take-off power.

The story of the Viscount development was typical of the long time required to develop the post-war generation of aircraft, for the initial design was in 1945, so seven years had gone in construction of engine and airframe, prolonged testing and development, and confirmation of performance and economics by ARB before issue of a C of A which rigorously established the envelope of flight variables which determine the take-off weight and altitude performance. Airline pilots found that the Viscount handled well at all speeds, with light elevator, moderate rudder, and good aileron response, but there was slight longitudinal instability necessitating concentration for accurate height holding, but helped to make landing easy, facilitated by a three-wheel undercarriage which allowed the machine to be flown on to the runway at almost horizontal attitude.

The Britannia underwent the same course of development, and now that initial adjustments had been completed and the Proteus engines found satisfactory, performance testing was proceeding though as yet the prototype had completed only 47 hours of flying. Nevertheless in the assembly shop the first of the production machines was already painted in BOAC colours although far from ready.

Echoing the Rome crash of the Comet came another when the first Comet 1A of Canadian Pacific Air Lines crashed at Karachi when taking off in the early hours of 3 March, killing all eleven on board. As before, the pilot lifted the nose excessively, took corrective action, but was too late to prevent hitting a culvert immediately beyond the perimeter fence. A contributory cause was lack of flying 'feel' due to the power-operated control. Undeterred, BOAC a month later opened a Comet service to Japan. The elapsed time for the 10,200-mile run was 36 hours — a valuable 15 hours shorter than the Argonaut schedule which included two night stops and a flight time of 44 hours against 28½ hours for the Comet.

On 1 April the internationally agreed tourist fares came into effect. More than 90 per cent of BEA's capacity would be available at these rates. At a Press conference Lord Douglas stated that cheap tickets on the London–Glasgow and Edinburgh runs worked out at 2¾d a mile — 'the lowest air fare in the world'. BOAC similarly introduced a tourist-fare service from London to Central Africa, terminating at Lusaka, for which 56-passenger Hermes airliners were used, and the programme would be extended to the Middle East, Singapore, Hong Kong, and to South Africa. Fares would be 80 per cent of the current first-class figure. Nevertheless BOAC was offering several Hermes IVs for sale, though it was suffering a setback because all their Boeing Stratocruisers were grounded due to engine seizures to three of these airliners in flight: American experience had shown this could result in a complete propeller flying off. Tourist Constellations were therefore temporarily substituted. Among those affected was Winston Churchill, the re-elected Premier, who was due to fly by Stratocruiser from Jamaica to catch the *Queen Mary* at New York.

Meanwhile BEA Viscounts were making freighting, proving, and training flights to Cyprus and Istanbul, and for better simulation passengers were carried, such as travel agency representatives whose interests would be helpful to the Corporation, for Masefield had a keen eye for publicity. On 18 April a twice-weekly regular Viscount service was instituted to Cyprus, though between Athens and Nicosia the BEA crews were deemed on charter to Cyprus Airways, a 46 per cent mutually owned subsidiary of BEA and BOAC which had Lord Amherst as chairman. In clear weather this was one of the most beautiful routes with its Alpine vista and classic Mediterranean shores, though it now had to be viewed from 20,000 ft or more, unlike the pre-war days, for nothing must hinder progress.

Or can it? There came startling news that on 2 May, the anniversary of the first scheduled Comet service to Johannesburg, that BOAC's Comet G-ALYV, with 43 aboard, had inexplicably crashed near Calcutta. The only radio signal had been a routine 'climbing on track' six minutes after take-off. Then silence. Eight hours later wreckage was found 22 miles northwest of the airport. It soon became obvious that there had been structural failure. Why? Presently the Court of Investigation reported that collapse had been due to 'over-stressing which resulted from either severe gusting encountered in a thunder squall, or overcontrolling or loss of control by the pilot when flying through a thunderstorm'.

That was the last of it as far as the public was concerned, but the Court recommended detailed technical examination to determine the primary failure and consider any modification necessary. There was no recommendation to ground the machine, so the Comet services continued.

Despite publicity, airliner accidents were so rare that passenger traffic seemed unaffected. In mid-March Princess Margaret accepted it as a matter of course to fly to Oslo in a Viscount chartered from BEA and piloted by Capt 'Bill' Baillie, the Corporation's chief Flight Captain. A week later, on 27 March, Lennox-Boyd opened the strikingly modern BEA Air Terminal at the former Festival of Britain South Bank site at Waterloo — but there was still no equivalent for reception of passengers at London Airport.

Thousands flew to London from the USA and the Continent to participate in the great occasion of the Coronation on 2 June of Queen Elizabeth II — a day of splendid pageantry and ceremony. At the end of that month the Queen Mother and Princess Margaret flew in a BOAC Comet to Salisbury, Southern Rhodesia. Capt Cane, flight superintendent of the Comet fleet, was in command. The Queen Mother was delighted with the smooth swift progress. An hour's stop was made at Rome; Athens was circled at 35,500 feet; on to Beirut for another stop; then Khartoum where Capt Rodney took over with a new crew; and so across the Sudan to Entebbe for breakfast at Government House. Two hours later the Comet was flying across Lake Victoria, soon to land at Salisbury, the Queen Mother and her daughter emerging exactly at the planned 10 a.m. Greenwich Time. An uneventful return was made on 16 July, to be greeted at London by the Queen and Duke of Edinburgh. The Queen Mother told Sir Miles Thomas: 'It has been a wonderful trip. I have great personal faith in the Comet' — a sentiment which everyone agreed, for there was pride in this beautiful jet airliner which was so splendidly leading the way to universal high speed travel.

BOAC now established a Britannia development unit. Prototype flights had shown that a stretched version was feasible, so the order for 25 was amended to fifteen of the present production, and the final ten changed to the even more economic Mark 300. That coincided with the end of the Brabazon. The Minister of Supply, Duncan Sandys, announced that this 230-foot machine, the biggest in the world, had completed almost 400 hours' flying and he was satisfied that all possible technical information had now been obtained, so he directed that it should be scrapped. That was the end of giant machines so far as Britain was concerned.

Britain's private air companies, somewhat freed from the restrictions of the Corporation's monopoly, had become fairly well established by now. They could not challenge BEA or BOAC on any existing routes, but the Government permitted them to apply for new routes which they were free to run at low rates if within the Empire. Over 200 applications were made, and 50 had been approved by the

MCA. Where they scored was in trooping contracts which they could undertake at a lower cost per head than by ship transport. However the independents still came under supervision of IATA to which John Sefton Brancker, that long-experienced executive of BOAC, was appointed as traffic director 'by mutual agreement with BOAC'.

At that time Sir Miles Thomas seemed to favour propeller-turbines rather than pure jets, for he considered a cruising speed of 450 mph was suitable, even though 100 mph less than projected pure-jet giants. His view was that a development of the Britannia with more powerful and economical turbines could fly from London to Japan over the Arctic fringes in two stages, and to Johannesburg or New York in one. 'Present evidence', he wrote, 'is that the so-called propeller is likely to be a good friend to airmen for years to come if only because it gives faster acceleration and can be used as a brake.' Nevertheless he must have been aware of the advanced-looking Boeing 707 jet transport design which had swept-back wings and engines suspended on pylons for easy access. A 500 mph cruising speed at 80 per cent power was expected, carrying 130 passengers. With an

BOAC advertising poster, *circa* 1953.

Passengers embark on a BEA Viscount at Gatwick airport.

all-up weight of 85 tons it was 20 tons heavier than the Brabazon.

September publication of BOAC's Accounts showed an operating profit of £103,875 for the year ending 31 March 1953 because the Board decided that the deficiency after payment of interest would be carried forward — so for the first time in the Corporation's history, no claim was made for a grant under the Act. The number of passengers carried had increased by 16 per cent to 290,629, whereas BEA, whose Accounts showed an overall loss of £1,459,131, carried 1,400,122, an increase of 23 per cent. Britain had therefore made a not unreasonable contribution to the total carried by the world's scheduled airlines.

A visible sign of progress was the constant succession of aircraft landing at Northolt, at the still unfinished London Airport, or at Gatwick which now had a single long runway. Three-quarters of the combined Corporation's 1¾ million passengers passed through Northolt alone, so it was clear that with eventual closure of that Terminus, London Airport would have to handle 2½ to 3 million per year by the late 1950s, and the Terminal Building must permit 1,200 passengers an hour to be dealt with.

London Airport was now the scene of competitors assembling for an International Air Race to New Zealand. BEA decided to show the flag, and with the co-operation of the MoS entered the prototype Viscount 700, now named *Endeavour*, flown by Capts Baillie and Johnson with Peter Masefield as team manager. KLM entered their latest Douglas D-6A, *The*

The air stewardess serves lunch in boxes, and hot soups and coffee from vacuum flasks.

Flying Dutchman. Though handicapped out of the race, the Viscount arrived first in the transport section, touching down in the dark with the twinkling lights of Christchurch in the distance, and the Douglas arrived nine hours later next day as winner. Enthusiastically Masefield cabled: 'Viscount perfect ride. Aircraft and engines magnificent. Four stops total 68 minutes on ground. What a prospect for Viscount earnings.'

In the Commons at the beginning of November, the work of the airline Corporations was debated as the result of typical political manipulation in which the Government was accused of supporting independent operators at the expense of the national airlines. This led to

At Ringway airport, Manchester, finely timed co-operation between the Post Office, British European Airways and Aer Lingus enables the swift delivery of mail to Ireland.

proposals in favour of merging BOAC and BEA. Conservatives argued that there was an air of complacency running through the Corporations' reports which bore no relation to the serious financial position existing. By comparison Trans-World Airlines made a profit of $7½ million despite tax payments of $10 million, and Pan American made $6½ million. A month later the second reading of the Air Corporations Bill was moved in the Commons by which BOAC's borrowing powers would be increased from £60 million to £80 million and BEA's from £20 million to £35 million in order to meet future re-equipment expenditure.

Confidence in BOAC was implied by the Queen and Duke of Edinburgh embarking on the flood-lit Stratocruiser *Canopus* early in the night of 23 November for the first stage of a Commonwealth tour. Watched by a cheering crowd they took off for Gander, where a twenty-hour stop was made before leaving for Montego Bay, Jamaica, where the Queen invested Capt Loraine, her pilot, with insignia of MVO whilst still aboard *Canopus*, and from the SS *Gothic* subsequently cabled Sir Miles Thomas: 'Please thank all members of your Corporation who helped to make our flight from London to Jamaica so easy and successful'.

Basic to success was the rigorous inspection and maintenance systems used by both Corporations. To improve operational economics it was vital that airliners were grounded for minimum time. To that end, instead of taking gantries and steps and platforms to the aeroplane, it was now warped into a dock of prefabricated platforms mounted on hydraulic jacks to vary their height. The ARB had approved progressive maintenance at 85 hours, 300, 600, 900, and 1,200 flying hours, the latter taking seven to ten working days and representing 25 per cent of the work required for the annual C of A renewal.

Though the margin between profit and loss remained small, and easily disturbed by strikes or grounding of aircraft, the auguries promised well once both Corporations were fully equipped with new aircraft. On 29 December ICAO announced that the world air traffic of all kinds in 1953 for the first time had exceeded 50 million passengers.

1954

Disaster on 10 January opened the New Year.

BOAC's Comet G-ALYP, flying from Rome to London on the final stage from Singapore, disintegrated into the Mediterranean ten miles south of Elba. Of the 35 on board there were no survivors. All Comet services were immediately suspended. Intensive technical examination was made in close collaboration with the de Havilland Aircraft and Engine companies, the ARB, MoT and MCA. Salvage operations began, for there was a good chance of retrieving a major portion of the wreckage. Explosion by sabotage was suspected, but not indicated by the fifteen bodies recovered. Anxious inquiry in the Commons led the Minister of Transport to stress the need to await the Inquiry findings before forming judgement on the cause, but he tried to allay fears of sabotage as that would frighten potential passengers away. Within a month wreckage was located at much greater depth than expected. Weeks of

the mud of the Bristol Channel.

For an hour Pegg had been flying this prototype at 9,000 ft above cloud — then fire broke out in the starboard inner nacelle. The fire-extinguishing system proved ineffective. Pegg headed for Filton, but an electrical short circuit caused the other engines to stop. Though the ingenious specialists on board managed to restart two, an immediate forced landing had to be made. On breaking cloud the only long enough area was the low-tide mud of the Severn, and there the big machine skidded along on its belly, effectively dowsing the fire and causing relatively little damage — but the rising tide swamped it and when retrieved next day the salt water had affected the alloy too much for repair. What with loss of this airliner and the Elba Comet disaster, British aviation had been very badly hit.

Even the Tudor was in trouble again. Thanks to the efforts of Freddie Laker, managing director of Air Charter Ltd, a full C of A had been granted for carriage of passengers. He was determined to establish a 'Colonial Coach' service between Stansted and Lagos carrying 42 passengers at cut fares. Within weeks partial power failure caused one of the Tudors to stall in cloud at 9,000 ft over France, and because of the automatic pilot, control was not regained until 2,500 ft, the heavy pull-out causing damage to the skinning.

To alleviate the fears of passengers in such emergencies BEA and BOAC planned to introduce a cabin talkie system on all their aircraft instead of using verbal and written methods and the captain adding an occasional air of assurance by walking through the cabin and talking to a few passengers. Stewardesses were being taught the elements of microphone techniques, and the pilots briefed to begin their speeches with: 'Good afternoon, ladies and gentlemen: this is Captain X speaking from the flight deck', then give location, height, speed, estimated time of arrival and a report on the weather at the destination. 'The idea seems commendable', said *Flight*.

Despite the unexplained Comet crash, BOAC announced: 'Subject to the outcome of the necessary flight tests being satisfactory, normal passenger services will be resumed with the Comet on the Johannesburg route on March 23. Other services will follow. The MoT and MCA, who have taken the advice of the Air Registration Board and Air Safety Board, concur in this decision.' Comets operated by

laborious toil ensued, but a large part of the wreckage was located and shipped to England so that the RAE could attempt to solve the jigsaw of pieces.

BOAC was still in difficulties with the Britannia. The second prototype had made its first flight on Christmas Eve, more than sixteen months after the first had flown. The BOAC *Review* observed: 'Overhanging the whole problem of delivery is the question of the certificate of airworthiness'. That was targeted for June 1955, though BOAC was urging it should be December of the current year so that Britannias could be put to immediate service in the summer. So far the first prototype had completed some 200 flying hours in 152 flights. As a gesture of assurance the unfurnished second prototype was flown to London Airport late in January, and Sir Miles Thomas flew back in it to Filton. A fortnight later it was spread-eagled on

French airlines also resumed services. Sir Miles Thomas signed a firm order for five Comet 3s which could carry 58 first-class passengers on stage lengths of 2,600 miles.

Meanwhile BOAC operations room at London Airport was staging a daily imaginary jet service to New York supervised by Capt Wilcockson, of earlier Atlantic fame. A sequence of drills sent the imaginary Comet on its journey with appropriate load and route, and the 'flight' stages and signals were recorded on the movements board. Gander played its similar part and 'supervised' it to New York for the return service. Vital sources of information were weather ships in the North Atlantic. Twelve nations shared the £6¼ million cost of the nine weather stations operated by 21 frigates.

But there were always new problems. BOAC was suddenly faced with an unpleasant and financially destructive situation when a meeting of 200 local trade union officials recommended that 1,500 BOAC maintenance staff should not participate in preparing four redundant Hermes which had been sold to Britavia 'unless satisfactory assurance have been obtained that they will not be engaged on flights which could be undertaken by BOAC'.

There were nineteen of these three-year-old machines standing disused at London Airport. Action by the engineers was clearly irresponsible, though Sir Miles charitably attributed it to 'confusion of thought'. Discussion led to the men agreeing to handle a machine if Britavia operated at wages and conditions equal to BOAC's and that the Corporation did the engine overhauls. Britavia replied that their conditions of pay were agreed by the National Joint Council for Civil Aviation and conceded that BOAC engine facilities would be used: but the ban continued. A month later Britavia announced they would issue a writ against BOAC for breach of contract, for they had paid a substantial deposit but were not even allowed to inspect the machines. At that the union officials advised the engineers to agree to service all the redundant Hermes.

While the controversy was at its height the strikers must have felt encouraged when Sir Miles Thomas said: 'Without letting go any secrets I can say that the financial year we are concluding at midnight will show a very substantial profit' — but he was referring to operating profits from which interest on capital would be deducted. However it was BEA's condition which was worrying, for on 1 April Lord Douglas said that the deficit for 1953–54 would show a slight increase, but should reduce

Located with the help of underwater television cameras, the first major section of the Comet's fuselage is hoisted up from the seabed mud off Elba.

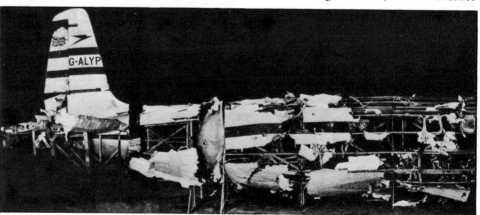

A reconstruction of the wreckage of the Comet, carried out at the Royal Aircraft Establishment, Farnborough, showing the rear fuselage and tail unit, starboard side.

by 32 per cent in the year ahead. Meanwhile the 52 member companies of the British Independent Air Transport Association had doubled their combined revenue in the course of the past year.

But now disaster struck once more, and again it was a BOAC Comet operating the scheduled service from London to Johannesburg. Two minutes after taking off from Rome on 8 April the pilot reported: 'Over Naples, still climbing' — then nothing. In the early hours next morning an air-sea search was initiated. Bodies and minor portions of wreckage were later sighted and recovered, but the area of impact was 3,000 feet deep, so nothing more was discovered. The mystery and horror of these successive Comet losses shocked the world. Britain pledged to spare no pains or perils to discover the cause of these disasters. John Profumo, speaking as Secretary to the MoT and MCA, promised that 'exhaustive investigations and tests will be carried out as a major national research by the Ministry of Supply'. All production of Comets ceased except for the 'stretched' Comet 3. Twice as powerful as the Comet 1, its all-up weight equalled a Stratocruiser. When completed early in May the maiden flight was postponed until assessment could be made of the cause of the disasters to its forebears.

That any and every country had its setbacks in developing advanced new aircraft was demonstrated when Boeing's huge four jet, swept-wing Stratotanker, forerunner of their airliner, moved gently down the runway for its first flight and suddenly the port undercarriage broke away so that the machine flopped like a vast wounded bird.

At the other end of the scale BEA was further probing the possibilites of helicopters, and on 15 June a scheduled passenger service using Bristol Sycamores was inaugurated from Southampton's Eastleigh Aerodrome to London Airport and Northolt. BEA also proposed to open a service next year between London Airport and the South Bank at Waterloo Bridge. As an initial trial run, John Fay flew an S.51 from Yeovil and landed on the derelict site on which it was planned to build a National Theatre — and that would entail removal of the BEA Waterloo Terminal office.

Not only bigger helicopters, but larger airliners were the subject of continuing investigation by Masefield and his staff, and a 60-seat airliner was envisaged of almost twice the all-up weight of the Viscount, and its design was proceeding at Vickers as the eventual Vanguard.

BOAC's need was an immediate substitute for the Comets. The Government sanctioned more American aircraft. 'BOAC is accordingly negotiating for six Stratocruisers from United Airlines, two Stratocruisers from Pan American, and seven additional Constellation 749 aircraft, four of which are being obtained from Qantas Empire Airways. The Corporation will dispose of Constellation aircraft when Comet services are resumed, and Stratocruisers with Britannias.'

At this point 47-year-old Basil Smallpeice, a chartered accountant who had joined BOAC three years ago from the British Transport Commission, was appointed deputy chief executive.

A few days earlier on 24 June Sir Winston Churchill and Anthony Eden had been passengers on the BOAC Stratocruiser *Canopus* on the scheduled London to Washington run, piloted by Capt Donald Anderson who had made some 430 Atlantic crossings in the last fourteen years. Interesting though this news snippet was for the public, the BOAC 'Monarch' Stratocruiser took pride of place on 1 July after crew and passengers, flying at 19,000 ft in clear weather 150 miles southwest of Goose Bay, observed a large flying object, accompanied by six smaller ones, keeping parallel with them for some 80 miles. Urgent radio from the Captain resulted in a fighter being scrambled to intercept, but just before it reached their position the objects disappeared, causing world-wide speculation in the Press.

More important was the mystery of the Comet disintegration now occupying the scientists with investigation on metal fatigue of the structure, strength of the cabin under pressurization, and possible excess wing-tank pressure due to the powerful fuel pumps. As yet there was no evidence of catastrophic cause, so Cunningham and his co-pilot Buggé were permitted to make the postponed flight of the Comet 3, and a long development programme followed. Meanwhile the new Boeing 707 prototype had flown, and within eight days had demonstrated a speed of 550 mph at 42,000 feet. For the time being it was still regarded as a military transport. Nevertheless the lead seemed to have gone to America.

Increasingly crowded skies led to anti-collision radar as a new requirement — highlighted on 11 August when a BEA 'Silver Wing' Elizabethan, carrying 23 passengers, touched an Air France DC-4 while they were flying blind in cloud in the Paris Control Zone; but the only damage was a small strip torn from the wing-tip of the Elizabethan, so it landed safely at Le Bourget, and the French machine returned to Orly. Eventually the French air traffic authorities admitted responsibility and said that no blame attached to either pilot. Because even on the ground there was risk of collision with such high-density traffic, the new central Control Tower at London Airport was being equipped with Decca radar airfield surface movement indicator delineating runways and taxi-ways with complete clarity. To ensure that operational staff, particularly flight crews, were kept fully aware of operational developments, BOAC formed a Flight Advisory Committee of representative experts led by Campbell Orde. Flying and engineering staff were to be encouraged to suggest improvements in every aspect of operations.

Thanks to Sir Miles Thomas and Basil Smallpeice, BOAC's operations for 1953–54 resulted in a gross profit of £2 million, reduced to £1 million after deducting interest on capital, and for the first time the Corporation became due for income profit tax, leaving a final surplus of £700,000. The four subsidiary companies, Aden Airways, Bahama Airways, British International Airlines, British West Indian Airways, had made a loss, but Gulf Aviation Ltd and Aeradio Ltd made a modest profit. A drop in freight ton-mileage was attributed to the greater space required for tourist travellers who from 1 November were further encouraged by a system of deferred payments known as the BOAC Budget Plan.

BOAC's average fare was £80; BEA's £16. Explaining the year's increased deficit of £1,773,797 Lord Douglas commented: 'BEA makes clear profits on the combined results of all routes which have a sector distance longer than 260 miles but incurs losses on routes short of that distance — which are in the majority'. BEA was therefore endeavouring to induce the Government to substitute for deficiency grants a system of payments for specific uneconomic but essential services. To help subsidize their training branch, it had been opened to foreign airlines operating Viscounts and so far eighteen pilots had taken the fourteen weeks' course and many engineers had been instructed in maintenance and overhaul.

The financial affairs of both Corporations were the subject of debate in the Commons on 15 November led by John Profumo, who referred to significant civil aviation milestones of the past year — particularly specific agreements for round-the-world partnership of BOAC and Qantas, and the Strasbourg Conference where the UK succeeded with important proposals for air transport within Europe.

Currently BEA opened a helicopter service between Gatwick and London Airport, the first flight carrying several hundred pounds of Redifon flight-simulator components which would be up-lifted by an RCAF aircraft at London Aircraft and flown to Canada. To supplement the existing Bristol 171s, BEA ordered two Westland eight-seat S.55 Whirlwinds costing £54,000 each. On signing the contract Lord Douglas warned that there was over-optimism among people whose imagination was fired by the idea of scheduled inter-city services using twin-engined helicopters capable of carrying 40 or more people, but a suitable civil helicopter was not likely to come in to service before 1958. Eric Mensforth, the managing director of Westland, mentioned they would probably build the Sikorsky S.56 powered with two gas turbines but Lord Douglas implied that even this machine could not fully meet BEA's requirements.

Though BEA was moving hopefully towards better economics with its increasing fleet of Ambassadors and Viscounts, BOAC was struggling to overcome the set-back of the Comet disasters. Their Stratocruisers and Constellations had been divided into separate fleets. BOAC and Capital Airlines of the USA announced: 'With a view to standardizing their respective Constellation fleets, BOAC and Capital Airlines have agreed that BOAC will transfer their seven Constellation 049 aircraft to Capital Airlines in exchange for Capital Airlines' seven Constellation 749A aircraft. A financial adjustment is involved. The exchange will be completed by June 1955.' The current market value of a Constellation 747A was some £500,000, £200,000 more than the 049s.

Because of the long delay before the Britannia fleet would be available, BOAC had to decide whether to purchase the long-range Douglas DC-7 equivalent. There were

The Royal Aircraft Establishment had the vital task of discovering what had caused the explosive cabin failure of the ill-fated Comet 1s. To that end, a complete Comet was tested to destruction in a huge container, using water pressure to simulate those strains experienced in flight. This resulted in the discovery that metal fatigue had led to local rupture of a skin panel.

rumours of negotiations for an R-R turbo-prop version, but no airline could afford mistakes when it came to transports of this calibre.

Said Sir Miles Thomas: 'We cannot carry passengers on promises. BOAC is a vigorously competitive international business and it is vital to offer present and future passengers aircraft which are as up to date as those of any competitors. BOAC is supporting the British aircraft industry with orders of more than £50 million for only two types of aircraft — the Comets and Britannias. Our policy is to buy British wherever possible, but it is also our statutory responsibility to operate the airline and to do this we must have the right aircraft. Moreover it is essential that we have them at the right time.'

For the past six weeks a public inquiry had been proceeding at Church House, Westminster, before Lord Cohen and other assessors to consider the cause of the Comet disaster at Elba. Research had been far-reaching, and now it was studied in detail based on the RAE *Report of Comet Accident Investigation* which showed that there had been structural failure of the pressure cabin due to metal fatigue, though it had occur-

red in a much shorter time than indicated by pressure tests in the specially built water tank at Farnborough. Despite hindsight criticism that de Havilland's pre-flight structural tests had been too optimistic, the firm was absolved from responsibility for the disasters though Lord Cohen recommended that the Comet be re-designed on the basis of thorough investigation of 'distribution of stresses throughout the structure in considerable detail, and the influences which determine both the high static load which it will sustain and its life to failure under repeated loadings'.

On Christmas Day BOAC were involved in still more trouble. Their Stratocruiser *Cathay*, commanded by Capt W.L. Stewart who had made over 300 trans-Atlantic crossings, was on ground-controlled approach to Prestwick Airport en route for New York in the early hours of morning under low cloud base and drizzle conditions, but apparently undershot the runway; the port undercarriage collapsed, severing the fuel lines in the wings, and the machine turned over and caught fire. Seven of the eight survivors were crew, but 27 passengers lost their lives.

Jet Set
1955-59

BEA lost another of the hard-pressed fleet on 16 January 1955, when Capt Waits, in taking off the Viscount *Sir Humphrey Gilbert*, mistook the end of a disued runway at London Airport for the correct one. During its run the Viscount struck a steel girder barrier which tore off part of the undercarriage and the two port engines, and ruptured the fuel tanks, but at least it did not catch fire, and only the Captain and one passenger were injured.

Shortage of aircraft was affecting both BEA and BOAC. As a result, ten BEA pilots were seconded to Lufthansa to operate their rival services for a year! BOAC's expedient was cancellation of the first-class return services from London via Manchester to New York, and the London–Cairo extension of the 'Monarch' service. There was also the problem of Comets cocooned and snow-covered, parked at London Airport — but in mid-February the Minister announced: 'Comet 1 aircraft cannot be made suitable for further airline use without extensive and costly modification. Certain of the aircraft which can be usefully employed for research and development will be acquired by the MoS.'

This was followed by a statement from BOAC: 'After studying the Cohen Report it has been decided to instruct the de Havilland Company to proceed with building a fleet of New Comets. The Corporation is satisfied that the cause of failures of the Comet 1 has been found out and can be eliminated by strengthening the fuselage structure. This the de Havilland Company will do in the design and construction of the new Comets. They will be flown by the makers and BOAC for many thousands of hours on service tests and route familiarization before they are put into passenger service.'

These were Comet 4s with more powerful R-R Avon 524s and greater full capacity to meet BOAC's North Atlantic requirements — but it would be at least two years before the prototype was ready. To make up the fleet requirements BOAC increased the order for Britannias to 33, comprising fifteen MK 100s,

eight long-bodied MK 300s, and ten MK 300 LRs with integral transfer tanks outboard of the standard tankage to give adequate range for the Atlantic route. Pending their introduction, permission was given for ten DC-7Cs to be ordered at the dollar equivalent of £13 million provided they were resold for dollars when the Britannia LRs came into service. Delivery was promised for late 1956.

This year the Brancker Memorial Lecture was given by Arnold Hall, the man who conducted the Comet investigation and had been knighted for his services. Ranging widely, he particularly expounded the problems of bad-weather flying, fog dispersal, use of the radio-beam (ILS) approach path and high-precision radar (GCA), and automatic landing using the magnetic field of a leader cable, and taxi-tracks with similar system, but hinted at 'radar–television' to provide a picture of the airfield ahead. He concluded: 'We must eliminate the not entirely incorrect idea that aviation still has hazards. Attention must be continuously directed to ensure that the fullest use is made at the earliest opportunity to those things which make for a safe, reliable journey at a reasonable price.'

Certainly London Airport provided every safety facility. The new central Terminal and tunnel access were opened on 17 April, coinciding with the summer schedules. Two BEA Viscounts made their respective arrival and departure under a cloudless sky at 7.30 a.m., and by midday the bright April sunshine had attracted lines of motor-borne enthusiasts to see the Terminal in action. The central area was dominated by the nine-storey Control Tower topped by the Control penthouse. Sixth and seventh floors contained approach-control facilities using Cossor airfield control radar linked to display consoles separately dealing with ground movements and flight control. In the approach-control room two radar controllers guided aircraft in from the Epsom and Watford stacks. Whether landing visually or GCA a three-minute landing rate could be achieved —

The futuristic-looking cockpit of the Comet 4B, 1959.

Detailed inspection and maintenance is the *sine qua non* of all airline operations. Here a Stratocruiser is undergoing overhaul in 'the Kremlin' at Heathrow.

6 June. BOAC's great Australian partner, Sir Hudson Fysh of Qantas Empire Airways, handed over his executive functions on 1 July to their accountant director C.O. Turner. On that same day 57-year-old Lord Balfour of Inchrye, better known as Harold Balfour the pre-war and war-time Parliamentary Under-Secretary for Air, became part-time member of the BEA Board. Because he had been a director of several small airline companies prior to 1938 there was speculation whether major changes were imminent in BEA.

but in the near future radar-monitored ILS landings were expected to improve this to 50 aircraft per hour.

All BEA routes now operated from London Airport, having moved from Northolt on 30 October after an eight-year association during which there were more than 300,000 aircraft movements carrying five million passengers. The last BEA aircraft to leave Northolt was a Viking on positioning flight flown by Capt Jimmy James, and this also signified the passing from service of these valiant interim machines. In the year ending 31 March BEA had carried more than 54 per cent of all traffic leaving the UK for Europe, and revenue earning had so increased that at last there was a profit of £52,000 after paying all costs, including £654,000 interest on capital and over £1½ million for amortization and depreciation.

But now came historic change. Churchill at 80 resigned the premiership. Elections in May resulted in victory for the Conservatives and Sir Anthony Eden became Prime Minister. That month another famous personality resigned: Capt O.P. Jones of the much-publicized jutting beard. At 56 he had completed 21,600 hours, crossing the English Channel 6,000 times and the Atlantic 300, carrying 140,000 passengers. Such long and devoted service earned an illuminated certificate.

Currently Major Thornton retired from the BOAC Board after nine years' valuable service, but would continue as consultant on commercial and economic matters. In his place novelist John Buchan's son Lord Tweedsmuir, a director of The British Steamship Co Ltd, joined on

At the end of July the long-promised helicopter service between the Waterloo site and London Airport began. On the first flight J. Boyd-Carpenter the newly appointed Aviation Minister, John Profumo, Lord Douglas, and Peter Masefield were passengers in the seaplane-like Whirlwind piloted by Capt 'Jock' Cameron. The pontoon flotation bags were mandatory in case of engine failure on the stipulated Thames entry route from Putney. The fare was 35s for the seventeen-mile journey, but even if the maximum five passengers were carried on each of the eight services a day there would be a loss of £322.

The full story of BEA's twelve-month transformation from loss of £1¾ million annually to a small but definite profit was revealed in their Annual Report published in mid-August. The major achievement was a 16 per cent increase in operating revenue for a mere 3·8 per cent greater expenditure, due to the economics of the Viscount and Elizabethan fleets, coupled with increasing popularity of air travel resulting in a smaller differential between the summer peak and winter trough of traffic. 'Looking ahead', the Report stated, 'the Corporation is well advanced with plans for a much faster, larger, and more economic successor to the Viscount, but sees no sign of a satisfactory large helicopter nearing the commercial stage.' Hope was expressed that work on Gatwick, essential to BEA's continued development, would proceed energetically. However a critic commented: 'BEA's organization cannot yet be regarded as economically sound. Compared with American airlines, the staff is far too large or productivity far too low. BEA has proved the technical merit of the Viscount but is not yet capable of exploiting its commercial characteristics, attributable in part to low utilization of aircraft and crews. In setting out operating costs, the

Report uses a BEA formula which, though efficient and convenient from an internal viewpoint, does not facilitate comparison with figures published in other sources of reference. A clear separation between the domestic and international routes would enable the Corporation to declare its "social services" deficit with a clear conscience and might force the Government to adopt a more positive policy towards air transport within the UK.'

A fortnight later came news that the meteoric, ever-friendly 41-year-old Peter Masefield had resigned from BEA to become the first managing director of the new Bristol Aircraft Ltd division of the Bristol Aeroplane Company Ltd. In a letter to the Aviation Minister he emphasized that his resignation did not result from differences of view on policy. 'My duties towards British aviation lie more clearly in making what contribution I can in the direction of the more pressing problems of British aircraft development and production.'

BOAC's Annual Report followed, but the reduction of profit from the previous year's £1 million to £260,000 indicated the set-back caused by the Comet 1 and delayed delivery of Britannias while competitors were increasing their traffic by some 20 per cent. 'It is impracticable', the Report stated, 'to estimate precisely the financial effect of the withdrawal of Comets. Residual expenditure and loss of revenue have to be written into the capital loss of £1,730,000. In addition, replacement Constellations and Stratocruisers could only be bought at top market prices in many instances greater than the cost when new, thus leaving a legacy of high operating cost during the continuing life of these aircraft in the Corporation's fleet.' The Report detailed BOAC's co-operation with British independent airlines, such as Airwork in establishing a North Atlantic freight service, agreement with Hunting-Clan for the new Africargo service, and a short-term charter agreement with Skyways to operate the BOAC freight service between London and Singapore. Coincidently Bill Lawford, the pilot who made the first commercial flight to Paris in 1919, died at the age of 70.

Adding to BOAC's troubles, their Argonaut *Altair* on the London–Lagos route crashed at Tripoli on 21 September after striking trees while approaching the airport terminal during a sandstorm. Fire broke out and the steward, stewardess, and thirteen of the 40 passengers were killed and seventeen injured.

Unfortunately these disasters were too widely publicized for people to realize they were comparatively rare compared with the enormous number of safe journeys made by every airline.

Now came another surprise announcement. On 3 October Whitney Straight wrote to the Minister: 'Would you be good enough to release me from BOAC because I wish to accept an invitation to join Rolls-Royce on November 1. Sir Miles Thomas, whom I have consulted, is agreeable. For the past twenty-two years I have been on the flying side of the aviation industry, of which sixteen have been devoted to public service in the RAF and the Airways Corporation, but for some time I have wanted to broaden my experience, and I feel fortunate to have the exceptional opportunity of joining Rolls-Royce. To leave old friends in both Corporations has been a difficult decision, but I am leaving at a time when the future has never looked more promising.' Boyd-Carpenter replied: 'The work you put in as deputy chairman of BEA and then on BOAC's Board, and in particular as deputy chairman in the last six years, is now reflected in the high esteem in which both Corporations are held all over the world. You helped to set the tremendously high standard.'

A significant pointer to the future was Pan American World Airways' announcement that they had placed orders for twenty Boeing 707 swept-wing Stratoliners and 25 Douglas DC-8s in the most expensive deal ever placed by an airline, for it totalled £96 million. The effects were bound to be far-reaching, for few airlines could stand the competitive pace of re-equipment on such a scale. Both aircraft, with their four podded under-wing jets, were hardly distinguishable from each other, though the DC-8 was slightly larger, carrying 108 first-class passengers or 131 tourist compared with 104 first or 125 tourist for the Boeing. Douglas guaranteed a cruising speed of 575 mph, but Boeing more cautiously said 'above 550 mph'. It seemed that Pan American had initiated a war of nerves, and it was certainly a knock to BOAC, for the Comet 4s only carried 60 first-class passengers and the cruising speed was 50 mph slower.

Strong Press opinion, largely unfavourable, followed news that Sir Miles Thomas, though still chairing BOAC, had joined the Board of Harry Ferguson Research to develop new designs of motor vehicles. However Sir Miles said he was 'merely acting in advisory capacity

Feet

Metres

Top: BEA's Westland Whirlwind Series 1 G-ANUK had a specially silenced 600 hp Pratt & Whitney engine, and was fitted with supplementary floats.
Above: The BEA Whirlwind landing in the heart of London at the South Bank site on inauguration of the helicopter service to London Airport on 25 July 1955.

production machine, G-ANBD, and both were formally handed over to the Corporation.

1956

For two months there had been constant queues for the London–Paris services because a strike of French airport staff in the autumn of 1955 restricted BEA to only five flights a day using the military airfield of Creil. Affairs dragged on until 1 January, when the French Air Force took over the control tower at Le Bourget. However reduction of facilities created hazard, for on 2 January one of the BEA Viscounts, flying over cloud, had engine failures due to water contamination in the fuel. Only one engine was giving full power with occasional bursts from the other three, but because he was using a trial Decca set the pilot, Capt Watts, navigated accurately to Cazaux and landed safely.

Matters had improved by 27 January, when BOAC had the honour of flying the Queen and Duke of Edinburgh to Nigeria. Three days earlier, six Canberra light bombers took off for 'Operation African Tour' in preparation for a ceremonial fly-past for the Queen at Lagos. The Argonaut *Atalanta*, commanded by Capt Parker, flew the Royal party on the first stage to Tripoli, where a second crew commanded by Capt Ballantyne took over for the final 2,000 miles to Lagos. *Flight* commented: 'While we do not advocate that a Britannia should be constantly at the Royal Command in the way that the Super Constellation *Columbine* is at the call of Mr Eisenhower, we are acutely aware that Argonauts and Vikings are no longer worthy to bear our Royal personages on their long and arduous journeys'.

Details of BOAC's plans to introduce Britannias to Commonwealth routes were given by Lord Rennell during a publicity mission to Australia, but whatever action the two Corporations took they were never free from criticism — possibly inspired by the non-scheduled operators. The Air League said that Britain was 'stumbling into the air age'. BALPA stressed the threat of the new American jet airliners, pointing out that 36 could carry as many passengers across the Atlantic as all airlines and shipping lines put together, and that BOAC would be unable to compete. That was because the Corporation had expended tremendous effort to use British aircraft which proved unsuitable. *The Aeroplane* blamed these on the Ministry 'which lacks expert know-

on a part-time basis'. This evoked from the *Sunday Express* the furious comment: 'If Sir Miles and Lord Rennell [Whitney Straight's 60-year-old successor] could not give all their time to BOAC they should get out of BOAC altogether and make room for men promoted from inside the Corporation'. Less bluntly, *The Times* doubted whether 'the British Overseas Corporation are arranging their highest affairs in fashion calculated to cope with the testing time just ahead in world flying'. On 22 November the new appointment of Sir Miles was questioned in the Commons, but the Minister replied that he was satisfied that additional work would in no way affect Sir Miles's duties as chairman of BOAC. Sir Miles and Sir Geoffrey de Havilland were at London Airport on 28 December to greet the arrival of the special Comet 3 in BOAC livery as the first jet airliner to encircle the globe. Here was practical exposition of the advertised performance figures, for so high was the average of 501 mph that the voyage had taken only 67 hours' flying time. For the moment this put the Boeing 707 and Douglas DC-7 in the shade.

Two days later, and seven years after the MoS had ordered the prototypes, the first available production Britannia, G-ANBC, which had been on route-proving flights, came flying in to London Airport, followed by the fourth

ledge' yet largely controlled what aircraft BOAC received.

Another writer commented: 'Far sounder patriotism would be displayed if BOAC was encouraged to operate the best aircraft, regardless of country of origin. What is needed, at least for BOAC, is greater freedom and fewer conflicting responsibilities.'

BOAC was having its own internal problems. BALPA was pressing for pay increases for first-class captains who now received £2,695 on the North Atlantic route, but whom it was hoped to up-grade to £3,299. More immediately worrying were the 1,000 engineering workers at Treforest who thought widespread unemployment would ensue when piston engines became obsolete and threatened that unless turbine engines were overhauled at their factory they would stop work from 2 April, and meantime banned overtime.

There were changes now at BEA. Anthony Milward was appointed chief executive. Suspicions of change at BOAC were also confirmed. On 7 March Sir Miles Thomas wrote to the Minister: 'I shall be grateful if you would allow me to be released from my responsibilities as chairman of the British Overseas Airways Corporation as soon as can conveniently be arranged . . . I feel I can now make more useful contribution to trade and industry in other directions. Although the challenge of bettering the affairs of BOAC is good exercise, working in a nationalized industry is not my natural bent.' Later he was reported to have said he was 'tired of irksome political interference and uninformed criticism from back-benchers'. There had, he emphasized, been no clash between himself and the Minister, but he added: 'You can either have an airline run as a competitive, keen commercial concern using the best available equipment, or you can have it as a

shop window for British aircraft you would not normally purchase'.

Within a month 49-year-old Gerard d'Erlanger was appointed chairman of BOAC and 60-year-old Sir George Cribbett, whose work at the Ministry of Transport and Civil Aviation had been concerned with international traffic rights of the Corporation, became deputy chairman, but Lord Burghley, who had served BOAC for ten years, terminated his part-time directorship. Basil Smallpeice was promoted to managing director; Keith Granville became his deputy and commercial director.

D'Erlanger told the Press: 'I regard myself not as a chairman on part-time duties, but rather as chairman of the Board, free of executive responsibilities allocated to others, but I will of course devote as much time as necessary to the conduct of the Corporation's affairs'. To consider future equipment requirements he appointed a committee comprising himself, Cribbett, Smallpeice, Sir Victor Tait, Keith Granville, Campbell Orde, Charles Abell the

chief engineer, Capt Tom Farnsworth the senior captain, and significantly Capt Tony Spooner who had recently evaluated the Boeing 707 prototype at Seattle. How would the committee react to this crucial issue? Would it recommend British-engined American jet airliners to maintain its competitive position in the early 1960s or wait until the late 1960s for a supersonic British airliner?

The capital cost was a vital factor, for though there had been a net profit of some £500,000 up to 31 March, d'Erlanger now announced a loss of £1½ million including capital charges. That

Above: Sir Miles Thomas (*left*), Chairman of BOAC, receiving the log book of the first Britannia, 1955.
Left: Sir Miles Thomas at the controls of the first Britannia 100 handed over to the company on 30 December 1955.

came as a shock, for it meant that after a lapse of four years the Corporation would again require government financial support. Though not connected with this loss, the retirements were announced of Sir Victor Tait the operations director, Sir William Cushion the supplies manager, and Sir Harold Whittingham the director of medical services, who was succeeded by Dr Kenneth Bergin, a keen pilot.

Though BOAC made this big loss, the preliminary trading results of BEA showed a net surplus of £500,000 — regarded as a big improvement on the previous year's £63,000. In expectation of 'our biggest summer yet' Lord Douglas estimated that each of the 29 Viscounts would earn about £47,000 a month throughout the season, and £35,000 for each of the nineteen Elizabethans. The Corporation proposed a big drive to increase the freight business as it was yielding 'really worthwhile results'. One of the BEA Viscounts was used by the Queen in July to fly to Stockholm and back, piloted by Capt Baillie the chief flight manager. A week after her return the crash of a BOAC Argonaut on taking off from Kano Airport, Nigeria, caused renewed anxiety on the risks Her Majesty ran in travelling by air, for of the 45 people on board the Argonaut, 32 died and eleven were seriously injured.

Meanwhile no time was lost by the BOAC committee in recommending close assessment of the DC-8 and Boeing 707 jet airliners. Campbell Orde left for the USA on 1 July to visit these two great manufacturers, and d'Erlanger was expected to join him later, accompanied by Capt James Weir who had just been appointed chief of flight operations.

That Sir Miles Thomas's judgement in ordering the Comet 4s was justified seemed endorsed by Capital Airlines of Washington D.C., one of the world's busiest operators, who currently ordered four Comet 4s and ten Comet 4As. Rarely in the history of British commercial flying had there been such welcome news, for hitherto no operators except BOAC seemed willing to commit themselves, particularly as the DC-8 and Boeing 707 projects had begun to assume the aspects of hard metal and hard cash, promising range and speeds beyond the Comet's attainment. Matching this order, BEA now signed a £25 million contract for twenty turbo-prop 50-ton Vickers Vanguards designed to carry 93 passengers for 2,600 miles. BEA's helicopter interest was also expanding, and on 2 July a Whirlwind service from Bir-

mingham to Leicester and Nottingham was inaugurated at Elmdon by the Lord Mayor and Mayoress of Birmingham, accompanied by Lord and Lady Douglas, and John and Mrs Profumo. On 20 July Lord Douglas and Anthony Milward visited Filton where Peter Masefield officially handed over a Bristol 173 helicopter — the first twin-engined helicopter to be used by an airline, and subsequently the two BEA executives flew back in it to Ruislip, piloted by 'Jock' Cameron, and accompanied by a Sycamore bearing Capt James, stalwart Henry Marking the BEA secretary, and Bob Whitby the performance and analysis manager.

1 August was BEA's tenth birthday. In that time it had become Europe's largest airline and had carried more than twelve million passengers, earning £113 million revenue. In honour of the occasion an anniversary party luncheon was held at the Savoy, attended by Harold Watkinson the Minister of Aviation, Lord Brabazon, MPs, former and current executives, airline representatives, and manufacturers.

Publication of the Accounts for the year ending March 1956 confirmed that the airline had improved its previous surplus tenfold, though the net profit after deduction of capital interest had whittled to £603. Scrutiny of the Report, contrary to Lord Douglas's earlier prognostication, showed that of all the 101 fixed-wing aircraft only the Viscounts made a profit, earning £1,138,605, whereas the Elizabethans lost £558,721 and the DC-3 Pionairs £722,195. Overall profit in fact had come from non-flying revenue such as ticket commissions. In view of this BEA made an 'upward adjustment' of 6 per cent on the London–Belfast fare and 10 per cent on all other routes effective from 1 December.

BOAC's Annual Report similarly showed that Sir Miles Thomas's estimate of £500,000 net profit had been over-optimistic, for the actual net surplus after payment of capital charges was £117,731 — less than half the previous year's. The decline was d'Erlanger's theme with warning that even when the Britannia and the DC-7C were available there would be heavy expenditure without appreciable attendant revenue. A significant fact was that more tourist seats were being sold than first-class, so there would be still more when BOAC, with other operators, reduced fares on the North Atlantic run in April 1958. 'The aircraft required for these services', said d'Erlanger, 'are the Boeing 707 and Douglas DC-8 which although powered by Rolls-Royce Conway engines will cost about £2 million each with spares provisioning; but they should pay for themselves within five years of being put into service — and it should not be overlooked that the lion's share of the revenue will be in dollars.' The next logical step, he said must be supersonics, and some 'very nebulous preliminary talks' had been held with various British manufacturers.

Delivery of the first four DC-7Cs for which Sir Miles Thomas had daringly signed the contract on 18 March 1955, nine months before the prototype flew, had been stipulated by 31 December 1956. The Americans capped this with 'first delivery by the vendor' on 17 October, and to the surprise of those fretting over the long Britannia delay it was ceremonially handed over by Donald Douglas to Lord Rennell two days ahead of schedule, and when the American Stars and Stripes and the Union Jack were drawn aside, the name *Seven Seas* and BOAC speed-bird insignia were revealed.

But where were the Comets? To fill the gap BOAC ordered fifteen Boeing 707-320s costing 44 million and issued a specification to de Havilland's for a comparable jet airliner, the 110-ton DH 118 powered with four R-R Conway turbo-jets giving superior performance to the Boeing and carrying 120 passengers, but it was never built. BEA more successfully issued a specification for a 600 mph swept-wing, short haul turbo-jet 75-seater for which de Havilland's tendered the DH 121 with triple jet engines in the tail.

These matters were aired in Parliament at the end of October, but achieved little prominence because of the political crisis which had developed when Nasser nationalized the Suez Canal Company. On 29 October the Israelis attacked Egypt. British troops were flown to the Mediterranean in 34 Britannia flights. When the shooting started in Egypt a further 34 trooping flights were made, but after the USA intervened withdrawal began on 6 November. It was a diplomatic victory for Nasser. Britain's gold and dollar reserves fell sharply. Expenditures by BOAC on the Boeing 707 and the proposed DH 118 were heavily criticized. Reginald Maudling, the Minister of Supply, admitted £6·5 million had been spent on developing the Britannia and £11·5 million on its Proteus. James Callaghan demanded: 'Why

The DC-7C, first introduced in January 1957 on the North Atlantic route. It carried up to 77 passengers at a cruising speed of about 340 mph.

is there no long-range British aircraft in sight twelve years after the war for BOAC to buy?' The Minister encouragingly replied that 'the long-range Britannia will be operating across the Atlantic before the American's long-range jet'.

That coincided with Lord Douglas's warning that unless BEA succeeded in 'beating our winter targets and hold[ing] down costs to offset the summer short haul the financial year is likely to end with a loss'. He cited the Middle East situation and the credit squeeze as the cause of unexpectedly low income. Ever since the previous summer, BEA had not once attained the budgeted revenues. Matters were made worse by imposition of a heavy petrol tax — but fortunately for BEA the kerosene-consuming Viscount would not be affected, though the piston-engined fleet would cost an extra £1,000 a day.

Beyond the scene of the Corporation's immediate affairs, though affecting their operations, were changes in the UK airways system as the result of representations made by GAPAN, BALPA, and the Guild of Air Traffic Control Officers (GATCO), backed by IATA and the British Independent Air Transport Association (BIATA) to whom the Ministry of Transport and Civil Aviation presented a new plan on 14 December. Currently there were six airways into London and another connected through the Midlands with Manchester. It was expected that the changes would simplify the task of individual controllers and expedite the

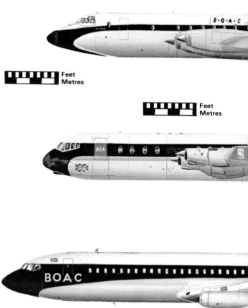

Sir George Cribbet (*left*) and Basil Smallpeice, making speeches on the departure of the inaugural Britannia 102 to Johannesburg, 1 February 1957.

handling of the increasing traffic between Britain and the Continent, but it offered no relief to the complexities of piloting. The next step would be introduction of a height level above the present 11,000 ft which would be inhabited by the big jets.

1957

On the last day of the old year the first long-range Britannia 312, intended for service with BOAC but as yet in Bristol Aircraft colours, made its first flight — but there would be another long sequence of test to establish its performance for the North Atlantic route. The shorter-range Britannia 100s were scheduled for the Johannesburg run and Kangaroo route to Sydney. All the crews had been flying American aircraft, and of the 750 pilots in BOAC only 48 had flown with Imperial Airways. Said the Britannia fleet manager, Capt Houston: 'Maybe the highly skilled, technically trained men who handle modern airliners are unromantic about their work — but they can become attached to some aeroplanes and not others. A pilot's hands and brain act in co-ordination to create a personal impression of the aircraft he is flying. He feels the tremendous power of the Britannia. An outboard engine can be cut and the machine still take the air in a fast climb. If he comes in to land with two dead engines on one side and without flaps he finds it as easy as a normal landing. The Britannia is a safe aeroplane.'

Contributing to that was the search radar so that the turbulence of thunder clouds could be avoided, and prominent landmarks established 120 miles ahead even on the cloudiest night. There was a lavish array of radio equipment — DME, ILS, two ADFs, two UHFs, two HF sets, all within easy reach of the pilots, and independent of the inter-phone system there was a first-rate address system to the passengers. The whole tenor of navigational development was towards automaticism, for celestial navigation, dead reckoning, and radio signals all involved errors making them only relatively useful. Under development was a new system of inertial navigation using a gyro-stabilized platform and a double integration that measured acceleration to show the distance travelled during a given time indicated on a dashboard dial.

At midday, 1 February Britannia G-ANBI, commanded by Capt Taylor, left London Airport on the first scheduled service to Johannesburg carrying a full complement which included Basil Smallpeice, Sir Reginald Verdon Smith chairman of the Bristol Aeroplane Co, and Sir Alec Coryton chairman of the Bristol Engine Co, together with nineteen first-class and 48 tourist passengers. With postponement of the in-service date still fresh in mind, many fingers were metaphorically crossed.

Concurrently a 'jet-age task force' appointed by ICAO reported on 'the world's outstanding case for improvement' — the North Atlantic. As many as 84 flights a day were made in the

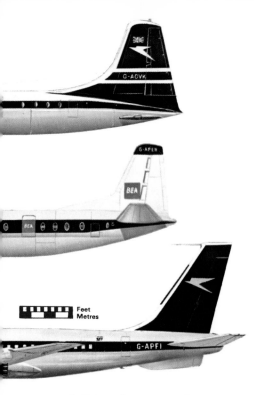

Feet
Metres

Left: Drawn to the same scale:
Top: Fifteen Britannia 102s were ordered, but the development programme was protracted, and they did not enter service until 1957.
Centre: As with all airliners, a 'stretched' version of the Type 700 Viscounts operated by BEA was eventually required, resulting in the Type 800 accommodating up to 65 passengers.
Bottom: Twenty Boeing 707-436s powered with Rolls-Royce turbo-jets were scheduled for 1959, but tail modification delayed delivery to 1960.

houses on the approach to Ringway Airport Manchester and all fifteen passengers and crew of five, as well as two occupants of the houses, lost their lives. A newspaper said: 'First clue to the cause was given by an eye-witness who saw part of the starboard flap buckle'. All Viscount 701s throughout the world were withdrawn from service, but flying was resumed within a fortnight after changing vital bolts which had suffered fatigue failure.

Accidents remained of deepest concern. The MCA issued a *Survey of Accidents to Aircraft of the UK*, but figures could be juggled to show how safe flying was; though in fact accidents had increased by 60 per cent from 1954 to 1955, the latter represented 95,000 flights per accident, but in terms of passenger miles was one in over 10 million, or over 32 million aircraft miles per fatal accident, and on that basis flying seemed fairly safe. Certainly the travelling public believed it safe. Despite gloomy forecasts there had been a big increase in traffic revenue, so BOAC and BEA by the end of their financial year on 31 March had a small surplus.

Both BEA and BOAC required more pilots to meet the envisaged programmes. The source now was the RAF by agreement with the Air Ministry who had requested the Commands for assistance with aircrew recruiting. BOAC required about 100 pilots during the next two years and BEA could absorb 40 in the current year.

It was a sign of the inflationary times that BEA discontinued helicopter passenger flying after five years of experimental schedules. Dr Hislop, the rotary wing technical manager, had joined Fairey Aviation, and now 61-year-old Reggie Brie resigned the management he had held for a decade. No large-scale helicopter passenger operations were proposed until bigger machines were available, but experimental flying would continue under management of 'Jock' Cameron, who had flown over 3,000 hours on helicopters.

summer of 1955, and at an annual 15 per cent increase that would mean 120 or 130 flights a day in the summer of 1959. This was significant because more than half the flights had 'substantial difficulties' due to defective communications or ATC services and inadequate position-fixing in flight. The report stated: 'In the absence of accurate information on the position of aircraft, safety demands that very large separations be maintained among them, which is one of the main causes of apparent congestion on the North Atlantic air space'. Adding point to the future problem the Government announced: 'The Minister of Supply, in conjunction with the aircraft industry and national airline Corporations, have embarked on a research project with a view to a supersonic airliner'. That was the beginning of aerodynamic experiments at Farnborough on slender wing deltas leading to Concorde.

Now came a surprising decision from BEA. Introduction of Britannias into service by BOAC had been matched by BEA's introduction of the 'stretched' Viscount 802 carrying 57 passengers in normal density or 65 in higher density. So successful had the sequence of Viscounts been on scheduled services that BEA decided to withdraw and sell the nineteen Elizabethans. The first two would come on the market in April, and successive pairs each month — a rate governed by delivery of the new Viscount 800s.

However BEA had a setback on 14 March when their Viscount 701 *Discovery* struck

The successive and disappointing delays which had preceded introduction of the Britannia 102s made it hard to accept that the all-important Britannia 312, which earlier in the year had successfully completed cold-weather trials in Canada, was experiencing late-hour teething troubles though needed for the scheduled Atlantic route in July. Now that it was at Filton after demonstration in the USA, there were reports that improvement to the specific fuel consumption of the Proteus 755 propeller-turbines was essential. Meanwhile the faithful eight-year-old Stratocruisers continued indefatigably on that route, having logged 190,000 hours and an accumulated 60 million miles. To hold position BOAC must continue to risk purchasing new types of aircraft and towards the end of May 35 Vickers VC-10 medium jet transports were ordered, adding £68 million to the £195 already at stake. Said d'Erlanger: 'My Corporation has every faith in the ability of Vickers-Armstrong to produce an airliner which, in partnership with our other new equipment, will help keep BOAC pre-eminent on the air routes of the world in a mid-1960 period and beyond'.

There were also raised eyebrows over a ten-year guarantee by BOAC of a £1·75 million profit for near-bankrupt Central African Airways in return for rights to operate the CAA services from the UK to Rhodesia and Nyasaland. BOAC would charter Argonauts to CAA and operate them in Corporation colours and with Corporation crews. How such profit could be guaranteed when it was three times BOAC's total net operating surplus in 1956 nobody could understand. A current decision to remove the Union Jack from BEA tickets, timetables, and literature provoked another outburst of protest, for the airline had been 'showing the flag' abroad by painting it on the fins of their aircraft. Anthony Milward in a letter to *The Times* on 6 June, explained: 'There must always be countries, of which the Near East is an example, who do not appreciate literature embodying the Union Jack. Our expensive time-tables instead of being prominently displayed are therefore thrown away or hidden behind competitors' publications. Our decision is dictated solely by commercial motives.'

In the following month Milward said BEA would decide 'within the next two weeks on our pure jet re-equipment programme. We will be meeting representatives of some of the four aircraft firms who may be able to achieve our requirements. Delivery would be needed by the end of 1962.' Clearly he had decided that pro-peller turbines were not the *sine qua non* of an economic service.

5 July was a nostalgic anniversary for BOAC and 'Pan Am' who jointly advertised in *The Times*: 'Tonight, on this twentieth anniversary of PAA's and BOAC's first trans-Atlantic flights, two modern airliners of these friendly rivals will exchange radio greetings in mid-Atlantic. It was on this day 1937 that the North Atlantic air route was simultaneously pioneered: westbound by Imperial Airways and eastbound by Pan American. To-day we proudly recall that historic first flight, and will honour the occasion once again by a friendly exchange of radio greetings.' So midway across the ocean the Captain of BOAC's Stratocruiser *Caledonia* duly talked with the Captain of the eastbound Pan Am Stratocruiser.

On 22 July the Commons debated the Air Transport Advisory Council's recommendation that Airwork and Hunting-Clan should be given a combined 30 per cent share in the new IATA approved third-class fare traffic to Africa, and the balance to BOAC who would exclusively have the higher-class traffic. There was immediate protest from BOAC trade unions that the new policy would threaten their members' livelihood. For the Opposition, Ian Mikardo declared: 'On more than one occasion we have raised the question of the erosion of the Corporation's services by feather-bedded concessions given to private operators. Most of the Colonial Coach services are bound to disappear in favour of the new level services. The Minister in a cowardly manner got the Advisory Council to do his dirty work. Members may wonder why the workers are so suspicious. Perhaps they noticed that the Minister had chosen to recruit his BOAC chairman from the Board of the company which finances the purchase of aircraft by private operators, including foreign operators. If the Labour Government are returned at the next election they will make drastic changes.'

In reply the Minister said: 'What matters is not what the Socialist party or the Conservative party decides on air transport, but the pattern which the world dictates. It is simply a piece of elementary justice to allow the independent airlines to keep the traffic they have created. There is no possibility that the Corporations can be other than the main flag carriers for this country.'

Exceeding even the most hopeful expectation, BOAC wound up its accounts for 1956–57 with a net profit of £303,352 instead of the £1½ million deficit d'Erlanger had predicted. The improvement was attributed to a 2 per cent increase in total load factor — or was it that BOAC was the one British commercial undertaking which had profited from the Suez Crisis? The customary Press conference was outspoken to an unprecedented degree, arising from a letter written by Smallpeice to the staff stating: 'We hoped to put the Britannia 312 into service last April, but delivery dates have repeatedly gone back. Even if the latest delivery dates are met, results in the current year will be over £2 million worse than they should have been. This is the measure of financial damage which late deliveries do to us.' Questions led to more revelations. The Britannia 312 was 10 per cent down on the lowest range performance guaranteed by the makers, so it would be unable to operate non-stop Atlantic services in the 1960s. Bristol refrained from replying, realizing the futility of counter-recrimination, particularly with their No 1 customer. Stupidly, BOAC began to publicize the frequency of engine changes and resultant irregularity of their Britannia 102 services.

'Things have got so out of perspective that it isn't funny any more. All aircraft have teething problems', declared Bristol's Britannia production manager when the prototype Britannia 312 on an ice-hunting sortie on 30 September was forced down at Miami because of compressor blade rub due to contraction of the casings. However there was soon cheering news that a

full C of A had been granted, with proviso that prolonged flight must be avoided in clouds above 16,000 ft in a narrow band of temperature above freezing and in heavy concentration of water or ice. 'The problem posed by this latest discovery has yet to be solved', warned the ARB.

BEA's Annual Report indicated a net profit of £216,770. A commentator remarked: 'The airline business seems to be a matter of putting a vast amount of money to work and being thankful if it yields one per cent profit. Every year is spent flying close to the break-even line, chased by fast rising costs and in pursuit of not so fast rising revenue. The margin between profit and loss is slender — too slender to withstand extraneous political and economic commotions, and too small to permit the build-up of capital for the renewal of plant which depreciates faster than in any other industry.'

Creating a considerable surprise was BEA's decision to place an order for six 100-seat Comet 4Bs with initial delivery towards the end of 1959 and completion by the spring of 1960.

Whereas the BOAC Comet 2Es were back in business, the Britannia continued to provide problems. The trade unions got into the act, demanding a public inquiry on the grounds that 'BOAC are losing hundreds of thousands of pounds because the Britannia is not a machine which they can operate to the full'. However the immediate engine problems had been overcome by fractionally cropping the turbine blades, and the Britannia 312 trans-Atlantic proving flights were resumed — but on 6 November the MoS Britannia 300 prototype, returning to Filton after a normal test flight, suddenly swung from one turn to another, went into a still steeper turn, lost height and struck the ground four miles from the runway, killing the crew of fifteen, of whom several were technicians from other companies. No cause could be immediately established.

Nor was BEA immune. One of their supplementary aircraft was the half-ton, 71-ft span four-engined DH Heron light transport used as an ambulance for emergency cases in remote Scotland. Dispatched from Renfrew to the Isle of Islay in bad weather, with low clouds, it was observed coming in to land, made a procedure turn, and disappeared. An hour later its wreckage was located a mile off shore, but none of the crew, including the nursing sister, had sur-

Left: G-AOVF was one of sixteen enlarged, longer-range Britannia 312s received in 1957–58, but the fin was too tall to enter the maintenance building and very long platform-ladders were required.

vived. Less than a month later, on 23 October, the flagship of BEA's Viscount 802 fleet, *Sir Samuel White Baker*, was coming in to land at Belfast under GCA control because of similar low cloud and rain, when it struck the ground and was completely destroyed, the crew of five and two passengers losing their lives. The intention had been to pick up the Minister of Supply and a party of journalists, and to that end a BEA official and his wife had been on board.

Whatever the losses, BEA's aim was to extend operations. Political unrest in the Middle East had caused a deficit of £73,000 for Cyprus Airways after four years of profitable trading, so BEA, who like BOAC had a 23 per cent stock holding, agreed to take over the majority of the routes, all of which were using Viscounts chartered from the Corporation. But financial problems were hitting the UK. Decisions on development of London Airport and for a small jet airliner for BEA were consequently held up. The Minister, Harold Watkinson, explained: 'The Government have tried to speak with utmost frankness about the measures we are taking to deal with inflation. We are determined to limit the amount of money going into circulation. Industries will find that the Government will not provide the means to enable any inflationary action.' Consequently the VC-10 was being privately financed by Vickers, but the proposed BEA triple jet would certainly require government support. It was another case of wait and see.

Amid all the clamour for official inquiries, criticism, and cash, the Russians suddenly riveted attention by sending into space the world's first little satellite. *Flight* commented: 'Some people have been frightened. Others have given new hope for a world wherein men of science and statesmen will show the way out of a morass of miseries and fears.'

It so happened that the Russians were also flying the world's largest airliner, the Tu-114, powered with four propeller-turbines and capable of 500 mph carrying 220 passengers — but it was the Britannia which became the world's first turbo-prop airliner to operate a regular service between Europe and America. El Al shook BOAC by advertising a trans-Atlantic

The new route over the top of the world!

service on 22 December. A few days later BOAC quietly announced that their own would open on 19 December but refused to reveal the timetable for a week. No sooner was it disclosed than El Al published a schedule which cut BOAC's time by one hour in each direction that day. But it did more. With a spectacular non-stop proving flight from New York to Tel Aviv, the El Al Britannia flew the 6,100 miles at an average speed of 401 mph, creating a distance record for a civil aircraft, and on 22 December that airline began a schedule of one flight a week with intention of increasing it to five within six months.

Another moment in history had passed almost unnoticed. On 12 December Capt Alfred Instone, that pioneer who in 1909 founded the Instone Air Line, died at the age of 73.

1958

The New Year's Honours of 1958 announced a knighthood for Gerard d'Erlanger and a CBE for Keith Granville. On the previous day Alan Campbell Orde had relinquished his appointment as BOAC's development director, and to many it was the loss of an old friend because of his long activity in British civil aviation. In the recent decade he had been very closely concerned with the design and operational evolution of the Comet and Britannia, and the specification of that Boeing rival, the Vickers

swept-wing, jet-powered VC-10, for which Basil Smallpeice now signed a contract for 35 with option on another twenty — the biggest single contract so far placed for a British civil aeroplane. Sir George Edwards described the design as 'the first big jet aeroplane to take advantage of modern design knowledge of one of the big handicaps of the pure jet — its airfield limitation. The VC-10 will come into service several years after the first US jets and consequently offers distinct improvements. Although it has a higher cruising speed, the significant advantage will be its ability to carry substantial payloads over long distances on routes served by or including "difficult" airfields, resulting in improved flexibility of operations and therefore better all round economy.'

Basil Smallpeice added: 'BOAC requires this aircraft primarily for its Eastern and African routes, therefore the importance of good airfield performance. The mounting of the engines at the rear will also give an exceptionally quiet and comfortable cabin, and its structural strength and power will make it as good an Atlantic aeroplane as any.' These days it was becoming difficult to distinguish between different types of aeroplane built for similar purpose, but the high T-tail of the VC-10 and tandem sets of jets each side of the fuselage between wing and tail would be distinctive.

On 7 January the scheduled BOAC Britannia on the New York to London run completed the journey in a record eight hours with the aid of a

The most important airliner of the 1960s — the Boeing 707-436, carrying up to 136 passengers at a cruising speed of 540 mph for up to 4,200 miles.

100 mph tail wind. A three-tier fare would be introduced on this route on 1 April, operating Britannia 312s and DC-7Cs with third, tourist, and *de luxe* class cabins, the third class being predominant with 54 seats on the Britannia and 37 on the DC-7C's. On the same day as the 'record', BUA introduced the world's first turbo-prop route to West Africa with the 53-seat tourist-class Viscount *Safari* which would operate initially once a week, replacing the former coach-class service which Hunting-Clan and Airwork operated before Ghana obtained her independence.

For a year battle had raged over the choice of BEA's jet airliner. Would it be the Bristol 200 project or the DH 121? The industry manoeuvred and regrouped behind the two contending designs, with Hawker Siddleley and Bristol in alliance and de Havilland setting up the Aircraft Manufacturing Co with their own chairman W.E. Nixon as chairman of the new company which included Hunting Aircraft and Fairey Aviation, but had only £100 nominal capital.

In the Civil Aviation Debate on 27 January Harold Watkinson, stated: 'The history of BEA's attitude was that to begin with, it favoured the Bristol concept, but after discussion and technical examination the final decision was in favour of the de Havilland design. I do not think there is now any aircraft manufacturer who has not had a chance of associating himself with this order if he wants to. The final detailed proposals from the de Havilland Group reached my Rt Hon friend and myself only this morning. They are being urgently examined.' Meanwhile the Bristol-Hawker Siddley Group was seeking American reaction to their own design and de Havilland's for theirs, for it was almost certain that the Ministry would give the order to the Group with the best chance of export orders. None were immediately forthcoming, but on 12 February conditional Government approval was given for the DH 121.

By then BEA was involved in the adverse publicity of another bad accident when their Ambassador *Lord Burghley* had crashed at Munich on 6 February on its third attempt at taking off on a snow-covered runway, and of the 44 on board, 23 were killed. Not even the Comet's accidents so forcibly impinged on the public mind, for the machine was carrying the Manchester United football team back to England from Belgrade. Engine failure as a cause

was eliminated and the effect of snow suspected. The aircraft had not been sprayed because it was in transit and only un-freezing snow was falling. In due course the German Inspector of Accidents issued a statement that the crash was due to icing causing the machine to stall. A long legal battle followed involving both pilot and passengers.

Whatever the setbacks, nobody could accuse either Corporation of lack of initiative. In the Middle East, BOAC had over £1 million invested in seven airlines as well as MASCO and British International Airlines in the Persian Gulf. Similarly BEA acquired a 33$\frac{1}{3}$% financial interest in Cambrian Airways operating in Wales. Surprisingly, BOAC now made a competitive move to include Europe in its international network by applying to the Air Transport Advisory Council for permission to operate Britannia 312s, DC-7Cs and Boeing 707s between London and Paris, initially twice weekly but on a daily basis — perhaps a *quid pro quo* for BEA's activities in the Middle East. At this point Pan Am announced that their Boeing 707 jet service across the North Atlantic would start in October. In effect the jet race with BOAC and their still undelivered Comets had started.

Not only deliveries but finances had slipped. BOAC had a deficit of some £2$\frac{3}{4}$ million for 1957–58 — the first for five years. Critics ascribed this as largely due to £2 million interest on capital, Treasury advances and bank loans as the price of the world's heaviest airline re-equipment programme. Watkinson in Parliament demanded that 'a constructive effort must be made to put the financial position right'. Crucial was BOAC's maintenance and overhaul work at nearly double the cost of most American and European competitors. A first step was dismissal of 650 engineering staff in the next two months, and 3,150 over the next two years. A union official declared: 'This is the beginning of a war — and a big one'.

There was at least satisfaction that on 9 April the first Comet 4 had been rolled out at Hatfield for engine run, though it was significant that the first DC-8 in the USA emerged that same day. On 27 April the Comet made its first flight, followed by others in steady succession.

In contrast to BOAC, BEA exceeded £1 million profit for the first time. Six Ambassadors had been sold, and there should be further improvement when the Viscounts took over virtually all the international services. But there was an immediate setback. BEA had chartered a Viscount to BOAC, but it hit Barwell hill, five miles short of Prestwick where passengers were waiting, and though the crew got clear despite injuries, the aircraft was completely destroyed by fire. That was the third Viscount written-off during the past seven months, and it increased disquiet not only in the public mind but in the insurance world because in the past year eleven transport aircraft on the British register had been destroyed. Then on 16 May a Pionair of BEA crashed in a storm at Nemours near Paris, killing the crew of three and increasing the disturbing total of BEA write-offs to six. But there had also been major crashes abroad by other airlines in one of which Capt J.R. Steer, BOAC's manager in the Far East, had been killed. Nevertheless two million passengers had safely crossed the Atlantic since the war.

Recently the Corporation had been conducting experimental helicopter night flying with a Sycamore at Gatwick, using a 'Cross of Lorraine' lighting pattern for a dummy heliport of 400-ft diameter, landing in visibilities as low as 100 yards, but trials had to end when Gatwick was opened to public traffic by the Queen on 9 June. A few minutes after the ceremony, commercial use of the airport began with a BEA DC-3 Pionair which left on a charter flight to the Channel Islands. BEA expressed intention of operating more international services from Gatwick, though the difficulties of connection with London Airport 25 miles away were likely to prove considerable despite the adjacent railway. However the Corporation, with an eye to helicopters, had received permission to operate an 'inner circle' service between London and Gatwick, and ultimately to Southend. To encourage Westland sales, Westland shrewdly obtained permission for a heliport site at Battersea.

On 30 July BEA's Ambassadors were finally withdrawn after the day's scheduled flight from Cologne to London. They had proved popular despite dangers inherent in a twin-engined machine, and in 6½ years since March 1952 the twenty Elizabethans had carried nearly 2½ million passengers at an average load factor of 64·5 per cent. BEA announced that: 'The Corporation believes there is a place in European air transport for higher speed jet aircraft, and for the mid-1960s envisages the DH 121 on longer international routes and the Vanguard on shor-

Top: Some of the nineteen Comet 4s at the Heathrow maintenance facilities.
Left: The chairman of BOAC, Sir Gerard d'Erlanger, receives the Certificate of Airworthiness for BOAC's first Comet 4 from Sir Geoffrey de Havilland.

ter international and domestic routes where operating flexibility is of primary importance. For the interim there is a clear requirement for limited jet operation to protect BEA's competitive position. For this reason BEA signed a contract for six Comet 4B aircraft to be delivered in the winter of 1959.'

The attention of both Corporations was therefore closely focused on the Comet testing. The prototype had successfully completed the 'hot and high' airport trials at Nairobi, and on 27 July the second Comet 4 made its maiden flight. Since then the prototype had made a quick dash to New York in a record 6 hr 27 min to confirm noise acceptance levels at the International airport, and on 28 August the official public début was made at Hatfield where 150 Press representatives and 50 other guests were given flights. Full certification was now the goal.

Another milestone was the retirement of Major J.R. McCrindle, the lawyer–pilot ex-managing director of Hillman Airways and British Airways Ltd, who in 1940 became deputy director-general of BOAC and since 1947 had been adviser on international affairs to the Corporation and its overseas associate companies.

A spectacular flight was now made by the

BOAC marks another historic occasion on 4 October 1958 with the opening of the world's first trans-Atlantic jet service using the newly certificated Comet 4. Centre of front row is the aircraft's commander Capt Roy Millichap.

'We were in good radio communication with Shannon, Gander, and London. The B-47 was cleared down to 31,000 ft and up we went to 35,000 waiting for clearance to 39,000. We finished lunch at 15.30 BST. Fifteen minutes later we were somewhere near the weather ship *Charlie* 900 miles from Gander and 1,450 from London, and going like a bomb. Gander was reached in 5 hr 28 min, having flown 2,360 miles at an average 430 mph. Maximum height was 39,000 ft, outside temperature −57 degrees centigrade. Refuelling took 1 hr 17 min. Gander was its usual dreary self and glad we were to get back into the Comet. For the 1,140 miles to Idlewild we had to mix it with 115 mph head winds which brought ground speed down to 335 mph. So we took 3 hr 25 min for the last leg, but arrived relaxed and exhilarated — and feeling very patriotic. We went to bed after carving a neat little 707 out of our courtesy soap and stuck pins in it. When we arrived back at London Airport there were painters' ladders against a big Pan Am hoarding which was shouting "First Atlantic jet service".'

Both the MTCA and Port of New York Authority had been co-operating on the jet noise problem, but residents near London Airport were soon up in arms because the 707 emitted dense black smoke when water injection was used for the Pratt & Whitney engines at take-off. However R–R Conways powered BOAC's 707–428s and were expected to create less nuisance.

Comet prototype which between dawn and sunset on 14 September, piloted by John Cunningham, flew the 8,000 miles from Hong Kong to London in 16¼ hours. Not to be outdone, the first Boeing 707 arrived at London Airport from the USA to demonstrate its capabilities, but had landed en route at Gander and Shannon to re-fuel because the steep climb-out necessitated reduction of gross weight from 105 tons, of which 45 was fuel, to 85 tons gross — so for identical ranges the Comet could carry the greater load of passengers. Nevertheless Pan Am announced that a daily trans-Atlantic service would be launched between New York, Paris and Rome on 26 October, and daily services to London three weeks later.

However BOAC was the winner. Duly certificated, a westbound Comet commanded by Capt Millichap and an eastbound Comet with Capt Stoney simultaneously made the world's first trans-Atlantic jet flights carrying fare-paying passengers on 4 October. One of the passengers recorded: 'It was just before 12.26 that we taxied out and 12.30 when Capt Tom Stoney turned on to the runway and started rolling. Sixty seconds later we were over Windsor and climbing like a fighter. At 12.46 we were over Filton. By the time we reached the Irish Sea we were at 32,000 ft — ground speed 465 mph with a 20-knot head wind. We hoped to be clear of this at 36,000 ft but opposing traffic in the form of a B-47 at 37,000 ft kept us down.

Tragic emphasis was given to the problem of increased traffic density by a mid-air collision near Nettuno, Italy, on 22 October between BEA's Viscount *Sir Leopold McClintock*, commanded by Capt Frank Foster, and an Italian Air Force fighter. The Viscount, flying at 23,000 ft, disintegrated on impact with fatal result to passengers and crew, but the seriously injured pilot of the fighter escaped by parachute. Anthony Milward immediately flew to Nettuno for the inquiry, at which he urged closer liaison between civil and military air traffic controls. Ironically the collision occurred while ICAO at Montreal was discussing air traffic congestion, and at Southend the Guild of Air Traffic Control Officers was holding a similar conference. Even more directly concerned was the Federation of Airline Pilots Association, whose secretary told the *News Chronicle*: 'The whole airway system in Italy is poor. There are consistent complaints from pilots, for air traffic control is mainly staffed, for economy reasons, by military personnel who do not stay long enough to learn the job thoroughly.' Pilots found it impossible to keep preventative watch with closing speeds so high and cockpit visibility often less than outside because of misted windscreen or sun glare, and in any case must concentrate on the mass of instruments or listening-in to radio aids.

Rarely were there complaints about London Airport. Already it was Europe's busiest air centre. In ten years air traffic movements had increased from 23,000 to 116,000, and passengers from 280,000 to 3·5 million. By 1970 it was expected that 13 million passengers would pass through, necessitating trebled aircraft movements. Nevertheless everything paled into insignificance compared with New York which was the busiest air centre of the world, and in the past year 14 million passengers had used the three main airports, almost matching the total of all Europe's airports put together.

However BOAC movements from London Airport came to a standstill in October after five engineers were dismissed for refusing to work overtime, and all went on strike. The Minister of Labour ordered a Court of Inquiry at which Clive Jenkins of the Association of Supervisory Staffs (ASSET) affirmed: 'The Government is progressively diverting traffic from the Corporations into privately owned profit-making airlines' — but his evidence was described as evasive and mischievous. Acid criticism was made of BOAC's and BEA's management by the chairman of the joint Shop Stewards Committee, who boldly affirmed: 'It is perfectly well known that I am a member of the Communist Party'.

In November the Court found that the overtime ban by the 4,000 BOAC engineering staff was unconstitutional and that the shop stewards' powers should be circumscribed — but criticized leadership at various levels on both sides, though agreeing there had been no undue delay by the employers in dealing with wage claims.

Christmas Eve, for BOAC, was another ill-fated day, for one of the Britannia 312s commanded by Capt Jackson on a local flight from London Airport crashed near Christchurch, Hampshire, and of the twelve BOAC employees on board, including five crew, nine lost their lives. The day was foggy; permission had been received to descend from 13,000 feet over Hurn to 3,000 feet, but below the cloud floor was fog and they flew into the ground because of the misleading nature of the three-pointer altimeter 'likely when the routine monitoring of the instrument panel has been interrupted during descent and then rescanned'. These were standard for all Britannias, Comets and Viscounts, so the ARB ordered them to be changed for an approved Kelvin Hughes design.

On Christmas Day and Boxing Day there were fatal accidents to foreign airliners. No previous year had so many tragedies, for there had been 50 crashes in the world's commercial flying taking the lives of over 800 passengers and crew. Nevertheless in terms of passenger-miles the global rate remained unchanged.

1959

On the night of 2 January 1959, Moscow radio announced the successful launching of the first rocket ever to escape from the earth's gravitational field, passing within 5,000 miles of the moon, and going on to become the first man-made object to orbit around the sun. The accuracy of guidance was even more impressive than the provision of sufficient rocket power.

Of more immediate concern to BEA was progress of the 60-ton Vickers Vanguard 951 of orthodox straight-wing design powered with four R-R Tyne propeller turbines and intended for short-haul routes carrying 139 passengers at economy rates. Piloted by 'Jock' Bryce and Brian Trubshaw, the prototype made its first short flight essay on 20 January, flying with undercarriage down from Brooklands to the Vickers flight test centre at Wisley. Subsequent flights revealed the usual array of snags, such as rudder hunting; nevertheless testing proceeded rapidly.

Though BEA had fought vigorously for a big fleet of jets to preserve its competitive position, it had agreed since 1952 to pool services with Aer Lingus, Air France, Alitalia, Austrian Airlines, CSA, Iberia, KLM, LOT, Lufthansa, Olympic Airways, Sabena, SAS and Swissair. The target advantages were prevention of individual excess capacity, joint economies in staff, station costs, promotional expenditure, and more convenient spread of services throughout the day instead of each line hogging peak times. The contentious step was now taken of pooling actual revenues with Air France and Swissair on shared routes.

With trans-Atlantic flying it was different. Here was intensive competition in which IATA ensured the same limitations for all, but when it came to flying across the USA the route was blocked. When Qantas and BOAC sought permission to fly between San Francisco and New York threats were breathed that if this was turned down 'the UK would have to review its policies as far as the US is concerned', for the USA domestic carriers were vehemently opposing the requests, particularly as BOAC had eyes on the long hop from San Francisco to Japan. Much depended on legal interpretation of bi-lateral agreements which permitted airlines to pick up traffic at designated terminals and set down at another, 'provided that the traffic concerned originates at or is destined for another country'.

Six of the nineteen Comet 4s had been delivered. The American Government agreed to BOAC's application for Britannia 312s to fly from San Francisco across the Pacific, enabling BOAC to announce that their first round-the-world services would begin on 1 April, with Comets flying eastward from London to Hong Kong in 3½ days, linking with Britannia 312s flying the westabout route from London in 4½ days. To aid navigation BOAC placed orders for the basic Decca system, and a Comet 2E was sent on a series of Decca demonstration flights in Europe and North America as an overture to an ICAO meeting called to adjudicate on the relative merits between this and the USA's controversial Vortac system. When a vote was taken the Vortac won by twenty votes to four, with fifteen abstentions, but IFALPA representing 30,000 pilots strongly opposed this and supported an 'area-coverage system with pictorial presentation'. Counter-moves seemed inevitable.

Some of the problems of airline operation were highlighted by two incidents in America, in the first of which a turbo-prop Lockheed Electra of American Airlines crashed into New York's East River at midnight on 3 February while using the ILS approach in fog and rain at La Guardia. Of 73 on board only eight were rescued alive. That same day a Pan American Boeing 707 carrying 124 from Paris to New York abruptly dived from 30,000 ft to 6,000 due to 'running away' of the Bendix auto-pilot which operated control and stabilization in three axes, auto-trimming, height lock, turn to pre-selected heading, glide slope lock, and manual bank and pitch command. This led Sir

William Hildred to warn: 'If manufacturers, inspired by dedicated project designers suddenly throw at us a supersonic aircraft which can do 2,000 mph before the rest of the system is in the phase to accept it, we shall be getting into something like chaos'.

In Paris, IATA agreed all-round increases on air fares for all classes and a jet surcharge on economy and tourist tickets. BOAC said they welcomed this, though formerly anti-surcharge — a change of mind due to their depressing finances, for the accounts for the previous year showed further substantial loss of £4·75 million, as well as a net capital loss on disposal of Argonauts, Constellations, and Stratocruisers. Sir Gerard said that BOAC on its own operations had broken even, but the associate companies had a bad year, change-over of fleets had been costly, interest on capital had considerably increased, and trading conditions generally had been very difficult, a contributory loss being the cost of the autumn strike at London Airport. Nevertheless BOAC had become number two major carrier across the Atlantic, with 28,000 passengers in the first quarter of the year thanks to tourist fares, though Pan Am remained leader with 54,000.

By a small margin BEA, for the fifth time in succession, managed to make a profit. Traffic had increased only slightly, but was greater than world average, and freight had increased by an encouraging 18 per cent to 26,500 tons, most of which was carried in the holds of scheduled aircraft on passenger services. Lord Douglas, who now had been chairman for ten years, declared: 'All is set for a good summer'.

As a first step a service between London and Moscow via Copenhagen was opened on 14 May using a Viscount 806 piloted by Capt McLannahan. Two days later an Aeroflot Tu-104A jet airliner made the reciprocal run by agreement with BEA, though the Air Ministry was concerned at the noise problem because of organized hostility around London Airport. Said a Russian official: 'No one ever complains of jet noise in Moscow'. Two flights a week with intermediate landing at Copenhagen were scheduled by each company at first-class fare of £142 4s and £118 16s tourist. BEA was offering package tours to Moscow for £120 inclusive and expected to break even with 51 per cent load factor.

On all its routes the signs were encouraging. Forward bookings were 'most promising', particularly for inclusive tours at lower fares. Sales of first-class seats also were increasing. Lord Douglas said: 'Our fares policy is to lower the price at one end of the scale and thus create a mass travel market, but we have no intention of throwing away our valuable first-class clientele because of our ambition to provide air transport for the masses, so we shall provide a better class of service at higher fares for those prepared to pay for it'. A further move was to bring Transportes Aéreos Portugueses (TAP) into the fold with an agreement for co-operation on the London–Lisbon route whereby TAP would charter Viscounts from the Corporation operated in BEA colours by BEA crews.

25 July marked the fiftieth anniversary of Blériot's flight across the Channel and coincided with a *Report on the Air Corporations* by the Select Committee on Nationalized Industries, in which BOAC was sharply reprimanded for lack of productivity in their maintennce department and big losses on subsidiary airways; a sufficient allocation for depreciation had not been made, so the financial results 'are not as good as they seem'. Nor were BEA's Annual Accounts 'a true indication of the Corporation's efficiency because losses on domestic social services are not published. The subsidy is paid not openly through the Civil Estimates, but quietly through the accounts of a nationalized industry. BEA would be wise to insist on placing the responsibility for these losses firmly where they belong.' Every aspect of operation was covered in this monumental report. Thus the extensive teething troubles of Britannia and Viscount led to the conclusion that 'the cost of introducing new aircraft into service falls too heavily on the Corporations, placing them at disadvantage compared with foreign competitors'. Of fares policies the Report said: 'Both Corporations were emphatic in their support of IATA: without it there would have been anarchy'. And of future 'jet' civil aircraft the Report quoted Lord Douglas's comment that 'the airline industry has gone a little crazy about jets and we have all got into the race in too big a way too quickly'. The Committee therefore warned that: 'A supersonic race might end in the airlines of the world suffering severe financial losses which they will be unable to make good without help from the governments'. Finally the Report suggested that the Ministry interfered with the Corporations to a degree far in excess of the statutes, and recommended that when the Minister wanted to override their commercial judgement he should publish a directive.

That modern transport aircraft had their problems was again emphasized when an American Airlines Boeing 707, taking off on a training flight, began to spin and crashed on Long Island. Newspapers headlined: 'Jinx strikes at Boeings again'. A Boeing representative said: 'The aircraft apparently got away from the pilot. Perhaps he made too tight a turn, or was demonstrating one of the emergency procedures to the others.' In fact, with a heavily swept wing an accidental sideslip, perhaps induced by sudden engine failure, creates roll in the opposite direction to that intended and may temporarily overcome corrective action. Every 707 incident was attracting maximum publicity, and a second appeal was made to Congress to ground these aircraft pending investigation.

In Britain the Air Registration Board, in the interests of economy and flight-testing, decided that their own pilots should participate in all future prototype tests, commencing with the Vanguard, and would include the Board's special safety trials such as abortive take-off, engine or systems failures.

At BEA's headquarters at Bealine House on 12 August a £28 million contract was at last signed for a smaller DH 121 of 47 tons instead of the original 65 tons; 24 were ordered and twelve were on option. Anthony Milward agreed that the DH 121 was virtually a Viscount replacement kept as small and light as possible, hence lower power, less fuel, and operationally less costly. Span was less than the original design, but the same fuselage diameter was retained and the fuselage length reduced. Delivery was scheduled for late 1963. As with all the new generation aircraft, controls had three separate hydraulic 'fail-safe' circuits, and each pair of ailerons was in two sections using only the inner portion at high Mach numbers. A prerequisite was fast turn-round, so there was an APU providing air for starting, cabin conditioning on the ground, and electric power.

BEA's impeccably presented Annual Report published in August confirmed that a profit had been made in 1958–59, but the net figure had shrunk from over £1 million to under £¼ million, for though traffic revenue had increased, operating costs rose more sharply. The report made a spirited defence of IATA and equally spirited attack on inclusive tours operated by the independents; but the Corporation's own pooling agreements were applauded as 'a means to achieve lower fares, not a monopolistic device to prevent them'.

'The biggest commercial and operational deal we have yet done', was BEA's description of their new consortium partnership with Olympic Airways of Greece whereby the latter's Comets would be maintained by BEA but operated by Olympic crews trained by BEA. The strategy would for a BEA Comet from London and an Olympic Comet from Paris to converge on Athens and fan out to various points to the east of Athens such as Nicosia and Istanbul.

An article in *The Financial Times Survey of Aviation* showed that Sir Gerard d'Erlanger viewed the possibility of Commonwealth partners and associates for BOAC in much the same light as Lord Douglas on European pooling. However the Association of BOAC and Middle East Airlines was in jeopardy despite the former's 49 per cent holding. It was a case of sensitivity to criticism, for Labour MP Frank Beswick had disparagingly referred to the arrangement as 'one big sieve through which public money had been poured', and MEA was piqued that BOAC appeared unwilling to defend its associate's reputation. BOAC's proposal to convert the original £5 million loan to equity capital was refused because this would give BOAC complete control of the airline, but eventually Sir George Cribbett, with his usual tact, patched up the rift and agreed, subject to Treasury approval, that BOAC would lend MEA an additional £1·13 million at modest interest and help secure modern aircraft to meet the economy-class competition in the Middle East.

Co-operation was becoming a general theme, though reports early in September that Bristol Aircraft and the Hawker Siddeley Group were conjointly designing and constructing a British supersonic airliner were officially described as 'premature'. Certainly no tender or design contract had been established, but three years earlier the MoS had appointed a Supersonic Air Transport Committee under the chairmanship of the RAE. Their report had been given to the Minister five months ago, proposing a Mach 1·2 medium-range airliner as

well as a long-range Mach 1·8–2·0 machine which had been heavily criticized as commercially unrealistic. Nevertheless Hall Hibbard, the Lockheed vice-president of Engineering, was declaring that a Mach 3, pointed-nose, windowless canard airliner was practicable, using a steel and titanium airframe powered with conventional turbo-jets: 2,000 mph should be the aim, he said. Britain, as ever, was inclined to compromise, although the Fairey D.2 Delta single-seater had been the first in the world to achieve 1,000 mph.

The cost of such machines was far beyond BOAC's reach. The Annual Report for 1958–59 published at the beginning of October showed a total deficit of £5,179,420 — the highest since 1949–50 despite carriage of 76,000 passengers. The accumulated deficit was nearly £14·7 million, for BOAC had taken to heart the Select Committee's criticism and had written-off £5 million as development expenditure which, Sir Gerard d'Erlanger explained, 'is because the Corporation is the first operator of any British type it purchases, whereas an American type would be fully developed by the time the Corporation acquired it'.

However, there was satisfaction that in the twelve months since introducing the Comet 4s into service, three-quarters of the westbound North Atlantic flights had arrived within fifteen minutes of the advertised time and the others within an hour of schedule. 'A remarkable performance, substantially better than that achieved by any other type of aircraft BOAC has ever had in service on these routes', said Basil Smallpeice. But though people had been attracted by the Comets they would be displaced from the Atlantic next April by Boeing 707–420s and used for the routes to Australia, South Africa, and South America. Meanwhile consideration was being given to a Polar route between London and San Francisco for the Boeings.

On the home front the MTCA finally closed Croydon on 30 September. One by one the aircraft took off, the last at 7.45 amid full airport illumination; then all lights were dowsed, and the familiar outline of the buildings was lost in darkness. For most of the tenant companies, Gatwick was the new future.

Parliament too had a new look. October elections brought the Conservatives back with a large majority under Harold Macmillan. A separate Ministry of Aviation replaced the MTCA, and Duncan Sandys, a man of deter-

Comet 4s being serviced at Heathrow. They were operated with great success by BOAC for a decade, and in 1969 they were sold to various British and overseas airlines.

mination and vigour, was appointed Minister. His first major action was to draft a new Corporations Bill, read on 29 October and 5 November, which would increase BOAC's borrowing powers to £180 million and BEA's to £95 million, representing increases of £20 million and £35 million. He also authorized economy fares to the West Indies, Africa, and Far East, provided they did not 'unfairly affect the colonial coach routes which the independent companies have so successfully opened up'.

He was present on 16 November when the first of BEA's 'stretched' 100-seater Comet 4Bs was handed over to Anthony Milward ten weeks ahead of contract. These had thrust reversers to brake the landing run, and five of BOAC's Comet 4s were being similarly equipped. That same day *Hansard* reported that both BOAC and BEA, after dismissing the idea of a merger, were making a joint survey with a view to achieving mutual economies 'without unacceptable loss of efficiency or revenue to either Corporation'.

BOAC and BEA had also combined to establish a new College of Air Training at Hamble with Capt 'Jimmy' James, the flight operations director of BEA, as first chairman of a Board elected from the two Corporations. The two-year course was for *ab initio* pilot-candidates of eighteen to twenty who passed the aptitude, fitness, and intelligence tests, or up to 23 for those with a university degree. To train each one to the requisite standard would cost about £4,000, towards which the Ministry of Education granted £1,000, and the trainee would pay £380 per year in fees, the sponsoring airline making up the balance — but on obtaining professional employment the new pilot

would have to refund £1,000 from his earnings.

Currently the long discussions between BOAC and TCA resulted in agreement to operate services between Canada and the UK in pool as from 1 March 1960. However BOAC's Boeings, following a series of operational disasters in the USA, had been held up because of 'tests required by the ARB'. Certainly development problems were not endemic to British aircraft alone, but Comet 4B proving flights were also delayed. The first was to have been a return flight to Nice on 1 December, but had to be cancelled because London Airport was closed by fog, and flooded Nice was experiencing the worst gales in living memory. 3 December was scheduled for a flight to Moscow via Copenhagen and next day from Warsaw to Stockholm and so to Oslo, but the Norwegian Parliament was debating aircraft noise as the result of the din made by a demonstrating Caravelle of Air Union, and to avoid inflaming the situation it was decided to postpone the Comet's visit. However flights continued to other countries, concluding with a run to Zurich and back in half the time taken by a Viscount. For the moment nothing more could be done because the pilots refused to take the Comets on revenue flights until their claim for a pay increase of £700 and reduction of two hours to the working day was settled — earning scant sympathy from the morning papers of 14 December for the 'Pilots' supertax strike'. The Ministry of Labour's conciliation officer was brought in, but only resulted in postponement of revenue-earning flights for over three months to 1 April 1960, and decision to review negotiations on 31 January and 29 February, any matters outstanding by 31 March being referred to arbitration.

Corbett Rejects 1960-64

Of those BOAC pilots who had pioneered the earliest trans-Atlantic flights, few were still in the Corporation's service. On 1 January the doyen of them all, Capt Arthur Wilcockson, who had commanded the first commercial Atlantic flights in 1937, retired as flight services manager amid an avalanche of good wishes.

A more formal send-off was on 25 January when Duncan Sandys, Sir Gerard d'Erlanger, Sir Aubrey Burke of de Havilland's, Lord Bridges of the British Council, and the Brazilian ambassador departed from icy London Airport in a BOAC Comet 4 which re-instituted, after a lapse of five years, the traditional route via sunny Madrid to the heat of Dakar, across the Southern Atlantic to palm-fringed Recife, and coastwise above the tropic forests to Sao Paulo, Montevideo, Buenos Aires, and over the snow-capped Andes to Santiago. Whether it could be justified remained to be seen, for within the keenly contested network of this route nine carriers were already operating.

The *Daily Mail* was forecasting 'BIG BOAC SHAKE UP', but the Minister was still in South America when he confirmed on 3 February that d'Erlanger had told him in November of his wish to resign as chairman on expiry of his current term of office, and that two days before the Comet's departure, Sir George Cribbett had said that ill-health necessitated his own resignation also. Questions in Parliament received the time-honoured evasive reply. The matter of future appointments was spun out for the next few months, during which Sandys was finalizing the Civil Aviation Bill to repeal the

monopoly clause of the 1949 Air Corporation Act and establish an Air Transport Licensing Board giving independents the same right as the Corporations to apply for routes. MPs were concerned this might lead to material diversion of traffic from established operations to the detriment of millions of pounds of public money invested in them. A sequence of amendments ensued.

Meanwhile the Minister announced: 'I am examining with the industry the problem of developing a supersonic airliner. I am placing separate study contracts with each of the major airframe groups [Hawker Siddeley and the as yet unnamed British Aircraft Corporation] and with each of the engine groups Rolls-Royce and Bristol Siddeley. They have been asked to study the technical issues involved including the question of optimum speed and economic prospects.' The rival consortia were also involved in the more immediate requirement of BOAC and BEA to equip the Vickers VC 10 and DH 121 with the auto-flare landing system.

In this age of mergers an ominous threat was raised for both Corporations by an amalgamation of Airwork Ltd, Hunting-Clan Air Transport Ltd, and the British and Commonwealth Shipping Group air transport interests to form British United Airways. *Flight* commented: 'This is the first round of the Minister's stated policy to create bigger and stronger groups in the airline industry'. Airwork was backed by the Blue Star, and Furness Withy Shipping Lines owned Air Charter, Transair, Morton-Olley Air Services, and had helicopter interests. The British and Commonwealth owned 50 per cent of Hunting-Clan, and were linked with the Union Castle line. The combined aircraft fleet of British United had a capacity of 28 per cent of BOAC's or 44 per cent of BEA's. The threat of domestic competition stirred BEA and its pool partner Air France to introduce tourist-class flights from April without meals, refreshments, or bar service, cutting the £16 16s Paris return day fare to £14 19s. Unimportant though this elimination of catering might seem, it had proved difficult to achieve in the face of resistance from other European airlines, though not prohibited by IATA who at least had agreed to reductions of tourist fares to many parts of the British Empire. But as the editor of *Flight* commented: 'Having put a cabotage pistol to IATA's head and forced it under duress to agree to reduce fares, Britain in effect gave thanks and pulled the trigger, for it always had the right to charge whatever fares it wished on sovereign routes'.

On 29 April BOAC's first 707–420 powered with R–R Conway jets arrived at London Airport after a non-stop flight from Seattle of 4,900 miles in 9 hours 44 minutes, piloted by Capt Tom Stoney. Two more were delivered in May. The initial BOAC batch of ex-Comet

BOAC's next choice for the future Atlantic service was the Super VC 10, which could carry 163 economy-class passengers instead of the 135 of the standard VC 10. A £25 million contract for ten was signed in 1960, but deliveries would not begin until 1965, and the last of seven more in 1969. A high tailplane and twin engine pods each side of the rear fuselage characterized this airliner.

pilots had taken a conversion course at Tucson, Arizona, described as 'one of the easiest we have done'. They now carried out eleven round-trip trans-Atlantic proving flights before the scheduled service was opened on 27 May. The next batch of pilots and engineers were already on a conversion programme at the RAF Station of St Mawgan, Cornwall. Initially each 707 pilot had a 35 to 40-hour stint on the Link flight simulator, which Capt Stoney said was 'an absolute Godsend'. After that there was a six-week ground technical course concluding with the routine ARB examination, for Type endorsement, followed by route familiarization as assistant pilot.

Sir George Cribbett now bade farewell as deputy chairman, though he continued as director of BOAC Associated Companies Ltd to which Keith Granville was appointed chairman. People would certainly miss Cribbett, the Whitehall formulator of Britain's international air policy of traffic rights based on the Five Freedoms. Clearly reorganization of BOAC was imminent. On 21 June came the not unexpected announcement that Sandys had selected as full-time chairman, Rear Admiral Sir Matthew Slattery, who had in turn chaired Short & Harland and Bristol Aeroplane Co. Some shrugged their shoulders, others were devastated including the senior staff of BOAC, though Sir Matthew's administrative and technical abilities were fully appreciated. But why had not Basil Smallpeice been selected? Why was a man with no airline experience chosen?

Meanwhile d'Erlanger was in office, and on 23 June signed a £25 million contract for ten Vickers VC 10s for delivery early in 1965. 'They are for the North Atlantic route on which the constantly mounting tourist traffic offers immense dollar earning opportunities', he said, and added that the order 'completes BOAC's current aircraft fleet requirements'. The new 'stretched' version had seats for 187 in threes each side of the central gangway, two galleys and seven toilets plus one for the crew. With a total payload of almost 27 tons and fuel reserves for one hour hold-off and a 230-mile diversion, the 160-ton Super VC 10 could fly just over 4,000 miles in zero wind.

MPs were tackling the Minister about congestion in the Terminal Buildings at London Airport, which he ascribed to so many large trans-Atlantic airliners arriving almost simultaneously due to unavoidable departure delays at New York, 'though usually the peak

arrivals of long-distance passengers coincide with the slack period of those from the Continent. Meanwhile we are pressing ahead with the new long-distance air station, half of which will be ready for occupation next year.' Unfortunately increasing traffic had a concomitant increase in the fatal accident rate to the world's airliners. In the first six months there had been 23, causing the loss of 590 lives and complicated problems of liability. BEA had already paid over £150,000 in personal claims arising from the Munich air disaster, and was now fighting a writ from Manchester United Football Club claiming a further £250,000 compensation for the potential transfer-fee value of players who were killed, loss of prestige, and loss of gate money.

Despite the legal fracas Lord Douglas was happy to write in the *BEA Magazine*: 'We have made a good start to another successful summer'. The Annual Report showed a profit for the sixth year in succession — this time a record £2 million largely because of the Viscount. Next would come the challenge of re-equipment with the Vanguard and newly-named DH 121 Trident. Lord Douglas boldly said: 'The rate of domestic travel is going up by such leaps and bounds that at the moment we don't much mind if the passengers we turn away climb on a train'. Anthony Milward endorsed: 'We have reached the point, and it happened suddenly last year, where the more we fly on the domestic routes the more we make. It is a breakthrough.'

BOAC however was less optimistic, for Pan Am and TWA were showing a traffic growth on the North Atlantic more than five times that of the Corporation. However Sir Gerard d'Erlanger on his last day as chairman on 30 July was able to show in his Report and Accounts for the year ending on 31 March that at least the parent Corporation had made a profit of about £¼ million, though this became a loss of more than £¾ million when BOAC Associated Companies' results were taken into account. It was a frustrating note on which to hand over to 58-year-old Sir Matthew Slattery, who took the news headlines at his first Press conference by revealing that the supersonic airliner was going to be built 'more or less regardless of the economic consequences' and then saying: 'I am probably getting old but I don't want to fly to New York in 2½ hours. I rather look forward to six hours away from telephones and perhaps a quiet snooze on the way.' On the basis that 'a country such as ours will be lucky to sell 25 aircraft' he warned they would cost £4½ million to £5 million each, and £½ million depreciation a year must be written off, 'and that is a hell of a lot of money. However, someone is going to do it, so we cannot be left out of the race.'

Undoubtedly there would be big problems. New designs of ever-increasing complexity invariably took longer to perfect than estimated. Even the conventional Vanguard in the last week of route-proving trials had serious engine difficulties necessitating reversion to further bench development, and away went all hope that BEA could put these machines into operation for the midsummer peak European services.

Statistics in the August issue of the *Board of Trade Journal* showed that for the first time in the history of British transport, more people now travelled trans-Atlantic by air than by sea, air traffic having increased by 23 per cent while shipping declined 14 per cent, resulting in 778,000 air passengers, handsomely exceeding the 635,000 who arrived or departed by sea. No wonder the great shipping lines had closely observed the trend and were amalgamating with airlines.

Every airline in IATA wanted to expand, but could do so internationally only by getting more traffic rights through bi-lateral agreements. At the sixteenth AGM of IATA in September the growing resentment of airlines at the increasing tendency towards national restriction and protection was evident. SAS, the host airline, was bitter with the Americans; Italy irritated with the British; Japan with the USSR; and within each country there were struggles. Thus Cunard-Eagle was fighting for a licence to operate passenger services across the world's most competitive international route — the North Atlantic — and BOAC was fiercely opposing. Nor was BEA immune from attack. Sir John Ure Primrose, a former member of the Air Transport Advisory Council, said: 'BEA's whole set-up in Scotland is ridiculous. They are not operating in the interests of the travelling public — we are only getting what they feel like giving us.' That was rejected by Sir Patrick Dollan, chairman of the Scottish Advisory Council on Civil Aviation, who until recently had been a member of BEA's Board. 'It is a mistake to think that every crofter in the High-

lands and Islands can afford to rush about in passenger aircraft', he said. However *The Times* also took up the theme, complaining that a fortnight's notice was necessary for a seat, whereupon a possibly 'inspired' correspondent took the opportunity to argue that other operators should be permitted to fly services in parallel with BEA.

Ever since 1958 there had been continuing discussion on low cabotage fares, leading to BOAC's challenge to IATA in September 1959. On 4 October Britain introduced the first of these services to East and Central Africa operated by BOAC's new competitor British United Airways with their 'Skycoach' 62-seat Viscount 810. Then on 10 October Cunard-Eagle inaugurated the first £130 Skycoach service to Bermuda and Nassau using the 113-seat Britannia 310 and would alternate with BOAC, sharing revenues on a *pro rata* basis. All passengers had to declare they had British residential qualifications in order not to undermine the IATA fare structure — though nobody could take responsibility for perjury!

On the South American trans-Atlantic run a small profit had been made by the BOAC Comets despite predictions of loss. 'When the route started', commented the route manager, 'every one had the impression that South America was difficult. In fact it is not difficult, but it is certainly different. It is no good banging your head against a brick wall; you're got to be flexible in your approach here.'

BOAC's Comet 4s, which had made history as the world's pioneer jet airline service across the North Atlantic two years earlier, were withdrawn from that route in mid-October and replaced by the Boeing 707s. The Corporation was now intent on a trans-Atlantic all-cargo service in rivalry with Cunard-Eagle, both applications having been approved by the Minister. Two of BOAC's ten redundant DC-7Cs had been flown to Douglas in Santa Monica for conversion to DC-7F all-cargo configuration despite Government reluctance to spend dollars — even though BOAC earned them!

As music of a more distant future, the Minister of Aviation announced that the long-awaited supersonic airliner design study contract, valued at £500,000, had been awarded to the British Aircraft Corporation for a Mach 2·2 delta airliner seating about 100. A report stated

Rear Admiral Sir Matthew Slattery, Chairman of BOAC between 1960 and 1963, and former Chief of Naval Air Equipment, explores the flight deck of a Comet 4.

that: 'BAC would guarantee to have the airliner for trans-Atlantic service with BOAC by 1970 and believed it might be done by 1968 if necessary'. The total development cost was estimated at some £50 million.

BEA was concentrating on the nearer target of the Vanguard. The combined Vickers and Corporation crews were intensively flying an 'engine assurance' programme with the first set of fully modified R–R Tynes. Three other Vanguards flown by senior BEA pilots were making three daily flights around the British Isles, each typical of BEA's stage length and procedures, and even the usual un-co-operative weather.

Increasingly the benefits of air transport were attended by the peril of collision, and this had been highlighted on 25 October when the Queen and Prince Philip were flying home from Denmark in an RAF Comet 2 at 35,000 ft and suddenly two German Sabre fighters were spotted on collision course.

'They had absolutely no business to be there', affirmed Sir Edward Fielden, Commander of the Queen's Flight. That was the crux, for the essence of air traffic control was to ensure proper separation between aircraft, but that was impossible when military aircraft strayed into the clearly defined airways, such as Red 1 in which the Comet was flying. Foreseeing increased hazards when supersonic aircraft were racing through the skies, a draft convention and protocol to establish unified control of

upper European air space had been announced in June by Duncan Sandys, who had just been replaced as Minister of Aviation by Peter Thorneycroft; Julian Amery had succeeded George Ward as Secretary of State for Air.

The new Minister was finding Gatwick a headache. Because BEA had spent £12 million on its base at London Airport, the Corporation refused to move to Gatwick unless foreign airlines could be persuaded to do the same. Thorneycroft told Parliament that when he had asked Air France to move some of the London–Paris services there the airline told him 'it strongly resents being made to use Gatwick Airport owing to the distance from London, as it would take 2 to 2½ hours for passengers to reach their hotels'. It seemed that Gatwick would remain seriously under-utilized.

On 2 December BEA's first Vanguard was at last established with a C of A, and was immediately flown from Wisley to Stansted where crew refresher training began. Airfield performance was well above original estimates: from a sea-level runway of 5,000 ft in standard temperature, the Vanguard could take off at a ton above the originally specified 59 tons; alternatively at the latter weight the runway length could be reduced by 1,000 ft. Certification marked completion of a 22-month test programme in which 190,000 miles had been flown by twelve aircraft in the course of 1,100 flights.

Just before Christmas there was a grim reminder of the crowded skies which the Queen's narrow escape had emphasized, for in the worst disaster in civil aviation to date a United DC-8 in the USA, having omitted to make the mandatory right turn over the sea for Idlewild, collided with a TWA Super Constellation which had failed to turn left for La Guardia — yet both aircraft that snowy day were supposedly under positive air traffic control. All 126 occupants of the two aircraft were killed and twelve people in Brooklyn. Insurance claims amounted to over £5 million.

Next day a USAF Convair came down in a crowded thoroughfare near the centre of Munich after striking the spire of St Paul's Church, and in addition to the twenty on board, many citizens were killed on the ground.

1961

At the beginning of 1961 BEA announced that its aircraft had carried more than 3,800,000 passengers during the previous calendar year, an increase of 600,000. Freight-ton mileage had gone up by 20 per cent, and already the Douglas DC-7 freighters were proving their value. The greatly increased traffic was making the manual method of booking and ticket sales obsolete. A system was needed whereby the telephonist/clerk on receiving an inquiry could slip a key-coded card into a box to interrogate a computer which replied with lights indicating whether the flight concerned was open or full. The American airlines had used such a machine, known as a 'reserviser', for ten years, and more recently had turned to 'fully integrated electronic booking'. BEA now followed suit with a decision to purchase at a cost of £2½ million a computer which would be installed at the Cromwell Road Air Terminal in 1963 and require a further £2 million for the complete electronics. Milward estimated that BEA would be carrying 6½ million passengers a year by the end of 1964 when the first stage of the system would be ready.

That BOAC and BEA would co-operate when it was to their joint advantage was indicated by the visit of Sir Matthew Slattery and Lord Douglas to the College of Air Training at Hamble, for they were concerned at the short-fall in the recruitment of budding airline pilots. Competition from universities and industry, reluctance of parents and headmasters to see boys embarking on a career with a degree of personal hazard, and a shortage of boys with adequate qualifications were the problems, for of 260 applicants selected for interview to fill 50 vacancies, only 41 were accepted, whereas 100 students a year was the requisite target, and each Corporation required 100 new pilots by the autumn of 1962.

For the moment there were problems with Viscounts. Central African Airways had discovered cracks in the spar-boom lug of the outer wing attachment, and Indian Airlines found cracks in a top spar boom. Vickers immediately recommended that all 390 Viscounts should be inspected ultrasonically as soon as possible, and the 86 with the earliest type of spar must be inspected within seven days. This kind of thing was a constant nightmare to all airlines because of loss of revenue, yet the first priority was to ensure structural integrity for the safety of their passengers.

Tariffs were the other bogy. In February an IATA Cargo Tariff Conference in Paris broke down largely because BOAC decided on cuts 'which would produce a lower overall rate than any other airline had recommended'. These were special commodity rates on which the trans-Atlantic freight business had been largely built, but now BOAC proposed to take unilateral action by making big reductions for heavier shipments and 'even lower rates for selected commodities to encourage greater use of air transport in specialized export trade'.

To that end the Vanguard had been designed with double-bubble fuselage giving a deep hold beneath the passenger deck, so that either passengers or freight or any combination of payload could be carried. It afforded a style of service veering from seasonal tourist holiday routes to the steadily developing internal network of trunk services, all of which had the same problem of differing loads of freight. Commercially it was therefore very versatile although its economic advantages were primarily apparent on sectors up to 500 miles. On 1 March the flagship *Vanguard* made its opening Paris run, undercutting Viscount flight times by fifteen minutes.

On the following day BOAC with their Boeing 707s inaugurated the Montreal–Los Angeles leg of their new route from London to California, and the pilots were the father-and-son team of Capt Gordon R. Buxton and First Officer Gordon J. Buxton.

In the House of Commons Peter Thorneycroft was asked about 'unnecessary and wasteful duplication of services between the two British airline Corporations, and the grave danger to BOAC's established position in the Middle East if there was a clash with BEA in that area'. Much more likely was a clash with BUA, for when Miles Wyatt, the BUA chairman, offered to discuss future relationship with the two Corporation chairmen, Lord Douglas refused, and though Sir Matthew Slattery made a friendly exchange of views a BOAC spokesman said: 'There is no truth in the suggestion that BOAC have agreed to meet BUA round a table with a view to resolving any matters that are shortly to come before the Civil Aviation Licensing Board (ATLB). However BOAC have certain fields in which they operate with BUA, for example routes to East and Central Africa, and there may well be occasions when matters of mutual interest will be discussed.'

The ATLB held its first public hearing of route applications on 14 March, chaired by 65-year-old Alfred Wilson, formerly adviser to the MCA; the other members had no aviation experience, but were elderly civil servants with

Sir Basil Smallpeice, Managing Director of BOAC, with Lady Smallpeice at Buckingham Palace on the occasion of his investiture with the Royal Victorian Order.

accountancy knowledge, and one was a barrister who was legal assessor to the General Medical Council. A spate of applications poured in to the confusion of all and the benefit of lawyers and Counsel. BEA even had to obtain approval for a new commodity rate to carry motorcar parts on the regular service between Birmingham and Manchester. In another case the bemused solicitor for British Railways requested adjournment to obtain data contesting allegations of dissatisfaction with the railway service in order to prove that air freighting was wasteful competition.

Confirmation that BUA could prove a dangerous competitor was an announcement by Vickers on 9 May that ten of their latest short-haul airliner design, the twin-jet BAC 'One-Eleven', had been ordered by that company. Intended as a rival to the DH Trident, the new machine seated 69 tourist passengers five abreast, and would cruise at 540 mph.

Suddenly the horizons of aerial transport were made insignificant by a monumental signpost in the progress of mankind. On the morning of 12 April Major Yuri Gagarin of the Soviet Air Force orbited the earth. 'I saw for the first time', he related, 'the earth's spherical shape. The earth is a delicate blue colour. The transition from blue to the dark of space is very gradual and lovely. When the weightlessness appeared I felt excellent. Everything was easier to perform. I could have gone flying through space as long as required, yet I was full of joy when I touched the earth.'

Less ambitiously, BEA's sights were still set on freight-carrying, and three AW 650 Argosys had been ordered at a cost of £1½ million to carry the more bulky freight, making possible 'a very great expansion indeed'. Lord Douglas said they hoped both to cut freight rates in Europe and to simplify them: 'There are 4,000 commodity rates. We hope to narrow these down to perhaps eight.' Milward tactfully qualified this: 'Our problem is to carry existing cargo at present rates, for BEA's first job is to make air cargo pay rather than cut rates, and just because we have bought a new freighter it does not mean we can cut rates straight away'.

Though provisional figures for BOAC's operations in 1960–61 indicated a probable overall loss of £1·7 million, BEA expected a net profit of at least £1¼ million — 'A creditable result for a year when profits throughout the airline industry have declined sharply, and great airlines well known for efficiency and profit-able operation have themselves sunk into the red for the first time in many a year', said Lord Douglas. BEA had carried four million passengers in the past year and was now the world's biggest passenger carrier outside the USA.

On 16 May the ATLB began hearings on Cunard-Eagle Airways' application for a North Atlantic route, with BOAC strongly opposing. A formidable array of Cunard-Eagle and BOAC executives was there to give evidence. Counsels spent hours questioning and wrangling, and there were barrages of statistics in the course of six long sessions, the last of which was on 30 May. A fortnight passed: then came the announcement that Cunard-Eagle had been granted a licence for a London–New York service, using Boeing 707–465s and Britannias at a frequency of once daily, from 31 August 1961 to 31 July 1976.

'We are surprised and deeply disappointed by the Board's conclusions', commented BOAC. 'We shall appeal in the strongest possible way. The Board's decision appears to accept material diversions of traffic from BOAC if Cunard-Eagle operate successfully. If that is the case BOAC's position will be undermined — yet BOAC had understood that Parliament's intention as embodied in the Civil Aviation Licensing Act 1960, was that this should not occur.' However in the Queen's Birthday Honours List there was at least an element of compensation for Basil Smallpeice, who was appointed KCVO.

Concurrently Lord Douglas accepted the Minister's invitation to continue as chairman of BEA until 23 December 1963, when he would be 70.

Meanwhile BUA agreed an *entente* with

Cunard-Eagle on their overlapping route applications, with mutual withdrawings so that each had a fair share. The twenty-first public meeting of the ATLB would deal with these and those of several other independents for European routes, opposed variously by BOAC and BEA. The meeting was scheduled to hear 69 statements in support of applications and 257 objections — a daunting affair. Key figures were the new chairman, Professor Jack, shrewd Ashton Hill of Cunard-Eagle and Henry Marking, the secretary of BEA whose expertise in argument and cross-examination matched the highly skilled and friendly advocacy of British United's Counsel, Gerald Gardiner. The whole complex issue of pooling and bi-lateral agreements, traffic and commitments had to be considered in detail, for the decisions would reach far into the future of British air traffic. Combined speeches totalled a million words during these historic meeting.

The 130-page Annual Report of BOAC, published at the end of July, was the fullest and frankest in the Corporation's history, and told the story of an airline in transition from the frying-pan where costs were too high into a fire where traffic was too low, resulting in an overall loss of £1·7 million and an accumulative deficit of £15 million. Sir Matthew Slattery said: 'We will need only a slight increase in fares to make us into a highly profitable organization'. Questioned on the prospects of the supersonic airliner, he replied: 'I don't want a supersonic transport at all. It is not going to bring lower fares or generate new traffic. I think it is going to be an infernal nuisance. However if BOAC is to remain competitive it must have a supersonic airliner.'

BEA's Annual Report, published in August, gave the Corporation's customary frank account of policy, but concluded with a warning that traffic recession might make profitability elusive in the current year, though for 1960–61 it had achieved £1½ million. BEA was concerned by the independents' bid for a major network of European and domestic routes, and so was seeking every means to extend its routes. Thus by chartering Comets to Transportes Aéreos Portugueses, entry was gained to the London–Lisbon–Madeira route in a clever move to outmanoeuvre BUA and Silver City, who were applying to the ATLB for this route. Though operated by BEA, the Comets would wear TAP transfers but operate the cabotage route from Lisbon to Porto Santo where ferry-boats connected to Funchal. Similarly BOAC had arranged to operate services with Air Ceylon, who would charter a Comet and BOAC crew for the London–Colombo–Singapore service.

The Royal Assent to the Carriage by Air Act, 1961, had recently been signified in the House of Lords, thus enabling the UK to ratify the 'Hague protocol' which doubled the limit of liability of an air carrier to 250,000 gold francs (£6,000 at that time). Attempts in the Commons to double that sum were narrowly defeated, though it was considered that 95 per cent

BEA Vanguard at Palermo airport, Sicily. This 118-ft-span airliner was designed as an economic successor to the Viscount. First flight was in January 1959, but the Vanguard did not go into service with BEA until 1 March 1961 — five years after ordering.

of litigation would disappear with higher limits of liability. All across te world accidents were increasing. The first 23 days of September were the worst in the history of global air transport, with 316 fatalities. Since the beginning of the year the total loss of life on the world's airways had increased to 995, though there was only one accident with a British airline — Cunard-Eagle's Viking hit a mountain 21 miles from Stavanger Airport, killing 36 passengers and three crew.

At the end of November BOAC's important appeal against the award of Cunard-Eagle's North Atlantic licence was adjudicated by Sir Fred Pritchard. Once again there was prolonged cross-fire by representatives of the two companies hurling statistics in the course of five days. On 10 December Sir Fred issued his report to the Minister of Aviation recommending that BOAC's appeal be upheld. Its acceptance was a stunning blow to the authority of the Air Transport Licensing Board. Sir Frederick even commented that the ATLB in granting the licence had not exercised its functions in the manner required by the Act 'To further the development of British civil aviation'. Clive Hunting, chairman of the British Independent Air Transport Association, commented: 'Presumably the decision means that no new licences of competitive nature can now be granted for at least five or six years'. It

also meant that Sir John Brocklebank, chairman of the Cunard Steamship Co, would reassess 'the extent of Cunard's investment in air transport'. Retrenchment began with the sale of their Viscount 707s.

Four days before Christmas BEA had another disaster, one of the Comets on the London–Rome–Athens–Istanbul–Tel Aviv route crashing a few seconds after take-off in the dark on the last sector from Ankara; fire started in the wing tanks after hitting the ground. Of the 34 on board, 27 were killed, including the flight crew of three and four cabin crew. Anthony Milward immediately flew out with a team to investigate, and on return said there was no evidence of pilot error but there must have been a mechanical defect. Subsequently it was found that the director horizon indicator was at fault, and de Havilland's immediately warned all operators that pilots should not rely solely on this instrument for pitch indication.

This accident increased the year's world total to 41 fatal crashes in which 1,258 passengers and crew had been killed — and yet that was a negligible risk in relation to the enormous mileage flown.

1962

In his 1962 New Year message to the BEA staff, Anthony Milward wrote: 'This aviation busi-

The twin jet pods in the tail show that these aircraft in the Vickers factory are VC 10s. The clean wing was the key to high speed, though seen here with the powerful landing flaps down. G-ARTA was the prototype.

ness is an odd affair. At a time when Air Union comprises four of our principal competitors in Europe, the Common Market is coming, and SAS and Swissair use each other's aircraft and equipment, it is curious that Parliament thinks the time is right for splitting British effort in Europe. Not only do we have to compete with our international friends but in future with other British operators as well. It is a strange British policy when already there are far too few passengers.'

The recession was continuing. High expectation of better economics rested on the DH Trident which made three initial test hops on 7 January; two days later, after waiting for suitable weather, the de Havilland pilots and crew of four made the first flight, watched by a thousand DH employees. As it accelerated down the runway the quietness of the Rolls-Royce Speys was noticeable. An hour later the Trident, distinctive in shape, was seen returning, made a slow fly past with undercarriage and flaps down for ground observation, then ten minutes later swept in to land. In the next issue of the *BEA Magazine*, Lord Douglas cheerfully wrote: 'BEA's hopes lie with the Trident in the same way as ten years ago our future lay in the equally revolutionary Viscount. It is the very last word in sub-sonic jet transport and is specifically designed for our particular network.'

Both the big Corporations were tightening their belts. In the *BOAC News*, Sir Basil Smallpeice wrote: 'We cannot relax efforts to keep costs down all round; we must intensify them. We have already taken steps to restrict spending on office redecoration and equipment and some building developments have been postponed; the buying of consumable materials and stores has been reduced; even tighter control of staff recruitment had been instituted, and all departments must examine their expenditure critically to see what can be cut or postponed without impairing our efficiency or ability to earn revenue.'

The BEA DC-3s would be replaced by Heralds for economy, and from 1 April the unprofitable international services to Budapest, Belgrade, and Ajaccio would be withdrawn; the thrice-daily frequency between Glasgow and Aberdeen cut to two; and all other Scottish services to one a day. Appeals were being lodged against the licences granted to the independent airlines on 22 of BEA's more profitable routes.

Nevertheless BEA was alive to all possibilities. A new line was all-inclusive holidays on attractive terms ranging from eight days in Paris for £25 8s to fourteen at Tangier at £66 19s. It was a theme the independents soon followed, led by Cunard-Eagle.

The Minister of Aviation was now negotiating with his French colleagues for financial and technical agreement between the British Aircraft Corporation, Sud-Aviation, and Marcel Dassault to design and construct the Mach 2·2 airliner. Foreseeing the problems of supersonic speeds, the air traffic control system was undergoing far-reaching changes. Soon there would be full radar coverage of route regions above 5,000 feet, new traffic control centres to which radar video would be fed, a new flight-plan processing system, and new equipment to interpret the radar pictures. All European countries were working to the same purpose under the general umbrella of 'Eurocontrol' and would be compatible with the envisaged American plan known as 'Project Beacon'.

What had become known as the Big Appeal hearings by BEA, British United, Cunard-Eagle, Starways, and British Railways against many of the European route decisions made by the ATLB, began on 9 April before Sir Arthur Hutchinson. Somewhat to the confusion of the appellants, Lord Douglas shrewdly timed an announcement that BEA would have a non-ticket 'walk-on' service in the autumn for the London–Glasgow route and probably for the London–Paris route next spring, and with one blow appeared to destroy the main justification for domestic competition. Certainly the appeal hearings appeared to be little more than a repeat performance of the ATLB hearings.

However Sir Arthur Hutchinson, a man of common sense, insisted: 'The ATLB are the experts and except in the most exceptional circumstances their decisions must always be final'. In the course of a month the hearings had occupied 11½ days and much complicated evidence. The Commissioner would now submit his report to the Minister, who would be the final arbiter.

While the hearings were still in progress a great man died — 76-year-old Sir Frederick Handley Page, pioneer aircraft constructor and pioneer of the air transport business. Even Lord Douglas, who had so tersely quarrelled with him when chief pilot of Handley Page Transport in 1919, declared: 'He was a good man in every way'.

On 6 June the Minister of Aviation stunned the entire aircraft transport industry by announcing that he had approved formation of BOAC-Cunard Ltd. BOAC held 70 per cent shares in the new company and was represented by five of the nine directors, with Sir Matthew Slattery as chairman and Sir Basil Smallpeice as managing director. Though Harold Bamberg, the tall young chairman of Cunard-Eagle Airways, was a member of the new Board, the combine was with the shipping company and not its air transport subsidiary. Initial capital was £30 million and the fleet comprised eight BOAC Boeing 707s and Cunard's two 707s. Sir Basil made clear that: 'For all practical purposes we are still the same people, doing the same work, flying the same routes, but adding the great marketing advantage that the name of Cunard means. As it is the intention that BOAC-Cunard should not, at any rate for the present, have any staff of its own, BOAC staff in the new company's area will continue to be BOAC staff on the same terms and conditions as before. Aircraft will have "BOAC-Cunard" on their sides, sales offices may have the new name across the front, and notepaper may carry the new heading, but our staff will still be BOAC's.' Though not directly concerned, Lord Douglas came into the act: 'The BOAC-Cunard agreement is bound to have profound effect on this country's civil aviation policy. The private airlines led by Cunard-Eagle and BUA have made great play of the advantages of competition between British airlines. Their arguments are rendered quite meaningless by this new move.'

Over-capacity was the looming problem. Because of that, BOAC reduced its order from fifteen to twelve of the standard VC 10s though the contract for 30 Super VC 10s remained unchanged and it was expected that by 1966–67 all would be delivered. Watched by the new Air Minister Julian Amery, Sir George Edwards, and Sir Basil Smallpeice, the prototype VC 10 took off from Weybridge in the late afternoon of 29 June for its maiden flight in the hands of Robb Bryce, chief test pilot of the British Aircraft Corporation, assisted by Brian Trubshaw the Vickers chief test pilot. After a 'completely successful' flight they landed at the nearby Vickers test airfield at Wisley. Though loaded to 80 tons, the big airliner with the aid of its advanced high lift system of almost full span leading-edge slats and big slotted flaps landed in less than half the 3,300-yard runway, though a touch of reverse thrust assisted the pull-up. But presently it was found that despite the clean wing, both climb and cruising speed were somewhat down and therefore the range was not up to specification. Stage-by-stage modifications were successfully initiated.

Five days earlier a Boeing 707 in BOAC's livery had opened the first service operated by BOAC-Cunard from London to New York and Bermuda via Manchester and Glasgow, carrying 38 passengers. However, financial problems seemed increasing at BOAC. A further economy drive was instituted 'using the Corporation's own methods staff supplemented temporarily by about a hundred specially selected from other departments'. Not only were there un-co-operative noises from trade union representatives but Kenneth Bevan, the financial comptroller, resigned. In a somewhat desperate attempt BOAC appealed to the ATLB to restrict the wide scope of charter flights 'akin to scheduled services' which Caledonian was inflicting on their traffic between London and Africa — but the Board refused to alter the licence because it was an existing contract but agreed 'that in reviewing "E" licences we should impose a general condition restricting Fifth Freedom charter flights to those not of the character of a scheduled service'. BOAC had virtually won, but BEA was set to compete against the independents for inclusive-tour charter work. Lord Douglas threatened: 'If private operators want competition they will jolly well get it'. The most prominent operator in that context was British United. Freddie Laker said: 'I am amazed that BEA appear to be so hysterical at a problem of which they don't yet know the extent. We believe in the spirit of co-operation, for there is little point in driving each other into the ground for the benefit of foreign airlines.'

At the end of August *Flight* commented: 'As usual the annual report for British European Airways sets an example of enlightened public accountability unmatched throughout the industry. It contains an admirably documented and analysed diagnosis of the malaise which has affected not only BEA but airlines generally.' Nevertheless it came as a shock that instead of the previous year's £1½ million profit there was as great a loss, though that was not the full story, for operating expenditure of £1¼ million was carried forward as a charge against future

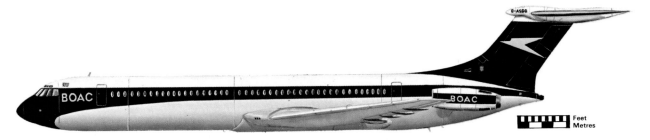

years. The published loss comprised a profit of £1·2 million on international services offset by a loss of £2·7 million on domestic services of which BEA had a virtual monopoly. The Vanguards made a loss of more than £2 million compared with a profit of more than £1 million by the Viscount 800s and £350,000 by the Comets. Thus the aircraft designed specially for BEA's routes lost money, and those bought to meet jet competition made money. At the annual news conference Lord Douglas said that there had been a lot of chit-chat about BEA joining clubs such as the French-sponsored European multinational airline Air Union, British United, and even BOAC. 'There is no question of joining any such schemes', he said. 'The only clubs I like are bridge clubs and night clubs', and he likened Air Union to 'a nest of Kilkenny cats fighting one another about shares of traffic'.

In mid-September the Minister of Aviation announced the European route decisions arising from the extensive appeals heard by Sir Arthur Hutchinson in the summer of 1961. All but two were upheld, and BUA had been awarded nine. Miles Wyatt said: 'Now that the battle between us and BEA has been resolved, we hope we can come to a reasonable working relationship for the benefit of British civil aviation as a whole'. Official comment from BEA was: 'These new private airline rights will mean yet more empty seats on the market. Everyone surely knows that airlines everywhere are suffering from too few passengers chasing too many seats — the natural road to ruin. It will now be even more difficult for airlines to hold down fares, let alone reduce them.'

The world's airlines from time to time had had their financial stringencies, but none had ever presented its shareholders with so great a deficit as the £64 million accumulated loss which BOAC revealed at the end of September in its annual accounts. In the accounting year of 1961–62 the operating deficit was more than £14 million and the upsurge in accumulated deficit was the result of 'rationalizing the value of the aircraft fleet by writing down the book

Above: BOAC's Super VC 10 Type 1151 to the same scale as its contemporaries on p.199.
Left: Jock Bryce, who piloted the VC 10 G–ARTA (pictured also on page 220) on its first flight, leaves the plane. He is followed by assistant pilot Brian Trubshaw, who later tested Concorde.

values of the Britannias, DC-7C's, and Comets into a capital loss of nearly £33 million'.

Sir Matthew Slattery explained: 'The Corporation has had to pay the heavy price of pioneering advanced technologies and of the technical troubles that compressed the useful operational lives of the Comets and Britannias into uneconomically short spans and made necessary the emergency purchases of Constellations, Stratocruisers, and DC-7C's that themselves had only restricted lives'. Of BOAC as an instrument of national policy, he said: 'To expect a company to do something that is not wholly commercial and then, when it has lost money doing it, to expect it to pay interest on that money is "bloody crazy" '.

There was a spate of rumours that BOAC and BEA would merge to counter a revised Air Union which was going forward as the biggest air transport force in the Western world. With the British moving towards the Common Market it seemed the time had come to reconsider the airline industry, but Lord Douglas dismissed that as absurd. 'This desire to dig up the plant of British air transport and examine its roots', he said, 'which has been going on continuously since air transport first started, must be resisted. It can only lead to frustration and confusion and in the end can do nothing but harm to the British airline industry.'

Evidence to the contrary was the Government's new Air Corporations Bill which proposed to extend BOAC's borrowing powers from the existing limit of £180 million to £300 million, and that of BEA from £95 million to £125 million. This meant paying yet more interest on money borrowed to pay interest *ad infinitum*. There seemed no immediate solution, so the Minister appointed John Corbett, an eminent financial adviser, to engage a London firm of chartered accountants to investigate BOAC's financial situation and advise what might be done to correct it. Sir Matthew Slattery said the inquiry was welcome and would help to evaluate the effectiveness of certain proposals, such as writing off the huge accumulated deficit, and subsidizing development flying of the VC 10, though these were matters of policy rather than accountancy.

In detailing to the Commons his criticisms of BOAC's financial history, Julian Amery said: 'Sir Matthew has asked that past losses be written off. I sympathize. I felt the same way when I reckoned up the interest on my overdraft, but I cannot see any reason why the Corporation should be specially exempted. To dismiss as "bloody crazy" the idea that one should pay interest on borrowed capital is not something which commends itself to me.' He then gave details of the Corbett financial inquiry.

On 29 November Amery made a statement in the Commons which would affect the future to even greater extent: 'I have to-day signed an agreement with the French ambassador for development and production of a supersonic airliner. This will be a joint project undertaken by Britain and France alike. The aircraft will be a slender wing airliner built mainly of light alloy. It will have a cruising speed of about Mach 2·2; that is about 1,400 mph. At this speed it would cut the Atlantic crossing from 7½ hours to about 3 hours and London to Sydney from about 27 hours to 13 hours. The design has been agreed between the French company Sud-Aviation and the British Aircraft Corporation. They will carry out the work on the airframe together, and make two versions — one with long range and the other medium range. Both will be powered by four Olympus 593 turbo-jet engines developed jointly by the British firms of Bristol Siddeley and the French Société Nationale SNECMA. First flight is

expected in 1966, and the aircraft should be ready for airline service by 1970. France and Britain will share the costs, the work, and the proceeds of sales on the basis of equal responsibility for the project as a whole. BOAC and Air France will be associated with the project from the beginning.' There were visions of swift trans-Atlantic flying which would put Britain and France into the premier position and establish a world market for supersonic airliners. Said Amery: 'This is a chance that will not return. It will have far reaching consequences in the technologies of metals, non-metallic materials, fluids, electrics, and electronics.'

Currently BOAC and Cunard-Eagle lodged with the US Civil Aeronautics Board an application for revalidation of their existing individual 'foreign air carrier permits' in the name of BOAC-Cunard Ltd. To their surprise the CAB examiner had already recommended that Caledonian Airways be granted a three-year certificate under the US Federal Aviation Act to operate unlimited trans-Atlantic charter flights. Caledonian now sought to intervene in the new application on the grounds that 'a full and complete disclosure of BOAC-Cunard's operations is required for the CAB to render a meaningful decision on the BOAC-Cunard applications'. That was the first time that one British airline had attempted to interfere with another in foreign proceedings. Certainly the mysteries of BOAC-Cunard were deepening. The company existed from the accounting point of view but not in respect of marketing, advertising, and promotion. Questions were beginning to be asked. BOAC-Cunard appeared to be more accountable to the Americans than to their own countrymen.

1963

At the beginning of January 1963 came news that Harold Bamberg had resigned from Cunard Steamship Co, Cunard White Star, and BOAC-Cunard, and with him went his fellow Cunard-Eagle director Norman Ashton Hill— which left BOAC-Cunard's Board wholly BOAC except for Sir John Brocklebank as chairman of Cunard Steamship. When in July 1960 Cunard Steamship had bought Eagle Airways for what was believed to be £1 million, Bamberg had surrendered autonomy believing that the move would ensure financial stability of his airline. Now he said: 'I was convinced that the proper thing would have been to have BOAC-Cunard as a holding company and to have let Cunard-Eagle and BOAC operate side by side in the Western hemisphere so that it would have been possible to get an operating yardstick for BOAC's efficiency. But as Cunard's only aviation expert involved, I was overruled.' On 14 February it was announced that he had purchased from Cunard a 60 per cent share in Cunard-Eagle, so after three years he was once again master of the airline he had founded in 1948. It must have increased his confidence that BEA's appeal to the Minister against the ATLB award of 'scheduled inclusive-tour' licences to Cunard-Eagle and other independents was dismissed by the new Commissioner, Sir John Lang.

BEA was no little concerned that first deliveries of the Trident might be delayed, because like the VC 10, maximum lift was below expectation, and considerable wing modification had been made including revised droop leading-edge flap settings, fitment of wing fences, small Kreuger flap, and retractable vortex generators. To date, 500 hours of testing had been completed, but there was still a long way to go before route proving trials could be commenced.

That kind of pre-operational testing had been initiated by George Woods Humphery for the later pre-war airliners to ensure that their introduction was free of major snags. Coincidentally, he died on 25 January, aged 70, the great part he had played in establishing the airlines of the 1920s and 1930s almost unknown by the post-war generation of airline pilots. As the autocrat manager of Imperial Airways he had taken it greatly to heart that the Cadman Committee criticized him for taking 'too narrow a commercial view of his responsibilities' — but still the same conflicts between commercial and political interests continued.

At the beginning of March BEA decided that instead of obtaining a special subsidy, the 'Highlands and Islands' services would be cross-subsidized from the other routes, taking the rough with the smooth, for the ATLB had agreed to increases of 5 to 10 per cent on domestic fares from 1 April. Deposits were required for long-term reservations and the balance paid within six weeks. A fine would be imposed for last-minute cancellations. However there would be stand-by fare facilities so that passengers could take a chance on seat availability, though it might entail waiting several hours. BEA's traffic director hinted that

first-class fares in Europe might be scrapped in favour of a one-class passenger service.

Helicopter services were also being planned. A BEA spokesman said 'We have all the experience we need, and given time and the right equipment believe we could put a helicopter service on a commercial basis'. To that end application had been made for Ministerial permission to buy two 25-seat Sikorsky S-61Ns at £250,000 each, for a service between Land's End and the Scilly Isles.

There were growls by Freddie Laker of British United that BEA was 'actively frustrating' the independent airlines' European licences. BEA denied this, but the pooling arrangements could certainly be used to defeat ATLB decisions on routes to the Continent. 'When law-abiding citizens have exhausted the processes of law as laid down by Parliament they accept the verdict, but not BEA', said Laker. Miles Wyatt endorsed this by commenting on the Genoa traffic rights: 'These lengthy and difficult negotiations have been made much more difficult by BEA's endeavour to frustrate them — in particular, by BEA's action in publicly applying to the Air Transport Licensing Board for the Genoa licence to be revoked at a time when the British Government was still actively negotiating with the Italian Government on our behalf. It is a sorry spectacle when a nationalized corporation publicly attempts to frustrate the Minister to whom it is responsible.'

A fortnight later Amery announced that Sir Matthew's appointment as chairman of BOAC would be extended for one year until 28 June 1964, and so would those of Sir Wilfred Neden, deputy chairman; Sir Walter Worboys; and Mr Lionel Poole. It was significant that John Corbett's Report had only just arrived on the Minister's desk, so the unusually short period of the extended term of office was presumed to give ample room for manoeuvre when the full facts had been considered.

Rumours of a merger between BEA and BOAC were now so extensive that Lord Douglas not only published his strong reasons against a merger in the *BEA Magazine*, but also wrote to 50 key MPs emphasizing the stability of BEA and stressing that there would be a conflict of interests under a single Board; profits on BEA routes could not offset BOAC losses; there would be no saving in operating cost and administrative saving would be small — so BEA in effect would become just the European division of BOAC, and the merged Corporation would find itself with 38,000 staff, so morale would suffer catastrophically.

Time was always the essence. Two-and-a-half years of planning and hard work had gone before the first BAC One-Eleven made its maiden flight an hour before sunset on 20 August, having suffered delays throughout the day from torrential thunderstorms and last-minute adjustments after taxi-ing and acceleration trials. Several thousand watched the eventual take-off with 'Jock' Bryce and 'Mike' Lithgow at the controls. Afterwards Bryce cautiously said: 'Everything went according to plan; we flew to 8,000 feet and did not exceed 180 knots'. Every one hoped this did not mean snags, for there were 60 of this impressive, rear-engined airliner on order of which 31 were exports — and that was encouraging.

There was little cheer in BEA's September Report for the year ending 31 March. The total operational costs, including 5·2 per cent interest on capital, exceeded income by some £1·6 million, though by paying £1·35 million of the year's costs out of reserves set aside during the seven profitable Viscount years 1954 to 1961 the loss was declared as £265,301. Milward, speaking in the context of the decline in first-class travel, said that poorly filled first-class compartments increased the problem of 'people clamouring to get on tourist class and being turned off because there isn't room for them'.

In the foreground of BEA affairs, though hidden from the public, was a dispute between the aircrews and senior management over changes in the promotion system proposed by the Corporation as part of the forthcoming introduction of Tridents; but compromise was reached— aided by BOAC's economy move in prematurely retiring 125 senior employees, including nineteen Captains who would be given a cash payment in addition to their normal pension.

BEA was now facing an all out challenge from Bamberg's British Eagle International Airlines Ltd, formerly Cunard-Eagle Airways Ltd (the prefix having been dropped on 9 August, thus ending the tenuous link with Cunard that had existed since 1953). Objection to the new name was lodged by BEA on the grounds that the initials BEIA could be confused with BEA; nevertheless on 3 November British

Eagle inaugurated their competitive daily service from London to Glasgow using Britannia 310s on hire purchase from BOAC unheedful of the risk to BEA.

On 22 October BOAC presented its 1962–63 Report. Because the combined deficit stood at £12·2 million compared with £19·9 million the previous year, financial experts considered this was an encouraging improvement, but the accounts contained obscurities and inconsistencies. Sir Matthew Slattery took an optimistic view, saying that results in the first six months of the present year were £3½ million better and 'extremely encouraging'. Asked whether he would object to publication of the Corbett Report, he said: 'If he has written the truth I wouldn't mind it being published'.

On the same day that the essence of the Report was made known, disaster struck. One of the prototype BAC One-Elevens dropped almost vertically in a nose-high attitude from 15,000 ft and crashed into a Wiltshire field, killing the Vickers test pilot Mike Lithgow, his ex-BEA co-pilot Dick Rymer, and the five Vickers technical crew. It was an accident which underlined the price still paid for progress. The 'black box' flight recorder showed that the machine had entered a 'super-stall' in which the elevators on the high tailplane locked fully up under heavy aerodynamic forces which could not be manually opposed. The engines had been opened fully without avail and the machine continued to drop flat until it hit the ground.

While this was happening there was political manoeuvring behind the scenes. Without showing Sir Matthew Slattery or Sir Basil Smallpeice his BOAC White Paper, let alone the Corbett Report, the Minister devised the resignation of these two exemplary men and in their place put 47-year-old Sir Giles Guthrie, whom few remembered as traffic officer in British Airways Ltd just before the war. His mandate was to produce within twelve months a sound plan for BOAC's future. Newspapers made little of it, for the impact was overshadowed by the assassination of President Kennedy in Dallas on 22 November.

In a BBC interview Amery alleged that Sir Matthew and Sir Basil had been guilty of 'very serious weaknesses in management', but the White Paper was a pitifully superficial document with scant justification for its assertion of 'need for stronger management'. Its 13½ pages merely re-stated well-known facts and overlooked the manner in which BOAC had almost halved the ton-mile cost in six years, had reduced the break-even load factor from over 60 per cent to less than 50 per cent, and had reduced engineering costs to 27 per cent lower than those of BEA.

There could be no criticism of Sir Giles Guthrie, who had been a member of the BEA Board since 1960, nor was there any question of his ability as a pilot in war or peace. A man of charm and wealth, he was associated with a number of financial companies, including Radio Rentals whose deputy chairman, Charles Hardie, a distinguished accountant, would join him on the Board of BOAC. 'Whether you are running an airline or any other commercial business', Sir Giles said, 'the principle remains the same — to achieve revenue and watch overheads. To begin with I shall look at every department, but I am not a believer in the hire and fire technique.'

The Times reported that Sir Matthew and Sir Basil would receive compensation totalling about £24,000. Sir Basil took his departure with good grace, urging his staff to even greater efforts: 'I would be less than human if after fourteen momentous and difficult years I did not have strong personal feelings about the situation in which we all find ourselves. We have lived through a period of great uncertainty and criticism, culminating in the White Paper which all ranks in the Corporation feel has been less than generous towards our ideals and achievements. However, if there is criticism, just or unjust, then let it be on me.'

On 2 December the White Paper was debated in the Commons, and Mr Cronin wound up for the Opposition by describing the sackings as 'the most disgraceful miscarriage of justice since the Dreyfus case'. This gave the Minister opportunity of saying that to secure balance on the BOAC Board between continuity and new men, he had asked Sir Walter Worboys, Mr Booth, Mr Granville and Mr Lee to remain on the Board, and Mr Milward and Mr Hardie had also been appointed. Three nominees had agreed to join when vacancies arose. He had therefore asked Sir Wilfred Neden, Lord Rennell, Lord Tweedsmuir, and Mr Poole whether, in the circumstances, they would be prepared to make way immediately. 'Sir Wilfred Neden at once saw the force of my suggestion, but the others have so far declined for reasons which no doubt seem good to them.' The appointment of Anthony Milward was warmly welcomed on

both sides of the House.

The hinged nose gives access to the capacious hold of a British European Airways Argosy.

1964

At a meeting of the BEA Board on 2 January 1964, 43-year-old Henry Marking was elected deputy chief executive, which meant that he would become chief executive when Anthony Milward succeeded as chairman on 1 April. After outstanding war service he had read law at University College, London, and was admitted as solicitor in June 1948 before joining BEA as secretary. For the past eight years he had been a member of the management committee and chairman of the forward planning committee, and his skilled advocacy in air traffic licensing had earned high praise.

Interviewed on his second day in office, Sir Giles Guthrie emphasized that the partnership between him and Anthony Milward would ensure discussion on joint problems and joint policies. 'It is the first time that both chairmen have been on each other's Board. Whereas in the past there may have been separate discussion by each Board on the same matter, neither knowing what the other was saying, this could not happen again. We both intend this co-operation to be a great success.'

Almost immediately a storm blew up over the relative merits of Concorde and the American supersonic Lockheed Mach 3 design which had a passenger capacity of 218, affording high earning potential. BOAC was pressing for approval to make a $600,000 deposit for six of these Lockheeds to the embarrassment of the Treasury who had just been rapped by Parliament for accepting a speculative estimate of £150–£170 million for the Concorde project without contacting the French Minister of Finance.

main runway, killing all 75 passengers and eight crew. The wreckage fell into a ravine, and could not be found until the next day.

In the cool March sunshine at Heathrow during the naming ceremony of BEA's first DH 121, Lord Douglas declared: 'While others wax lyrical about supersonic airliners, I pin my faith on the Trident', then with a last side-swipe at BOAC added: 'We have bought British

Amery had written to Sir Giles on 1 January: 'The choice of aircraft is a matter for the Corporation's judgement. If national interest requires some departure from the strict commercial interests of the Corporation, this should be done only with the express agreement or request of the Minister.' Then on return from a fortnight's trip to Peru, Mexico, and the USA where he flew in a McDonnell Phantom at Mach 2·1, he told Sir Giles that the Lockheed would not be permitted for the time being. As compensation in this early crisis of Sir Giles's management the Minister now allowed him to see the Corbett Report, though still refused to publish it. Equally BOAC refused to make public the BOAC-Cunard agreement, and in explaining this to the House, Amery said: 'BOAC has also had discussions over a possible merger with BUA, and feels that future negotiations of this kind might be hampered if the party with which it was negotiating knew of the details of the agreement in question'. Already BOAC-Cunard had applied to the ATLB for revocation of British Eagle's licence for a trans-Atlantic all-cargo service, which British Eagle then requested transformation into an inclusive-tour licence for flights across the Atlantic on behalf of Sir Henry Lunn, the travel company.

Shortly afterwards British Eagle had a bad set-back, for on 29 February one of the Britannia 312s on a schedule run from Heathrow to Switzerland in overcast conditions hit the Glungezer peak six miles short of Innsbruck's

aeroplanes not because we were directed to do so, but because we consider them to be the best available tools for the job in hand'.

Negotiations were also proceeding with Hawker Siddeley for part exchange of the three Argosy 100s for five of the latest Argosy 220s which had wider loading doors permitting use of cargo pallets nearly twice as big. At Heathrow BEA could unload and reload an Argosy in 30 minutes using a conveyer table and fork-lift trucks, and was handling large loads of merchandise and machinery which previously had been turned away as too bulky.

On 31 March Lord Douglas retired after sixteen years as full-time chairman. To the accompaniment of skirling bagpipes he mounted the embarkation steps of a Trident for his farewell flight on its first scheduled service to Zurich. In a last message to his staff, Lord Douglas wrote in *BEA Magazine*: 'The financial year which ends on March 31 has been the most successful in BEA's history. Provisional estimates indicate that the profit will be approximately £3 million. This is BEA's biggest to date, exceeding by about £1 million our best results in 1959–60 when we made just over £2 million.' On 1 April Henry Marking was appointed to the BEA Board as chief executive. A month later the Scilly Isles helicopter service was opened, for which purpose BEA Helicopters Ltd, a new £1 million subsidiary, had been registered, with Lord Balfour of Inchrye as chairman.

At BOAC it began to seem that the Corbett Report had not been necessary because Sir Matthew's and Sir Basil's management over the past year had resulted in a profit which Sir Giles Guthrie estimated at more than £3·5 million. Traffic revenue, including that earned by BOAC-Cunard, exceeded £102 million — over £9 million higher than the previous best. There was still a link with Basil Smallpeice, for he had joined the Board of the Cunard Steamship Co Ltd.

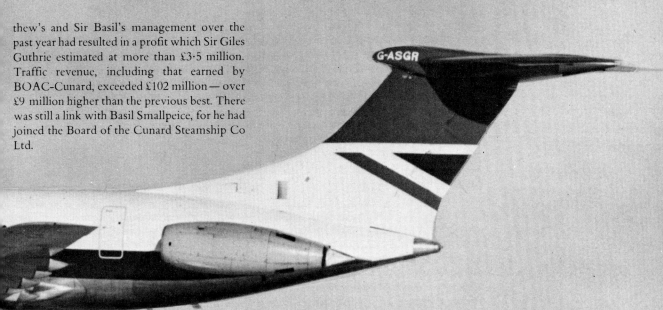

G-ASGR

BOAC's aircraft were now resplendent in new uniform which bore a golden speed-bird across the centre of the fin, rendering the Boeing and VC 10 *marque* instantly distinguishable. From 1 June a new eleven-man management team would meet weekly to implement Board policy. They were Keith Granville, deputy chairman; Gilbert Lee, chairman of BOAC Associated Companies; Ross Stainton, commercial director; David Craig, senior general manager; Derek Glover, financial director; Capt Dennis Peacock, flight operations director; Charles Abell, chief engineer; John Gorman, personnel director; Winston Bray, planning director; Robert Forrest, secretary and solicitor — and of these, Granville, Craig, Stainton, Abell, and Peacock would meet daily under Sir Giles.

Six of BOAC's fourteen Britannia 102s had been bought by the new firm of Euravia. That coincided with the death of its original inspirer — that great figure in British aviation, Lord Brabazon of Tara, who died on 17 May. A week later the recent deputy chairman of BOAC and founder of Britain's original bi-lateral agreements, Sir George Cribbett, died.

There was still concern about the BAC One-Elevens, though British United had already accepted five. Sir Giles Guthrie was not convinced of their suitability for BOAC, nor of the VC 10s, so he informed the Minister that all 30 Super versions should be cancelled and Boeing 704–420s substituted. At least £50 million of public money was at stake. This involved the highly controversial issue of the conflicting

interests of BOAC and the British aircraft Corporation. The Minister prevaricated, and on 20 July told the Commons: 'Sir Giles has agreed that BOAC will take seventeen of the 30 Super VC 10's to meet estimated requirements up to 1967, and thereafter a further ten. This leaves BOAC with two Super VC 10's above estimated requirements after 1968. Of the thirteen surplus Super VC 10's, the RAF will take three.'

Thus in little more than six months Sir Giles had his original agreement with the Minister flouted twice, but Amery endeavoured to cover up. 'What I always said is that the chairman of BOAC should give us his judgement on commercial solutions and that he should not seek to determine what the national interest is. Many of the troubles of the Corporation have arisen from the fact that the chairman sometimes thought he was judging where the national interest lay.' He did not mention that the other difficulty was the ministerial assumption of technical and financial aeronautical judgement.

Explaining to his staff, Sir Giles said: 'Speculation infers that BOAC is anti-VC 10. This is rubbish: we are merely pro-BOAC. The VC 10 is operating well in Africa and the Middle East and we hope to operate this aircraft for many years to come. It really is "swift, silent and serene". The plan I put to the Minister covered future routes and aircraft fleet. We intend to withdraw completely from the East coast of South America because it is likely to lose us £1¼ million a year. We plan to cut the

Wearing the eventual British Airways livery with quartered Union Jack, the re-painted prototype Super VC 10 G-ASGR was initially used by Vickers for trial installations and demonstrations, receiving its C of A in December 1964. It carried five crew, seven stewards, and could accommodate 163 economy-class passengers.

extensions from New York to Washington and from Nassau to Lima, and we want to concentrate European calls at Rome, Zurich, and Frankfurt. We also want to fly the South Pacific before long, and are looking at future routes across Central Asia to the Far East. We have been talking to the Russians in Moscow about this.'

On 22 July the Commons debated 'The Report from the Select Committee on Nationalized Industries on the British Overseas Airways Corporation', but it was more a debate on the Minister's much-publicized VC 10 directive to Guthrie. Amery declared that despite the Select Committee's view he found no evidence of Government pressure on BOAC. Roy Jenkins, for the Opposition, then instanced the combination of pressure from the Minister and Vickers to make BOAC order more aircraft than required and proceeded to attack the Minister tooth and nail, saying that for eighteen months he had done nothing about relations with the Corporation except set up 'that ridiculous cloak-and-dagger accountancy exercise, the Corbett Committee'. Amid the medley of attacks from other MPs came constructive intervention from Sir Richard Nugent, chairman of the Select Committee: 'Is it really practicable in 1964 to build a national aircraft for a national airline? The minimum number for economic production is substantially more than the commercial interests of the Corporations permit them to take. Should we not look forward to international co-operation in construction?'

Praise for the rival Trident was given by Anthony Milward at the Press conference marking his first AGM as BEA's chairman. Full tribute was paid to Lord Douglas's years in command during which traffic increased thirteenfold, the unit cost of production almost halved, and average fares were reduced by 5 per cent. 'These figures', he said, 'testify to the success of his leadership.' BEA was now carrying nearly six million passengers a year and was the world's fifth largest passenger carrier. Emphasizing that it was no sinecure, Milward said: 'On the London–Frankfurt route, the hottest and most competitive on which there are eighteen different jet airline services a day, we couldn't hold our own with the Viscount but with the Trident we have increased our load factor by 10 per cent since June'. He prognosticated that by 1970 BEA would have an all-Trident fleet in Europe using a developed version seating 95 passengers flying a stage length of 1,500 miles. Asked about British Eagle he said: 'I understand they have applied for a licence to operate BAC One-Elevens on domestic services. I suppose this is the sort of competition that the present Government requires. We would have to counter with Tridents, but would make domestic economics impossible and the consequences could be very serious.'

But what of British United Airways? BOAC having dropped the South American services because they did not pay, BUA now took them over. That was regarded as scandalous by the Opposition. The Minister explained: 'In the light of the great value attached to the economic and other bonds between the country and South America, the Government was bound to view the withdrawal of BOAC with regret but decided that the heavy expenditure involved in supporting the service could not be justified'.

Elimination of the service left BOAC with even greater excess staff, to which end Sir Giles was negotiating with the unions, but probably 7,500 of the 21,686 staff must lose their jobs by 1968, of which 3,500 might have to go in the immediate future. 'A streamlined, highly efficient organization providing first-rate service at a profit is the objective', reminded Sir Giles, despite earlier 'hire and fire' comments. Dispute followed with the Treasury over the generous amount of severance pay proposed, for it might have repercussions in other nationalized industries.

Though the two Corporations had become great empires beset with many problems, the activities of newly formed BEA Helicopters Ltd at Penzance was like a return to pre-war days. Said a visitor: 'The atmosphere is that of a friendly airline. One could wish that some of the traffic staff at London could have a refresher course in this atmosphere of outback friendliness. Whether it is the traffic officer in his little hut by the railway station, the ground crew working all hours, or the pilots, there is a feeling of pioneering and pride.'

Both BEA and BOAC now had to face big wage increases for the thousands of engineering workers of up to £4 per week spread over the next three years coupled with reduction of hours from 42 to 40, elimination of clocking-on to give white collar status, and three weeks' holiday. In return the nine unions concerned agreed to such management rights as work measurement, elimination of demarcation disputes, and improved efficiency. When BEA applied for a 5 per cent increase in domestic fares the ATLB unfeelingly turned it down.

However BOAC was less dismayed. The Annual Report showed that revenue for the first time exceeded £100 million, and the operating surplus of £8·7 million was the highest ever, but after paying interest the net profit dropped to £1 million.

'If BOAC were as inefficient as the White Paper implied', wrote Sir Giles Guthrie, 'it could not have achieved the dramatic recovery which the figures for 1963–64 disclose. The new Board takes no credit for the results. The foundation had been laid by its predecessors. The operating plan had been worked out in detail, capacity allocated, sales target fixed, but were sufficiently flexible to take full advantage of the upsurge in traffic that occurred.'

Co-operation between BOAC and BEA was increasing. Spurred by the Select Committee's June report expressing concern that there was no engineer on the BOAC Board, Beverley Shenstone, the 58-year-old chief engineer of BEA, was appointed technical director of BOAC, and BEA assigned Kenneth Wilkinson, an expert in performance and analysis, as his successor. Shenstone, a lanky Canadian, was a well-known figure whose academic knowledge and accomplishments were widely recognized.

There were changes, too, brought about by Labour's victory at the polls. The new Minister of Aviation was Roy Jenkins, a young economist of smoothly engaging personality and brilliant mind, but there was concern at the appointment of a trade union official, Frank Cousins, as Minister of Technology — a new department that certainly would be concerned with aviation. There was uneasiness that on 26 October the Government statement on Britain's economic situation called for reduced spending on 'prestige projects' and revealed that the French Government had been told of Britain's wish 'to re-examine urgently the Concorde project'. Three days later Roy Jenkins flew to Paris for talks with his French opposite number Marc Jacquet. On return he denied that the Government wanted to cancel Concorde: but in any case General de Gaulle had told his ministers that cancellation was impossible. Jenkins therefore said there would be an urgent review, and if the Government

was convinced that the project was in the best interests of the two countries they would go ahead. The cost would be at least £280 million plus substantial sums after the C of A had been obtained, and might spiral higher. Sir Giles Guthrie expressed no public opinion other than that Concorde must not be made obsolete in less than seven years if it came into service.

Though the Concorde future was uncertain, BOAC and BEA benefited in other ways from Roy Jenkins' dispassionate review of aviation. BOAC had asked whether it could now bid for trooping contracts — hitherto the unwritten prerogative of the independents. In the House on 25 November, the Minister agreed, and also permitted reduced-fare *ad hoc* trooping on scheduled services. This seemed fair since there was now equality to operate limited scheduled services.

Meanwhile BEA in conjunction with Okanagan Helicopters of Vancouver had formed a new operating company, International Helicopters, which would charter long-range S.61Ns from the two holding companies for operation in the North Sea oil exploration concession areas held jointly by Shell and Esso.

The result of Jenkins's aviation activities became apparent on 9 December when he announced that a Committee had been appointed 'to examine the future place of the aircraft industry in the British economy. Lord Plowden has accepted the Government's invitation to serve as chairman.'

Plowden had been chief executive at the Ministry of Production during the war, chairman of the Economic Planning Board 1947–1953, chairman of the Atomic Energy Authority 1954 to 1959, chairman of the Committee of Inquiry into Treasury control of Public Expenditure, 1959 to 1961. His distinguished committee of eight comprised the former First Sea Lord, two outstanding MPs, senior executives of the Royal Dutch Shell Group, Bank of England, Atomic Energy Authority, Transport Aircraft Requirements Committee, and for good measure the chairman of the TUC International Committee. Their deliberations were likely to affect the entire future of the British aircraft industry. No previous Committee ever had so wide a mandate. Concorde would certainly be one of the major considerations, and by now the estimated cost of bringing it to certification stage had risen to £350 million, shared between Britain and France.

Waiting for Edwards 1965-69

When Parliament reassembled on 19 January Roy Jenkins announced: 'We have completed the review of the Concorde project which we set in hand in October and have exchanged views with the French Government. We still retain some doubts about the financial and economic aspects. We have, however, been impressed by the confidence of our French

However it was the solidarity of the independents which was affecting BEA. Appeals by the Corporation against the ATLB's approval of 46 applications by nine independent operators for inclusive-tour charters to Majorca were dismissed. There followed a plea by Harold Bamberg to end the hostilities against British Eagle. 'There is room for both of us,' he

partners, and the Prime Minister has informed the French Prime Minister that we stand by the Treaty obligations which the last government decided to enter, and in the coming months we shall discuss with our partners the detail programme of development and production.'

Concern over the Government's latest aviation review was reflected by private meetings of industrial leaders and public demonstration of aviation employees — but all became temporarily subdued on 24 January when it was learned that Sir Winston Churchill had died that day. Over half a century ago he had experienced the magic of flight as a would-be pilot, then in war days used aircraft for journeys that were to mould victory, and in peacetime travelled by airline on his journeys abroad: as a visionary he had said 'Civil aviation is the greatest instrument ever forged for international solidarity'.

said. 'We are very willing to work more closely with BEA so that our competitive services do not clash if they will do the same thing with us.' But BEA was considering a charter subsidiary to compete more effectively with the independents. Improved passenger-handling facilities were being installed including the first powered passenger gangways at Heathrow.

BOAC was also introducing new facilities. An automatic Collins International Data Information computer had been installed at Heathrow House, near the airport, and was brought into action on 3 February to process and route the 45,000 messages a day hitherto channelled manually to the network from the airline's London Headquarters. Sir Giles said it would save £80,000 a year, and his technicians were exploring its uses for service control, passenger checking, and pre-flight load controls.

BOAC now received a big push forward. On 1 March the Minister announced the intention to write off the entire accumulated deficit of £80 million and to establish a reserve of £30 million against contingencies because 'long-haul air transport is peculiarly susceptible to trading fluctuations and the effect on revenue'.

On 1 April the Super VC 10, ordered by BOAC in June 1960, began the new 'Monarch' service which took over from the Boeing 707s with six flights a week London–New York–Bermuda and return, and one flight a week to San Francisco via New York. Soon there would be fifteen flights a week across the North Atlantic using five of these resplendent machines. To counter competition in 1968 of the envisaged 200–250-seat Boeing 707-820 development, BOAC was asking BAC to con-

Sir Giles said: 'The planned rundown in numbers is going well and we are just under 19,900 for the first time since 1960, and with the help of the Unions a great deal has been done to agree proper pay scales on a longer-term basis'.

That was also a problem which BEA was facing. Their pilots were claiming higher pay and shorter hours. The counter-opinion was that pilots in any case worked very short hours, for a Comet pilot averaged 27 hours a week and a Viscount pilot 33 hours, but that ignored briefing, preparation time, and snag reporting,

Trident two

G-AVFA

sider a stretched version of the Super VC 10, with the equivalent seating accommodation. Pilots liked the VC 10, for it had a spacious flight deck and was much nicer to fly than the Boeing 707, though as a revenue-earner it was no better.

That BOAC had managed to make a profit for the year 1964–65 was announced on 1 April by Sir Giles Guthrie who said the figures were provisional, 'but we expect to show a net profit of over £7 million. This is the largest operating surplus BOAC has ever had and the first clear profit for eight years. It has been achieved not only by raising our revenue to a record £114 million, but by holding down expenditure. We are in the black and we are going to stay that way.' Economy was certainly the watchword.

as well as time spent on overnight stops. An 18 per cent pay increase spread over three years, with 8 per cent back-dated to October 1964, had been offered to the Corporation's 1,000 pilots, whose salaries now ranged from £1,300 a year for a Viscount First Officer to £4,700 for a senior Captain flying Tridents or Comets. American pilots had obtained much higher remuneration. Soon there was deadlock and a 24-hour strike was called by BALPA, but withdrawn when Anthony Milward said: 'The famous 55 points of grievance have been practically demolished. We have told BALPA that we are willing to grant a 5 per cent back-dated pay rise on the understanding that talks on productivity continue.'

BEA's operational policy of profit through

The Hawker Siddeley Trident was originally sponsored by BEA and is notable for the three-engine arrangement of two on rear stubs and one in the fin. After intensive trials the prototype C of A was issued in April 1968. A contract for 24 was signed in August 1959. The airline now has fifteen Trident Ones and 1As, sixteen Trident Twos, and 25 Trident Threes. The British Airways livery applied from 1975.

Above: The value of the twin-turbo powered Sikorsky S.61N was its ability to operate in reasonable safety from city centre areas.

Right: Carrying 22 passengers, the Sikorsky S.61N amphibian was ideal for operations between Penzance and the Isles of Scilly — a service initiated by BEA Helicopters Ltd in 1964.

Feet
Metres

high revenue rates and high load factors was criticized by Roy Jenkins. Milward immediately visited him to outline plans for development of the London–Paris route which he stressed was 'operated under conditions laid down by the British and French Governments, and these include a stipulation that the two national carriers shall operate in pool'. That in effect eliminated the competitive spirit of securing customers through efficiency, low cost, and good service. Possibly Jenkins' comment was to stimulate interest in an 'Airbus' for cheap travel which he said was being explored conjointly with the French, and 'if we see a project coming out we would be extremely keen to do it with them'. However the Rolls-Royce investigation revealed insufficient demand to cover the high cost of developing the requisite engines.

There was a brief reminder of BEA's interim years when it was announced that Peter

Masefield had been appointed chairman of the British Airport Authority which had received the Royal Assent on 2 June. Early next year he would have overall responsibility for running London Heathrow, Gatwick, Stansted, and Prestwick. A week later Heathrow was the scene of another significant moment in aviation history when a BEA Trident carrying ten passengers from Paris to London made the first ever automatically flared commercial landing. That was the result of BEA's original specification to Hawker Siddeley that Duplex Autoflare equipment must be fitted. For several years it had been under development by the Aviation Division of S. Smith & Sons during which thousands of experimental landings had been made by various aircraft; but the Trident was the first to receive ARB certification.

Such developments were costly but essential to improve safety and regularity. However BEA were well placed, with a net profit of some £1·3 million for the 1964–65 financial year on a total turnover of £66 million. With that con-

234

solidation, BEA proposed to cut charter rates by 20 per cent to all destinations, and already more than £1 million of business had been booked, largely by the travel agents Thos. Cook. Though BEA Helicopters had made a loss of £36,648 the Scilly Isles service was continuing, and the North Sea operations by International Helicopters started on 9 July with the first crew transfer to an oil rig and entailed the longest over-sea flight yet made by a BEA helicopter.

The MoA 'had rescued BEA's follow-on Trident order from becoming one of those never ending serial stories' by approving the purchase of fifteen MK II, and the contract was signed on 26 August for delivery in the summer of 1968. BEA was also proposing a short-haul Airbus for use in the next decade, and it was hoped that the October meeting of the European airlines technical committee would lead to a joint specification.

An airliner of this type was of no interest to BOAC, who admitted 'keeping in close touch with Boeing and Douglas'. The year's profits at £8 million proved greater than Sir Giles had estimated in April. He forecast that the current year should bring slightly better results; but in succeeding years, BOAC could not be expected to earn at the same rate in an era of rising costs and constant pressures to cut fares, but reaffirmed that the 'superb' VC 10, stretched to seat 265 passengers, would be bought only if price and timing were right.

That rival to both BOAC and BEA, British United Airways, appeared to be in trouble. In a surprise statement the retirement of its managing director, 43-year-old Freddie Laker, was announced. Laker said it was 'a matter of personal principle', but he would continue his aviation career, perhaps starting his own business again. Three months after leaving he formed Laker Airways, though he refused to name his backers. Meanwhile BUA succeeded in gaining from the ATLB the rival British Eagle's domestic trunk rights. That meant BEA would have to face jet competition from BUA's One-Elevens.

International Helicopters now ran into a management problem. Okanagan pulled out and sold its 50 per cent holding to BEA Helicopters. In a powerfully worded statement Okanagan's president declared that he was originally told by the MoA that no licence would be granted unless BEA Helicopters Ltd was made partner. 'It soon was apparent that BEA wanted

to take over management of International', he said. 'We were offered two alternatives: either we withdraw from management and BEA Helicopters continue, using Okanagan's equipment, or Okanagan buy out BEA who would go in to North Sea helicopter operations competitively. Okanagan recognized that in addition to licensing problems it would be competing on an uneconomic basis with a Crown Corporation, so decided to sell out.'

BEA's increasing concentration was on air freighting, so additional cargo services were being added to those existing to Paris, Frankfurt, Turin, Dublin, and Glasgow, using Vanguards with forward compartments stripped to accommodate eight tons of freight but with 71 passengers in the other compartments, supplemented by similarly stripped Viscounts with a capacity of three tons of cargo and 36 passengers.

BEA now suffered another disaster, for on 27 October one of their Vanguards on the Edinburgh–London run crashed 1,000 ft short of the Heathrow threshold on its third attempt at landing in fog on a monitored ILS approach, caught fire and disintegrated, killing all 30 passengers and the crew of six. It was BEA's first fatal accident since the Comet crash at Ankara in December 1961.

Because both Corporations were already under State control they were less affected than the rest of the British aircraft industry by prospects of nationalization which was the purpose of the Plowden Committee when appointed more than a year previously. At last, in mid-December, Plowden's voluminous report of 139 pages was issued, but argued less vehemently than expected for 'some degree of public ownership of the two main airframe groups'. The range of subjects, logically if not fully analysed, dealt with guide lines for future policy, international co-operation, Defence procurement, exports, decision making, industrial organization; but there was special mention that whatever types were built by British manufacturers they must be targeted towards export appeal and not the particular needs of the Corporations, therefore the airlines would be permitted to purchase foreign aircraft.

Though legislatory matters seemed so prominent in airline operations, it was the detail organization which made success or failure. From the faraway days when a devoted mechanic judged the airworthiness of an aircraft by eye or by the sound of its engine, maintenance had become a paramount science and provisioning was a system of mathematics. The box of sandwiches which a passenger bought for his death-defying flight from London to Paris had become an ordered meal which required a complex string of operations to reach the stewards' galley. Even then, the airline caterer could be fined $25,000 if he gave passengers a meal better than the IATA regulations specified.

1966

A new Minister, like a New Year, brings hope of better things. In this critical moment in the history of Britain's aircraft industry Roy Jenkins, at the beginning of 1966, was promoted to Home Secretary, and Frederick Mulley succeeded as Minister of Aviation. The month was also notable for the election of a woman to the BEA Board — Mrs Alison Munro, 'who comes to us with a wealth of experience gained in the Ministry of Aircraft Production during the war and recently as Under-Secretary, Overseas Policy Division, Ministry of Aviation. I believe she is the first woman to be appointed to the Board of any state-owned airline in the world', said Anthony Milward. But she was not: Pauline Gower, head of the Women's section of the Air Transport Auxiliary, had been a prominent member of Viscount Knollys's war-time BOAC Board.

BEA was again battling with the independents. The new Appeal Commissioner, Sir Harold Kent, in recommending acceptance of part of the appeal by British Eagle against an ATLB decision to revoke its domestic trunk licences said: 'British Eagle have shown that the competition of their services with those of BEA produced an improvement in the latter's services which was not maintained after British Eagle's withdrawal. The evidence is convincing. I accept that competition benefits British civil aviation.' Commenting on evidence of BEA's 'sandwiching and swamping' of Eagle services, he said: 'These tactics go beyond legitimate competition between the public Corporation with unlimited frequencies and an independent airline granted a licence to provide a limited alternative service'. And that meant there were now three operators on the London–Glasgow route: BEA, BUA, and British Eagle, with a total passenger potential of 600,000 a year.

That was chicken feed compared with the Atlantic run. Capacity rather than supersonic speed was certain to be the requirement, so the big American delta-winged airliner designs had been put aside. Instead Boeing, Douglas, and Lockheed were concentrating on breathtakingly huge and heavy wide-bodied jet airliners which would have a gross of 220 to 270 tons depending on whether passenger capacity of 350 or 500 was the objective. At the beginning of January Boeing promoters discussed with BOAC a design seating 400 on two decks. BOAC technicians were undoubtedly impressed — but the immediate economics, as well as the Plowden arguments, dictated development of a Super-Super VC 10 as a joint venture with Europe. Meanwhile the two Boeing 707-336Cs had been flown to England. Both bore the BOAC-Cunard inscription, and 'BOAC CARGO' was superscribed in bold letters above the central cabin windows. On 13 January they began a twice-weekly service between London and New York via Manchester and Prestwick.

While the two Corporations were separately involved in consideration of Concorde prospects, big capacity 'Jumbo' jets, Super VC 10s, and the Airbus, there was increasing awareness that they presented new safety problems. The world-wide safety record for the first 35 days of the New Year had been bad, for 300 were killed in five scheduled-airline accidents. But now in the first week of March came disaster to a BOAC Boeing 707–436 which, minutes after leaving Tokyo International for Hong Kong under visual rules, had disintegrated, pieces falling on the lower slopes of Mount Fujiyama, 50 miles from Tokyo, and other wreckage spread over a wide area, so none of the 113 passengers and eleven crew had survived. There were ominous implications, for this time the accident could not be ascribed, as so often, to 'pilot error'. As with the Comet, here was a fatigue failure. Inspection of other 707s revealed hair-line cracks in part of the empennage structure, though Boeing said the sequence of break up had begun with the starboard wing and/or forward fuselage, other structural failure following as secondary effect. Inspection of all 707s and 720s which had flown more than 1,200 hours was instituted, with more detailed inspection for those above 1,800 hours — a period which fourteen of BOAC's Boeing Fleet had exceeded. Twenty-two instances of cracks were found in 63 aircraft. BOAC suspended all services, for six of their nineteen 707s were suspect. All tails were modified in that area, and flying then resumed under even more stringent inspection schedules.

Elections at the end of March brought a Labour victory — so aviation policy was unlikely to change, but there was a big switch in the battle between airlines and British Rail when electrified trains between London and Manchester were inaugurated on 18 April, cutting the terminus to terminus express time from 3 hours 40 to 2 hours 40. That was only fractionally longer than block-to-block airline time, after which passengers still had to reach the city centres. Both BEA and BR began an advertising campaign of disparaging references to each other.

More soberly, BOAC was conducting a recruitment campaign 'to meet future requirements for experienced crews on its expanding world-wide VC 10 and 707 jet services'. Senior pilots were already earmarked for a future fleet of Boeing 747s, which now had become inevitable because Juan Trippe had just ordered an initial fleet of these machines, and if BOAC was to keep in the race Sir Giles Guthrie must do the same. He had good reason to be buoyant, for a net profit of £8 million in an operating surplus of over £20 million was revealed in the current annual accounts for 1965–66. In the May issue of *BOAC Review* he wrote that: 'We foresee a need for the large-capacity "Jumbo" for the high density routes and a somewhat smaller though still large type for other long sectors on our network'.

There were suggestions that BEA should take over BOAC's surplus VC 10s, but Milward said it was 'absolutely impossible to think that we can keep our airline going on somebody else's cast-off long-range jets. No other European airline is thinking of using 707s or DC-8s for short-range work.' He also denied that BEA's commuter-jet requirement would undermine the Anglo-French Airbus project. It would merely, he said, defer it to 'a more realistic date, say 1975, when I believe that a 250–300 seater will be required'. Milward was widely held in high regard. With twenty years of airline experience behind him, he was was now awarded a KBE in the Queen's Birthday Honours List.

Automatic landings with BEA Tridents had been intensively progressing to the extent of 1,200 touch-downs — but now the blind fates struck again. A Trident on pre-delivery test flight crashed near Norwich on 3 June, spinning into the ground in a flat attitude, wrecking the machine and killing the test pilots, Peter Barlow and George Errington, and two test staff. Once again it was the deep stall. Ironically the famous and gently sardonic Errington was not only an honorary BEA Captain but a contributor of articles on safety to the aviation press, and he would have been the first to point out that the fatal stall had been a deliberate experiment and would never be encountered in the course of routine operations.

In the height of summer considerable attention focused on delays in the BEA services, resulting in adverse Press publicity. A reporter commented: 'Tempers at Bealine House, in the passenger cabin, and evidently on the flight deck, have become ruffled under the glare of publicity'. There were major problems with the Tynes powering the Vanguard, and hydraulic failures with the Trident. One pilot went so far as to say that he was 'ashamed and embarrassed' at having to apologize for the delay to his aircraft — and that led to an uncomfortable interview with his flight manager, Capt Priest.

Four hundred BEA pilots next sent the Government a precedential vote of no confidence in the management. Parliamentary questions showered on the Minister. Would he institute an inquiry into the partial breakdown of BEA's domestic services during June? Would he direct BEA to re-equip its fleet? 'No direction or inquiry is called for', Fred Mulley replied. 'The technical difficulties which interfered with domestic services are of a temporary nature and do not indicate basic inadequacies in BEA's management.'

'Why the pilots blow their tops without using the proper methods of communication, I don't know', mused Sir Anthony Milward on returning from a Norwegian holiday. When his chief executive Henry Marking was asked whether pilots were irritated by poor promotion prospects he said that every BEA copilot would probably have his command by 1976. That discontent persisted was shown by the growing number of resignations because of better promotion prospects elsewhere.

BALPA wrote to its 950 BEA members asking them to list their grievances as evidence to make the Minister change his mind. Fewer than 90 replied, thanks to the conciliatory activity of Henry Marking who had told the pilots: 'Neither I nor my department heads and their staffs have been sitting back complacently hoping things would right themselves. Our bad operational performance has not happened suddenly: it is the culmination of what has been happening for a long time. You will know better than I of slacknesses which have crept into some of the things BEA does. We have got to correct this, and I look to you to help me by checking it when you come across it. I know you want to do this, but have sometimes felt it useless because no one took any notice of your reports. I have heard expressions of anxiety lest BEA becomes a third-rate airline. My policy is to make BEA not only Europe's foremost airline but second to none in the world.'

It was certainly not being helped by the Government, for the foreign travel allowance was reduced to £65, with a maximum of £15 in sterling cash. BOAC reacted by cutting the cost of package holidays to the sterling area resorts of Bermuda and the Bahamas. BEA took a gloomier view, for the new limit would have a depressing affect on the more expensive nonsterling areas such as the French Riviera and Scandinavia.

As expected, the Minister ruled on 2 August that BEA must choose its 'commuter jet' fleet from aircraft available from the British aircraft industry. 'Those under consideration are developed versions of the VC 10, Trident, and BAC One-Eleven. The Government is prepared to give launching aid but I have told BEA that it must hold over such part of its approved orders as will produce savings of £5 million in the investment planned for 1966–68.'

As to BOAC, the Minister said: 'After careful investigation, the Government had authorized the Corporation to acquire six Boeing 747 aircraft for delivery in 1969 and 1970. These will be very large aircraft with about 400 seats, suitable for the busiest long haul routes on which they will give very economical performance. No British aircraft are available that could fulfil that role. These American aircraft will earn in foreign currency far more than they will cost.'

Not only big aircraft but a multi-computer was engaging BOAC's attention. Known as BOADICEA, it cost £33 million and was expected to save £48 million by 1980 through eliminating manual work. Housed in a £1½ million building already under construction at London Airport, it would be connected to a £6¼

million communications system which would link 100 BOAC stations throughout the world and deal with all passenger reservations and check-ins by November 1968. The system would also be used for planning and budgeting; flight operations and flight planning, with ability to analyse alternative routing; engineering and maintenance control and scheduling staff information; financial data processing; and acquisition of statistical records from information fed into the system. This was indeed a splendid instance of forward planning. BEA followed suit with £250,000 of electronic devices to accelerate check-in facilities at the Heathrow Terminal.

There ensued on 16 September the surprise decision that: 'On the proposal of Cunard Steamship Co Ltd, BOAC has agreed to acquire for cash Cunard's 30 per cent holding in BOAC-Cunard effective on 15 October 1966. A purchase consideration of £11·5 million is related to Cunard's proportion of the estimated net asset value of BOAC-Cunard. After that date the air routes now operated in the name of BOAC-Cunard will be 100 per cent BOAC.' The Steamship Company thus avoided having to raise at least £25 million over the next five years for a 30 per cent share in re-equipping the airline with Boeing 747s and BAC/Sud Concordes, for it already faced serious capital problems in modernizing its maritime fleet, so the £11·5 million refund would be available to invest in container ships.

Decision on BEA's fleet was also imminent. The Annual Report confirmed a net profit of £1·3 million, resulting from a £2·9 million surplus on international services and a loss of £1·6 million on domestic services. To ensure better profits both the Trident 3 with 136 seats and the BAC One-Eleven with 99 seats were being considered. 'Part of the exercise', said Marking, 'is that BEA should buy or hire BAC One-Eleven 300 Series aircraft with 79 seats to cover the period until the BAC One-Eleven 500 is available.' Guardedly, Milward wrote in the *BEA Magazine*: 'We are delighted that we can stay British as we always have done. The aircraft we are going to get will be the best that the industry and ourselves can plan. I am thankful that the decision has been taken. Hard bargaining between the two manufacturers involved is now the order of the day — and may the best man win! BEA's whole future depends on these orders.' There was no indication as to which of the two he preferred.

Meanwhile critics of Concorde were far from elated by the Committee of Public Accounts' revelation that the estimated cost had risen to £500 million. Deeply concerned, the MoA appointed John Hamilton to 'direct and co-ordinate the execution of all the technical, financial, and administrative tasks relating to the Concorde project which fall within the responsibility of the Ministry of Aviation, in accordance with the policies, plans and estimates of time and cost approved by the Anglo-French Concorde Directing Committee'.

The foggy days of November were affording further opportunity for Auto-land trials with the Trident. On a day in which all other flights had stopped because of visibility little more than 50 yards, the Trident, piloted by Jimmy Phillips, made three landings at fog-bound Hatfield. 'It was all very relaxing — even more than practice-landings under the hood', said the pilot. A few days later the One-Eleven using the rival Elliott automation system emulated the Trident with four landings at Gatwick in minimal visibility. Then the Trident made a riposte on 24 November with six fully automatic touch-downs at Heathrow in 50 yards' visibility and flew through fog to Manchester to pick up Henry Marking and bring him back.

The technical background of such developments had been one of the responsibilities of the MoA, but on 21 November Prime Minister Harold Wilson announced: 'I have decided that the present responsibilities of the Ministry of Aviation form a closely linked group that should be transferred to the Ministry of Technology. The organization for research, development and procurement on aircraft, guided weapons and electronics will remain broadly in its present form — but under the Minister of Technology it will make a significant contribution to achieving our aim that the Department should be a major instrument of progress in the engineering and electronics field.'

Early in the following month Viscount Knollys, that omniscient chairman of BOAC from 1943 to 1947, died at the age of 71 after a long illness. Since retirement from the airline he had been deputy chairman and then chairman of Vickers Ltd until 1962, and from 1959 to 1965 was chairman of the English Steel Corporation — yet his memorial was the foundation of post-war BOAC.

Decision on BEA's medium-haul requirement had been hanging fire while Government changes were being made, but on 16 December, despite earlier concern over the fatal structural collapse of a Trident in the USA during a thunderstorm, the president of the BoT, Douglas Jay, gave approval for the purchase of eighteen BAC One-Eleven Series 500

British Airways requirements led to the 'stretched' Trident Three of 1969, which carried 135 passengers instead of 99, but had 700 miles less range.

airliners. An option on a further six depended on whether runways at Guernsey and Jersey could be lengthened for them. Already BEA was evaluating a stretched version of these airliners known as the Two-Eleven powered with R–R Conways, though they would prove costly to integrate with the Corporation's engineering organization. As an alternative there was the stretched Trident 3.

Engine maintenance requirements were becoming increasingly onerous for both Corporations. Consideration was therefore being given to forming a jointly owned engine company which would take over BOAC's engine base at Treforest in South Wales where nearly 1,000 engineers were employed, giving ample potential for overhaul and repair of engines from other airlines as well as their own.

1967

BOAC opened 1967 with an option on ten more Boeing 747s, with delivery from 1972 onwards. On 19 January Sir Giles Guthrie, not to be outdone by Henry Marking, flew in the Super VC 10 Elliott automatic-landing development airliner, and three such landings were made at RAE Bedford. Sir Giles said: 'The landings were excellent, although conditions were bad because it was very bumpy and there was a 20-knot cross wind. I was extremely impressed, and I know BOAC and Elliott's have developed a British system which leads the world.'

Although BEA was already certificated to make fair-weather 'auto flares' with the Autoland Tridents on scheduled passenger services, and was heading for a true blind-landing system, Sir Giles stole their thunder by announcing that BOAC would be the first-ever airline to use a fully automatic landing system. That the Elliott system had certain advantages seemed likely because BEA specified it 'for comparison purposes' in the contract for One-Eleven 500's signed on 27 January.

Meanwhile BOAC was in trouble with an unexpectedly heavy modification programme for the Boeing 707s to extend the structural fatigue life from 30,000 hours, which was imminent, to 60,000 hours. Sir Giles Guthrie explained: 'One of the two work lines will have to be kept going until June. The cause? First the immediate rectification work when fatigue cracks were found last spring in the tail assembly bolts of some 707's and subsequent perma-

nent modifications which came on top of the "face-lift" given to each 707, including fitting VC 10 type economy-class seating at 34-inch spacing. There have also been delays in the VC 10 winter checks aggravated by shortage of spares.'

A recruiting drive for 200 maintenance staff helped to bring the engineering maintenance division 'up to the planned 1967–68 strength within the next two months' — yet two years earlier the airline had begun decreasing the engineering strength to a target of 1,830 by December 1966. Evidently the Corporation had over-cancelled both its Super VC 10s and staff, so the £4¾ million golden handshakes had been partly wasted. BOAC's shortage of capacity soon attracted comment. The *Daily Mail* said: 'An airline that thinks more about economics and balance sheets than about putting aircraft in the air and keeping them there is heading for trouble'. The Corporation's explanation of cancelled services, originating from the loss of their 707 at Tokyo a year ago, did not dispel belief that the planning department had got its sums wrong in July 1964.

Though it was generally believed that the policy of British airlines towards Concorde was cold indifference, Sir Giles Guthrie declared: 'Absolutely not — this is rubbish. BOAC will need Concorde, and we will also need the American Mach 3 SST; they are complementary, but they must be commercial propositions. Within the past two weeks I have advised the Government that production of Concorde should start. The manufacturers say that by 1967 they must purchase the metals needed to meet the 1971 production deadline. It is for the Government to take this decision.' The issue was now in the hands of John Stonehouse, the Minister of Technology, regarded as one of the most able of Labour's young men. He also had to reach agreement with the French on the thorny question of the Airbus, for Lufthansa and Air France confirmed a requirement for a 250-seat short-haul version; but BEA was out of phase with the majority conception and remained more interested in the Boeing 727-200 and its derivatives, or the BAC Two-Eleven. Sir Anthony Milward remarked: 'Some papers say we have plumped for the Two-Eleven because it is the most expensive to develop and will thus be quickly rejected by the Government, leaving the way open for a renewed attempt to get Boeing 727-200s in its place. No such Machiavellian tactics have ever passed my mind!' But from Budapest, on opening a direct BEA service a few weeks later, he said: 'Every week that goes by drives us nearer and nearer to buying the Boeing 727, and once we go American we cannot change direction again'. But matters dragged on. The Minister seemed more interested in a scheme of 'noise certification' for civil aircraft.

In April there was every indication that BEA's results for 1966–67 would show an operating surplus of about £5·5 million, and after payment of interest the net profit would be 'not less than £500,000'. Much more encouraging was BOAC's announcement of a record £23·5 million profit, the interest on capital having been outweighed by gains on aircraft sales, principally Comets. As *Flight*'s editor commented: 'These are golden years for long-haul airlines. The massive deficits are old history now. The country has decided that if the Corporation is forced to do anything against its will, then the taxpayer will foot the bill. Airlines justify high profits on the grounds that heavy capital expenditure will be needed on Boeing 747's and supersonic aircraft.'

In mid-month BEA staged 'operation automatic' in the most ambitious programme of auto-pilot flying so far undertaken by an airline. During a seven-day series of flights on normal passenger services the Auto-land Trident, using manual control only for take-off, logged 34½ hours under auto-pilot during which 27 automatic landings were made at fifteen different airfields in nine European countries. With increasing availability of Tridents modified to Auto-land standards all pilots would be encouraged to use automatic flight, but not until over 3,000 landings had been made would genuinely blind landings be permitted.

The independent airlines were facing different problems. Safety had been deteriorating. Two accidents at the beginning of June involving inclusive tours resulted in the deaths of 160 persons, including crew. This brought the total number of British independent airline accidents in the past ten years to 26 and a total of 709 fatalities, compared with eleven accidents and 321 fatalities for BOAC and BEA combined. Repercussions followed. Douglas Jay instructed the BoT to make 'a special review of the performance of all operators of British-registered commercial aircraft'. The directors of flight safety began re-appraising stricter enforcement of existing legislation and compliance with 'approved' operating standards —

but there was no uniformity of navigational facilities between secondary airfields and large busy terminals, and aircraft equipment that seemed the latest in technological development six years ago was comparatively inaccurate compared with the latest product. There was also the question of age of the aircraft itself, for many had been bought secondhand from the two Corporations.

Labour's bias against private venture airlines was strong. Both Guthrie and Milward had been haled before a sub-committee of the Select Committee on Nationalized Industries in which Ian Mikardo had asked such questions as: 'What support has the Minister given you in your competition against private airlines?' In the course of questioning Sir Anthony said that the amount of checking by government officials of BEA's capital investment plans was particularly irksome. 'We had ten people from the Board of Trade, Ministry of Technology, Treasury, and Department of Economic Affairs in one office asking the same questions and sending to the next meeting different people who all repeated the same questions.'

Problems over pilot's pay were again looming. BEA pilots had offered a 'productivity' deal, but the BoT turned it down as contravening the Prices and Incomes Board [PIB] requirements. BALPA therefore recommended a salary structure based on seniority and an hourly rate varying with aircraft type, miles flown, and aircraft weight. This seemed a preliminary move which had the Boeing 747 ultimately in view, for the latest design figures showed even heavier all-up weight, and by 1971 it would have take-off certification at 316 tons.

Decision on the Anglo-French-German Airbus was incessantly expected, but not until 25 July was tripartite decision reached to initiate the design stage, largely due to John Stonehouse who in effect awarded a £50 million contract to a foreign company, Sud-Aviation, to design and build an aircraft for which it would have complete technical control — the assumption being that a British contract for the engine development would be a *quid pro quo*. In the USA both Douglas and Lockheed were designing a rival for their own domestic trunk routes, using a triple-engined wide-bodied cabin seating 250 to 350, though the Lockheed CL-1011 (TriStar) proposal was somewhat smaller than the Douglas DC-10, which seated nine abreast compared with the Lockheed's eight.

The weeks rolled by. In mid-August BEA published the accounts for 1966–67 which showed a reduction in net profit to £708,296 compared with the previous year's £1·3 million. Competition from independent airlines and British Rail on domestic services was described as the major problem. A large part of the Report was devoted to the re-equipment issue — 'a subject which dominates all others in BEA to-day' — and warning was made that: 'The concept of the European Airbus must not be allowed to confuse a clear-cut issue that it is imperative, for commercial and competitive reasons, that BEA take delivery of a second phase of aircraft not later than 1971'. In commenting on the financial results Sir Anthony Milward stressed that because of the economic squeeze and the £50 maximum overseas spending allowance the chances of a profit for 1967–68 were nil, and he could not understand why air travel should be so completely victimized. 'You can buy a German car any day if you have the money, but you cannot have more than £50 travel allowance to go to Germany to see where it is built.'

BOAC's results for the year proved the best ever, for there was a group net surplus of nearly £24 million, and for the first time passengers had exceeded 1½ million. But earlier the Corporation had lost its appeal against the approval by the ATLB of licences for British Eagle and Lloyd International to operate inclusive tour charters between London, Bermuda, and Bahamas. This was still a sore subject, and the Annual Report warned: 'If the inclusive tour holiday market is made available to non-scheduled airlines, the traffic on which scheduled carriers rely for the development of their services will be diluted by this unnecessary competition'. Appeals were now launched against British United Airways, British Eagle, and Trans-Globe Airways to revoke their inclusive tour charters to points in East Africa at a non-standard tariff of £150 — but these too were dismissed by the BoT. So many of the independents had fallen by the wayside, that their official Association was currently dissolved, but gave a last kick at the ATLB, saying: 'It can no longer be pretended that the Board are competent to fulfil the duty of satisfying themselves of the all-round competence of applicants for licences'.

Towards the end of September Douglas Jay implemented the statement he had made in the Commons two months earlier that: 'The

Government has decided to institute a broadly based inquiry into the civil air transport industry . . . While the inquiry must be thorough, it is also important that it should be completed quickly. I hope it will be able to make a first report with recommendations in spring 1968.'

To that end Sir Ronald Edwards, the 57-year-old chairman of the Electricity Council, was appointed chairman of the Inquiry Committee, and 60-year-old Sir Hugh Tett, the chairman of Esso, became deputy chairman. Neither had any airline experience, but Sir Ronald had been Professor of Economics at London University, and Sir Hugh was a governor of the London Graduate School of Business Studies. The other members were a trade union official, a banker, a State Corporation chairman, and A.G. Manzie of the BoT as secretary. To quell the inevitable outcry that committees of this kind comprised mainly men who knew nothing of aviation, S.F. Wheatcroft, an airline economics consultant, was appointed assessor, and Capt F.A. Taylor, a former Pathfinder and a current airline Captain, was added to tell them how aeroplanes flew. The whole future of British airlines would depend on the recommendations of this Committee.

On 12 October a new threat to flight security caused great concern. A BEA Comet disintegrated above the Turkish coast killing the 59 passengers and seven crew. Urgent inves-

The British Aerospace Corporation Super One-Eleven 500s had twin tail-mounted jet pods and carried 99 passengers. BEA began operating eighteen on the German network in 1968/69; four more were subsequently obtained, and in 1974 British Airways added seven of the smaller 400 version to the fleet.

Cambrian British Air Services Super One-Eleven 500

tigation proved conclusively that an explosive device had been detonated within the cabin causing rupture of the controls, and in the ensuing dive the aircraft broke up. The urgent question was how to deal with terrorists. Judicial aspects of law still had to be unravelled.

To some degree that endorsed action by BOAC pilot members of BALPA who had warned they would support strike action if no progress was made in revising their pay structure by the end of October. Limited 'work-to-rule' began on 1 November, based on a twelve-point directive which could well delay flights for an hour or more, though BALPA described it as 'the greatest act of moderation possible'.

Three weeks went by without results, other than increased efficiency of ground crews to maintain serviceability, so the next phase was put into operation which could lead to wholesale cancellations. At that, Ray Gunter, the Minister of Labour, called a meeting between representatives of BOAC and the pilots. Nothing was immediately achieved. The pilots threatened a series of 48-hour strikes from 8 December, but BOAC capped this by threatening to shut down completely unless 'industrial order' among the pilots was restored. The pilots immediately struck; 32 flights had to be cancelled and the 900 passengers re-allocated to other airlines. BOAC were well aware that a

shut-down would cost £2·5 million a week in lost passenger revenue, two-thirds of which would be foreign currency. Gunter set up a Court of Inquiry. Meanwhile a similar situation was arising between BEA pilots and their management, the BALPA members backing a motion to work-to-rule on similar lines to BOAC pilots, and 80 senior BEA Captains gave three months' notice of resignation from voluntary training duties.

While the undercurrent of dissatisfaction was rolling to a climax, BOAC received permission from the BoT to order five more Boeing 747s. That was followed a month later by rejection of BEA's requirement for two BAC Two-Elevens, and instead the Government agreed to share the cost of launching the stretched 3/3B verson of the H-S Trident. The new president of the BoT, Anthony Crosland, said that the decision against the Two-Eleven was because sales prospects did not justify the estimated

£120 million development cost. Instantly Autair International, in association with Clarkson's Tours, announced a firm commitment for three, and on the following day Laker Airways ordered another three.

But now Concorde re-entered the news. Everyone had long been familiar with its shape and expectations, though stunned by speculation that the cost was now estimated at over £600 million — yet five years ago it had been £160 million. On Monday, 11 December, Concorde became reality, for amid pomp and ceremony the huge upward hingeing doors of the Toulouse flight hangar rose precisely on schedule and Concorde 001 was towed out, gleaming in the pale winter sunshine. Speeches followed. Anthony Wedgwood Benn, the new Minister of Technology, ended his with: 'Our years of co-operation have only been marred by one disagreement. In English, Concord ends with a plain "d". With splendid extravagance our French friends have added an extra "e". No amount of argument or discussion, no series of committees or ministerial meetings have ever produced agreement on this point. I have therefore resolved it myself. From now on it will be spelt with an "e". That letter symbolizes Excellence, England, Europe, Entry and Entente — that alliance which binds our two countries together.'

At that, Concorde was pulled in, and the hangar doors closed.

1968

The Edwards Committee visited Switzerland in the second week of January 1968 for talks with civil aviation authorities. Similar discussions were planned with key countries across the world. Fifty airlines had been approached for evidence and considerable written testimony had been received. *Flight* reported: 'The Committee has had a number of formal briefing meetings and this has helped fill in the background, since the majority of its members are completely new to the industry and its mysteries'.

At ATLB there was another round of sporadic battling. Sir Giles Guthrie was leading BOAC's objections to applications from British Eagle and Caledonian Airways to operate scheduled services on North Atlantic routes. Nobody believed that both independents would be permitted to compete with BOAC, yet a fortnight had to be expended in sifting the evidence of many people and then it would be months before a decision was reached — so no plans could be implemented for the summer trans-Atlantic traffic.

The effects of devaluation on holiday traffic abroad could be disastrous, said Sir Anthony Milward. 'We have to charge higher fares for a holiday which needs be shortened owing to further diminution of the value of the £50 travel allowance.' An American commentator wrote: 'If there is any hope at all for Britain to climb out of the present economic morass, it lies in massive development of modern technology to increase the productivity of its labour force and make its goods competitive once more in the international market. All new directions in modern technology are polarized around the aerospace industry.'

What European eyes focused on was the Concorde. It was becoming known as the Discord. Not until mid-February did it have the first engine run. The French Transport Minister in explaining delay in flight testing said: 'The date of February 28 was a working hypothesis rather than a definite date. As a result of British delay in production of the final engines, the Concorde is at present receiving provisional engines which will be utilized only for ground tests.' The British Press was quick to make capital from these comments to the detriment of the Concorde project, though British employment was greatly benefiting not only from the major contractual work at Bristol and Rolls-Royce but by some 323 sub-contractors employing over 12,500 workers at 355 centres. 'Virtually every major town in Britain', reported the SBAC, 'has one or more factories contributing to Concorde.'

On 13 March the House of Commons voted up to £125 million to finance Concorde production, in addition to the shared cost of the prototype. Wedgwood Benn, who had constituency interest at Bristol as well as being Minister, was emphatic that: 'If this country wishes to remain in an advanced technology it has to support the engineers engaged in the production of this aircraft, for this is not private enterprise but a national enterprise'. Total estimated cost of the Anglo-French supersonic programme was now some £850 million. Here was one of the biggest gambles in the history of commercial aviation.

Delay was symptomatic of the modern world. The BoT report on the previous autumn's dispute between BOAC and BALPA had just been issued. BOAC was criticized for missing a favourable opportunity of negotiating during the pilots' 'reduction of co-operation' campaign. No mention was made of management criticism, but conciliation was in the air, and a deal was mutually agreed by which the pilots received a 10 per cent pay rise this year and $7\frac{1}{2}$ per cent in the next two, in return for productivity concessions including an increase in the number of duty days away from home and abolition of the requirement for a fourth pilot on trans-Pacific sectors. However that still had to be agreed by the BoT. Again the weeks began to mount.

Luck narrowly averted a major disaster at Heathrow on 8 April when a BOAC Boeing 707 was turning on course shortly after take-off for Australia. Trouble showed on No 2 engine, and before it could be shut the low-pressure compressor disrupted and severed the fuel pipe. The crew omitted to close the low-pressure fuel cock. Kerosene flowed into the engine pod and ignited. A skilled cross-wind landing was made on the nearest runway but by then the flames had consumed so much of the port wing that it broke off, and, when the machine stopped, the fire consumed most of the fuselage centre-section and rear fuselage — but the crew managed to evacuate 110 of the 126 on board, though the machine was destroyed. By long odds the same Boeing had been involved in an engine disintegration the previous November. The burn-up was a bad setback and meant serious loss to revenue, so accelerated delivery of a Super VC 10 was requested but proved impossible, nor could Boeing quote less than a year for a 707-465. However Saturn Airways saved the position by releasing one of the three 707-320Cs they had on order. Luckily BOAC was in a strong financial position these days. Provisional unaudited figures showed a Group profit of £21 million in the year ending 31 March, and though this was a reduction of £2·9 million, that was attributable to the Israel–Arab War which had shut down an important market.

BEA on 17 April received the first fully certificated Auto-land Trident 2, and it was officially named at Heathrow by Lady Milward. Sir Anthony said that the first few would be used on an *ad hoc* basis to back up the Trident 1 services, but regular services would start on 1 June on the London–Milan run. To meet the ever-increasing need for freighters, five Vickers Vanguards were scheduled for conversion and renamed Merchantman. The airline's new cargo terminal at Heathrow would come into use next year and was to be named Cargo Centre Europe.

Another step towards safety was taken on 16 May when a BOAC Super VC 10 made that Corporation's first automatic landing with passengers aboard, touching down at Heathrow after a scheduled flight from Chicago and Montreal; the 146 passengers were not told of the landing until after touch-down had been safely made.

Pilots, it seemed, were still essential — but the pay and productivity deal which BOAC and BALPA had jointly sent to the BoT had run into trouble because the two parties could not agree on how much productivity could be achieved. BALPA estimated a $12\frac{1}{2}$ per cent rise; BOAC stood firm at only $1\frac{1}{2}$ per cent. The pilots therefore decided to reinstitute last year's 'restriction of co-operation' campaign from midnight 24 May — so the dispute was referred to the Prices and Incomes Board.

Though it certainly had nothing to do with his criticism of the pilots, Sir Giles Guthrie announced that he wished to resign when his term of office expired on 31 December. Anthony Crosland invited him to remain for a second five-year term, but he declined, saying he had never intended to serve longer than to achieve his brief of bringing BOAC back to profitability. There was a feeling that the Government's refusal to let him deal directly with Ministers explained his refusal, and possibly there had been talk of a BOAC merger with BEA to which he had not agreed, for on 14 May Lord Beswick, Government spokesman on aviation, said: 'It is a matter of some regret that over the years, when one has contemplated the possibility of one Corporation, no one name has ever leapt to mind as leader of such a unified Corporation'.

A week later the Government nominated Charles Hardie, the part-time deputy chairman, as eventual successor to Sir Giles in part-time capacity for one year. Hardie, skilled in accountancy, already held seven or eight other active directorships. To assist him, Keith Granville, that stalwart of Imperial Airways days who was now full-time deputy chairman, accepted the duties of managing director. Announcing these appointments, Anthony Crosland explained that because the Edwards Committee was due

BOAC routes, 1969.

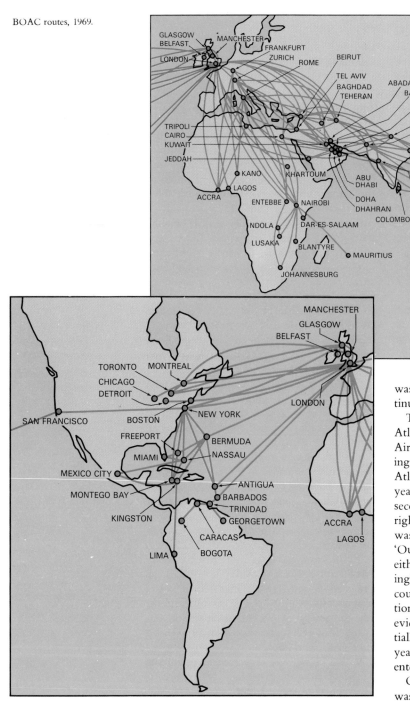

BOAC routes, 1969.

to make its recommendations in the first part of next year, his aim had been to maintain the *status quo* and avoid changes in the Board before the end of 1969, so he had invited those in BOAC and BEA whose appointments terminated within that time to continue until the end of the year. Thus, Sir Anthony Milward, who

was due to retire next March, agreed to continue.

The involved case of BOAC's objections to Atlantic rights for British Eagle and Caledonian Airways now reached solution with the surprising decision that there should be no trans-Atlantic independent competition at all. Seven years ago the ATLB had been in favour of a second trans-Atlantic carrier and had granted rights to Cunard-Eagle, though the decision was reversed on appeal. The Board explained 'Our decision might have been different if either applicant had been able to show convincingly that even in the circumstances of to-day it could successfully establish its proposed operations'. The Board accepted the Corporation's evidence that it intended to bid for a substantially larger share of the market in the next three years, and the fact that it was now a profitable enterprise was a convincing factor.

One of the side effects of this important case was increasing rumour that the Government was considering a merger between BOAC and BEA.

For the moment the latter was more concerned with its 200-seater problems. Asked whether he would order the A-300 Airbus by the July deadline, Milward said: 'There is not the remotest chance. Instead we can look around at the Lockheed 1011 and Douglas

DC-10. We shall not need an Airbus until about 1974.' In high hope that it would be abandoned, Lockheed was going to great lengths to sell their triple-engined 1011 with availability in late 1971, and on 18 June flew journalists from all over the world to see the mock-up at Burbank, USA.

Two days before that flight BOAC was grounded by the long-threatened strike of pilots protesting against the time taken to get the new agreement. Twelve hours of talk at the Department of Employment and Productivity on 1 July induced the pilots to call off the strike on promise of implementation at the end of the month subject to agreement of the Prices and Incomes Board. However the disruption was such that services could not get back to normal until 9 July, for some 800 flight staff had to be re-established overseas.

Next day Anthony Crosland announced that in recompense for BEA operating a new fleet of aircraft not of its choosing: 'I have agreed to make assistance available in the form of an initial transfer of £25 million, with a possibility of a further £12½ million if needed in the period April 1, 1972 to March 31, 1975'. As the 26 Trident 3Bs would cost £83 million, Sir Anthony Milward would go no further than describe the settlement as: 'Fair — but not generous'.

On 8 August BOAC published its Annual Report, confirming a profit of £21 million. Already the shadow of the Edwards Committee was evident, for Sir Giles said: 'The recommendations could have considerable effect on our intentions, not just in detail but on a broad front. We are confident however that they will take full account of BOAC as a valuable asset belonging to the nation as a whole and there is no reason why its strength should now be dissipated.'

BEA was in a similar category, but in a poor way, for the accounts published on 20 August — the day when the airline began using a new livery and a symbol based on the Union Jack — revealed a heavy net loss of £1·8 million after paying £5·9 million interest and writing off £1·7 million of aircraft introductory costs. At the usual Press post-mortem a week later, Sir Anthony Milward, white-haired, affable, and outspoken as ever, said that despite the loss BEA was not ashamed, for it had not cost the taxpayer anything in the past fourteen years and had helped the country considerably through foreign exchange earnings. Asked about the

A-300 Airbus he said: 'We still don't know what it is or what it costs, and the project is surrounded with more talk and less action than almost any other. What BEA still wants is a 200-230 seater with wide fuselage, so the Corporation is interested in the Three-Eleven for which there could be a requirement for perhaps twenty by 1973.'

Taxi-ing trials of the BAC/Sud Concorde prototype 001 commenced on 20 August, and in the course of a week it made eighteen ground runs, and was then returned to its flight hangar for flight test preparation.

Three weeks later, with no rhetoric, no bands, but watched by several hundred who had helped to build her, the Bristol-built 002 at Filton was rolled out to the ground-running bay for check of engines and systems before similar taxi-ing trials.

Even more important for the next decade of commercial aviation was the roll-out in the USA on 30 September of the enormously impressive Boeing 747, construction of which, as well as its vast factory, had been completed in astonishingly short time, for the project had been launched in the spring of 1966 when the Airbus and Concorde had long been subjects of contention. Europe would have to wake up if it could ever compete again.

At home the affairs of the pilots had not been settled by the agreed date of 31 October, so they refused to fly more than an average 45 hours a month or more than 10½ each duty day, and were considering resignation *en masse*, then rejoining as freelances with individual contracts. At the last moment the Prices and

Embarkation time for a BEA Trident at Heathrow airport, using twin entrances.

Incomes Board broadly approved the agreement for an hourly-rate pay structure and bidding for blocks of work in order of seniority so that each pilot could set his own earnings level. Nevertheless on 1 November BOAC threatened to dismiss all BALPA members who claimed that the Corporation was lax in negotiations and not interested in a productivity deal, but at the eleventh hour withdrew its threat because 780 of the 1,080 pilots said they were willing to face dismissal. Talks on pay and scheduling therefore continued, for the PIB adjudication grandiosely pontificated: 'There should be no automatic relationship between pay and the weight and speed of an aircraft. A change in pay should reflect changes in job content identified through techniques of job analysis.'

BOAC was still battling against the independents, and had secured revocation of British Eagle's inclusive tour charters on the London–Bermuda route. Indignantly Harold Bamberg said: 'This decision once more highlights the protectionist attitude in favour of the national airlines'. But it meant more. The revocation of the Caribbean inclusive tour licences caused Hambro's Bank to withdraw support, and on 6 November the British Eagle companies were closed down. With invariable acumen BEA applied for licences to operate several British Eagle routes, and BOAC obtained approval to purchase that company's leased Boeing 707-320C. Sir Anthony was conciliatory: 'There certainly will not be any crowing in BEA that Eagle has disappeared. There has been more than a suggestion that Eagle's failure is in some way BEA's fault, but one person who has not said this is Mr Bamberg himself. We all work in a difficult industry with an extremely narrow dividing line between profitability and failure whether we are nationalized or privately owned, the difference being that it is extremely unlikely that BEA would ever be allowed to go bankrupt. I wish we could as a nation stop arguing private versus public ownership. Could we not call a halt to all this and accept, for better or worse, that this nation has a mixed economy and will always have one?'

Certainly there was no differentiation between independents and the two Corporations at the new 160-acre Cargo Terminal at Heathrow, to which the 1,000-yard entry tunnel was officially opened on 9 December. The buildings for the independent airlines, both British and foreign, were ready except for fittings, and

some of the warehouses would be occupied early in the New Year. The joint warehouse for BEA and BOAC had been constructed, but lagged behind the rest of the development by six months. Heathrow had become the third port in Britain in terms of cargo exported or imported, with London and Liverpool docks still in the lead.

There followed the world's greatest technical experiment yet made. On 21 December the Apollo 8 rocket was launched to make man's first orbit of the moon carrying Frank Borman, James Lovell and William Anders, and on the 27th they triumphantly terminated this epic with a splash-down in the Pacific after re-entering the earth's atmosphere at a velocity of 25,000 mph. It was a feat of technology, navigation, and courage that astonished and changed the world just as the Wright brothers had 65 years earlier.

Almost unnoticed by the world's Press, Russia's supersonic Tupolev Tu-144 made its maiden flight on 31 December — but the geometrically similar Concorde prototypes were still being prepared.

1969

'£1,000 million Concorde' was a scaremongering newspaper heading in January 1969 — and it was almost true if £30 million was included for experimental establishments, £60 million for special tooling provided by the

British and French governments, and provision through the Industrial Expansion Act for £125 million as production-learning costs. Though some was recoverable, the Anglo-French total was probably some £970 million — but that was infinitely small compared with the American space research programme.

On 9 February the USA secured another hit with the first flight of the Boeing 747 flown by Jack Waddel, who reported over the R/T that the machine handled easily and a speed of 300 mph had been reached at 15,000 feet. In Europe the question of the Airbus A-300B versus the BAC Three-Eleven remained at deadlock. However on 2 March, a year late, with André Turcat at the controls and crew of three, that splendid supersonic airliner Concorde made its first flight, climbing straight ahead to 10,000 feet leaving the undercarriage down and the nose visor in fully dropped position, swept steadily round until twenty miles down-wind and head back, landing 29 minutes after take-off without perceptible flare, a puff of smoke billowing from the tyres. BOAC's Keith Granville enthusiastically said: 'It was a soaring triumph for everyone involved with this spectacular aeroplane'.

In the same week, on the basis 'If you can't beat 'em join 'em', Henry Marking established a BEA charter company to handle non-IATA operations, and appointed the flight operations maestro Capt W. Baillie as manager. When the Comet 4Bs were withdrawn from scheduled services in June he would be allocated seven, based at Gatwick with a staff of 200. There were immediate rumours that BOAC intended to set up a similar subsidiary, though it had no surplus aircraft at the moment but might buy second-hand Boeing 707s. There was immediate 'inspired' outcry that nationalized airlines were spending public money on holidaymakers who did nothing for the balance of payments — but this was the market at which the Lockheed TriStar aimed its unbeatable economies on all ranges from 500 to 4,000 miles, making even the One-Eleven and VC 10 obsolete.

BOAC was now in even greater difficulty with the pilots. Devoted and highly skilled at their job, they were nevertheless in deadlock with the management, who a fortnight earlier had offered a new pay scheme that raised questions of redundancy for the many senior pilots over 50, whereas BALPA insisted on the established trade union principle 'Last in first out'. No agreement was reached between BALPA and BOAC management. Consequently the BOAC pilots went on strike at midnight on 30 March following useless intervention by Mrs Barbara Castle. The strike hit the Corporation's plans for the inaugural Polar route service scheduled for the following day. The mediator, Professor Wood, who had chaired discussions since July of the previous year, resigned. The Trade Union side of the National Joint Council for Civil Aviation met to discuss the dispute, and optimistically appointed Mark Young of the ETU and Clive Jenkins of the ASTMS as 'peacemakers'. Negotiations over Easter weekend led to calling off the strike on 5 April after a six-day stoppage which cost the airline more than £3 million, but it was symptomatic of the complete distrust between pilots and management that neither party came face to face during the Easter negotiations, the success of which was largely due to Clive Jenkins, and led to a guaranteed basic salary for senior Captains of £6,750 which by bids for blocks of flying could rise to £8,400 a year. Meanwhile the pilots had further problems, for three senior BALPA executives — chairman, industrial relations director, and public relations adviser — resigned.

Politically of great concern was Britain's resignation from the A-300 Airbus, disappointing all who believed that the principle of collaboration was the only course for the ultimate viability of the European transport aircraft manufacturing industry. Wedgwood Benn had

The impressively large Boeing 747 proved to be the world's most economical airliner, and was first operated by BOAC in 1971. Eleven were taken over by the British Airways Board in April 1972 when it assumed control of BOAC and BEA. Subsequently, eight more were obtained and seven very long-range versions powered by Rolls-Royce RB211-524 engines.

decided that the £60 million share would not be a good investment, but Hawker Siddeley remained ready to play a key part as a private venture, and Rolls-Royce in any case would benefit if the Airbus went ahead.

However the Anglo-French Concorde had successfully proceeded to its next phase, for on 9 April the British-assembled prototype 002 made a successful initial flight from Filton in the hands of Brian Trubshaw, watched by almost the entire personnel of the BAC factory and huge crowds outside the airfield. Spellbound they saw it, looking like a praying mantis, run down the runway, lift into a climb, and set course for the longer runway at Fairford, twenty miles away, where the flight test programme would be conducted. Meanwhile in France Concorde 001 had completed eight more flights and had reached the crucial threshold of Mach 1 — but even that achievement lost prestige publicity with the resignation of General de Gaulle from the Presidency on 28 April.

On 2 May the long-awaited report of the Edwards Committee was published as a bulky volume of 300,000 words and 38 appendices. Almost two years had been spent in achieving this excellent primer on British air transport which basically advised a strong Civil Aviation Authority to regulate greater competition between Corporations and independents. A national Air Holdings Board was proposed with sovereignty over the individual identities of BOAC and BEA, but domestic services would be run by a co-operative British Air Services responsibile to the Holdings Board, and the private airlines, of which BUA and Caledonian were specifically mentioned, should combine into a 'second-force' operator in which the Holdings Board would have shares and directors in exchange for concessions on the North Atlantic and Paris routes. *Flight* commented: 'The Holdings Board has merit, for there seems no other way of avoiding costly duplications like the Vanguard and Britannia, or separate city terminals and overseas offices, incompatible multi-million pound data-processing systems, duplicated engineering projects departments. Cross-posting of the chairman of the Corporations has achieved little or nothing, so co-operation will have to be imposed if the vast investments of the future are not wasted.'

The proposal for a national Air Holdings Board was described by Sir Anthony Milward

Spanning 195 ft and weighing 325 tons all-up, the Boeing 747-136 can carry 404 passengers cruising at 550 mph for some 5,000 miles, and has a usable fuel tankage of some 120 tons — enough to keep the average Mini going for over 100 years or drive 50 times round the world!

Mr Keith Granville (knighted 1973), Chairman of BOAC 1971–72.

Super VC 10s, the Government was now pushing the Air Corporations Bill through Parliament to provide financial aid of at least £25 million and perhaps £37·5 million for BEA to operate the Super One-Elevens and Trdent 3Bs instead of the Boeings of their choice. Somewhat confusingly the BoT Minister said that such public dividend capital would not make any difference to BEA's financial performance, whereupon the Opposition spokesman interjected: 'The real test comes when an airline has to resort to the market for additional capital. A nationalized Corporation does not resort to the market, but to the Treasury, and because it is a nationalized industry it clearly cannot be left to get into real financial difficulties, so it is never likely to resort to the Treasury in vain.'

Meanwhile there was opposition by the 3,000 engineering and ground staff of BEA and BOAC to the Edwards Committee's proposal for a 'second-force' airline. At a Heathrow meeting chaired by Clive Jenkins they unanimously decided to express strong disapproval of any 'hiving off' of the Corporation's services to any such privately owned airline. Any attempt to dismember BEA or BOAC, warned Jenkins, would be met by political activity and, if necessary, by national action. One of the likely contenders, Autair International, currently announced abandonment of its entire scheduled network through lack of a subsidy, but proposed to concentrate on inclusive tour holidays, and to that end changed its name to Court Line — the name of the shipping, hotel, and travel group of which it was a wholly owned subsidiary.

as 'a distinctly curious idea' because if the Board exercised the defined 'wide-ranging responsibilities' it would immediately be the overall authority merging the identity of the two Corporations. If it forced BEA to take undesirable actions, the BEA chairman would be able to say it was not our fault'. Responsibility, said Milward, must be in the hands of one man alone — either the Holdings Board chairman or the Corporation's chairman, not both.

BEA was expected to make a profit of about £3 million in the financial year which had just ended, said William Rodgers, the new Minister of the BoT — but that had only been achieved after crediting £2½ million for increased depreciation of the Comet and Viscount fleets and £5 million compensation for abandonment of the American aircraft purchase. However the Minister assured MPs that the outlook for the next few years was promising.

Profitability was also the theme of BOAC. Keith Granville was able to announce at the inauguration of the Polar service to Japan on 5 May that the Corporation had made a surplus of £21 million on the operating account for the year ending 31 March. A 25 per cent increase in capacity was planned for 1970–71 to meet consolidation and expansion of the Polar service. A few days later the BoT gave permission for purchase of two more Boeing 707-320Cs and spares at a cost of £8 million; as no alternative British product was available, exemption from import duty was permitted. Having also given BOAC £30 million inducement to operate

Once again voyaging into space overwhelmed all other news. On 21 July man stood for the first time on another planet. On their TV screens 600 million people watched and heard the bulky figure of Neil Armstrong climb backwards down the aluminium ladder, set foot on the moon, and comment: 'That's one small step for a man, one vast leap for mankind'. Would the successors of BOAC one day use an orbital airliner to speed in minutes from London to Australia?

At least BOAC was heading towards prosperity. The Annual Report published in mid-August confirmed a profit of more than £21 million despite the pilots' strikes resulting in £11 million lost revenue. Explaining the need for enormous capital expenditure in the

1970s, Charles Hardie said that a grand total of £680 million would be required between now and 1978. 'That is the key to commercial success. The more capital you invest now, the more you can plan your expenditure. Here lies the future. Capital equipment at a known fixed cost during its useful life.' However he played down the recommendations of the Edwards Committee, but warned that if BOAC's scheduled routes were taken away on the scale envisaged and redistributed elsewhere, there would be 'major staff reduction and cancellation of forward aircraft purchase orders'. That would be the end of BOAC, for the world's airlines were intent on imminent use of the Boeing 747 Jumbo jet.

BEA's profit proved half a million greater than predicted, but the Annual Report revealed that the British Air Services subsidiary had lost £533,000; the Scottish division £423,000; BEA Helicopters £48,000. However it was on the subject of new aircraft that Sir Anthony Milward sounded a grave note: 'If Britain does not build a new generation jet transport her chances of remaining in the manufacturing race are very slight. BEA needs an Airbus by the spring of 1975 and that means delivery in the previous autumn. Five years is the shortest time for building and developing an airliner. If work on the A-300B or Three-Eleven does not start before the end of this year, BEA will be forced to buy American equipment, and by 1985–90 its whole fleet would be American.'

Within a week the Government issued its White Paper on policy. 'This is a major charter for the British industry', said the new president of the Board of Trade, Roy Mason. A Civil Aviation Authority would be established to regulate the entire economic, operational, and technical environment of the airline industry. The BoT would be responsible for laying down the objectives and policies and implementing their execution. Under these two departments would be an Airways Board to control the public sector airlines and ensure that the fleets and routes of BEA and BOAC were planned and marketed to the best overall advantage. There would be a continuing and promising role for independent airlines having the necessary financial strength and competence. There was no hint of a merger for the two Corporations but licensing of a second British carrier on scheduled routes was favoured 'where it can be shown that such competition would be in the public interest'.

BUA's reaction was likewarm. 'It is like being invited to dinner and being given nothing to drink', said Anthony Cayzer, the BUA chairman.

At the beginning of November came the death of 76-year-old Lord Douglas of Kirtleside — that great RAF officer who after the last war had made a new career in civil aviation, first with BOAC, and then as chairman of British European Airways. As Anthony Milward said: 'He piloted the young BEA out of the converted war plane and piston engine era into new endeavours where the gas turbine, first in turbo-prop and later in pure jet form, was to rule the skies. Under his guidance BEA became a leader, commercially and technologically among the world's airlines. For all his firmness and ruthless adherence to the course decided upon, Sholto Douglas was a soft spoken man who liked every one in all walks of life and was correspondingly trusted by every one.'

A few days later the BoT invited Sir Anthony Milward and other Board members to serve a further year after their terms of office expired next March. In the *BEA Magazine* Milward wrote: 'Although I expected to retire next March on reaching the age of 65 I am accepting this further appointment in hope that I may be of some assistance in this critical period in seeing that the White Paper legislation is the best that can be devised for this country and our Corporation'. He remained strongly opposed to any thought of a merger between BEA and BOAC 'which are just about the two most prosperous airlines in their respective spheres in the world to-day, and this has not come about by accident. It is because of good management and staff, good aircraft, good operating abilities, good marketing, and a fanatical concentration on our respective specialized jobs. Had the Edwards Committee looked further they would have found we were almost unique in the profitability field — certainly BEA is one of the few operators making substantial profits in the short-haul world. Additionally we have built up business to where 20 per cent of all European passengers fly BEA.'

The Corporation's chosen airliner, the Trident 3B, made its maiden flight at the beginning of December. Without BEA there would have been no Trident, and the advanced systems developed in conjunction with BEA had kept Europe right in the forefront of air transport technology. The dawn of full blind-landing capability was at hand.

Wings across the World 1970-74

Flight's editor, J.M. Ramsden, opened the new decade with a critical recapitulation of the previous one. Of its beginning he wrote: 'As the sixties dawned the Ministry of Aviation was formed. It brought every thing aeronautical together — airlines and manufacturers, recognizing the national importance of aviation by putting it under a Cabinet Minister. But to the Labour Government the MoA became the Temple of Profligacy, and in mid-decade they tore it down. Aviation was ignominiously bundled into the basement of a new Ministry of Technology under a junior minister. The inadequacy of the civil service in that decade was measured by the number of outside committees to which it passed its aviation problems: Corbett, Plowden, Cairns, Lang, Wilson, and Edwards — to name only some of those set up to deal with pressing crises. But there is time for wiser counsel to prevail; and it is a matter of record that in its 1969 White Paper the Government accepted competition as having merit in principle. The other major principle established in the sixties was that BOAC and BEA would no longer be regarded as captive markets for the national aircraft industry. This caused temporary, and in the case of the VC 10, avoidable damage. But in the seventies it will mean that aircraft will be built for world markets instead of being tailored too closely to the rather specialized needs of BOAC and BEA.'

Meanwhile American manufacturers were sweeping the board, and though four years earlier the Government had said: 'In no foreseeable circumstances will the Corporation be allowed to buy any more of these machines', BOAC had ordered not only the Boeing 707s but also the big 747 Jumbo jet whose full certification had been achieved less than a year after the first flight. Tests included take-offs at 320 tons, and diving to just under Mach 1·0. On 12 January the first of these 'giant' airliners, the *Clipper Constitution* owned by Pan Am, crossed the Atlantic, loomed impressively in the distance and majestically landed at Heathrow. Drawing into its temporary handling bay, 362 passengers were disgorged who boarded the disembarkation buses and cleared Customs within half an hour. A publicity flight for officials and journalists was arranged for 2·15 p.m., but there were starting problems with one engine, so the machine was almost two hours late — but everyone waited in subdued excitement and all were staggered by the size of the commodious cabin and the relaxed sense of safety it ensured.

Though first deliveries to BOAC were scheduled for April, the BALPA pilots of the Corporation refused to go to Seattle for training until their pay claim for flying this new type had been agreed. Nevertheless BOAC and BEA were facing a happier outlook for travellers because the Government had lifted the £50 currency restriction and substituted a £300 limit. Sir Anthony Milward said with relief: 'It will cause the greatest joy to those who believe that travel is one of the basic freedoms of man-

Concorde takes off, shimmering in the heat haze of its powerful jets.

kind'. Flying was also becoming safer. Though the world's airlines had 48 fatal accidents in the past year, only one had been British and that was a training flight. Statistics showed that there was only one fatality in every 15 million miles, and in terms of journeys made this was many times lower than for travelling by railway.

There was hope that supersonic travel would soon be available, for the Ministry of Technology had agreed test routes for Concorde 002 in which the extent of the sonic boom would be measured during sustained cruise at Mach 2·2, for though this could be calculated, it was the 'quality' which determined the nuisance value. Noise was of such concern that on 5 March the BoT issued revised instructions for minimum-noise departure routes from Heathrow in which airliners must achieve initial height at steepest possible angle of climb before entering the long fuel-economy trajectory of their flight plan.

An unexpected reaction to the Edwards Report now occurred. Alan Bristow, who had succeeded Freddie Laker as managing director of BUA, suddenly resigned. That seemed to indicate possible financial difficulties. Thereupon BOAC secured permission from the BoT to make a takeover bid. BOAC's chairman said: 'The deal will strengthen British competitiveness against foreign airlines'. In swift rivalry, Caledonian Airways applied to the ATLB for licences to take over the BUA scheduled routes. A week of manoeuvring followed, during which Caledonian and Laker made individual approaches to British & Commonwealth Shipping, the owners of 90 per cent of the BUA shares, and Bristow, who had his own helicopter company, also made an offer. Clive Jenkins proclaimed that any move by the private sector to take over BUA would be resisted by industrial action. To those who proposed bidding he said: 'Just you bloody well try'.

An about-turn by the BoT followed, and its president Roy Mason told the Commons on 18 March that he had been misled by British & Commonwealth and would therefore withhold the approval already given in principle to BOAC.

'All this indicates how much civil aviation in this country remains a political football', wrote Sir Anthony Milward. 'BEA, which had no part in these discussions, has received the brunt of attacks from those who do not like nationalization, and this encouraged people to draw comparisons between our domestic operations and those of BUA, but it would be unwise to believe that their domestic routes in Europe are cheaper, better, or more luxurious than ours. We have a wonderful record of expansion, regularity, and safety. I see no point in decrying our efforts to make a politician's holiday.'

Promptly he made takeover bids for a number of scheduled routes operated by BUA, including London–Rotterdam which had offered stiff competition to BEA. Others were for routes between London and Genoa, Madeira, Seville, Canary Islands, Tunis and Ibiza, representing an important part of the European scheduled routes. Here BEA had an advantage over BOAC because the conditions of sale stipulated withdrawal of applications by those bidding for BUA. One of these was Caledonian who complained that not only had it been denied information supplied to BOAC but a further £22 million was now required in guarantees on aircraft leased to BUA. The outlook for the formation of a second-force airline began to look bleak.

A basis for settlement between pilots and BOAC was now proposed by BALPA which would give Boeing 747 Captains £11,000 per year maximum instead of £8,578, though it still left unsettled whether the crew should comprise three pilots or two and a flight engineer. Agreement proved impossible, so BOAC abandoned plans to operate the type for the time being, although delivery of the first 747 had been made on 22 April. Keith Granville said the cost of postponement would be enormous and the long-term effects very serious. 'BOAC had offered £10,400 a year as soon as services began, rising to a maximum of £11,440 by June 1971 — but BALPA objected that these top-of-the-scale figures were misleading, and have constantly refused to agree to arbitration. We are back to square one.'

It seemed unlikely that BOAC would be able to put these machines into service before the autumn because from the moment that crew training started it would take 88 days to mount the first flight. The fourteen return services a week between London and New York would now be operated with 707s or VC 10s with resultant decrease in planned capacity and returns. Nevertheless the airline stressed that operationally it enjoyed excellent relations with its pilots.

Cashing in on the re-equipment problems of the two British Corporations, Lockheed began

Ross Stainton, Managing
Director of BOAC 1972–74.

a series of eye-catching advertisements: '*Cruise ship of the future*: Attractive cabin divided by two broad aisles under room height ceiling. Passengers have a surprise in store: a kind of comfort they never dreamed possible on an airliner. They will find the TriStar jet makes the trip a small vacation in itself. Just like a cruise ship.' But it soon transpired that the Lockheed Aircraft Corporation was in grave financial difficulty and that Douglas with similar problems had found it expedient to merge with McDonnell, and was now known as the Douglas division of McDonnell Douglas. At the beginning of June even the great Pan American airline admitted: 'We are in trouble, but the most important thing is that we know it'.

At Heathrow all was ready for an influx of 747s. The new Terminal 3 was opened on 2 June as part of the £13 million expansion scheme to handle these and other large aircraft. For the first time passengers had separate buildings for arrivals and departures, and it was considered that the combined Terminals would have capacity to handle more than 2,700 passengers an hour in both directions, with a peak flow of 900 in fifteen minutes. There were now ten stands for the 747s, and 30 acres of concrete apron and taxi-ways. A 900-ft long moving walkway connected Terminal 3 and the new Boeing pier. In the course of the year it was expected that four million passengers would use Terminal 3, increasing to $7\frac{1}{2}$ million by 1975 of whom at least 60 per cent would be carried on the 747s.

Elections in mid-June resulted in Conservative victory. Edward Heath appointed Geoffrey Rippon as Minister of Technology and Michael Noble as president of BoT on a 'care and maintenance' basis pending changes in the autumn. The new Government considered it important to form the second-force airline as soon as possible, and named Caledonian Airways and British United as the founder members who would be 'assisted by a limited transfer of routes from the public sector'. On 3 August the go-ahead was given for the new national carrier on lines proposed by the Edwards Committee. The BoT made it clear that no compensation would be paid to BOAC because the licence to operate a route was regarded as having no inherent value, though the Corporation represented that in profit terms the reallocated routes were worth £750,000 to £1 million.

BOAC could afford to ignore this, for the accounts showed the highest ever operating surplus of £31·1 million, giving a net profit of £19·3 million, though £2·5 million less than the previous year. Charles Hardie quixotically said: 'It is very gratifying that since reconstruction, the airline had earned enough in profits to repay with full interest the £80 million had that sum not been written off!' Traffic had increased 20 per cent, revenue by 17 per cent, but partly offset by increased staff and operating costs, which individually totalled £57 million. Although output for each of the 22,400 employees had increased 17 per cent, with earned revenue of £9,073 per person, the Americans with TWA achieved £11,600 for each of their 39,700 employees, so there was still great scope for improvement.

BEA also issued their accounts for 1969–70, and although domestic services had operated at a loss of £1·1 million the international routes boosted the overall operating profit to the biggest ever of £11 million, resulting in a Group profit of £6.53 million. Sir Anthony Milward pointed out that BEA was now the seventh largest airline in terms of the number of passengers carried, the other six being in the USA. He warned of the perils of the 'second-force' airline where 'unbridled competition on domestic routes would be a disaster'.

Though the chairman of the BAC Weybridge division announced at the SBAC Air Show in September that BEA had decided to buy the Three-Eleven, it was only half the story, for the Government still had to decide whether to back this airliner or the A-300B Airbus over which the British, French, West German, and Dutch ministers were still conferring. There was a low quick warning from Milward that if BEA was forced to buy an aircraft it did not want then government aid would be demanded to ensure that the new equipment operated profitably.

The unimaginable was always happening. That autumn came the most serious hijacking yet experienced, for the Arab-Israeli conflict brought successful attacks on five jet airliners involving 692 passengers and 60 crew. Four of the aircraft were destroyed on the ground by Arab guerrillas after the occupants had been let out, but 54 passengers and crew were retained as hostages, and only delicate negotiations by the International Red Cross on behalf of the several national airlines eventually resulted in their release. The attempt on the fifth machine, an El Al 707, had been foiled, and it landed at Heathrow with one of the two hijackers dead and a steward seriously injured. Increased use of magnetic detection equipment to screen passengers for weapons was instituted at Heathrow and other major terminals — but lawyers seemed unable to formulate international legislation to deal with hijacking.

Every possible safety precaution was the hallmark of Concorde. Mechanical, structural, and thermal-fatigue tests had been intensive. There was full exchange of information with BOAC, but the Corporation was making a cautious approach to supersonics. The managing director, Ross Stainton, said: 'Magnificent as Concorde is as a technical achievement, a rational assessment of cost and benefit to the air transport industry has yet to be made. Use of this aircraft would entail heavy demand on limited investment funds with as yet no certainty of increased returns.' Research and development costs had reached £825 million, but it was hoped that the series of flight tests would be completed by mid-December, for on 4 November Concorde 001 in almost routine manner, achieved the designed cruising speed of Mach 2 at 52,000 ft.

A new look was given to governmental responsibility by abolishing the Ministry of Technology. A Ministry of Aviation Supply took over aerospace research, development, and procurement, headed by Frederick Corfield, a lawyer who had been shadow aviation minister and chairman of the Conservative aviation committee for three years. A Ministry

of Trade and Industry was established, headed by John Davies, which would deal with civil aviation regulations.

These changes entailed much internal rearrangement, so there was unlikely to be immediate decision on Concorde production, Airbus, or BAC Three-Eleven, but at least agreement was reached on 20 October that Caledonian would purchase the entire ordinary share capital of BUA for £6,900,000. Adam Thompson, the chairman and managing director of Caledonian Airways became chairman of the combined airlines.

Changes were also being made at BOAC and BEA. On 27 November it was announced that at the year's end Henry Marking, chief executive of BEA, would succeed Sir Anthony Milward as chairman, and that at BOAC Keith Granville, the managing director, would succeed the recently knighted Sir Charles Hardie — but because the Government intended to establish an Airways Board with 'strategic control', the appointments were for three years instead of the usual five.

Both Corporations were suffering falling profits. By autumn BOAC's operating surplus had decreased from £19·6 million to £9·6 million, and BEA expected to lose about £2 million on its domestic services during the 1970–71 financial year.

Scarcely had legislation been formulated to establish a Civil Aviation Authority and an Airways Board than the Government decided there was no money for the BAC Three-Eleven nor any return by Britain to the European A-300B Airbus consortium. However BEA would be free to buy TriStars, VC 10s, or even the A-300B if it ever went into production. The TriStar had the edge on the others, for 25 per cent of its value was British as it was powered by R-R R.B.211-22 engines which had Government launching aid of up to £89 million. Rolls-Royce certainly had high hope, for the TriStar's maiden flight of 2½ hours on 16 November at Palmdale, USA, earned high commendation for the turbo-jet.

In Parliament Michael Noble, Minister for Trade, made a Christmas gift to the new British second-force airline by announcing: 'I can say tonight that BOAC will cease to serve Lagos and Kano in Nigeria and Accra in Ghana after March 31, 1971, with the intention that Caledonian/BUA should serve them directly from London thereafter'. BOAC's revenue from these West African routes amounted to

Some of the 146 passengers disembarking from a BEA Airtours Boeing 707 introduced in 1971.

£4 million a year, but to ensure the promised £6 million revenue package for the combine further routes were to be added. Mr Noble made the placatory comment: 'When we realize that BOAC alone has an annual route revenue of over £200 million, and in normal times expects and plans for it to increase by 14 to 15 per cent, the whole matter is put in proper proportion'.

1971

At the beginning of January 1971, a valedictory letter to *The Times* from Sir Anthony Milward mourned the end of the BAC Three-Eleven which had been 'swept under the carpet and all but forgotten except by those intimately concerned. Many attempts had been made to lessen the impact by saying that there are other aircraft to follow and that all is not lost. I hope this is true, but must declare my conviction that BEA will probably never be able to buy another British aircraft.'

Initial confirmation of that view was an order by BEA Airtours for turbo-fan Boeing 707-120Bs for delivery towards the end of the year. Meanwhile BOAC was moving towards

a similar non-IATA charter subsidiary. Rumours were mounting of a BOAC/BEA merger because legislation was being drafted 'to secure the gains and economies which would result by treating the resources and the route networks of BOAC and BEA as a single system'.

As a step towards better things BOAC's pilots and management had at last reached agreement. Senior pilots, whatever the aircraft, would receive £9,000 a year, representing a rise of £400, and the bid-line system was dropped. The previous offer of £11,500 had been rejected because it was not pensionable, but the new salary would secure a pension of between 35 and 60 per cent for Captains according to length of service. The first BOAC operations to New York with the 747 were therefore scheduled to begin in April, increasing from twice weekly to daily flights in May. A further batch of 747s would shortly be delivered, and BOAC and BALPA agreed to carry out an evaluation aimed at two-pilot operation by the late autumn.

Because of their colleagues' success, the BEA pilots threatened a 'work-to-rule' in support of negotiations for similar pay, adding to the frustration of a management already involved in a Press advertisement campaign explaining the airline's side of the engineers' work-to-rule dispute which had been going on since mid-December, followed by a five-day strike at the end of January which grounded most of the airline services. BEA employees now attempted to get BOAC workers to join in the strike, but they were unsuccessful, so the red flag was eventually hauled down and normal work recommenced.

A shock to the nation was the collapse of Rolls-Royce — a catastrophe of major dimension which also entailed repudiation of contract with Lockheed who had everything at stake on the TriStar and was still in deep financial trouble. Parliament was told: 'As a measure to ensure continuity of the activities of Rolls-Royce which are important to our national defence, to our collaborative programmes with other countries, and to many air forces and civil airlines all over the world, the Government have decided to acquire such assets of the aero engine, marine, and industrial gas-turbine engine divisions of the company as may be essential for these purposes. However the Government have no liability in respect of the contract between Rolls-Royce and Lockheed, but the Government will explore, with the Receiver, the future of the R.B.211 engine and also undertake urgent discussions with the Lockheed Corporation and with the United States Government.' For Daniel J. Haughton, the Lockheed chairman, that meant vast and immediate problems.

Major changes in BEA were announced on 11 March by Henry Marking. He had already promoted Ken Wilkinson, the chief engineer, to deputy chairman, deputy chief executive, and managing director of Mainline. Decentralization was the plan — with ten divisions, each directly responsible to the Board but operating as individual enterprises, though BEA Airtours, BEA Helicopters, British Air Services controlling Cambrian Airways and North-east Airlines, would continue unchanged, and nor would BEA's hotel interests be affected. 'People work better in smaller units', said Marking. 'It's hard to get personal loyalty in a monolithic organization, but I want it to become fashionable for staff to transfer from one unit to another to gain experience and make life more interesting for all.'

Headlines arising from the Civil Aviation Bill presented to Parliament this same day struck the key-note clauses which provided for a British Airways Board to oversee BOAC and BEA with obvious intent to merge them later in accordance with the Edwards' recommendations. At least one airline independent of the Board would be established. BOAC and BEA had to accept the inevitable.

Concorde also was making headlines, for the British 002 had been grounded since the end of January after an intake control mechanism failure on the French-assembled 001, but on 3 April trials recommenced amid increasing vociferation from the anti-Concorde lobby. Decision on production was still in abeyance, though several airlines were examining the profit potential with fares surcharged 50 to 70 per cent above economy-class travel. But would people pay for speed? Whether Concorde could comply with the noise level stipulated by New York was another query, though Washington was almost certain to accept it. BOAC's interest was confirmed by selection of Capt James Andrew, the flight development manager, as their first Concorde pilot, for he had been associated with the project ever since 1964, and would now make regular sorties on the flight deck of 002 and subsequently participate in route-proving trials aimed for 1973.

There was also more hopeful news of the TriStar. On 14 May Haughton boldly signed a contract in London for Rolls-Royce to produce the R.B.211 provided he obtained Congressional approval for a loan guarantee by the US Government. Pending this settlement the British Government agreed to continue financing the engine until August. To consolidate the relationship with Rolls-Royce, Haughton sent the demonstration TriStar from Le Bourget to East Midlands Airport near Derby on 5 June for the benefit of the engine employees, 10,000 of whom queued to walk through the cabin to see the beautifully appointed mixed-class seating layout. Next day the TriStar flew over Rolls-Royce factories at Barnoldswick, Glasgow, and Belfast before heading back to the USA.

In mid-summer BEA Airtours purchased seven ex-BOAC Boeing 707–436s to replace its time-expired Comets. They would be converted to a 189-seat layout by BOAC's engineering department. Conversely BOAC cancelled its option on four Boeing 747s because the pilots' strike had wrecked the re-equipment timetable.

However, six of these splendid giants had already been accepted and a further six would arrive between autumn and next spring.

Meanwhile BOAC was being challenged with characteristic élan by Freddie Laker who announced that his airline had applied for a new low-fare, no-frills scheduled service between London and New York — yet IATA was warning the world governments of the increasing impact of independent airlines on the profitability of the major airlines. On that basis BOAC immediately lodged opposition to the Laker Airways application, aware that a long, long tussle would follow.

The Corporation experienced a new kind of piracy on 22 July when a VC 10 en route from London to Khartoum, was ordered to land at Benghazi 'for the safety of the souls on board' because two Sudanese officers were passengers. Capt Bowyer, the pilot in command, demanded clearance back to Rome, but the Libyan authorities threatened to shoot the airliner down unless he carried out instructions. The two Sudanese insisted he must not endanger the passengers, so Capt Bowyer circuited the airport to burn off fuel and landed. The Sudanese were removed by Libyan security men and executed within hours despite strong Government protest to Libya at the outrage and an appeal to Sudan's President Numeiry for clemency.

BOAC's new subsidiary, British Overseas Air Charter, began operations in August with a series of regular flights to the Far East, charging £85 for the single journey to Bangkok compared with £220 by scheduled service. Caledonian/BUA had been licensed for a competitive service, and Keith Granville was facing a worrying future, for profits in the accounting year 1970/71 had dropped by more than £19 million to less than £3·5 million. 'Nevertheless', he said, 'the airline had fared better than most of its competitors.' He warned that President Nixon's measures to bolster the US economy would affect BOAC adversely in the short term: 'In common with the world's major airlines BOAC is largely a one-product business upon which chill winds have a habit of blowing from time to time. Many airlines have tried to mitigate this by widening their investment base, but none has succeeded to the extent of obtaining substantial relief in the lean years. Unless our total revenue gets back on target we will be hard put to make a profit at the end of the current financial year.'

BEA's profits were similarly down, achieving only £524,000. As with BOAC, capacity was less than in the previous year and cargo had slumped, but passenger traffic had risen marginally and costs much more. 'Although this result is disappointing', said Henry Marking, 'it was achieved in an extremely difficult year for industry in general and civil aviation in particular. Had BEA the same type of capital structure as BOAC the profit would have been £5·75 million. I imagine that the system will change, for it would be illogical for BOAC and us to go into the British Airways Board next year with different capital structures.'

At the ensuing Press conference, Marking announced cuts of up to 50 per cent in fares on trunk routes, though international agreements still had to be obtained from IATA where the only possible objector was Lufthansa which had already refused agreement to advance-purchase fares on the North Atlantic. However BEA was prepared to go it alone with a four-month advance booking period and tickets covering a minimum of six nights' absence and a maximum of two months. In the forefront, BEA had Caledonian/BUA, now named British Caledonian Airways, as the potential rival.

Britain's Civil Aviation Act, 1971, became law on 5 August after considerable amendment and improvement, establishing the Civil Aviation Authority (CAA) as an equivalent of the American Civil Aeronautics Board (CAB), and also the British Airways Board for which David Nicolson, a specialist in corporate planning, was appointed chairman with mandate to select eight members in consultation with the Department of Trade and Industry.

The TriStar was now given the green light; on 9 September the US Government approved a $250 million emergency loan guarantee. However there was still the A-300B Airbus prospect to decide, for Air France was about to order six, with option on a further ten. BEA continued side-stepping.

On 2 October BEA's recent accident-free record ended with another disaster when a Vanguard on scheduled flight from Heathrow to Salzburg, cruising in good weather, partly disintegrated and fell to the ground near Ghent killing all 55 passengers and eight crew. Though ten years old, it embodied fail-safe design, and recent inspection during conversion to Merchantman freighter class showed the structure to be in sound condition despite logging 20,000 hours. Could this accident be

British Airways TriStar. There were policy and governmental delays in 1971/72 over ordering TriStars, but they eventually came into service in 1974.

due to a Comet-like cabin failure? A height limit of 10,000 ft was imposed on all Vanguards. Corrosion was discovered in the rear pressure bulkhead of the crashed machine, so strengthening modifications were made. Leak testing and X-ray crack detection tests followed, and the machines were cleared with 'no defects to compromise safety'.

There were still pilot problems. Few, except participators, could understand the mental and physical demands, let alone the high level of skill. BEA pilots, through BALPA, were still endeavouring to secure the same pay award and conditions of service which BOAC pilots had received. But the latter remained uneasy. At the crux was the airline's obligation to provide a

36-hour rest period which must include two full nights' sleep within a seven-day working period. Instead, the re-scheduling of services, particularly for Boeing 707s in the Caribbean, led to rosters giving only six nights' sleep in eight working days, and that was considered a flight-safety risk. The Dept of Trade & Industry therefore instructed BOAC to make changes in four of the schedules.

BEA was meeting head-on competition with

British Caledonian Airways, which on 1 November opened the first independent cross-Channel schedule from Gatwick to Le Bourget since the 1930s. Advertised as the 'Golden Lion' service, it was claimed to be the fastest link between the two capitals, with a total city-centre journey time of 2½ hours, and was the third which British Caledonian had inaugurated on international routes hitherto served by BOAC and BEA.

By now Britain and France were more in accord over the Concorde. On 10 December the British Secretary of Trade, John Davies, after a 1½-hour flight on the prototype 002 in company with the Minister of Aviation Supply Lord Carrington and other important officials, declared: 'Every one of us in the Government feels no effort must be spared to see that Concorde gets the support which this great project deserves. If you had doubts on cancellation you can banish them now.'

Extolling the virtues of the aircraft, he later said: 'We had a really remarkable experience. It is extraordinary to be in that aircraft at 50,000 feet or more flying at twice the speed of sound, talking amiably with one's friends as if it was the most ordinary flight in the world. It is obviously a fabulous aircraft.' A fortnight later the first pre-production Concorde had its maiden flight. Asked what it was like to fly, Trubshaw said: 'It is an ordinary aeroplane which has to be flown by ordinary people. All the fuss and drama have gone. You operate it as a normal commercial aeroplane and handle it as such.'

1972

Peter Masefield received a knighthood in the 1972 New Year's Honours list. He had been an aviation zealot from earliest days at Cambridge and on his vacation course in 1933 he had helped to rig HP 42s at Croydon. Tall, facially cherubic, eyes twinkling behind glasses, he had a statistician's mind and outstanding competence, whether in long-term planning at the MCA or turning BEA into a profitable and highly skilled business, and in the past six years had done the same for the British Airports Authority. Typical was his judgement: 'It is easier for aviation people to learn business than for business people to learn aviation'.

But it was increasingly onerous to run a great airline. In the past calendar year BOAC had carried 2,053,000 passengers and just over 67,000 short tons of cargo, yet there had been 500,000 seats unfilled. Reduced fares seemed the probable solution, but there was still intense argument about it at IATA. As an initial move, BEA announced abolition of first-class accommodation on the domestic routes and replacement by improved economy-seats bookable at £2 premium for those who valued

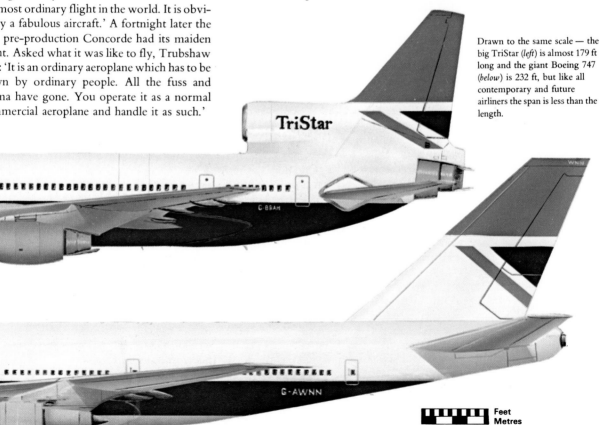

Drawn to the same scale — the big TriStar (*left*) is almost 179 ft long and the giant Boeing 747 (*below*) is 232 ft, but like all contemporary and future airliners the span is less than the length.

Feet
Metres

greater leg room and comfort. 'You can never
charge enough in first class to pay for it', said
Wilkinson the managing director Mainline.
Losses on the domestic routes were running at
almost £2 million a year, so it was hoped that
the new arrangement would restore rather
more than half. The Trident 1s with the new
seats were introduced on 1 February and soon
proved popular. However, 'a loss for BEA in its
1971–72 financial year seems unavoidable',
warned Henry Marking. Nevertheless BEA
Airtours intended spreading its wings beyond
the Mediterranean, and had even applied for
licences in the traditional preserves of BOAC,
whose subsidiary, British Overseas Air Charter
Ltd, was mainly active in Far East charters,
flying non-affinity passengers under special
exemption granted by the British Government.

The newly formed British Airways Board
had set up a joint managing directors' sub-
committee comprising Kenneth Wilkinson and
Ross Stainton, financial director Derek Glover,
and planning director Stephen Wheatcroft. The
Board was weighing the Airbus Industrie's
arguments against those of Lockheed for the
TriStar. Significantly, a ten-man team from the
ARB had started certification studies of the
TriStar at Palmdale, and their test pilot, John
Carrodus, had flown the prototype as a pre-
liminary to official flight testing.

Concorde was becoming a prime objective
for BOAC, and in mid-January Keith Granville
with other members of the Board participated
in a test flight. Afterwards he said: 'We look
forward to being able to buy Concorde, which
is a magnificent British achievement. It has long
been BOAC's policy to go supersonic as soon
as it is practicable to do so.' Questioned as to
whether it would be profitable, he added: 'I
would have bought it already if there was such a
profit report. If someone offered us a project for
an aircraft such as the Concorde now is, we
would probably say that it was not on. But it is
here, and that alters the situation.'

On 1 April the new CAA began business
with overriding responsibility for the whole of
British air transport, from financial fitness of
participants to handling qualities of supersonic
airliners, seeking to ensure that British airlines
provided services satisfying all substantial
categories of public demand. Major changes of
Parliamentary responsibility followed six days
later, Michael Heseltine from the Department
of the Environment becoming Minister of
Aerospace with responsibility for air transport,

and Cranley Onslow, chairman of the Conservative aviation committee, became Parliamentary Secretary for Aerospace. On 13 April John
Davies, Secretary of State for Trade and Industry, announced that BAC and Aérospatiale had
authority to build six more production Concordes, bringing the total to sixteen. Cost of
this Anglo-French enterprise had risen to
£970 million — but at least it provided some
26,000 jobs in the UK alone, and it was estimated that a single Concorde could cross the
Atlantic four times a day, earning £10,000 of
which half would be foreign exchange.

The commercial take-off for Concorde came
at last on 25 May when Keith Granville signed a
£115 million contract for five, including spares,
simulator, and hangar. He said: 'This is the
most significant single contract undertaken by
BOAC since its purchase of the world's first jet
transport twenty years earlier. We have complete faith that Concorde will make it possible
for BOAC to lead the world successfully into
the supersonic age. It will cut the round trip to
New York by almost half. A passenger leaving
Sydney in the afternoon will arrive in London
the same evening, local time. Leaving London
at lunch-time he will arrive at dinner-time in
Johannesburg after a flight of little more than
$7\frac{1}{2}$ hours.' A week later Concorde 002, commanded by Brian Trubshaw, took off from its
test base at Fairford for a sales mission extending to Japan and back. Full operations were
envisaged for 1975 — but development costs
were still leaping skyward. There were
demands in the Commons for an inquiry into
the shortcomings of financial control 'that too
often characterizes the actions of governments'.
It was ten years ago that Concorde had been
started as an Anglo-French project for which a
total of £85 million had been budgeted. The
reassessed cost now stood at £1,070 million.

There were rumours that BEA had settled for
six TriStars, but the British Airways Board had
still to approve. Half BEA's revenue was coming from sales on the Continent, thanks to
growing middle-class prosperity, and Germany was the major potential followed closely
by Italy. The possibility of profit had been
badly shaken by a big pay increase for
40,000 BOAC and BEA workers, and the
pilots' threatened work-to-rule remained the
sword of Damocles. As BALPA was a trade
union, George Woodcock had been appointed
arbitrator. The GAPAN was aloofly critical,
but Capt Ron Gillman, the Master, said it was

not surprising that pilots picked for their initiative became disenchanted with the rigid routines and procedures of airline operations. Perhaps the ghost of Major Brackley was at his side when he had said: 'Every airline should have a pilot on the Board who has no other managerial responsibility or Trade Union commitment and serves solely in advisory capacity'.

Matters worsened. BEA offered rises of up to £800 for a senior Captain, giving a total of £8,850 per annum, but a ballot on 13 June resulted in a clear mandate for strike action, though many were prepared to accept the pay offer as it brought near parity with BOAC. BEA made contingency plans but to no effect when a world-wide stoppage of air services was threatened by the International Federation of Airline Pilots because of universal failure to step up action against hijacking and sabotage.

For the moment all was overwhelmed by a BEA Trident crash shortly after take-off from Heathrow on 18 June under gusty conditions with low cloud, and the 109 passengers and nine crew were killed. The flight recorder indicated that the leading-edge droop slots had started to retract, causing the airliner to enter the stall regime and assume a marked nose-up attitude, during which the Trident dropped flat. Next day a meeting of pilots heard a speech pre-drafted by the deceased Captain in which he deplored industrial action — but it failed to secure support. The atmosphere became less tense when BEA's deputy chairman, Kenneth Wilkinson, agreed to meet the pilots at a discussion chaired by Capt Gillman. Then in a final round of negotiations under the aegis of the National Joint Council for Civil Aviation, agreement was at last reached for pay rises close to the original demands, and revised two-man crewing was approved in principle.

In. July Michael Heseltine decided that all activities of BOAC and BEA would be brought together under a single top management of what he referred to as the British Airways Group. In anticipation he allocated £200 million 'public dividend capital' for purchase of Concordes and TriStars, saying: 'I expect that the British Airways Board will reach a decision in the next few weeks on ordering their short/medium-range wide-bodied aircraft. I met the chairman of Lockheed last night and told him I recognized that the need for a de-

cision was urgent.' On 7 August he announced both the go-ahead for development of the R.B.211-24 engine and authority for BEA to order six standard TriStars with option on six more. Type certification had just been granted by the CAA, and the first machines were destined for the Court Line early next year.

The British Airways Group became established on 1 September, but caused little immediate change in the functioning of the two Corporations. David Nicolson was appointed chairman with Keith Granville as deputy chairman and Henry Marking as chief executive, their statutory posts on BOAC and BEA going to Ross Stainton and Kenneth Wilkinson as chief executives, with each airline retaining its commercial independence. Immediate action of the Board was to set up task forces to study integration and rationalization of route structure and aircraft fleet and investigate BEA and BOAC commercial efforts in Continental Europe, charter marketing activities, engineering facilities for wide-bodied jets, possible integration of BEA and BOAC Cargo Centres, catering, motor transport, computer systems.

Meanwhile Freddie Laker, sublimely indifferent to the rival potential, was presenting his case to the CAA for his 'Skytrain' low-cost, scheduled trans-Atlantic daily service, for which £37.50 would be the single-way summer charge and £32.50 in winter. Within two months the controversial plan had been accepted with the proviso that Stansted must be the terminal. Optimistically the CAA stated: 'We believe that operators on other European routes to New York will find no need to match Skytrain fares, since the demand for which it caters will be largely confined to limited catchment areas in the vicinity of the cities served'. Instead, the doorway had been opened for mass travel.

The British Airways mainline fleet for the 1980s was now type-cast with Concordes, Boeing 747s, and TriStars, but left open for a 200-seat, 500-mile range aircraft for routes where TriStars would be too big and Tridents too small. Would the Airbus come into the picture after all? To handle the incipient traffic BEA had installed a new computer system (FICO) which could handle some 7,500 transactions daily, dealing with aircraft operational status, flight schedules, public inquiries, and crew movements.

Though a loss on the year's workings had been expected, the BEA Annual Report pub-

Power-pods for the
Rolls-Royce R.B.211-22B
turbo-jets of the TriStar. Clean
aerodynamics and great thrust
result in a top speed of 610 mph
and cruising at 575 mph.

lished on 24 August revealed a net profit of almost £250,000 after crediting £8 million compensation from the Government for the delay in delivery of the Trident 3s and Super 1–11s. BOAC fared worse with £1·4 million deficit, the first loss in eight years, but Keith Granville blamed this on 'blatant activities of dubious charter operators whose services are becoming almost indistinguishable from normal scheduled services except for the prices offered'. Then British Caledonian came under fire because their North Atlantic services would result in an 'estimated loss of revenue to BOAC of no less than £11·5 million over the five and a half years of the British Caledonian projection'. But there was also the USA where 'for many years American operators have been grossly over-providing capacity on the North Atlantic, particularly on the Chicago–London and Washington–London route'. Nevertheless BOAC remained a financially strong airline with reserves of £77 million.

Edward Heath, speaking at the AGM of IATA in mid-September said: 'Realism to-day all too often means putting fares up. Instead it should consist of straining every nerve to bring prices down — and nowhere more so than in a growth industry such as air transport.' It was therefore not wholly coincidental that Britain's CAA announced plans to introduce advance booking charters on the North Atlantic from 1 April, and invited British airlines to apply for licences. Passage could be booked 90 days ahead but the minimum group must be 50 and only round trips of at least fourteen days were allowed. Flights were not subject to price or capacity control.

BEA's commercial relations manager said that unless a 10 to 15 per cent increase in fares was granted losses could reach £5·3 million next year. 'If everyone seeks to deal with inflationary situations in this way', commented Lord Boyd-Carpenter, the CAA chairman, 'the inflationary situation will be aggravated.' There would be no need for increases, he argued, if BEA could get its labour relations in order and thus decrease staff costs and if British Caledonian reduced frequency in order to gain heavier load factors.

Consideration was being given by David Nicolson to using BEA TriStars on some BOAC routes, and BOAC VC 10s on BEA routes. BOAC might also need something smaller than the Boeing 747 for some long-haul services and he thought a twin-engined version of the TriStar might do. As to Concorde: 'We are large enough now to take on this totally new development. It is difficult to predict what profit could be made when you don't know where you are permitted to land, where fly across, and who else is going to have it. But despite uncertainties, the Concorde has tremendous advantage for all of us, not least in terms of leadership and prestige.'

Both Corporations were having a re-shuffle following the departure of Kenneth Wilkinson, chief executive BEA, to become managing director of the recently nationalized Rolls-Royce (1971) Ltd. Philip Lawton was appointed BEA group director and Roy Watts became chief executive; Ross Stainton was made group director of BOAC and Cyril Herring became group director of British Air Services — these titles reflecting the holder's 'overriding British Airways Group responsibilities'.

1973

1 January 1973, marked the entry of Britain, Ireland and Denmark into the new Europe of the Economic Community — and yet Anglo-French aerospace co-operation had largely failed. Britain had a big industrial share in the A-300B but was buying American instead; Britain and Germany had refused to support the French policy of an independent European space launcher (ELDO); there were disparate views on aero-engine policy; no agreement over weapons had been possible and the French had pulled out of NATO; only the Anglo-French interest in Concorde and helicopters seemed mutual.

At the end of January the British Airways Board recommended, and the Secretary of State for Trade & Industry agreed, that as from 1 April 1974, BEA and BOAC would fully merge under the name of British Airways — an ironic reminder of Edward Hillman as the tough pre-war rival of Imperial Airways. The conjoined airline had the most comprehensive route network in the world, extending half a million miles with 200 destinations in 84 countries, and the 220 aircraft would be the world's largest passenger fleet. To handle passenger and charter selling in the UK, a joint sales unit, British Airways Travel, with staff of 2,800, was being formed by Henry Marking.

British Caledonian joined the big league of airlines on 1 April when their Boeing 707, with Lord Mountbatten as distinguished passenger,

made the first of its twelve-times-weekly trans-Atlantic flights, though was diverted from New York to Boston because of bad weather. On this fiercely competitive route the biggest carrier between the US and Europe was now TWA which had 1,789,315 passengers in 1972; Pan Am with 1,742,446; BOAC was third with 989,000, so the intrusion of a rival was neither welcome nor a tribute to the Government's interpretation of economics.

Quickly it became evident that rationalizing BOAC and BEA into British Airways would take longer than the Government expected. An exasperating problem was the necessity of cautious co-operation with trade unions fearful of redundancies, yet it was essential to increase productivity closer to that of the USA. For the time being the individual names of BOAC and BEA would still be used, though a new-style livery and colour scheme would be adopted by the combined aircraft fleet. Conflicting application for services to East and West Africa by BOAC and British Caledonian had been resolved by the CAA permitting BOAC to operate through West Africa, but as that area was *de facto* the British Caledonian sphere of influence, the State airline was restricted to services through Lagos or Accra and it was specified that only Concorde could be used. In East Africa British Caledonian was awarded compensatory rights to Nairobi subject to the existing 70:30 formula governing the relative activities of the two airlines in Africa. However the proposed dual assignment of British Caledonian and BOAC on routes to the Far East, Australia, and Canada, was described by the Corporation as economic lunacy, so a major test case of the big principles involved was likely.

At the Paris Aero Show held at Le Bourget, Concorde and its similar Russian rival the Tu 144 were on view to the world. The perils of emulation were only too tragically evident — for in their determination to show the handling quality of their machine, the Russians pulled the Tu 144 into a steep climbing turn and in the subsequent diving descent the outboard portion of the starboard wing collapsed; the aircraft rolled on to its back, the ruptured fuel lines ignited, and an explosion completed destruction of the wing before the machine hit the ground in flames, killing the crew of four and eight spectators, bringing the 1973 Salon to a sombre end.

Discussions with Russia for a supersonic

trans-Siberian route round the world had proved unfruitful, so in June British Airways settled for an alternative route to the Chinese People's Republic via Europe, the Middle East, the Indian sub-continent, and Hong Kong — and Keith Granville, who had just been knighted, signed an agreement to that effect in Peking. This made the UK the only country with an airline serving both Communist and Nationalist China.

To implement the British Airways network of world routes the group planning director, Stephen Wheatcroft, envisaged that in addition to Concorde, nine types of subsonic airliners would be required by 1988 ranging from 150- to 600-seaters for specific stage lengths and take-off capability. 'There is nothing really surprising that we shall want new aeroplanes in the 1980s which are much larger than the Boeing 747', he said. 'What may seem surprising is the scale of the requirement. My projections for 1988 indicate that we shall be carrying as much as 64 per cent of the total passenger traffic in aircraft considerably larger than the Boeing 747.' That was because the fastest growth sector was leisure and personal holiday travel requir-

ing low fares feasible with large aircraft at low frequency.

Not only future aircraft but the Tridents and One-Elevens and eventual TriStars had to meet revised noise abatement standards. Emphasis was on relief of disturbance to people several miles from airports. Even more stringent noise standards would be mandatory for future aircraft after a specific date not later than 1980 so that 'aircraft noise should not exceed the noise of ordinary busy city streets'. Concorde was one of the problems, and Michael Heseltine stated: 'Manufacturers are studying a number of possible improvements relating to noise for introduction after the aircraft enters service'. There was now no hope of this dramatic aircraft receiving its C of A in the third quarter of 1974 as previously thought, but early 1975 seemed possible.

The more immediate requirement was three additional BAC One-Elevens for the Scottish services of the British Airways regional division. Quietly domestic though that route seemed, it could have its alarms. On 9 September emergency evacuation of two Viscounts took place at Edinburgh after a warning

The fourth, sixth and eighth production Concordes on the final assembly line at the British Aircraft Corporation's Filton works. Even-numbered Concordes were assembled at Filton and the odd-numbered aircraft at Aérospatiale's Toulouse plant.

British airways

Above and right:
Concorde's narrow fuselage is almost as long as a Boeing 747 but lifts only 100 passengers, though it carries them at 1,350 mph through the stratosphere compared with the Boeing's 550 mph.

telephone call of a bomb on one of them — but it proved a hoax. Nevertheless hijacking and bomb threats had become a world-wide scourge. So far in 1973 there had been ten attempts, all of which failed. Although the USA and Israel adopted armed sky marshals to combat that potential hijacker, prevention on the ground was widely accepted as the more effective method, so airport security measures had been greatly strengthened.

The huge oceanic spread of the Atlantic was no environment for hijackers, for their requirement was usually escape to a country other than the route destination — but it was a battle ground for cuts in fares. The US Civil Aeronautics Board had refused proposals from British Airways, British Caledonian, and Lufthansa for £65 advance-booking return fares, but now a formidable ally was found in Ralph Nader's consumer organization, for it battled in

the American Court of Appeal against the CAB, who were judicially instructed that fare cuts proposed by foreign carriers could not be overruled.

On the home front British Airways remained in open conflict with British Caledonian who had applied for licences to points already served by the State airline or within its presumed exclusive preserve. In Singapore, Henry Marking told the Confederation of Australian Travel Agents that British Caledonian's application for a route there via Bahrein or Karachi was unnecessary as his airline and Singapore International 'could easily cope with the market at prices the public would accept'. British Caledonian's marketing director hit back that this statement was 'typical of the paranoia prevalent in the upper echelons of British Airways. It is regrettable that this monolithic Corporation loses all sense of reason and sight of the basic facts when talking about British Caledonian.'

British Airways now announced that the abbreviations BOAC and BEA had been replaced by 'British Airways Overseas Division' and 'British Airways European Division'. Though now effectively a single unit, the past year's financial reports for BEA and BOAC were issued individually in September for the last time. BEA had made an operating profit of £11·4 million which after paying interest became a net profit of £477,000 — but that excluded the now independent Scottish Airways and Channel Islands Airways whose accounts turned the profit into a net loss of £1·2 million. Over 180,000 flights had been made, carrying 10·5 million passengers, and a further 12,500 flights carried 140,000 tons of freight.

By comparison BOAC had an operating surplus of £22·7 million compared with its disconcerting low of £2 million in the previous year, so there was now a net profit of £8·2 million. Entry into the low-fare market resulted in 2·8 million passengers, and 88,000 tons freight and mail carried in the course of over 3,000 mil-lion miles. Nevertheless BEA and BOAC were running at far under capacity, and so was every other airline. On the North Atlantic alone there were 46 competing carriers, and the result was a shambles of surplus seats and lost revenue.

To show the flag, Concorde, with the name 'British Airways' on the port side of the nose and 'Air France' on the other, made its first sales visit to the USA, and on arrival in Texas was greeted with superlatives, having first flown via Las Palmas to Caracas on 18 September. Nine days later it was back at Paris Orly after little over $3\frac{1}{2}$ hours from take-off at Washington's Dulles Airport carrying full payload of eleven tons and sufficient fuel for a 250-mile diversion. The French Minister of Defence pronounced: 'The profoundly significant crossing of the Atlantic has ensured the future of supersonic flight'. However Concorde did not have the prerogative of international demonstrations, for on 18 October the first prototype A-300B Airbus called at Heathrow on its way back to Toulouse after a tour of South and North America where it was received with friendly indifference, so great was the potential of American machines from Boeing, Douglas, and Lockheed.

Committed as it was to TriStars, the European division of British Airways now ordered a further three, bringing the total to nine with a further nine on option. As an example of American selling zeal, Dan Haughton, chairman of Lockheed, flew the 6,000 miles to London to speak at the annual luncheon of the Air League. 'All the predictions are for tremendous traffic growth', he enthusiastically said. 'For the same fuel, a TriStar will lift one-and-a-half times the passengers of a 707. Don't think I don't think the 707 is a good aeroplane — it's just obsolete.'

In the Middle East there was war, and on 31 October the 90 members of the Association of European Airlines met in Brussels to discuss the problems of fuel supplies and prices resulting from that conflict. This was the new bogy. In the past decade fuel bills had been steadily rising, but now they might double by 1975, and because fuel cost was 10 per cent of the total operating cost for scheduled services, and even more for charter airlines, fares would surge up. Airlines were playing the fuel scarcity problem on a day by day basis while working on contingency plans, for on the Eastern route there was grave shortage, and on one day Istanbul had no fuel at all. British Airways tried shutting down the central engine of Tridents to economize, but this produced excessive heat in the other two. Slight reduction from a cruising speed of Mach 0·8 ensured a 4½ per cent saving in fuel, but entailed complex re-scheduling and reprint-ing timetables. As an immediate expedient BEA Airtours and other inclusive-tour operators imposed a surcharge, for they were losing an average of £3 per passenger on such flights. Difficulties in the USA resulted in the Senate giving the CAB authority to regulate airline activities in order to cut fuel by 20 per cent, and thousands of airline staff became redundant. In the Commons on 7 December Heseltine announced: 'I have decided that the airline industry must reduce consumption by a total of 95,000 tons for the period November 20 to December 31 — that is by an average of 17 per cent'. To achieve that, British Airways announced no less than 40 per cent cuts to its services during the remainder of the month.

Prince Philip with test pilot Brian Trubshaw (*right*) and other members of the Concorde team, after he had flown the aircraft.

Henry Marking said that unless more fuel became available there would be no guarantee of seats for 150,000 holidaymakers over Christmas.

British Airways was also hit by the Chancellor of the Exchequer's 'mini-Budget' necessitated by the troubled British economy, for the airline was not only instructed to reduce its 1974 capital expenditure by £25 million but was under government pressure to begin a 10,000 reduction in staff as from 1 April. All government-financed projects were being reviewed, and the British and French governments were discussing reduction of Concorde production from sixteen to only five.

The fuel shortage had led to long overdue capacity cuts on the North Atlantic route. 'Our fears are now respectable', said David Nicolson. 'Over the past ten years an average of 45 out of every 100 seats has been flown empty. The British made no secret of their desire for a degree of rationalization. If capacity was designed to achieve a year-round industry load factor of 65 per cent, or even 70 per cent, competition in the market place would be no less intense. Hopefully it would become more ethical. Not only would saving of fuel be prodigi-ous and the environmental effect positively beneficial, but we would make more effective use of our crowded air space and be less profligate in the use of airport capacity. This is of particular interest in Britain where the prospect of a new airport at Maplin raises enormous economic and ecological problems.'

1974

There had seemed every prospect that 1974 would be a year of gloom and despondency for all airlines — but British Airways, after two months of reshuffling its plans in the face of the fuel shortage, managed to retain its 200-odd destinations, though frequencies would be cut. Charter airlines were treated a little more favourably than British Airways because they would have less chance of survival if services were reduced, whereas British Airways could cut 20 per cent of its scheduled 6,000 flights without too severe a financial impact.

One of British Airways' increasingly important areas was Scotland, formerly regarded as a 'social service' run at a loss. In the coming year there would be continuing expansion of North Sea oil-related aviation activities,

The first British production Concorde flew on 6 December 1973 and obtained its C of A exactly two years later after the most extensive test programme in the history of civil aviation. Meanwhile the French and British prototypes had made many record-breaking supersonic flights.

for there were now significant increases in air travel to Aberdeen and to Lerwick in the Shetlands which were becoming 'boom' towns. Permission was therefore obtained to purchase two Hawker Siddeley 748As and already British Airways Helicopters and the rival Bristow Helicopters Ltd were beginning to find lucrative returns from carrying crews to oil rigs.

Increasing fuel costs led the sixteen airlines operating scheduled British domestic routes to apply to the CAA for a 20 per cent increase in domestic fares from 1 March, and in due course that was agreed, but even then did not enable British Airways to break even, for the calculated loss on domestic routes was £1·6 million for the 1974/75 accounting year. Examination of traffic prospects for the Overseas and European divisions resulted in decision to retire the eleven-strong VC 10 fleet and the remaining five Vanguards from passenger service, though three of the latter would be converted to Merchantmen for the Cargo division.

Meanwhile the war between British Airways and British Caledonian continued unabated. An announcement that bookings for the British Airways holiday travel divisions were 127 per cent greater than last year caused British Caledonian chairman Adam Thompson to fulminate: 'Is it necessary to use taxpayers' money to subsidize the entry into the tour market of a nationalized Corporation? Undoubtedly they are going to lose a bomb.' Gerry Draper, director of the BA travel division, said this was absolute nonsense, and predicted increased profit for 1973–74. 'No doubt Mr Thompson's remarks are prompted by BCAL's very unhappy experience in the cut and thrust of the European package market.'

However Thompson also vehemently objected to British Airways Overseas division's recent decision to serve Los Angeles non-stop from London. 'Traditionally BOAC operated to Los Angeles only via New York', he said. 'In 1972 the licensing authorities stated that BOAC's services on the Los Angeles route "were clearly inadequate" and gave BCAL a licence to operate direct services. Before we could commence operations, BOAC commenced direct services. Now BCAL has been forced to ask for the British Airways direct service authority to be revoked in order to avoid wasteful duplication.'

Elections on 28 February resulted in no clear victory, but on 4 March Edward Heath resigned and a minority government was formed by Labour's Harold Wilson. As news value that was less than the previous day's hijacking of a British Airways VC 10 on flight from Beirut to London by two Arab terrorists who forced it to land at Amsterdam and then blew the machine up after releasing all 92 passengers and ten crew. But even that was overshadowed in the public mind by a terrible disaster the same day when a DC-10 of Turkish National Airlines crashed nine minutes after take-off from Paris Orly, killing all 347 on board, many of whom had been originally booked on British Airways flights which had been cancelled because of a strike by the ground staff at Heathrow. The wreckage indicated the possibility of sabotage, but eventually it was established that there were structural and control failures due to incorrect latching of the rear baggage-hold door — but few realized the years of legal battle this would entail to establish liability.

In the Commons, Anthony Wedgwood Benn, the new Secretary of State for Industry, had cancelled the project to use the Maplin Sands site near Southend as the third London airport, and was also reconsidering Concorde after finding that the latest modifications might add £220 million to the £1,070 million development cost, and probably the net loss on sixteen production machines would be £200 to £225 million. 'In view of the size of public expenditure involved and the importance of decisions that must now be made', he said, 'I thought it right to place these facts before the House and the Country before any decisions are reached.'

On 3 April British Airways followed British Caledonian in transferring cross-Channel flights to the new Charles de Gaulle Airport at Roissy-en-France which was planned to become Paris's premier air transport hub, for Le Bourget and Orly had reached passenger saturation and were now surrounded by built-up areas. British Airways, despite the fuel crisis, was predicting a record summer inflow of holidaymakers to Britain. More walk-on piers were therefore being installed at Heathrow to eliminate the need for aerodrome buses to carry the passengers to and from the aircraft. To ensure swift transit of aircraft, fully automated air traffic control was being installed, broadly following the established pattern in the USA.

In the same week as the terminal change, Sir Hudson Fysh, one of the great collaborators of Imperial Airways and BOAC, and co-founder of Qantas, died aged 79. Under his management the work of Qantas had been crucial to the war-time 'Horseshoe' operations by flying the 3,513-mile stretch between Perth and Ceylon, whence BOAC, the part shareholder of Qantas, took over. After the war the Australian Government acquired the BOAC share and became the company's sole owner, but Hudson Fysh remained managing director until 1955 and then was chairman until retirement in 1966, a doyen of airline founders.

Earlier forebodings of a difficult year were proving well-founded. Henry Marking told his staff that the airline was likely only to 'just about break even' for the current year. 'Quite unprecedented problems have built up for British Airways and the rest of the airline industry.' Inflation would add 35 per cent to last year's operational costs of £500 million. 'Even with fare increases', he said, 'the airline cannot hope to get enough extra revenue to prevent this swallowing up the profit previously forecast.' The fuel alone would be £110 million, whereas last year it cost £70 million and the year before was £48 million. Wage rises, higher pensions, and increased national insurance contributions would add more than £30 million. Navigational charges would rise by £7 million and general costs by another £27 million.

Having overcome pilot pay and crewing problems, the Overseas division now had an unofficial strike of cabin staff causing a loss of upwards of £400,000 a day. On multi-sector routes the stewards and stewardesses wanted a maximum duty day of 10½ hours instead of 12½, though the legal maximum was 14 hours — which on any count was a very long time; but they also wanted the regulation three-day break periods increased to four days if the previous flight entailed a time change of five hours or more. 'Jet-lag' fatigue had become one of the difficulties, and there was no let up for cabin crews. Not many investigators understood the chronic feeling of fatigue that came from months of hard flying, particularly for the pilots who from high motivation would usually cover up the symptoms. The practical effect could be dangerous, for it might lead to unawareness of accumulated errors, and allow the elements of an operation to lose their correct sequence. Such things were rarely perceived by managements with no personal experience of prolonged flying year in and year out.

The problems of airline management were mounting. Knut Hammarskjold, director-general of IATA, declared at a London confer-

ence attended by international airline operators and officials: 'The dominant note in to-day's arena is the world economic situation: the energy crisis, commodity prices and shortages, wildly fluctuating exchange rates, a serious balance of payments problem, and the present hyper-inflation. We find a changed travel market with tourism dominating. Profibility has declined as a result of deteriorating yields, nowhere more evident than of the North Atlantic.' David Nicolson endorsed this with: 'The statistics may astonish you and certainly horrify me. Take 1973 as an example. The average load factor on British Airways services between Britain and the USA was nearly 55 per cent. As the total load capacity we offered was equivalent to about eleven Jumbo jets a simple calculation shows that we operated the equivalent of nearly five of them completely empty a day — and yet we did much better than the industry average on these routes. Taking all thirteen North Atlantic carriers with their 51 Boeing 747s a day, they operated the equivalent of 25 of them empty. These are statistics that send a chill down the spine of every senior airline executive who is concerned about profitability.'

Although unilateral British cancellation of Concorde had seemed probable, there were now strong signs that the Government's review was leading to second thoughts — or perhaps it

Concorde heads for the stratospheric heights of 50,000 to 60,000 ft, far above other high-flying airliners.

was prompted by the march of 2,000 BAC workers to Westminster to insist that the Concordes should not be cancelled. Certainly Concorde secured world-wide publicity in June when 002 flew from Paris to Rio and back between breakfast and supper after spending 90 minutes at Rio for lunch. A week later it flew supersonic from Charles de Gaulle Airport to Boston in 3 hours 9 minutes on a flight pattern which took it to 56,000 feet. Noise measurements at Boston Airport taken by the Massachusetts Port Authority were reported as 'encouraging in comparison with the Boeing 727'. Meanwhile Henry Marking was assured that the Government would underwrite the financial risk of operational losses on Concorde.

British Airways had allocated £36 million for the imminent entry into service of its nine Tri-Stars, the first of which would be delivered at the end of July. Very extensive equipment was required, such as an engine test cell, automatic test gear, an engineering ground simulator which could reproduce 385 engineering faults, a flight simulator, systems trainer, and a passenger cabin mock-up for crew training. Some £3·5 million had to be spent on moveable support items and £500,000 on fitting out four TriStar departure gates at Heathrow. Yet retrenchment was the objective. Marking said that the management was having to 'consider very seriously, withdrawing and selling up to thirteen Trident 1C's next year and the remaining seven in 1976'. The airline was faced with a probable £10 million loss and would have to reduce staff by 2,000 within six months and delay the next pay increase until 1 April next year. Finances had been damaged, he said, by 'unconstitutional and unofficial industrial action and failure to follow established negotiating procedures designed to settle all differences without resort to strikes'. There were now some 49,000 employees in the UK and 7,000 abroad.

A fortnight later he warned a mass meeting at Heathrow: 'By the end of September there will not be enough in the kitty to pay the wages. The cash is not coming in. We shall either have to get it as part of our public dividend capital or borrow it.' Nevertheless the accounts for the past year showed a profit, but that was before the fuel crisis — and certainly there was cash available for new aircraft because an order was placed for three more Sikorsky S-61N helicopters for late 1975 delivery to reinforce the ten

operating from Scottish bases in support of the oil rigs.

The financial brinkmanship of airlines was dramatically revealed when the Court Line Group, the largest holiday air transport business, announced on 15 July that it was going into liquidation. The two TriStars and nine One-Elevens were grounded and the CAA revoked their licences. That left 49,000 tourists stranded overseas, 40,000 of whom had booked holidays with Clarkson's and the others with Court Line subsidiaries. Swiftly the Association of British Travel Agents, with whom Court had lodged a £3 million bond, coordinated with British Airways, British Caledonian, Laker Airways, and Dan-Air to bring back the stranded passengers — though there were immediately difficulties because some hoteliers demanded that bills be paid before they left. That left about £1 million to recompense the 100,000 who had booked subsequent holidays at considerable outlay; most was likely to be recovered because the Government had agreed to acquire the Group's shipbuilding assets for £16 million. A political storm followed. David Nicolson at a Press conference in August warned of 'an icy wind of change which had been blowing over the air transport industry since the beginning of the year'. British Caledonian had lost £2·4 million, and even the giants Pan Am and TWA in the USA seemed likely to lose $70 million each this year.

British Airways was weathering the storm. The first Annual Report by the centralized management of what was now Europe's largest carrier showed a profit of £60·9 million before interest and taxation, an increase of 79·6 per cent for the opening year of operation, resulting in a net profit of £16·6 million compared with £5·2 million for the previous year. Nicolson was not optimistic: 'We were forecasting a profit of £80 million for the current year but are now faced with a possible loss of £14 million, and the latest figures show it might even be £18 or £20 million'. To the Captains flying the infinities of sky across the world this empire of cash calculations was so remote that there seemed no contact. Yet the burden of it all fell fundamentally upon these pilots, watching, checking, listening, deciding, concentrating intensely as they flew blind through the overcast, made their approaches, landed, conscious that safety fundamentally depended on them and their quick reaction to emergencies.

In September the CAA began talks with British Caledonian on rationalization of routes and services with those of British Airways. Relations between the two transport businesses was better than might be expected from their public opposition. British Caledonian already had engines overhauled by British Airways and was keen to enter an agreement 'to provide mutual establishment of a more logical, efficient and economic route structure during a period in which both carriers, as well as major foreign airlines, are going through a very difficult time'. British Airways agreed to 'give consideration to any proposal that would not weaken our operations'.

Meanwhile the North Atlantic fare levels, types of fare and capacity remained in the melting pot. However British Airways, British Caledonian, Pan American, TWA, and National Airlines agreed to reduce capacity by 20 per cent. British Airways forecast a loss next year of up to £30 million, and British Caledonian seemed unlikely to improve on last year's £1·5 million. Both Pan American and TWA were in difficulties following refusal by the CAB to grant a $10 million monthly subsidy. KLM was pruning its services, and Sabena was asking for a subsidy of £11 million. British Airways plodded on but sought a 12 per cent increase in fares on its three main domestic routes, having discovered that anything greater reduced the traffic.

In the October elections Labour just managed to win with a majority of three. This was unlikely to produce greater industrial efficiency, but at least political continuity should ensure that Concorde would not be scrapped. Symptomatic was an immediate strike by engineering ramp supervisors at the European division of British Airways. There were problems too at British Caledonian: falling business caused 800 employees to be sacked, yet each man earned about 10 per cent more revenue for that airline than did his better-paid colleagues and rivals in British Airways. Seven One-Eleven 500s would be sold, but the long-haul fleet would be increased with two Boeing 707s. 'If we hadn't taken this action we should have found outselves in a Court Line situation by the middle of next year', explained Adam Thompson.

The arrival at Heathrow on 28 October of British Airways' first TriStar was the signal for renewed activity on the industrial front. The Transport and General Workers' Union ramp staff and loaders refused to handle TriStars unless paid an extra £5 a week; the Association of Licensed Aircraft Engineers objected to the CAA's appointment of inspectors with authority to check out aircraft; flight engineers demanded talks on security and terms of employment as TriStar crews; and BALPA was again endeavouring to secure pay increases in separate categories for wide-bodied and narrow-bodied aircraft, and a supersonic premium for flying Concorde. Away went the planned service entry date of the TriStar and with it the vital revenue. Compensation agreements with the staff made heavy lay-offs uneconomic, for it would cost equivalent of two years' salary for each man. As things were a loss of about £15 million seemed inevitable.

Because of their different missions the operational unification of the Overseas and European divisions of British Airways was more difficult than a mere matter of centralized office routines. The conjunction of the engineering divisions presented big problems; even the few minutes' walk between their two big bases emphasized the separate identities. More than a re-grouping of equipment was required, for the task of maintaining aircraft in the highest state of efficiency and safety was dependent on detailed monitoring and analysis, recording and forecasting by specialized groups under the respective chief engineers. In all, some 10,000 were involved in this costly work, and their trade unions would have a big say, so a 50/50 management/union study group was being organized. Meanwhile the engineering services were earning £25 million in export work employing a tenth of the engineering manpower.

British airline policy in its entirety was being reviewed by the British government. Peter Shore told the Commons that the problem was 'whether there genuinely is room for two airlines in the way that the Edwards Committee originally recommended'. Michael Heseltine, the former Minister of Aerospace, requested Shore to 'accept that while the review is taking place there is no purpose in BCAL developing or investing in any of the routes that are the subject of the review'. The chairman of British Caledonian countered with a strong plea that UK air transport policy should be taken out of politics, for it was quite wrong to decide future ownership of the industry as a short-term answer to world-wide economic problems.

Into the Future
1975-80
and on

A lone Iranian hijacker seized a British Airways One-Eleven on 7 January during a flight from Manchester to London and demanded to be flown to Paris. The pilot eventually landed at Heathrow where airliner and crew remained for nearly eight hours of threats and evasions; then to give the impression of proceeding to Paris, flew to Stansted where the hijacker unsuccessfully attempted to escape and was found to have merely a toy pistol when arrested. The affair raised the whole question of airport security, for it was British practice to screen only 50 per cent of domestic passengers except on routes to Belfast and this man had not been checked. Meanwhile international law on air piracy remained inconclusive.

Five days later British Airways introduced Europe's first 'shuttle' service on the London–Glasgow route, using nine 100-seat Tridents. No booking was required for a guaranteed seat, and the regularity of hourly departures gave competitive advantage over other modes of transport. 'It is never likely to achieve a profit', growled Adam Thompson of rival Caledonian, 'and in abandoning the profit motive British Airways are using their financial position to compete unfairly.' Success was immediate. In the first week there were 11,716 passengers in the course of 195 flights including 45 back-ups to ensure no passenger had to wait. On 1 February the airline began selling the shuttle tickets on the aircraft. Immediately 450 protesting clerical workers went on strike, bringing the European divison almost to a standstill, and Henry Marking had no alternative to abandoning this time and cost-saving plan, but after months of parley with the Arbitration and Conciliation Service it was eventually established.

Both British Airways and Dan-Air had applied to the Civil Aviation Authority for revocation of the Laker Skytrain licence, but were rejected with the unequivocal statement that: 'The only reason why Skytrain services have not already been in operation for the past two years is that the United States authorities have engaged in unconscionable procrastination'. Freddie Laker triumphantly said: 'The authorities' decision is a shot in the arm for natural justice'. However the CAA cautiously suggested that the Laker services should not start until 'the market has resumed a healthy rate of growth'. Undoubtedly it was already improving, for Ross Stainton as chief executive of British Airways Overseas Division said: 'Cheap advance-booking charter and advance-purchase excursion fares are attracting inquiries at the rate of several hundred a day'. He envisaged 180,000 low-fare passengers being carried between Britain and the USA in the current year.

The biggest source of passenger business for Britain's air transport industry had become Spain. On the scheduled services British Airways and Iberia expected to share 780,000, and the charter subsidiary British Airtours expected

The flight deck of Concorde had three crew, and like the similarly manned Boeing 747 had three independent computer inertial navigation systems and fully automatic flight control and stabilization, together with weather radar.

300,000 to Spanish destinations, bringing the total British Airways share of that market to 11 per cent. On other routes operations would be cut back 10 per cent because a reduction of one million passengers was predicted, and the airline's all-cargo aircraft on short-range routes had long been unprofitable. A deficit of over £2 million was predicted for the year ending 31 March; consequently British Airways announced that a reduction of 1,300 from the 49,000 UK work force must be made, affecting all divisions in all regions. Aircrews would also be reduced by redeploying or placing on leave 400 pilots for a maximum of three years in order to sustain the Hamble Air Training College plan to produce the next decade of new men. At the end of three years it was estimated that 650 pilots would have retired, and the grounded crews could then rejoin, reinforced with 250 Hamble graduates — but it was a fair certainty that those pilots 'on leave' would seek other jobs.

Concorde now received a big boost. After long deliberation the US Federal Aviation Administration issued a draft 'environmental impact' statement recommending a total of four daily flights into and out of New York Kennedy Airport and two into and out of Washington Dulles. Permission was still subject to a public hearing. Pilots and flight engineers from British Airways and Air France had already begun training at Bristol and Toulouse for Concorde shadow services and endurance trials planned for the summer. Pending satisfactory outcome in the USA, the two airlines agreed to introduce supersonic services on the same day, probably early January 1976. Said Anthony Benn, the Secretary of State for Industry: 'It is important that a joint partnership over many years by the two countries, which makes the rest of the world's airlines obsolescent at a stroke, should not be masked by competition between the two airlines' — but he also said that no further construction beyond the sixteen production aircraft would be authorized.

On 18 April the great anti-noise hearing opened in the USA. A vociferous battle mounted, but after five hours of heated debate the Environmental Protection Committee of New York City Council rejected the resolution which would have banned Concorde from landing at New York with the qualification that flights should not begin until there was proof that the aircraft met existing US standards as

regards noise, pollution, and safety.

In any case British Airways' timetable for operational introduction of Concorde was likely to be delayed because BALPA was demanding £17,000 a year for 'supersonic' pilots, and had banned further training until settlement was reached. But why pay more for Concorde when the BAC chief pilot described it as suitable for any airline pilot — by which he meant those accustomed to the techniques of recent jet airliners? These demands gave the erroneous impression that supersonic flying must be dangerous. 'For us, Concorde is just the same as any other commercial aircraft and will be given no special priorities', ruled Alan White of the CAA. However this epochal airliner still had to obtain its C of A, and that required the programme of proving flights.

For the non-stop London–Los Angeles route British Airways had leased McDonnell Douglas DC-10-30s from Air New Zealand with the intention of phasing out the 707s in favour of these as a 'running mate' to the Boeing 747. Though the Los Angeles service was technically British Airways the same aircraft continued from there to Auckland as an Air New Zealand flight with ANZ crew, and Peter Shore confirmed in the Commons that the CAA had given this arrangement 'full and unconditional approval'.

Industrial action on any occasion that could be turned to advantage was an ever-increasing threat to enterprise. British Airways maintenance men at Heathrow now went on strike to secure higher wages for working on the European division's TriStars. All flights from Heathrow had to be cancelled from 6 a.m. on 2 June. These 550 men were causing such loss of vital revenue at a difficult time that three days later the airline again had to come to terms — but to get the business moving again wasted still more days. Marking warned that all staff must be prepared to switch jobs within the airline or else there would be redundancies, and to that end the unions agreed to co-operate in filling 290 urgent vacancies. Some were filled by Hamble cadet pilots still awaiting a flying job despite the recent grounding of airline Captains. These Hamble courses were stopped for the time being, though the College continued on a much-reduced scale to meet RAF and overseas requirements.

That same month the Queen's Birthday Honours announced the award of Knight Bachelor for David Nicolson as chairman of

British Airways. A few days later Sir Peter Masefield, the one-time chief executive of BEA and recently chairman of the Airports Authority, became a non-executive director of Caledonian Airways Ltd, the parent company of British Caledonian Airways, the rival of British Airways. Was there some political issue behind this? If so, it was submerged by the resounding 'yes' of the referendum for entry into Europe.

On 19 June the first Concorde training flights were made by the four management pilots and four senior training Captains selected by BEA, but secrecy surrounded the enhanced pay terms agreed with BALPA. On 7 July, commanded by Capt E.C. 'Mickey' Miles, Concorde 204 made the inaugural non-scheduled flight to Bahrein. Despite an hour's delay in trying to disconnect the nose tow bar and re-slot 204 into the take-off pattern, Henry Marking was happy to tell reporters: 'Speed, speed, and more speed is the order of the day'. Unfortunately the eighteen-mile wide 'sonic boom carpet' only permitted going supersonic over the Adriatic, so it took 3 hr 49 min before the touch-down at Bahrein — too late for the official reception,

In the next few months over 400 hours were achieved, in the course of which Concorde flew the most intensive programme ever undertaken for certification of an airliner and was tested not only in the Near East, but North and South America, Africa, India, Malaysia, and Australia.

Though the Civil Aviation Act gave the 'second force' a bigger chance to compete with British Airways the suspension of British Caledonian on the North Atlantic and Eastern USA was causing controversy as to whether its activities should be taken over by British Airways in order to reduce the latter's losses. The idea of healthy competition was beginning to wane. The Laker Skytrain, if it became effective, was threat enough. But at least the British Government's decision to provide launching funds to develop the Rolls-Royce 50,000-lb thrust jet turbines to power Boeing 747Bs for British Airways indicated determination to hold on to British long-distance routes as well as the certainty of increasing exports.

In contrast to the big Boeings, British Airways was now introducing two 46-seat Hawker Siddeley 748s ordered specifically for the uncertain weather of the Scottish routes at a cost of £2 million to replace the 71-seat Viscount 800s which were limited to 45 passengers on the service between Aberdeen and Sum-

burgh — the front line 'oil-rush' air base. The flight manager said: 'The crews relish this new aircraft and this type of demanding flying, and the enthusiastic and happy base atmosphere is the reason why we have got it into service so quickly. The Sperry flight-director system, costing £100,000 per aircraft, and the new Plessey radar ensure precision type approaches down to the minima permitted in the prevailing poor visibilities.'

The long-awaited UK civil aviation policy review was published at the beginning of August, and could be summarized in Peter Shore's comment: 'In future it should be our general policy not to permit competition between UK airlines on the long-haul schedule services'. However British Caledonian survived intact, with precedence on the long-haul scheduled routes to South America and West Africa, and would continue to compete with the national airline on domestic and European routes. Shaw said that with existing over-capacity on the North Atlantic it would be 'a major inconsistency to hold out hope of an early go-ahead for Skytrain while cutting off British Caledonian's line of return to that route'.

Two days later the next round of Licensing hearings on the UK routes began with British Caledonian applying for tariff and frequency changes on British Airways' London–Glasgow shuttle and the scheduled London–Edinburgh service, claiming that no operator could make a profit on UK domestic trunk routes. 'With British Airways ten times the size of BCAL it is obvious who can bear the losses longer', said British Caledonian, and asked the CAA 'to restore the balance' and prevent British Airways from 'selling pound notes for 70p'. British Airways mounted an effective counter attack, backed by an unprecedented number of letters in support of the shuttle. A week passed, and the CAA rejected the British Caledonian application, saying that no conclusive evidence had been presented to show that BCAL would suffer from the introduction of the shuttle. Surprisingly, despite continuing confrontations at the CAA, these rival airlines were not spurred by animosity, and now began negotiating route exchanges to implement the Goverment's revised policy on long-haul competition.

British Airways Helicopters by this time had expanded considerably to cope with the North sea oil business, and recently had obtained a

£14 million contract from Shell for operations over the next five to eight years. Three more S-61N amphibians had been purchased, but the big problem was shortage of helicopter pilots. This was no job for amateurs. The work was hazardous. Relief of oil crews and carriage of equipment must be conducted round the clock in all weathers across the gale-lashed North Sea, navigating by automatic Decca Danac with monitoring systems by radar — but for operators like British Airways and the rival Bristow Helicopters here was a fortune.

Nevertheless when the Annual Accounts of British Airways were published at the beginning of September there was a net loss of £9·4 million though turnover had risen by 15·6 per cent to £748 million. In that context Sir David Nicolson attributed £11 million income erosion to 'unofficial, and in my view quite unnecessary industrial action', for there had been 25 damaging industrial disputes in 1974–75. Sir David added: 'Plans have been formulated which could give the airline an operating surplus in the current year, although much depends on the degree of acceptance by the staff'. Part of the problem was rivalry between European and Overseas divisions. 'Some people think they are still Imperial Airways', sourly commented one executive. But as *Flight*'s editor said: 'British Airways, after the US carriers, is at the top of most traffic and industrial-performance columns — market shares, foreign currency earnings, safety, and support of its national aircraft industry'.

Talks between British Airways and British Caledonian were proceeding in an increasingly co-operative atmosphere, but when giving the British Commonwealth Lecture on 9 October, Sir David Nicolson still had things to say on Government attitude towards commercial aviation. 'It is not for British Airways to concede route transfers which would be against the interest of the airline and its staff. We should therefore be particularly opposed to any transfer to British Caledonian which damaged British Airways financially or resulted in resources, whether people or equipment, becoming surplus. British Airways has invested many millions in future equipment and it would be ludicrous to imagine that the whole operation, including commitment for manpower, should be subject to arbitrary transfer of route licences.'

In yet another financially co-operative venture, the European division leased two Douglas DC-9s from Cyprus Airways together with flight-deck crews to resume the services to Cyprus. Direct flights had ceased with the closure of Nicosia Airport after the previous year's Turkish invasion. Recently Cyprus Airways had been using Larnaca Airport for DC-9 flights to Athens, whence British Airways Tridents took over the passengers for the London route, but in future DC-9s would be used throughout.

At home, the half-millionth passenger flew on the London–Glasgow shuttle on 17 November, just ten months after starting the guaranteed seat service. So popular was the route that revenue had increased 50 per cent, and it was expected that the operation would break even next year despite the disastrous loss of £3 million in 1974. In fact the European division was now hopeful of all round profit in the current financial year, for the summer traffic had been 'a welcome boost to morale'. Holiday traffic had shown improvement beyond all expectation; only Portugal, because of civil disturbance, was one-third down on last year's figures.

The next procurement decision facing British Airways was replacement of the regional division's 31 short-haul Viscounts which would all be retired by 1978–80. 'As to long-haul aircraft', British Airways told *Flight*, 'the first option is not buying anything at all'—for the airline was well supplied with Boeing 747s, 707s and VC 10s, and was committed to the long-range Boeing 747-236B with deliveries starting in 1977. Despite use of the DC-9s on the Cyprus run, the airline did not accept the McDonnel Douglas contention that an intermediate type was needed by 1978, probably because the Lockheed TriStar 500 was sufficient back-up. Meanwhile there was Concorde which now had its full C of A after thirteen years' developing and testing.

New aircraft availabilities in any case might result from the nationalization of the British aircraft and shipbuilding industries which was approved by a narrow margin on 2 December, and would embrace 43 companies employing 170,000 people. 'This Bill', pretentiously said Eric Varley, the Secretary of State for Industry, 'deals with two industries in need of structural change and reorientation. The Bill deals with the real world of the shop floor, the research laboratory and the sales contract, not with arid political generalities or statistical abstractions.'

Sir David Nicolson was strongly opposed to

nationalization. Earlier he had said: 'Just because Government has money in the business there is no reason why it should try to run that business. I believe it is wrong to ask public Corporations to carry out uneconomic projects without proper, prompt and clearly identified compensations. I also believe it is wrong to use public Corporations as economic regulators of political instruments, whether to keep prices down or to aid technology, without proper thinking.' Accordingly he resigned as from 31 December and was succeeded by 60-year-old Sir Frank McFadzean, of the Royal Dutch Shell Group, who had a formidable record in big industry but was not an airline man.

1976

The opening problem of 1976 was whether confrontation with the USA on Concorde operations should be avoided. Hopes for an unconditional all-clear for flights into New York had withered in the face of concerted opposition from environmentalists, community groups, public officials, and the Airport Operators Council International. Asked about Concorde's noise, Gerald Kaufman, the new Industry Minister, said: 'We claim that though it is greater than that of the 747, it is broadly comparable with 707 and DC-8 types which makes tens of thousands of flights a year in and out of New York and Washington. To listen to our opponents you would think we were asking for non-stop take-offs and landings at all hours of the day and night whereas we are only asking for four and two respectively.'

Since it was a dead loss to keep Concordes grounded until permission was achieved for flights to the USA it seemed reasonable to secure a measure of revenue and certainly valuable experience by operating a service to oil-rich Bahrein. On 15 January, Henry Marking handed to Frederick Page, the chairman of the BAC commercial aircraft division, a £20·5 million cheque for Concorde G-BOAA which had just been delivered from Fairford to Heathrow. Six days later G-BOAA lined up at 11·35 GMT for take-off to Bahrein, with Capt Norman Todd as commander. At exactly the same time Capt Pierre Dudal, with Brian Trubshaw in the 'jump' seat, set out from Paris with their French-built Concorde outward bound for Rio de Janeiro. Aboard the British machine were Henry Marking, Eric Varley, Ross Stainton, Sir George Edwards, and Alan Greenwood of

BAC, senior engineers, journalists, and 30 fare-payers, totalling 100 passengers in addition to the flight crew, two stewardesses and four stewards in special uniform. 'The normality is just unbelievable as we tuck into smoked salmon, roast duckling, strawberries and cream at 1,350 mph some where over Greece', wrote J.M. Ramsden. 'Two hours since take-off and we are passing Crete and Cyprus. We are across Lebanon and Syria in under six minutes, then along the Iraqi–Saudi border. Light fades over the vermillion desert as our speed hastens down the fast sinking sun. My next glance at the window meets darkness as if we had snuffed the day. We start descent. In five minutes we reach subsonic on the meter. At 325 knots I can see the necklaces of Bahrein pricking out the darkness. Six minutes later we feel the touch-down. Every one claps. Whatever happens now, man has attained supersonic age.'

Temporizing, the American Transport Secretary on 4 February gave limited permission for Concorde to land at New York and Washington Dulles for a trial period of sixteen months. 'A firm decision at this time neither to admit nor ban Concorde would be irresponsible', he said. American opposition immediately mounted. New York State legislation swiftly followed with revised aircraft noise limits which would effectively ban Concorde, and the environmentalists and anti-Concorde groups filed an appeal against the decision to permit the trial period. Weeks of struggle lay ahead.

Newspapers, ever on the lookout for damaging snippets, were criticizing Concorde's operational serviceability on the Bahrein route — yet there had been only one turn back and that was due to an engine component scheduled for modification; all passengers had transferred to the stand-by Concorde. Apart from the inaugural run the load factor had averaged 42·5 per cent in the sixteen journeys to date, but this meant a loss of £800 each flight. Air France was doing better, for there had been a 58·3 per cent load factor on flights to Rio, and 1,137 passengers had been carried at slight operating profit. In mid-April the New York Port Authority was insisting on a six-month evaluation of Concorde noise at the airports of Paris and Heathrow before considering use of New York Kennedy. An appeal to the US Supreme Court was therefore mounted.

Except for the Concorde reverse, all British Airways routes were doing well. The London–Scotland shuttle was an outstanding success with departures every two hours, using six 146-seat Trident 3s with seven 100-seat Trident 1s available as back-ups. The European holiday business was flourishing, and for the first time in the Overseas division's history the total revenue on East-bound routes to the Middle East, Far East and Australasia exceeded North Atlantic revenue. The total number of passengers on all routes topped the three million mark for the year, representing 12½ per cent growth. The eighteenth Boeing 747 had been delivered, so the entire Australian services would use this high-capacity aircraft. The London–Hong Kong service would be the testing route for an 'executive cabin' 747 service demanded by passengers paying full fares.

In a move to ensure unification of engineering activities, Kenneth Wilkinson, who had originally joined BEA in 1946 as a performance analyst, resigned as vice-chairman of Rolls-Royce and rejoined British Airways as group engineering director with the formidable task of eliminating old rivalries and integrating the separate Overseas, European, and Regional engineering departments and the Treforest engine overhaul company.

In mid-May President Giscard d'Estaing flew to the USA in Concorde, landing at Andrews Air Force Base near Washington on what was described as a State visit but in fact designed to impress the proceedings of the US Federal Appeal Court which opened on 19 May to decide the validity of the Transport Secretary's favourable ruling on Concorde. Nine judges of liberal view were assigned, although only five would hear the case, and they soon decided that the Transport Secretary had acted constitutionally on all issues. The way was open. On 24 May British Airways G-BOAC and Air France's F-BVFA touched down at Washington Dulles Terminal in a double coup of technology and showmanship achieved by a flight of just under four hours. Thousands were there to see these machines. 'Concorde is a technical triumph', said the receiving American Minister, greeting Gerald Kaufman as he stepped from the British machine. 'We look forward to the sixteen-month environmental trial.' Lord Beswick, chairman designate of the British Aerospace Corporation, drew the lesson: 'People said Concorde would never fly. People said it would never get into the USA. The record gives us confidence in Concorde's future.'

Emulating the French Premier, the British Prime Minister, James Callaghan, expressed his own confidence in supersonic travel by chartering a British Airways Concorde to fly him and senior members of the Government to Puerto Rico on 26 June for an International Economic Summit meeting. The 4,550 nautical-mile outbound non-stop flight of 4 hours 10 minutes was the longest so far made by Concorde.

On the newly established Washington run the novelty of supersonic flight was ensuring a load factor of 91·6 per cent based on a maximum of 71 seats offered from London and 76 for the return, depending on wind direction and strength, which at supersonic height could attain over 100 mph. Regardless of airline economics, delivery of Concorde 208 was currently delayed by BAC workers striking in protest against closure of the Fairford testing base.

Summer subsonic traffic was booming. The European division was experiencing a 15 per cent traffic growth on services into Britain, and visitors from Scandinavia and Germany had increased by one-third. Roy Watts, chief executive of the division, said: 'People are flying into this country from all over Europe to take advantage of the bargain prices afforded by the new value of the pound. Austria now finds it as cheap to fly with us for a three-night holiday in Britain as to spend the same three nights in a first-class hotel in Vienna.' Air France and British Airways were co-ordinating an almost hourly 'air bridge' between Heathrow and Charles de Gaulle Airport. Air France's general manager said: 'Co-operation with British Airways had been perfect and we are getting over 77 per cent load factors'.

At British Airways the long-awaited agreement establishing a common pilot-force had been signed with BALPA. This comprised four groups, the first of which were pilots who joined shortly after the war and were now close to retiring age which ICAO had agreed would be a mandatory 55 after December next year; second were those after the initial post-war intake up to the pre-Hamble era of 1963; next were the Hamble graduates up to 1972, and fourth were those on the common seniority list since 1972. The aim was better operational flexibility, particularly when aircraft types were transferred from one division to another, as with the TriStars on the Overseas routes.

Replacements for the big fleet of Tridents and the One-Eleven 500s would soon be required, and a 160/180-seater was visualized. That brought the Airbus A-300 into the picture again, but British Airways did not want this twin-engined 220-seater, though France was apparently bartering its purchase as a pre-condition of the European Consortium Aerospace membership. McDonnell Douglas plunged in with advertisements for the DC-10 offering a collaborative agreement which would benefit the British economy to the tune of £300 million and 13,000 jobs — but at a Board meeting on 6 August the British Airways executives came to preliminary decision in favour of the Lockheed TriStar 500.

Presenting his first Annual Report of British Airways, the chairman, Sir Frank McFadzean, reported a net loss of £16·3 million for the 1975–76 financial year compared with the previous year's loss of £9·4 million. 'Not a result I feel proud about', he commented. 'Nevertheless we hope it will be recognized, first, that we have survived an industry-wide blizzard better than most of our rivals; second, that in operations, marketing, innovation, and staff relations we achieved a positive improvement over 1974/1975; and, third, that we face the future with greater strength.' Indications were that by 1985 the annual number of passengers on scheduled services could be 25 million, compared with the current 14 million. To match that growth as many as a hundred new aircraft would be needed over the next ten years — from short range up to 1,000 miles, and very long range of over 5,000 miles. That would represent an investment of about £100 million annually.

McFadzean said: 'Last year's report spoke of "Resistance to change" as a delaying factor in the integration of the former British European Airways and British Overseas Airways, and the Board recognizes that minorities of 50,000 people could not, and should not, be arbitrarily disrupted. We believe our commitment to participatory study groups, in our planning of organization developments, is the right approach.'

Interesting facts emerged. British Airways now flew to all six continents, serving 158 cities in 78 countries, and the scheduled route network of 400,000 miles was the longest of any airline. During the last year 13,792,239 passengers had been carried, of which the international passengers totalled 9,340,806 — more than any other airline. In booking reservations, the UK staff took more than 5,250,000 telephone calls, and over 3,000,000 meals were served on the domestic and European flights. British Airways had interests in 45 hotels offering 22,000 beds in twenty countries, and booked over one million bed-nights for visitors to the United Kingdom. British Airways Helicopters, in addition to the oil-rig shuttles, had carried 80,170 passengers between Penzance and the Isles of Scilly. Outside contracts by the airline and its subsidiaries amounted to £77 million, of which £25 million was contributed by the engineering facility and £20·5 million from International Aeradio Ltd for provision of communications and technical services. Above all, the 455,000 flying hours without fatality matched the best of other airlines.

Alas! the safety record of British Airways was immediately broken, for on 10 September their Trident 3 G-AWZT on scheduled service from Heathrow to Istanbul with 58 passengers and crew of nine was involved in a mid-air collision with a DC-9 of Inex Adria at 33,000 feet when some twenty miles north of Zagreb. There were no survivors. An international inquiry would follow, but it appeared that air traffic control at Zagreb was at fault, and five controllers were arrested.

At the beginning of October, the Fairford test base dispute having collapsed, British Airways received its third production Concorde, and now stepped up the service to Washington with three round trips weekly. Five thousand passengers had flown on British Airways Concordes to the USA, maintaining the high load factor. There were still protests about take-off noise, and the sonic boom was sufficiently severe at Alderney to necessitate moving the French route slightly north. Air France was now offering 100 seats on the eastward run and 90 for the westward because the lower temperatures of autumn resulted in less fuel consumption, affording a higher payload. British Airways continued the policy of prudence, limiting the seats respectively to 90 from Washington and 70 from London.

At the end of November British Caledonian took over British Airways' mid-Atlantic routes from London to Caracas, Bogotá, and Lima in compliance with the new UK civil aviation policy of 'spheres of interest'. Sir Frank McFadzean earlier had said: 'We accept the outcome of the review as something we can live with, and hope that we can look forward to a period of stability in this respect of civil aviation policy so that we can plan ahead with greater confidence'.

The British Airways Board on 5 November decided to apply to the Secretary of State for Trade for permission to make organizational changes proposed by the airline's special committee chaired by Peter Hermon, the Group Management Services director. Sir Frank assumed the additional duty of chief executive, and the posts of managing and deputy managing director were abolished. Unification was the objective — four years after the merger of the two nationalized Corporations!

The airline head office and those of the three operational divisions were all at different locations, and the divisions had been inward-looking and defensive towards the HQ organization. Problems everywhere tended to lead to committees, and as members were usually equals this was no substitute for management. Communications often involved re-presentation both from HQ and from each division, so no corporate face was presented to the world. Thus at Heathrow there was no one person in charge. There was not even cohesion in the commercial organization as each division had separate organizations for traffic sales. Planning tended to become the summation of divisional plans for which the Executive Board became a forum for settling differences rather than a focus of decision for efficient operation. Sweeping changes were therefore organized.

1977

Though complete integration of British Airways management organization had been targeted for 1 January in the Queen's Jubilee year of 1977, this proved impossible because of plan modifications, but was expected to be 'fully effective' by 31 March. Commercial operations were to be headed by Ross Stainton who was appointed co-deputy chairman, thus equating with deputy chairman Henry Marking who had special responsibility for planning, legal, and international affairs. Roy Watts was Stainton's director of commercial operations, and Basil Bampfylde became controller of route divisions of which there would now be six — Western, Southern, Eastern, UK and Ireland, South and West Europe, North and East Europe. Concorde operations acquired special status in the department of commercial operations. Stephen Wheatcroft was made director of subsidiaries with special responsibilities for the

airline's Associated Companies, British Airways Helicopters, and International Aeradio. A significant appointment was that of Bob Whitby as adviser on future aircraft under the planning director Alec Finlay. Capt Tom Nisbet as air safety adviser reported directly to Sir Frank McFadzean.

British Airways, Air France, and the British and French Governments now decided to proceed with a law suit against the Port Authority of New York over the ban preventing Concorde landing there — for the issue had been successfully stalled for three months. The threat elicited guarded support for a permit from President Carter and led to delaying the court battle. So far Air France carrying 28,700 passengers had lost some £21 million; British Airways with 18,000 passengers had lost £10 million — yet both the airlines and the manufacturers were encouraged by the first year's operations. Despite the relatively narrow cabin of VC 10 proportion, passengers enjoyed the experience of high-speed flight, and pilots had no complaint except that they wished their seats were more comfortable — but that did not mean they could relax, for every thing must be done with absolute accuracy, and factors affecting cruise fuel consumption and CG position had to be closely monitored when the tactical situation was changing so rapidly with the aircraft flying at a good 20 nm a minute.

Since every man had to be a specialist, occasional accidents in training seemed inevitable. Thus on 17 March a British Airtours Boeing 707-436 crashed during a practice sortie at Prestwick, the aircraft yawing and rolling to the left when rotated at take-off during a simulated engine failure. The port wing struck the ground and its engines broke off, then the machine rolled the opposite way, tearing off a starboard engine. Fire broke out and largely destroyed the centre fuselage, but none of the four crew members was seriously hurt.

Though this made headline news, the effect was negligible compared with a runway collision at Santa Cruz Airport, Teneriffe, between two Boeing 747s owned by Pan Am and KLM, for 580 were killed. This was the world's biggest aircraft disaster — yet it was on the ground. Complex investigation followed, revealing confusion over air traffic instructions causing the Pan American aircraft to miss its turn-off to a taxi-way. The insurance bill was likely to be $200 million, two-thirds of which would be on the London market.

Once again British Airways became involved in that misnomer 'industrial action'. The maintenance engineers at Heathrow took unofficial action by banning overtime and shift working from 3 April. The airline warned that those not reporting for their shift would be dismissed. The ultimatum was rejected and 4,000 men were dismissed for breach of contract. Flight cancellations began. The strike was costing £3 million a day, but the chairman continued his uncompromising line because other unions at Heathrow indicated support for the management, but by the time revenue losses reached £31 million compromise was reached by meeting part of the engineers' claim and agreeing to consider independent negotiating machinery instead of the customary National Joint Council for Civil Air Transport. Concurrently the Government stated that no further expansion of Heathrow would be allowed until Gatwick was fully utilized to handle its potential of 16 million passengers a year. The Government estimated that if it had not intervened, three-quarters of a million charter passengers, mainly carried by British Airways, Pan Am, and TWA, would have used Heathrow next year. It was hoped that by 1982 three to four million passengers a year, of which one million were charter passengers, would have transferred to Gatwick.

In May the Rolls-Royce-powered Boeing 747-236 entered service. These magnificent airliners were capable of taking off at 365 tons, although would be used at 355 tons initially — which was almost 30 tons more than the Pratt & Whitney-powered versions. Their empty weight was just over 166 tons, and for maximum range 120 tons of kerosene was stowed in the seven tanks, but for such hot-and-high airports as Nairobi the all-up weight was limited to 335 tons which reduced the payload to 29 tons. Using suitably placed intermediate stops the Boeing was the world's most economic airliner and could carry 450 passengers if need be. A participating pilot wrote: 'By any yardstick the Boeing 747 is a remarkable aeroplane. Doubts about its size and complexity, voiced before the first example was built in 1968, have long since evaporated. It is a delight to operate, easy to fly and almost invariably provokes lasting admiration among pilots. The manufacturer has incorporated various airframe improvements in the 200 Series aircraft which are offered for a minimum of twenty years' service. The four Rolls-Royce engines represent 25 per cent of the value of the aircraft, underlining Britain's ability to compete with the best the US can offer.'

In the USA, the Court of Appeal refused to delay the Concorde case any further and set the hearing for 1 June. No decision emerged. Instead the Court asked the appropriate US Federal Government Departments to submit briefs as 'friends of the Court' by 6 June. The British and French Governments requested leave to intervene and were similarly asked to file briefs. Three US Appeal Judges unanimously rejected the previous findings but a fresh hearing in the District Court was stipulated to decide whether the New York Port Authority had treated Concorde fairly and reasonably in imposing its ban.

US/UK talks laboured on a new Bermuda

The British Airways version of the Boeing 737-200, which first flew in April 1971, was a unique combination of proven and new, updating a fifteen-year-old design with latest computer techniques.
Bottom: Portrayed to the same scale, the 200-seat, twin-engined short-haul Boeing 757 successor was given British Government clearance in late 1979 for British Airways to purchase nineteen for delivery in 1983.

Agreement. Midnight 2 June was the deadline for expiry of the 1946 agreement. Not until ten minutes later did the US negotiator and the chief of the British delegation initial a preliminary document clearing the way for an agreement to be completed and signed in Bermuda in July. There would then be a capacity control jurisdiction requiring each country to file its plans and forecasts of traffic; permissible growth would be averaged, and new provisions for fares consultation would enable airlines to know their government's policy before appeals were made to IATA. Even before the Bermuda Two Agreement was signed, US carriers were asking the CAB to approve steps which would further dilute the North Atlantic fare yields in an effort to compete with the low-cost Skytrain service which Laker had at last been permitted to operate. British Airways countered with proposal for a Skytrain-style service to New York at £149 return, but with guaranteed seat and food services instead of the 'no-frills' Laker standard.

'In return for a few significant gains, British air transport will be substantially worse off because some of the broad ground rules for international air transport, enshrined in Bermuda One, are undermined. In view of the importance of Bermuda Two to every nation's air services, and most of all to our own, there ought to be no misunderstandings or glossing over of the factual position', wrote Sir Peter Masefield to *The Times*. He said the most important gains were the opening of new North Atlantic routes, some rationalization of Fifth-Freedom rights into Europe within five years, the move towards capacity control, and new ways of agreeing fares and rates; on the debit side there was a disturbing retreat from the principle of fair and equal opportunity.

In England air travel chaos was threatened. Three separate disputes were causing long delays at Heathrow and other major UK airports. In the first, Air Traffic Control assistants seeking a 17 per cent pay rise reimposed a work-to-rule and refused to operate a computer which co-ordinated movements handled by the London Air Traffic Control Centre. The second involved 620 catering staff who stopped work for two days, refusing to clean incoming aircraft in protest against reductions in staff. That resulted in overnight delay to a Nigerian Airways Boeing 707 charter flight to Lagos, and next day 100 or so passengers boarded the aircraft and staged a sit-in. The third was a

threat by 4,000 maintenance workers to strike in support of their shop steward Jack Gatsky, who was sacked after publicly criticizing the airline's safety standards. However he admitted he was not qualified to comment and apologized, but by then 40 flights a day were being cancelled. Major disruption during the August Bank Holiday weekend seemed inevitable, for on 22 July a ballot of the 850 Air Traffic Control assistants decided on a strike which Government intervention failed to avert. Drastic rescheduling followed and this led to a booming trade for air-taxi operators. For ten weeks these strikes disrupted all flying, which in the case of British Airways resulted in a loss of £30 million.

However, the British Airways Annual Report published in August was encouraging, for the financial year 1976–77 showed dramatic improvement. Group turnover had climbed from £916 million of the previous year to £1,248 million, and the net profit was £35 million compared with a loss of £16 million in the previous financial year. Nevertheless McFadzean, who declared that he had 'the reputation of being a hard and ruthless person', warned there was a long way to go before the airline met his efficiency standards, and he instanced the industrial relations scene of 87 disputes involving 52 stoppages where the common element was the complex and unwieldy pay structure. Thus in one part of the airline alone, comprising 5,200 employees, there were 90 different pay grades. To overcome the anomalies the Board therefore proposed to the trade unions the formation of a British Airways Council composed of elected employees and managers.

On 1 September, Henry Marking, that earlier outspoken chairman of BEA and currently deputy chairman of British Airways, left full-time employment with the airline to become chairman of the British Tourist Authority, though remaining a non-executive Board member. There was no hint of a clash with McFadzean, yet to many it had seemed inevitable. he had joined BEA in 1949 in a temporary job as assistant solicitor, but so outstanding was his ability that by 1970 he was the fifth chairman of BEA, and had seemed certain to take over as chairman of British Airways when Sir David Nicolson resigned in 1975 — but in the event McFadzean, the outsider, had been appointed. For his outstanding services Marking received a KCVO.

While the battle for Concorde was swaying to and fro, Freddie Laker was facing more opposition from British Airways, British Caledonian, and the British Airport Authority, but secured substitution of Gatwick for Stansted, so preparations were completed for the inauguration of the Skytrain service on 26 September. Queues were reported both at Gatwick and New York, and British Airways and Pan Am, who had been running a competitive no-booking service from Heathrow, found on the opening day that all Skytrain stand-by passengers had secured seats, leaving theirs only partly taken.

Concorde prospects also received a blow when the Public Accounts Committee announced that: 'There appears to be no practicable possibility of production beyond the sixteen aircraft authorized', for it was estimated that the Government would lose £200 million on Concorde production even if the five unsold Concordes found customers at a price comparable with that paid by British Airways and Air France. New York as a terminal became even more essential to encourage other airlines to buy these costly supersonic aircraft.

The extended hold-up by New York Port Authority seemed all the more biased when the US Transport Secretary announced at the end of September that Concorde had passed its test of environmental acceptability at Washington Dulles Airport and that flights could continue. On 17 October the US Supreme Court turned down, without comment, the New York Port Authority's request to delay Concorde flights in order to lodge formal appeal.

British Airways and Air France snatched the tactical advantages and began a short series of proving flights in to and out of New York Kennedy. None of the Port Authority's noise monitors recorded a reading above the normal limit set for all aircraft. Take-offs, however, had their danger, for the noise abatement procedure involved a turn through 90 degrees initiated at only 100 feet. With a view to inaugurating the passenger service in a month's time, a booking office was opened, Air France offering a daily flight, but British Airways was temporarily restricted to two round trips a week because of shortage of qualified Concorde pilots.

1 November brought Concorde into the headlines again, for the Queen and Prince Philip flew home from Barbados in the Concorde flag ship after their Silver Jubilee Canadian and Caribbean tour. This was a record flight which covered 4,200 statute miles to London Heathrow in 3 hours 42 minutes at an average of 1,134·5 mph, piloted by Capt Brian Walpole. During her Jubilee year the Queen had made more than 60 flights in Britain and abroad, including her first helicopter and supersonic experience. By using the Concorde she had been able to open the Barbadian Parliament on the morning of her departure and the British Parliament in London next day.

Three weeks later there was a tumultuous welcome for Concorde when Air France and British Airways inaugurated the regular New York services on 22 November. At the Waldorf Astoria the City tycoons held a crowded reception in the huge grand ballroom. On the dais were leading representatives of commerce, finance, multi-national corporations, senators, and even trade unionists. Enthusiasm ran high. 'That Concorde was a dangerous monster exists only in the minds of those against progress', declared the chairman — and Britain's Trade Minister sealed the felicitations with an announcement that on 7 December Concorde would carry a party of American businessmen and trade unionists to London to promote Anglo-American trade.

Certainly British Airways' intention to purchase more American aircraft for delivery in 1979–82 was confirmed. The choice according to Ross Stainton was between the Boeing 737-200 and the DC-9-40, and possibly the Boeing 7X7, and he said: 'I can't take any view other than that our job is to keep British Airways in the forefront and to go where the most competitive equipment is'. That irked the British Aerospace management who were pushing their X-Eleven project — and it also led to a surge of salesmen from the rival American manufacturers. Gerald Kaufman carefully interpolated 'whenever possible' in stating that 'all British airlines should buy British', and in Parliament there were even demands that Ross Stainton should be dismissed if British Airways failed to buy the One-Eleven.

Nor was the route for Concorde to Singapore free of contention, for it got off to a controversial start on 9 December because Malaysia immediately vetoed flights over its territory for fear of sonic booms. This was temporarily solved by limited permission from Indonesia to re-route through their skies, though only for three return services. The diplomatic wires hummed; but for the time being

Opposite: British Airways routes
across the world in 1980.
Bottom: The European
spider-web of British Airways.

the Bahrein–Singapore sector had to be cancelled. The Malaysians were holding Britain to ransom, demanding material concessions for additional rights before permitting Concorde overflights. An escalating cycle of retaliation seemed likely.

1978

1 January 1978 brought a new management structure to British Airways, for deputy chairman Ross Stainton had replaced Sir Frank McFadzean as chief executive — a position he had held *locum tenens* since last September, when Sir Frank had suffered a heart attack but continued as non-executive chairman. Roy Watts was given responsibility for finance and planning, and the new director of commercial operations was Gerry Draper who had been head of the airline's marketing and sales division for the past five years. Peter Hermon became management services director and with Draper was appointed to the main Board as an executive member.

At the beginning of February a Boeing team visited British Airways to continue discussions on the 7X7 derivative of the 737 in the form of a 120-seater twin jet, and was offering British Aerospace a major partnership in construction. Equally pressing was the Airbus Industrie with participatory offer of a European 150-seater which would have a 75 per cent similarity in aerodynamics and systems to the A-300, but their case was considerably weakened because the Air France airline was hoping to purchase Boeing aircraft to replace the time-expired noisy Caravelles. The American sales team had not long returned to the USA when Boeing announced that the original 7X7 design was programmed as the 757 narrow-bodied twin jet seating 160 to 180 passengers six abreast. However Eric Varley told a French audience that the British Government was 'giving priority to Europe in its moves towards a new airliner programme' and assured them that 'no negotiations had been made' during the visit of the Boeing team. Huge sums were at stake for new equipment before the end of the century.

But a big question mark was also emerging. Looking into the future, Willis Hawkins, Lockheed's visionary president of engineering in California, said: 'The fuel shortage is going to catch up with us. The optimists give you to 2010 AD and may be you can put it off to 2020, but countries like Japan may be facing it in five

years. In place of kerosene, hydrogen is a beautiful thing to use as fuel. You can make it more easily out of coal than you can make jet fuel. It enters the engine as gas and burns clear. It would make a cargo version of the TriStar 500 carrying 100,000 lb of cargo 4,000 miles weight 1,200,000 less. To fill it with hydrogen fuel you would need 155 tons of coal to make the hydrogen, but 200 tons to make kerosene for the same mission, and the liquid hydrogen tank is substantially a safer container than a standard fuel tank.' One thing was certain: costs would soar. The capital expenditure in hydrogen plant alone would be breathtaking, whether coal were the basis or eventual synthesis from water.

That the future of British air transport depended on Anglo-American co-operation was certainly the view of British Airways, for approval was now sought to buy nineteen Rolls-Royce-powered Boeing 114-seater 737s at a cost of £140 million. 'We believe in fostering a new concept of trans-Atlantic approach to building, choosing, and operating a new civil aircraft, encouraging British and American manufacturers to combine the best airframe with the best engines to produce the best and most saleable aircraft', said the management, but though British Airways was heading the queue for the Boeing 757 powered with Rolls-Royce R.B.211-535 engines the time was not yet expedient to place an order. The fleet strategy was to reduce the number of types, excluding Concorde, to four: 747, TriStar, 737, and 757, the latter giving a major opportunity for Anglo-American industrial partnership, yielding a possible 20,000 jobs in the British Aerospace airframe and engine industry.

British Airways Helicopters concurrently confirmed an order for two Sikorsky S-76 helicopters. 'The pace of our expansion over the past twelve months has been tremendous', said managing director Capt 'Jock' Cameron. Designed purely for the civil market, the twin-engined S-76 had a cabin for fourteen and was notable for a retractable undercarriage combined with flotation gear packed on the inside of the retraction doors. Cameron also had an eye on the twin-rotor Boeing-Vertol Chinook which could fly to the furthest oil rig with a 44-passenger load, and there was the possibility that one day this type might take over the short-haul routes and even the London–Paris run. A time-saving shuttle run between Heathrow and Gatwick opened on 9 June, using a

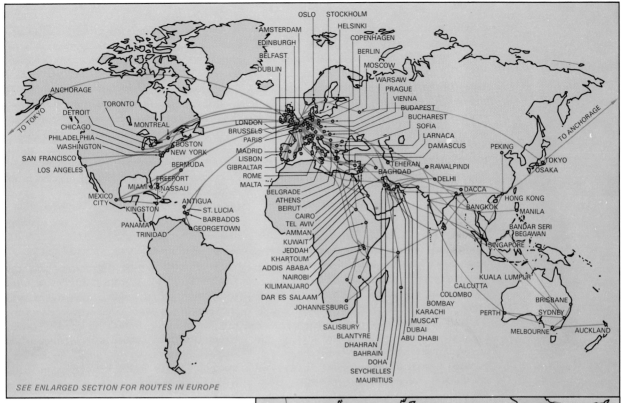

SEE ENLARGED SECTION FOR ROUTES IN EUROPE

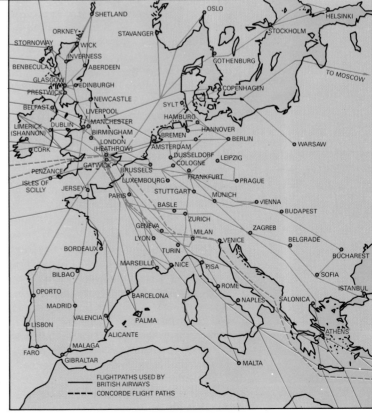

FLIGHTPATHS USED BY
BRITISH AIRWAYS
- - - CONCORDE FLIGHT PATHS

BAH S-61N aircraft, operated by BCAL on behalf of BAA.

Increasing intrusion of trade unions into business matters on which they were unqualified to speak had become a sign of the times. Boeing's offer of subcontracting the 757 wings to British Aerospace was described by a group of unions at the BAC Weybridge plant as 'totally unacceptable', alleging that the firm would lose money on the deal — but in fact feared that the American hire-and-fire practice would be adopted to avoid losses. Employees everywhere turned a blind eye to their lack of productivity compared with USA operations, and inevitably Britain was becoming at risk in competing with the rest of the world.

Despite similar protests by the unions against British Airways' intention to buy the nineteen Boeing 737s, Trade Secretary Edmund Dell announced permission at the beginning of July 'following exhaustive discussions'. As a sop to domestic opinion, the airline offered to purchase three to six additional One-Elevens. Meanwhile Lufthansa and Swissair were putting their money on the Airbus for deliveries in early 1983, but British Airways remained intent on the Boeing 757 which 'would provide five times as much work for the British aircraft and aero-engine industry as would the proposed European project, assuming 1,000 Boeings are sold by 1990'. A hopeful indication was BALPA's agreement for two-man crews on these machines because of the automatic flight control system (AFCS), visual approach monitor (VAM) and performance data computer (PCDS) which enabled a two-man crew to have constant information on the most efficient way to operate the aircraft under particular conditions of flight.

In publishing the Annual Report for 1977–78, British Airways made a direct approach to the employees with a dramatically simplified, eye-catching synopsis which explained the enormous cost of operations and relatively small profit. As the full 66-page Report stated: 'Profit, before cost of capital borrowing, was £65 million. This profit could have been increased by a further £40 million if certain well publicized external and internal events had not taken place.' After providing for interest, currency losses, and taxation, the net profit was £33 million compared with the previous £35 million but included a tax adjustment of £14·5 million.

Sir Frank McFadzean wrote: 'The main deterioration in our operations resulted from industrial disputes. Prerequisite for survival in a growing competitive market is a greater degree of stability in industrial relations.' A special tabulation comparing pay and productivity for 1974, 1975, and 1976 between British Airways and the average of eight foreign airlines showed that on both accounts the 57,000 British Airways employees achieved under 60 per cent of the foreigners' yield. There was the warning that: 'Productivity must be improved to the level of our most efficient competitors by greater aircraft utilization and restricting the increase in staff numbers, within a framework of corporate growth. Manpower control has never been easy, and implementation of the detailed strategy postulates considerable changes in attitudes.'

A change in viewpoint was Sir Frank McFadzean's conclusion that 'Concorde is unlikely to make a profit on normal accounting principles', and he revealed that British Airways was discussing with the Department of Trade new arrangements to ensure that losses on Concorde would be covered by the Government either by

writing off the airline's investment in these airliners or taking over these machines and allowing British Airways to operate them as a contractor. The prime problem was that unless Concorde could make an immediate turnround after each flight it could not pay — but there was insufficient demand for that to be practicable. So far Concorde had lost the airline £17 million, discounting interest on capital borrowed to finance their purchase. Optimistically Ross Stainton said: 'We are very far from being reluctant to operate this aircraft. It is good for our image. All we have to do is to continue delivering a reliable service and we have to make it self-supporting. That's our task. I don't see why we shouldn't get on with it.'

The Annual Report also warned that the scene was set for scheduled airlines to offer competitive prices, and that 'approval of Skytrain services between London and New York is a complicating factor'. Sir Freddie Laker, recently knighted, opened his new London–Los Angeles Skytrain service on 27 November, using DC-10-10s. British Airways reciprocated with details of its three-class service between Britain and the USA. From 29 October passengers paying the full economy fare would travel 'club class' across the Atlantic in a cabin set apart from discount-fare travellers and would be entitled to some of the benefits enjoyed by first-class travellers, such as free drinks, in-flight entertainment, and choice from a new menu based on Elizabethan cooking. At airports they would have separate check-ins, and were entitled to stop-overs and exchange routing. Substantial price cuts on eighteen European routes would follow on 1 November by agreement with IATA. Indicating the shape of things to come in the USA, the House of Representatives passed a Deregulation Bill by which the CAB's authority over domestic routes would end in 1981, followed by closure of its jurisdiction over fares and rates in 1982, so that US domestic air transport would then become a free market. Would Europe follow suit?

On 12 October the first of British Airways' new TriStar 500s was rolled out at Lockheed Palmdale, USA. Princess Margaret rescheduled a private visit to California in order to baptize the new airliner during a pleasant Anglo-American ceremony at which the Lockheed vice-president extolled the virtues of TriStar and its derivatives, and Ross Stainton gave an enlightening glimpse of British Airways' intention to cater principally, though not exclusively, for low-fare passengers. 'We believe that is the only way any major scheduled carrier is going to survive. After all we ourselves invented the low-fare scheduled service concept with ideas like APEX and ABC fares, and that was where the whole low-fare movement began a decade ago. To the extent that governments push on with deregulation, the ruling fact in our business in the next decade is going to be competition. It is not a question whether we should be in the low-fare mass market but of how we do it, for we shall go on offering the whole range from very high quality first-class service to a good but very basic low fare product which may be based on stand-by fares or include a simple form of seat reservation. Our job is not simply to get costs down, but to ensure they are comparable to competitors in relation to the revenue we get back. That is a crucial point.

'We recently announced our three-class fare structure, with all three carried on one aircraft — first, club, and discount. That certainly is right at present, but may not be a long-term answer. We shall need separate, very simple check-in facilities for discount passengers, and the fare will entitle them to only a straightforward end-to-end journey with no stop-overs. I can envisage do-it-yourself reservations where the prospective passenger consults a TV display to see what is available and at what price, and then makes his own booking entry into the computer. Ticket issue, at least for simple journeys, may be a matter of pushing a credit card into a slot and getting back a pre-printed ticket, probably incorporating a boarding card, with a passenger seat number printed on it. Baggage handling may be the passenger loading his single permitted suitcase into a container at the airport.

'There is also the airport problem. For years, successive governments have failed to tackle this. It is no longer a question whether we need a fourth terminal at Heathrow but a question of where and how we are going to find room in this country to handle all the passengers. Rapid action is needed to provide extra airport capacity, particularly in the South of England. British Airways may have to think in terms of using a whole range of airports, each perhaps handling an autonomous part of the operation. Hitherto this has been anathema because unity is cheap and diversity expensive — but it may prove more efficient, for people tend to work better in small groups where they can actually see the end product and feel they are doing a worthwhile job. Above all we must maintain the quality in terms that matter to the customer — safety, punctuality, reliability, cleanliness, courtesy. That is what brings the customer to our door.'

With November came fog and prospect of delay for many travellers — but British Airways was scoring with the automatic landing systems it had pioneered for the One-Elevens, Tridents, and TriStars whose crews had to satisfy stringent requirements before achieving approval for such operations in specific categories relating horizontal visibility and decision height.

Less than ten years earlier it had been difficult to convince people that there were any benefits in automatic landings. Since then the practice had matured from a novelty into a genuine time, cost, and energy saving asset, reducing the number of cancelled services due to bad weather and certainly adding enormously to safety of operations.

In very different sense British Airways helicopters had added to the safety of oil rig workers by carrying them ashore when the seas would have made voyages highly dangerous, and there had been many search and rescue missions from Aberdeen and Sumburgh, one helicopter crew earning international recognition for saving the lives of eight seaman when their trawler ran aground on the west coast of the Shetland Islands. They had also proved profitable, so the Board agreed in December to order three Boeing-Vertol Chinooks at a cost of £17 million for delivery late in 1980 in expectation of increasing the present 108 million passenger miles to 225 million by 1990. The Chinook would meet ICAO noise requirements and the interior could use Boeing 727 components, including windows, seats, and luggage bins, and fuel tanks would be fitted in enlarged wing-like sponsons.

The business of British Airtours was also booming, the turnover having increased during the year from £26·6 million to £32·6 million. Nine Boeing 707s were employed for flights conducted by a wide variety of tour operators, as well as long-haul flights to the USA West Coast and the Far East. Soon the 707s would be time-expired (after some twenty years in airline service), so Airtours now signed a contract for nine 737s for delivery in readiness for the 1981 summer tour season.

1979 and on

The great consortium of British Aerospace became a full partner in Airbus Industrie on 1 January 1979, with the major task of building production Airbus wings. Laker Airways was the only immediate British customer. Would British Airways be forced to follow suit?

Concorde planning was the more immediate concern. On 9 January the USA ratified the C of A, thus clearing the last obstacle to Concorde interchange services by Braniff from New York to Dallas/Fort Worth in conjunction with British Airways and Air France who registered a US-incorporated subsidiary to comply with the FAA laws on registration of foreign-owned aircraft. Concordes would be chartered on an hourly leasing fee of $2,000, including flight and maintenance, and four-fifths of the through fare from London or Paris to Dallas adverted to British Airways and Air France. Three days later, using one British and one French Concorde, the service was inaugurated by Braniff crews. The French machine carried 86 passengers, the British 90, and with splendid showmanship they touched down on parallel runways almost simultaneously, parked facing each other, then dipped noses in salutation to the applause of a delighted crowd while a band played 'The Yellow Rose of Texas' and 'The British Grenadiers'.

However at home British Airways was encountering problems. The icy weather necessitated cancellation of many flights from Heathrow, snow eliminating 150 of 180 scheduled flights on one day alone. Then a 24-hour strike by 'short-haul' pilots, protesting against use of a 'long-haul' TriStar on the London–Paris route, caused practically every domestic and European service to be cancelled. Sir Frank McFadzean called the strike 'A callous and cynical act not expected from skilled and responsible people', and said that it brought 'disgrace and humiliation to the airline'. Underlying the pilots' action was discontent that they seemed 'poor relations' in the airline's career structure. One pilot publicly said he was 'sick and tired of our scruffy fleet. Many aircraft need an interior re-fit' — but at least the hard wear and tear was due to intense use, though not improved by the industrial malaise which seemed to be affecting all classes of employees. However a two-day meeting between management and pilots cleared many misunderstandings and even established a project team to consider Boeing 757 flight-deck operations,

though little was done about integrating the long- and short-haul pilot forces, each with its own negotiating section in BALPA.

Running an airline seemed a continuous process of negotiation. For fourteen months the Government of Malaysia had been holding out against the British Government over Concorde, but now agreed to allow overflights to Singapore and a thrice-weekly schedule was resumed on 24 January. As a political gesture the Concordes were painted in the colours of British Airways on one side and those of Singapore Airlines on the other. Despite a stop of an hour at Bahrein for refuelling, the flight time of 7 hr 27 min was nearly half that of a subsonic airliner for the 7,400-mile journey. Optimism ran high, for there was an encouraging flow of bookings. Sir Frank McFadzean had persuaded the British Government to write off the £160 million capital cost of the Concordes and spares in return for 80 per cent of their surplus earnings. That liberated the operation from the annual £15 million depreciation charge and virtually gave British Airways the five Concordes — but though McFadzean also proposed that the two additional machines stored at Filton should be retained in Government ownership and operated by the airline under a leasing agreement, this was 'kept open' by the Government because of British Caledonian's interest in chartering them.

A few days later the Queen and Prince Philip flew to Kuwait in a British Airways Concorde to begin a three-week tour of the Middle East.

Marking another step forward, a contract for nineteen Boeing 757s, costing £300 million, was signed on 2 March by Sir Frank McFadzean — the biggest ever by a British airline. Sir Frank said: 'The 757 was established beyond doubt as the right aircraft for the job. It is the right size, slotting between the 737's we are buying and the TriStars, and it has the right economics with the lowest fleet-mile costs of any short-haul airliner of comparable size and performance.' British Caledonian countered with purchase of six Airbus A-310s which would replace the One-Elevens and 707s and could be used on a new network to twenty European cities at fares cut by 40 per cent. 'Air transport in Europe needs fresh thinking and radical changes', said the affably shrewd Adam Thompson, and added: 'I would be surprised if British Airways welcomes our proposals'.

North Atlantic fares were causing concern. The negotiator of the Bermuda Two Agree-

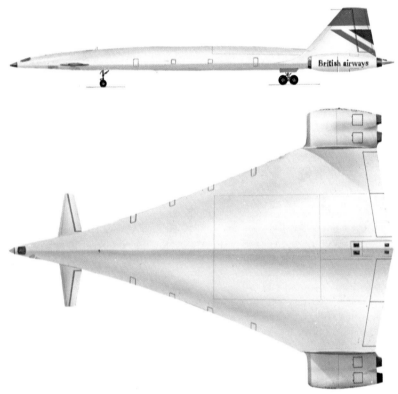

British airways

ment, Sir Patrick Shovelton, who was now director-general of the Council of British Shipping, declared that fares must go up, otherwise there was 'danger of the sort of *débâcle* we witnessed in the European tour market some years ago'. American airlines were applying for a 7 per cent surcharge to meet sharply rising fuel costs. OPEC oil ministers, who earlier had agreed to raise prices by 14·5 per cent in stages, met again at Geneva on 26 February and imposed the full increase forthwith. Two days later IATA members hurriedly discussed fares in the wake of shortages caused by the Iranian troubles and soaring free market prices. Clearly the world was on the threshold of the predicted energy crisis in which costs would steeply increase as oil diminished.

Twenty years earlier very few realized that a fuel shortage lay ahead. There was reminder of those days with the death of Willard Whitney Straight at the age of 66 on 5 April. To a few war-time contemporaries he was remembered as the keen young RAF officer setting up radar stations at the time of the Narvik campaign, and later as Air Commodore in the Middle East Transport Command. Some in British Airways knew him as BEA deputy chairman after the war, and in 1947 as the 34-year-old managing

director of BOAC who in pre-war days had made his mark in commercial aviation. In 1949 he became deputy chairman, leaving in 1955 for high position on Rolls-Royce of which he eventually became chairman. Cultured, lively, adroitly businesslike, he was essentially an airman — so pilots had faith in him.

To most British Airways manual operatives he was probably unknown. Pay, not people, was their idiom — so a new productivity deal at Heathrow giving an average increase of 14 per cent, and up to 25 per cent for some, was described both by management and shop stewards as 'a milestone for industrial relations'. Here was a fresh attempt to reconcile the deep differences between the old BOAC and BEA engineering departments. For more than 30 years it had been a case of 'us and them'. The 1971 merger had even made matters worse with duplications and reduced efficiencies, partly because the BEA section was organized for short-haul work and continuous quick turn-rounds whereas BOAC was geared to long routes with aircraft strung across the world at many support stations. As a result, job demarcation, discrimination, and even union collision were barriers to unifying the two separated big maintenance factories at Heathrow. The management could only gamble that the new agreement would ensure efficient running of the programme under which 100 aircraft would be bought over the next five years at a cost of £1,000 million. Some 14,000 workers were affected, and the deal was designed to overcome much of the over-manning problem, so there would be non-replacement on retirement of 1,500 engineering staff. McFadzean ascribed the excess manpower to the enforced operation of more diverse aircraft and engines than any leading competitors. 'This albatross was not put round our necks by previous management but by successive governments intervening in the airline's affairs', he said.

On 30 April, the first of British Airways' TriStar 500s seating 202 in economy class and 30 in first, was delivered from California to Heathrow in a flight of twelve hours controlled by the 'management' system which was switched on at 1,000 ft after take-off and flew the machine the whole way until the approach at London. Sir Frank McFadzean said: 'It is this aircraft, more than any other at this crucial time, that is showing us how to squeeze the maximum revenue-earning work out of every drop of fuel we burn'. Kenneth Wilkinson explained that the combined technological refinements built into the TriStar represented a 7 per cent improvement in fuel consumption. 'Over our projected fleet of six 500s, spending an average of about 4,200 hours in the air during a year's operations, this represents more than £1 million savings on fuel bills. At today's fuel prices we estimate that every one per cent improvement is worth £30,000 for each aircraft. As fuel costs rise this "discount" provided by the design becomes even more important.'

Early in May the Conservatives displaced Labour at the polls. Their aviation policy had been declared. No regulatory change for UK civil airlines was expected. British Airways and British Caledonian would remain flag carriers within their spheres of influence, but other independents were likely to be given greater opportunity to compete with the big two. British Caledonian currently established a new line of operations by taking over the helicopters operated by Ferranti and registering British Caledonian Helicopters Ltd.

Crucial to European flying was whether the lead of the USA should be followed in 'deregulation' of domestic carriers, giving freedom to start new services and set fare levels in competition with established scheduled carriers. Sir Freddie Laker was spearheading the attack and threatening to take the British Government to the European Court of Justice on grounds that its regulatory policies were a breach of the Treaty of Rome provisions on competition. However, other leading European airline industrialists attacked deregulation at a conference on International Aviation organized by Lloyd's in New York. Ross Stainton declared: 'Sovereignty deserves more respect than is accorded by some protagonists of deregulation. Respect for the customs and courtesies of one state to another rules out behaviour that, from overseas, looks remarkably like an outbreak of arrant aerial Imperialism.'

There was every sign that this new move was unacceptable internationally — but Laker would persevere. That the Conservative promise of encouraging competition was being upheld was emphasized by a CAA decision in June that the British Airways licence for the Aberdeen–Wick–Sumburgh service would be withdrawn despite the airline's investment and awarded to the charter operator Air Ecosse, and the Gatwick–Aberdeen route transferred to Dan-Air. This was immediately followed by permission to Laker Airways for unrestricted trans-Atlantic Skytrain services, allowing seat reservations, excursion fares, and cargo carriage at the basic Skytrain fare to and from London, New York, and Los Angeles.

Meanwhile the huge rise in OPEC fuel prices caused British Caledonian to drop all plans to fly Concorde to West Africa and the USA. As Thompson said: 'It has proved impossible in to-day's circumstances to find any combination of routes which could produce an adequate return for the company'. Fuel accounted for one-third of Concorde's operating costs.

The Press was stirred to both headlines and sage editorials on 21 July when John Nott, the Trade Secretary, announced that the Government would offer to the public, and to the airline employees in particular, a substantial shareholding of some £150 million in British Airways, and would give up control of the investment programme. The latter involved £2,400 million in capital expenditure over the next five years which would now have to be raised by the airline's own financing from internally generated funds or by borrowing in commercial markets, and the Government estimated this would save about £1,000 million after taking into account the reduction in borrowing for new aircraft.

British Airways was promised that constituent parts of the business would not be hived off, nor would there be radical re-organization of route allocations, and that the management would be completely free to order any type of aircraft. In future it would be a case of 'no profit, no cash: no cash, no new aircraft'. Ross Stainton, now 65, had just been elected chairman on the retirement of Sir Frank McFadzean and cautiously commented that 'the Board will be discussing the Government's statement shortly in order to come to a view' — but in *British Airways News* he assured all employees: 'The Board is not going to abdicate its responsibility to lead and direct simply because we may be entering a period of uncertainty. The Government decision just adds sharpness and urgency to our need to get on with running the best airline in the world.'

At the end of July Ross Stainton announced that British Airways had made a net profit of £77 million for the financial year 1978–79, and was budgeting for a pre-tax profit of £150 million during the current financial year ending 31 March 1980 — though escalating fuel costs could well upset all predictions, and already the Trade Department had requested a cut back of 5 per cent on the budgeted fuel requirements. That bill next year was likely to be 70 per cent higher despite operating Boeing 737s which used 25 per cent less fuel per passenger than the Trident 3, or the Boeing 757 which was still better and might save 30 to 40 per cent dependent on type of operations. As Stainton indicated, British Airways found itself 'on a voyage which is taking us past the Scylla of low fares and the Charybdis of soaring fuel prices — and the navigation is tricky'.

Deputy chairman was Kenneth Wilkinson, former chairman of BEA. Roy Watts, the re-shaper of the airline's plans and fleet for the 1980s, rose to chief executive. Stephen Wheatcroft, the director of subsidiaries, became director of economic development; Howard Phelps, the personnel director, was made operations director responsible for day to day flight requirements at Heathrow and Gatwick; Roger Moss finance director; John Garton, engineering director; and Ted Gosling, personnel director.

Forty years earlier, on 4 August, 1939, the Bill establishing BOAC had become law, establishing the Corporation as a legal entity three months later. Sixty years ago, on 25 August, 1919, the world's first international scheduled air service had been inaugurated on a shoe-string by that grandfather forebear of British Airways, Air Travel & Transport Ltd. And now in this year of anniversaries Britain's major airline was again at the crossroads, an epoch completed, a new era about to begin beset with the difficulties of reorientation and the impact of the Government's promotion of competition instead of state monopoly.

What will be the airline's course in the next 60 years? The first decade is not difficult to foresee. The next generation of airliners already under construction have an expected 'life' until 2000 AD. Roy Watts prophesied: 'In Britain alone by 1986 the annual market for package holidays will have doubled from 3 million to 6 million, and one in nine of the population will be taking a package holiday abroad every year compared with one in eighteen to-day. They will be prepared to accept limited choice, high load factors, simple service, and very basic ground facilities in return for excellent value for money. The bulk of this growth will be on the long-haul routes relatively free from land or sea competition, but we expect the short-haul market of the UK to grow by 27 per cent between now and 1986 during which the long-haul market will have doubled. I regard it as absolutely certain that a stretched Boeing 747 will be in fairly widespread use by 1986, carrying 580 passengers in an all-discount layout, but I do not believe there will be a second generation supersonic transport in service, nor do I think that city centre to city centre aircraft will be an everyday feature.'

The decade to 1990 is bound to be a period of change and adjustment and intense competition, yet it is a mere moment in time. The long Concorde development shows how the years fly by in meeting a single specific requirement — yet by 2000 a subsonic 1,000-seater could be operating, or even capacious 'lifting body' prototypes flying at hypersonic speeds which would enable any point in the globe to be reached in $1\frac{1}{2}$ hours or cross the Atlantic in 45 minutes. The crucial problem is not the design of such aircraft but whether a vast industrial complex can be established for the manufacture of liquid hydrogen or alternative fuel on a commercial scale before the natural oil runs out. But whatever proves feasible, one thing is certain: British Airways will remain at the forefront, fulfilling its motto 'To fly, to serve'.

Index

Acknowledgements

All photographs save those listed below appear courtesy of British Airways:

Aero Pictorial Ltd: page 9.
BOAC: pages 91 (right), 107 (top), 203, 213, 252, 257.
British Aerospace: pages 38, 48, 49, 80, 93, 135 (left), 150 (bottom), 152 (bottom), 189, 220, 273.
British Aircraft Corporation: page 269.
Hawker Siddeley: pages 6–7.
Imperial War Museum: pages 11, 120, 121, 125, 128 (both), 129, 131, 138, 143.
Keystone Press: pages 53 (main picture), 65, 105 (right), 109, 156, 195 (bottom left), 205
   (bottom left).
Popperfoto: pages 8, 12, 13, 16, 31 (right), 53 (inset), 135 (right), 180, 186 (both), 218.
Radio Times Hulton Picture Library: pages 31 (left), 39, 146, 161, 169, 173 (bottom), 183
   (bottom), 184, 192.
The Royal Aeronautical Society: pages 7, 11 (top), 104 (left), 272.
John W.R. Taylor: pages 26, 43 (bottom left), 52, 79 (bottom), 158 (top).